THE GERMAN EDUCATION SYSTEM SINCE 1945

Editor: Iván Tapia
Translated by Vera Heidingsfeld and Timothy Nevill
Title and Book Design: Graphicteam Köln
Printer: Nettesheim Druck GmbH & Co. KG, Köln
Printed in the Federal Republic of Germany

CHRISTOPH FÜHR

THE GERMAN EDUCATION SYSTEM SINCE 1945

1997 INTER NATIONES · BONN

Dr. Christoph Führ, historian (b. 1931).
From 1957 to 1965 personal assistant in the secretariat to the Conference of Ministers of Education. Since 1965: German Institute for International Educational Research, Frankfurt/Main. From 1986 to 1996 lecturer at the Johann Wolfgang Goethe-Universität, Frankfurt/Main.

Publications include: *Das k. u. k. Armeeoberkommando und die Innenpolitik in Österreich 1914–1917*, Vienna 1968. – *Zur Schulpolitik der Weimarer Republik*, Weinheim 1970, 2nd ed. 1972. – Numerous books, essays on and reviews of educational policy. Editor together with Prof. Dr. Wolfgang Mitter of “Studien und Dokumentationen zur deutschen Bildungsgeschichte”, Böhlau Verlag, Cologne (around 60 vols.).

Preface

Today education and knowledge have become crucial factors determining the situation facing our country" – declared Federal President Roman Herzog at the 15th congress of the German Society for Educational Science, meeting at Halle an der Saale in March 1996. He outlined the magnitudes involved in the educational sector as follows: "Ultimately many million 'customers' exert an impact on our education system – children, school pupils, trainees, students, course participants – and almost a million people offering 'services' – educators, teachers, trainers, professors, lecturers – with a total budget of 250 billion DM, amounting to 7% of the gross domestic product in state and economy". In 1995 these 'customers' included 12.3 million youngsters at school and 1.9 million students, instructed by 724,200 teachers and 114,000 university lecturers, amongst them about 42,000 professors. At a time of difficulties for public budgets schools and universities are today faced with great problems.

An attempt is made in what follows to sketch the diversity of our education system. This is closely linked with our country's federal structure, which is deeply anchored in German history. Like its predecessors in 1979, 1988, and 1992, this publication was written for Inter Nationes, and thus primarily for foreign readers rather than for German use. It will also appear in several languages. Developments from 1945 to the present day will be outlined in 20 chapters.

A preliminary survey of the history of German education since 1945 is attempted in the "Introduction". Reference is also made to the Soviet Occupied Zone and the German Democratic Republic (GDR) where that is indispensable for understanding the current situation. A more detailed description of the GDR education system would have exceeded the limits of this book. In addition there are many excellent studies of that subject, such as those by Oskar Anweiler and Siegfried Baske (see bibliography). The chapters that follow provide accounts of developments in the Federal Republic (including the New Laender from 1990). Chapters 2 to 4 cover the federal structure and the most important institutions co-ordinating educational policy – e.g. the Conference of Laender Ministers of Education, the Federal Ministry of Education, Science, Research, and Technology, and the Federal-Laender Commission for Educational Planning and Advancement of Research –, the influence of interest groups and churches, consultative bodies such as the Science Council, and educational research. Chapters 5 to 17 describe the education system from kindergarten to adult and further education. The last three chapters deal with current issues, view German education in the European and international context, and conclude with a summing-up.

The need to keep the text's length within bounds meant that some topics could not be treated in detail. Those included scholarship and research, curriculum development in the context of didactic and epistemological changes, nationwide competitions for school pupils such as the highly successful annual (since 1973) "German History" event, the much discussed theme of "violence in schools", loans and scholarships as a means of assistance, the role of army colleges, such current concerns as sex education and drug counselling, advice about schooling and studies, and German schools abroad. The administration and financing of education are also only treated somewhat peripherally.

This report is based on a wide range of official material. Authoritative statistics come from the Ministry of Education, Science, Research, and Technology's handy "Grund- und Strukturdaten 1995/96" ("Basic and Structural Data 1995/96") and the excellent "Statistische Veröffentlichungen der Kultusministerkonferenz" ("Statistical Data", published by the Conference of Laender Ministers of Education). The data mentioned in the text refers to the 1994/95 school year and the 1994/95 winter semester. Where more recent figures are not available, we had to be satisfied with older ones. Just a few days before this work was completed the Conference of Laender Ministers of Education published the 1995 figures for pupils, classes, and teachers. These could no longer be taken into account in the main body of the text but are included as an appendix.

The need for concision spoke against the fashionable practice of constantly making specific reference to both male and female members of such groups as pupils, students, teachers, etc. So it goes without saying that both sexes are meant in any general references.

This book owes a great deal to the energetic and critical support of Barbara Launer who is heartily thanked here for over two decades of close co-operation. The number of those who once again constantly supplied me with information, advice, and assistance is too great for adequate individual mention. Important suggestions came from Marianne Exner and Iván Tapia at Inter Nationes. Rapid and comprehensive help was provided by Jürgen Schlegel, secretary-general of the Federal-Laender Commission for Educational Planning and Advancement of Research, and by colleagues whom I still know from my "administrative phase" as schools expert in the Conference of Laender Ministers of Education's secretariat (from 1957 to 1965) even though their careers have sometimes taken them in other institutional directions: Gerhard Fengler, Peter Fränz, Franz Letzelter, Harald Kästner (who knows most about our school system), and Dieter Rübsaamen. Important material was supplied by Gerhard Schreier of the University Rectors Conference. The German Institute's research library and the Berlin-based library for research into educational history were as helpful as ever. Marion Bierwagen, Birgit Bittorf, Christa Förster, Sonja Hartung, Andrea Mennaa, Albrecht Denzer, Hartmut Müller, and Christian Ritzi stand here for many others. Heartfelt thanks must also go to Hermann Avenarius, Hans Döbert, Peter Döbrich, Peter A. Döring, Rüdiger Haug, Christoph Kodron, Renate Martini, Ute Mengels, Maria Miclescu, Wolfgang Mitter, Hasson v. Recum, Angelika Schade, Ulrich Schäfer, Gerlind Schmidt, and Manfred Weiss of the German Institute of International Educational Research. I owe to my friend Bernard Trouillet, whose life is devoted to Franco-German understanding, intensified awareness of the advantages and disadvantages of the German education system as compared with France.

The earlier presentations of the German education system – dating from 1966, 1973 (both together with Walter Schultze), 1979, 1985, 1988, and 1992 (only concerned with the five New Laender) – were mostly translated into English, French, Spanish, and Japanese. This publication also belongs within an institutional tradition launched with Hans Heckel's worthy "Übersicht über das Schulwesen im Bundesgebiet" ("Survey of the Educational System in the Federal Republic of Germany") in 1952. If these surveys are read synoptically, one gains a differentiated overview of the history of German education during the post-war period.

Of course each depiction is at the same time a personal interpretation of the education system, shaped by the writer's experiences. With this publication the author takes leave of educational research after almost 40 years, thinking back to the highly instructive "apprenticeship" with Kurt Frey (1913-1993), secretary-general of the Conference of Laender Ministers of Education, and with Hans Reimers (1908-1989), director of Hamburg's Senate and chairman of the School Commission.

On a foggy day in autumn 1950, after completing the university entrance qualification, I came – together with my 16-year-old brother Fritz –

to the Federal Republic as a refugee from the GDR, carrying only a brief-case: Illegally across the green frontier in the Southern Harz mountains. Among the formative experiences for me in the Federal Republic was the freedom of choice at the universities of Tübingen and Hamburg, and then a similar freedom at the German Institute of International Educational Research in Frankfurt/Main from 1965 to 1996.

At the end attention returns to the beginnings, to my time at school in the humanist *Gymnasium* (established in 1524) in the former free imperial town of Nordhausen in the Harz, destroyed in 1945, and, after the war, to the Humboldt school there. Amid the confusion of war and the ruins of the post-war world, Kurt Sachse and Friedrich Rabenald, senior directors of studies, continued to uphold a general education devoted to Classical Antiquity, Christianity, and German Classicism, untroubled by the spirit of the age under Nazi and communist dictatorship. This work is dedicated to their memory.

Frankfurt/Main, September 1996 — Christoph Führ

Translator's Note

Since there is not always an exact English equivalent for the German secondary and vocational schools, the German terms have usually been used in the text. In the tripartite secondary system, the *Hauptschule* is a general, non-academic school providing a secondary education usually up to the minimum school leaving age, the *Realschule* is an intermediate form of school between the *Hauptschule* and the *Gymnasium*. The *Hauptschule* and *Realschule* together are roughly equivalent to the English secondary modern school. Where English terms have been used for the sake of readability, "secondary modern" has been used for the *Hauptschule*, "intermediate school" for the *Realschule*, and "grammar school" for the *Gymnasium*.

Glossary

Berufsaufbauschule – vocational extension school
Berufsfachschule – full-time vocational school
Berufliches Gymnasium – vocational gymnasium
Berufsoberschule – vocational secondary school
Berufsschule – part-time vocational school
Fachgymnasium – technical gymnasium
Fachhochschule – degree-granting college of higher education roughly equivalent to a polytechnic
Fachoberschule – technical secondary school
Fachschule – technical school
Gesamthochschule – comprehensive university
Gesamtschule – comprehensive school
Grundschule – primary school
Gymnasium – grammar school
Hauptschule – non-academic secondary school roughly equivalent to a secondary modern
Integrierte Gesamtschule – integrated comprehensive
Kolleg – sixth-form college
Kooperative Gesamtschule – co-operative comprehensive
Kunst- und Musikhochschule – college of art and music
Mittelschule – middle school
Oberrealschule – upper level intermediate school
Pädagogische Hochschule – college of education
Realgymnasium – intermediate gymnasium

Realschule – intermediate school
Regelschule – norm school
Sekundarschule – secondary school
Technische Universität – technical university
Verbundene Haupt- und Realschule – combined secondary modern and intermediate school
Volksschule – elementary school
Wirtschaftsschule – trade school

Contents

Appendices

Theodor Haecker 1927/1946:

Some ages have believed, and this is still the case at present, that the legacy of Classical Antiquity – philosophy, art, and scholarship as exists only in the West – and humanitarianism, as an idea only known in the West, can be preserved and implemented despite, or even because of, emancipation from the one and only faith. That is mightily misguided. Without Christian belief Europe is only a grain of sand amid a whirlwind of opinions, ideas, and religions.

Eduard Spranger 1947

An education ... that does not awaken youth to a sense of conscience and personal moral responsibility is not worthy of that name.

Friedrich Meinecke 1948

Personality entails the shaping of one's own existence by way of liberty. Freedom leads directly to self-limitation, to self-discipline – not to self-obsession. ... Viewed from the stand-point of universal history, these ideas of liberty and personality are at the heart of the concepts of 'Europe' and the 'Christian West'. Today those ideas are the focus of a worldwide struggle.

Ernst Jünger 1968

What should ... happen in a situation where it is scarcely possible to speak any longer of 'education' despite a pedagogic fury extending as far as the jungle? ... How should one set about education today without those concerned, submerged in commonplaces, being led around in circles? ... It is highly questionable whether human beings become better through 'education', but they certainly become more intelligent and more dangerous.

Wolfgang Hildesheimer 1991

There may be values which are eternal – even though people want to doubt that today – but there do not exist any rules of human co-existence and communication that survive for generations. The future is uncertain, and each new stage of development ultimately finds us unprepared..

1 Introduction

Anyone who wants to understand the diversity of today's German education system must know its history. A comprehensive historical survey is not possible here because of the limited space available. We largely restrict ourselves to the post-war period after 1945. The history of the Federal Republic of Germany since its foundation in 1949 is the Germans' greatest "success story" in this century. This was an ascent out of the darkness of national catastrophes. Mention need only be made of the years 1918, 1933, and 1945: the end of the first world war and rule by the Kaiser, the replacement of the Weimar Republic by Nazi tyranny, and the conclusion of the second world war started by Hitler in 1939. Hitler's dictatorship was the nadir of German history. Germany lay in ruins and was divided into zones by the occupying powers. During the Cold War Germany became a sphere of antagonism between the great powers. The two German states established in 1949 – the Federal Republic of Germany and the German Democratic Republic – were divided by the "Iron Curtain" with its mines and barbed wire, and from 1961 by the Wall in Berlin.

Germany has been reunited since 1990. Reconstruction of the school and university system in the five New Laender – Mecklenburg-Western Pomerania, Brandenburg, Saxony-Anhalt, Saxony, and Thuringia – and in East Berlin constituted a great challenge during the past six years. Time is required for "inner reunification". German educational policy is increasingly becoming a part of domestic politics within a united Europe.

Despite economic well-being it should not be forgotten that for some two decades now the Federal Republic has experienced a degree of structural unemployment which in winter 1995/96, with over four million people out of work, achieved a level reminiscent of the world economic crisis at the start of the thirties. Unemployment and the difficulties facing public budgets are at present exerting a multiple impact on the education system. After reunification the struggle against unemployment is the main political challenge at the end of our century.

Let us first recollect the course of educational development in recent decades.

1.1 Two Basic Elements in East and West

When in 1906 Friedrich Paulsen published his "Historical Development of the German Education System", he retrospectively put emphasis on "two ongoing basic elements: progressive secularization and nationalization of the education system, and constant extension of school education to ever greater numbers – so to speak, the democratization of education". Paulsen's diagnosis applies to the twentieth century as well as to the 19th.

"Democratization of education" – viewed by all social forces in the West as part of the development of a basic democratic order – led after 1950 to the greatest expansion of secondary and higher education in German history, and to the development of an exemplarily differentiated vocational school system. The percentage of those qualified to enter university thus rose between 1950 and 1994 from around 4 % to 25.9 % (and if colleges of higher education are also included to 34.9 %). In the same period the number of students rose from around 100,000 to 1.7 million (with the share of women students increasing from some 20 % to the current 46 %, thereby more than doubling). This expansion disrupted all planning, leading to a crisis of overloading throughout the university system. For university graduates (especially teachers) it has been difficult to find adequate employment since the seventies. Nevertheless, educational policy is still under the spell of growth-oriented planning.

In the East too reconstruction of the education system got under way with the objective of democratizing schooling. However, education was intended to serve the development of socialism, and was thus soon dictatorially reshaped by the Socialist Unity Party on behalf of the class struggle. During the fifties and sixties the construction of universities and colleges was pushed ahead so as to create a new class of socialist leaders. From the start of the seventies the number of students in the GDR – unlike in the Federal Republic – was gradually reduced (1972: 161,000 – 1985-90: around 130,000 students). About 12 % of an age-group received education up to the level of university admission. There were also cutbacks in correspondence courses, which had been developed on a broad basis, and evening studies were terminated. Despite that, the GDR had problems with finding appropriate employment for graduates, as became apparent in the "winding up" of the unusually over-staffed academies and the reconstruction of the education system after 1990.

With regard to nationalization, state and society, schools and universities have long been closely interrelated in Germany. The education system is largely dependent on public backing. In the East there was a "state monopoly of schools and universities", whereas in the West private schools are guaranteed the support of constitutional law. The large majority of private schools and colleges are maintained by the churches, particularly the Catholic Church, but predominantly financed out of public funds. In the West in 1990 some 540,000 pupils attended private schools (around 6 % of the then total of c. 9.05 million at school), and only around 27,000 students non-state colleges (1.6 % of all students). What Paulsen comprehended as "progressive nationalization" is particularly apparent today in the form of increasing "legal underpinning" of the education system.

"Progressive secularization" does not only receive expression in the declining importance of the two main churches whose social position within education initially seemed unusually strong after 1945 because of the part they played in resistance against the Nazi regime. In the West there was also discussion of the constitutional guarantee of a right to religious instruction on a voluntary basis, which apparently is often in danger – to the extent that it is offered at all – of being comprehended as a form of "social studies". In the East religious studies were banned from the curriculum until 1990.

1.2 The Post-War Situation

Unconditional capitulation on the 8th of May 1945 did not only lead to the end of the "Greater German Reich". Traditional national and patriotic educational objectives were also called in question. In November 1945 Ernst Wiechert, the teacher and writer who had been imprisoned at Buchenwald in 1938, declared in his "Speech to German Youth": "We once had a fatherland that was called Germany". How far-reaching this "collective loss of meaning" was could hardly be foreseen at that time, accompanied as it was by a provisional end to patriotic endeavours on behalf of "preservation of German educational unity". These had got under way towards the close of the 18th century with extended discussion of German national education from the perspective of freedom-loving citizens of the world. During the 19th century that increasingly succumbed to the influence of excessive nationalism until finally Adolf Hitler wanted to see young Germans brought up as "fanatical nationalists".

After millions of people had paid for that with their lives, the vision of a united Europe became for many – at least in the West – a "substitute fatherland". Carlo Schmid wrote: "After the collapse of 1945 there were virtually only Europeans in Germany". For decades the Cold War between the USA and Soviet Union, as global powers with allies, left divided Germany in a bi-polar sphere of tension, shaped by the two blocs. In 1949 two completely different and opposing German states and social systems came into existence. Schools and universities were drawn into intellectual and political disputes, becoming an arena of struggle. Only with dissolution of the blocs and the reunification of Germany in 1990, accompanied by intensified integration of educational policy within the European Community, did a new chapter begin in the history of German education.

At the end of the war many German schools and universities had been destroyed. Lack of classrooms, teachers, and textbooks affected lessons. Many teachers and professors were removed from public employment – for a time or for ever – because of their Nazi involvement. External reconstruction of schools and colleges took over a decade. The West had to accept and integrate some twelve million refugees and expellees from Central and East Germany – one of Germany's greatest achievements. Schools and universities played an important part there. In the course of reconstruction refugees were completely integrated – despite cultivation of close ties with local loyalties. The GDR also took in four million refugees up to 1949, and almost half of those moved to the West before the Berlin Wall was built in 1961.

In the West Laender and local authorities became responsible for education in a resumption of the country's federalist tradition, and the central authorities only took on limited responsibilities, mainly in the university sphere, in 1969. As early as July 1945 the Soviet military authorities in Berlin set up the German Central Administration for National Education under Paul Wandel, a Mannheim communist who had returned from exile in the Soviet Union. The Ministries of Education in the Eastern Laender that existed until 1952 only played a subordinate part in the Soviet Zone of Occupation. When the GDR was established in 1949 the Ministry of National Education became responsible for the entire education system, receiving directives from the Socialist Unity Party's central committee. In the East the constitution and administration were shaped by socialist centralism; in the West federalism and political pluralism prevailed. Federalism also entailed a risk of a splintering of the education system, but the Laender Ministries of Education were aware of the necessity of voluntary co-operation. That has been guided since 1948, even before the Federal Republic was set up, by the Standing Conference of Laender Ministries of Education and Cultural Affairs and its secretariat. The first (and for 42 years only) all-German gathering of Ministers of Education took place in

February 1948 in the Hohenheim district of Stuttgart. Even at that time differing objectives in reconstruction of the education system became clearly apparent. The Cold War then getting under way for decades prevented almost all contact in the educational sphere.

Prussia had played a leading part in German educational policy since the beginning of the 19th century. Once Prussia no longer existed, no other Land predominated in educational policy in the West after 1945. None of the Laender in the Federal Republic was large enough to be able to take over Prussia's leading role. The former Prussian provinces of Schleswig-Holstein, Hanover, Hesse-Nassau, Rhineland, and Westphalia were quickly incorporated in new Laender. These shook off Prussian traditions and strove to develop their own identities. Through progressive division within ongoing "Berlin crises" and finally construction of the Wall in 1961, West Berlin increasingly became peripheral. East Berlin became the "capital of the GDR". With the fall of the Wall and reunification Berlin as capital is now faced with new cultural and political tasks.

Until 1990 Germany remained a disputed geographical concept with regard to its frontiers. In the East cultural landscapes of great educational and traditional significance had been lost with East Prussia, Pomerania, and Silesia. They had been closely linked with the names of Kant, Hamann, Herder, Eichendorff, and Gerhart Hauptmann, with the universities of Königsberg and Breslau so rich in tradition, and with the technical colleges at Breslau and Danzig.

1.2.1 Coming to Terms with the Past

Since 1945 a shadow has been cast over the history of German education by National Socialist rule and its crimes. It only gradually became apparent what a historical burden had been imposed by the extermination of Jews murdered in concentration and prisoner of war camps. Soon after 1933 some 1,700 Jewish scholars, including over 300 university professors, were driven out of office, often by way of degrading terrorist methods. Most of them, including such globally celebrated scholars as Albert Einstein, emigrated to the USA and England. Retrospectively, Austrian historian Friedrich Heer wrote: "Germany is irreplaceably impoverished by the removal of its Jews ... Everything there has become provincial". Heer sums up: "From the 18th to the 20th century German intellectual life is inconceivable without the explosions of Jewish input. From Moses Mendelssohn, Heinrich Heine, and Karl Marx to Sigmund Freud and Albert Einstein, German-Jewish thinkers and philosophers (just two names from their great number: Simmel and Husserl, Heidegger's teacher), political scientists, doctors, psychologists, depth-psychologists, biologists, chemists, physicists, bacteriologists, jurists, writers, and critics established the arena for German intellectual life". After 1945 only a few of the well-known Jewish emigrants returned, including historians Hans Rothfels and Hans Joachim Schoeps, and philosophers Helmuth Plessner, Karl Löwith, Max Horkheimer, and Theodor W. Adorno in the West, and Ernst Bloch and literary scholar Hans Mayer in the East (which they once again left in the sixties).

Frankfurt philosopher Theodor W. Adorno once declared with regard to "education after Auschwitz": "The demand that there should never be another Auschwitz is the prime demand to be made on education. It is so much more crucial than any other that I do not feel any necessity to justify it". "Reappraisal of the past" became a leading task for schools, universities, and research institutes in the West – as is demonstrated by many publications and exhibitions (inclusive of catalogues), and by the establishment of the Munich Institute of Contemporary History (1950) and corresponding facilities in the Laender, for instance at Hamburg. Attention was also devoted to elimination of nationalistic depictions of "the enemy" in school history books where the Brunswick-based International Textbook Institute under Georg Eckert led the way. In the East the Socialist Unity Party viewed itself as an embodiment of the communist antifascist resistance, accusing the West of perpetuating National Socialist, militaristic, and imperialist tendencies. That charge, of course, was unfounded.

Discussions about the Nazi regime were taken seriously in the West – despite one-sided claims to the contrary. They led from the Nuremberg trial and its successors by way of the Eichmann trial (in Jerusalem), the Auschwitz trial (in Frankfurt/Main), and other trials up to the "historians dispute" in the eighties. As early as 1960 outbreaks of swastika-daubing in a number of cities led immediately to resolutions by the Conference of Laender Ministers of Education on devoting greater attention to Nazi crimes in history and civics lessons.

One of the central issues in reappraising the past was and remains the evaluation of National Socialism. As early as 1946 Freiburg historian Gerhard Ritter, who was close to the resistance movement and in 1944/45 was arrested by the Gestapo, wrote: "Germans' national self-confidence is today deeply shaken ... It would be not merely unwise, but also untrue and unjust, to want to depict our people's political past as nothing but a single chain of mistakes and misfortunes. No matter how tragic its course may have been as a whole, it is not possible to speak of clear-cut 'inevitability' ".

The German resistance movement against Hitler became a beacon for the "other Germany" with its Christian, socialist, cosmopolitan, and humanistic educational traditions. All levels of the population were involved in this – workers, aristocracy, middle-class, churches, trade unions, army officers, professors, and students. Development of German democracy in the West after 1945 would have been even more difficult without the libertarian and democratic fundament preserved during the Nazi period.

1.2.2 Return to Educational Traditions

In 1945 it was not only many of Germany's cities that lay in ruins; so too did the traditional educational world. Publisher Peter Suhrkamp, a teacher at the reformist Wickersdorf community school in the twenties and later incarcerated by the Nazis, in 1947 declared: "The destruction of this war entails something more terrible than ruins. Those do not completely reveal the destruction; part exists within ourselves".

With what educational traditions should, could, a link be re-established in 1945? On what foundation should intellectual redevelopment of Germany and reconstruction of the German education system be based? What elements had stood the test? There was great discussion of such matters in the initial post-war years – sometimes still in all-German terms – despite all the outer restrictions, hunger, and lack of accomodation. Friedrich Meinecke, the elderly and esteemed Berlin historian, sought to establish a way in his 1946 book "The German Catastrophe. Reflections and Recollections". He concluded this work with the words: "Our German state has been crushed, much German land has been lost, and foreign rule has become our fate for a long time ahead. Will the German spirit be successfully saved? Never before in its history has it been exposed to such a test of endurance".

However, there were not only such expressions of despondency. Frankfurt legal historian Helmut Coing retrospectively stressed: "Despite everything a mood of profound inner joy prevailed among many people. The war was over, the dictatorship ended. Life again lay in front of us with all of its possibilities. There predominated an openness to all forms of intellectual and spiritual expression – scholarship and literature, music and the visual arts – as I never again experienced in my life". That experience and assessment of the situation explain much of the elan of reconstruction. Educationist Eduard Spranger paid high tribute to students in the post-war period: "Never has a generation studied in more tragic circumstances than between 1946 and 1949. Even outwardly it lacked means, was inadequately nourished, in poor health, badly accomodated, and often completely homeless. This generation had learned little or nothing at school. It had suffered the most terrible fate of waging a war in whose purpose it could – at least at the end – no longer believe. ... Naturally it was inwardly completely disoriented and confused, but at the same time was assailed from all sides by the victorious powers with remedies and attempts at re-education. ... If I affirm out of 40 years experience ... that those who studied between 1945 and 1949 were the most serious and best students I have ever encountered, I am not alone in that view".

In the East too a link was initially established with the neo-humanistic and reformist traditions of the Weimar Republic period. However, differing, even opposing, stands were adopted. In the West, for instance, Eduard Spranger, who in 1946 moved from Berlin's Humboldt University to Tübingen, embodied a continuation of early 20th century humanitarian education and philosophical idealism into the sixties. Other educationists such as Theodor Litt, Herman Nohl, Wilhelm Flitner, and Erich Weniger – just to mention a few – exerted a decisive influence during the first decade and a half. In the East, on the other hand, such a leading socialist reformist educationist as Heinrich Deiters – Spranger's successor at the Humboldt University – was increasingly pushed onto the sidelines as part of the "Sovietization" of education. In 1953 Deiters had to concede that his opponents in the Socialist Unity Party had "a different idea of education" – a dogmatic communist approach where the emphasis was on instruction in "hatred of the class-enemy".

Educational developments in the East led to a radical break with tradition after 1945. Intermediate schools (*Realschule*) and grammar schools (*Gymnasium*) were eliminated as part of the drive towards unified schooling.

1.2.3 Re-Education and Reforms in the West

During the initial post-war years the Western occupying powers endeavoured in their zones to implement their particular views about the role of schools and universities in re-education. Cultural officers provided ideas that turned out to be fruitful over the long-term, receiving expression in objectives laid down in new Land constitutions and legislation on schools and universities. German politicians also stressed the need of qualitatively new political education for the young. Hesse Prime Minister Karl Geiler thus declared in February 1946: "We Germans are faced with an educational task ... We have to introduce an intellectual and psychological reshaping of our people".

Theodor Heuß was also aware of many young people's political homelessness during the post-war period. As Württemberg-Baden's Minister of Education in 1946 he told teachers at the recently established Protestant Academy at Bad Boll:

"We have experienced the breakdown of innumerable civilized values and are faced with enormously difficult tasks ... How will it be possible to make a start on recreating within the German people respect as a force in human existence; how will it be possible to help those Germans who experienced that time, who had to experience the madness of overrating the significance of things German before being plunged into the depths, to get beyond being bogged down and becoming psychologically depressed, so that they do not regard gloomy defiance, which is only cowardice in the face of realities, as courage? Will it be possible to take the decisive step of creating the forms and content of a sense of German nationality which makes us proud and thankful to be German, despite all we have experienced?"

That question is still topical today. As the first President of the young Federal Republic Theodor Heuß was also a stroke of political good fortune. Heuß came from long-established Württemberg Liberalism, had been shaped by the school of Friedrich Naumann, the Saxon national-liberal clergyman, and made a name for himself during the Weimar Republic as a journalist and German Democratic Party member of the *Reichstag*. During his period of office from 1949 to 1959, Heuß embodied the best traditions of the educated German liberal bourgeoisie. At the same time he represented a Swabian expression of continuity of liberal thinking from the *Kaiser's Reich* to the redevelopment of democracy. Through many speeches to school pupils and students, and through visits to schools, universities, and student hostels, he took on – in the public mind – the secondary job of "Federal Minister of Education and Culture", an office that has in fact only existed since 1969. In 1946 Heuß saw the Allied military governments on the one hand as "executive organs of a complete military victory" and on the other as "auxiliaries of German restoration".

The occupying powers furthered the international exchanges of experience that had been largely broken off after 1933, and, for instance, made possible study trips by education experts to the USA under the auspices of the Fulbright Program. Thanks to American assistance in 1950 Hesse was able, following a suggestion by Minister of Education Erwin Stein, to establish the "College of International Educational Research" at Frankfurt/Main, which in 1964 became the German Institute of International Educational Research. Empirical research incorporating international experience was intended to complement traditional humanistic research at universities.

The occupying powers also played a large part in establishing universities at Mainz, Saarbrücken, and Berlin (Free University). These new universities were closely linked with discussions about reforms, getting under way amid a world still in ruins (see section 15). Berlin's Free University was set up on the initiative of students who were excluded by the Socialist Unity Party (SED) from the Humboldt University in the Soviet-occupied Eastern Sector. It is an irony of history that a university created at the start of the Cold War with American assistance – whose name embodied an anti-totalitarian programme and whose first rector was Friedrich Meinecke, a liberal historian – in the sixties became a stronghold of radical leftist students, some of whom even obstructed university professors in their teaching and research.

1.2.4 Restoration or a Fresh Start

It is disputed up to the present day whether the kind of sweeping structural reforms carried out in education in the East under the influence of the Soviet occupying power with clear-cut ideological objectives would have been possible in the West. On the one hand, the occupying powers had no agreed objectives with regard to structural reform of the education system, on the other, federalism resulted in differences of emphasis. As early as 1950 reconstruction of the education system in the West, mainly following on from developments in the Weimar Republic, was criticized as being only “restoration”. This combative slogan was mainly used by Walter Dirks and Eugen Kogon in the “Frankfurter Hefte” in a political confrontation with the then Federal Chancellor Konrad Adenauer. This evaluation was again much used in the sixties to legitimate educational reforms at that time. Even in 1989 the former Hesse Minister of Education Ludwig von Friedeburg regretted the “lost opportunity” in 1945: “Never before in German history had the situation so urgently demanded overdue educational reform”. However, Friedeburg also conceded that “Material and staffing problems were primary, not issues within the organization of the education system”. Did the situation really demand reforms as a matter of urgency? Was it not much more necessary to fulfil the simplest preconditions for organizing schools and universities before thinking of reforms? In 1945 Herman Nohl told teachers in the British zone: “Schools' difficulties are so great that it seems almost ridiculous to want to come with demands. ... There is a lack of classrooms, of all teaching aids ... Classes are overfull ... Both pupils and teachers are physically and mentally run down. In that situation it seems meaningless to think of putting forward plans for reform. One is happy if the most primitive school set-up ... functions”. It should also be remembered how difficult communications were during the initial post-war years, even within a zone let alone between zones. Some time passed before post, telephone, and railways operated relatively smoothly.

Dirks' and Kogon's evaluation thus distorts realistic assessment of those developments. Viewed superficially, it may seem as if, for instance, the re-introduction of church primary schools, abolished by the Nazis, mainly in the Western Laender ruled by the Christian Democrats points towards "restoration". However, it should not be forgotten that this reinstatement of church schools occurred in completely changed social circumstances compared with the twenties. Up to 1945 there had been relatively clearly divided Protestant and Catholic regions. The great movements of refugees and expellees in the post-war years led, however, to a hitherto unknown mixing of populations. Protestant refugees streamed into previously closed Catholic towns and localities (and vice versa). That soon made it seem impracticable to structure primary schools in terms of religious beliefs over the long-term. In the sixties religiously segregated primary schools and secondary moderns thus vanished almost completely – with the agreement of the churches but almost unnoticed in public discussions.

The upper-level school system in the West was not simply restored either. In the post-war period there were a number of new developments including new types of school. Only at that time was the number of intermediate schools increased to meet needs. Only since that time (and not in the 19th century already) can one speak of a completely developed three-tiered school system. Alternative forms of access to university were established. In short, after 1945 there were many new beginnings so that at the start of the fifties public debate about supposed "school chaos" got under way. Individual Laender began to develop in different directions. The Prime Ministers' Düsseldorf Agreement of 1955 and its revision in the Hamburg Agreement of 1964 assures up to the present day a largely unified structure within the education system. It can thus be retrospectively stated that educational redevelopment in the West was more akin to a fresh start than to restoration.

The (former) Federal Republic was also "much more homogeneous" (M. Rainer Lepsius) in its social and cultural structure than the German Reich. Mobility within the country played a considerable part in that. Advancement through education was of particular importance for refugees and expellees. Their striving for education and wish to advance themselves inevitably supplied special motivation.

In the West re-emergence from the ruins brought an affluence unprecedented in Germany. This development began with the currency reform of 1948. Only then did the "social market economy" get under way. According to Hans Rothfels, who returned from emigration to Tübingen in 1951, economic recovery was based on "simple diligence, dedication to working one's way up, and willingness to lend a hand wherever possible. Another marvellous aspect should be remembered too. In the stories told about those years you time and again encounter the fact that, amid all the chaos, alongside hard-heartedness and pushiness, goodness and readiness to help manifested themselves to a degree seldom previously experienced. Never were things more joyfully shared as during a time when next to nothing existed to be shared". It is true that at the start of the fifties there were still great difficulties in the vocational integration of young people, but full employment soon prevailed after years of great joblessness.

1.3 Socialist Educational Reforms in the East

The initial emphases in educational policy were established – as previously mentioned – by the German Central Administration for National Education, set up by the Soviet military authority in July 1945. Reverting to the proclaimed objectives of socialist educational policy at the end of the 19th century, the establishment of private schools was banned in the Soviet occupied zone and East Berlin. The secularization of schools was implemented and religious instruction no longer tolerated. The churches then developed classes in religion attended on a voluntary basis, but these only reached a small percentage of pupils. The consequences of decades of atheistic upbringing and radical secularization of the education system became apparent with reunification in 1990. The reintroduction of religious instruction in state schools, in accordance with the Basic Law, led to many problems and differing solutions in the New Laender.

The "construction of socialism" left multiple traces in education. The autumn 1945 "land reform" led to the dispossession of "Junkers" and "Lords of the manor", quickly followed by far-reaching ousting of the bourgeoisie from "property and education". Classes that for centuries had shaped and influenced education and culture in town and country thus vanished. With the introduction of production co-operatives in agriculture and trades, and nationalization of the health service and industry, there came into existence a "new society" that increasingly differed from the West in terms of tradition, mentality, and ideas about education. Over the decades there developed a new, socialist-oriented, and broad-based educated class. The stages of that development are sketched in what follows.

In May 1946 the reform of schooling got under way with the "Law on Democratization of the German School", drawn up by the Berlin central administration and constituting the basis for similar legislation in Thuringia, Saxony, Saxony-Anhalt, Brandenburg, and Mecklenburg. This "unified school law" linked educational reform and old social democratic and communist objectives. The traditional school hierarchy with a structure of primary, intermediate, and higher institutions was abandoned.

Eight years of primary schooling for everyone were now followed by four years of upper school with specializations in modern languages, mathematics and natural sciences, and classics.

After denazification in 1946 only about 8,000 of the 28,000 or so teachers in general education remained. Some 28,000 new teachers were then trained, but over half of them had not received any higher education and came from the families of workers, both industrial and agricultural, skilled and unskilled. By 1949 these new teachers accounted for around 70 % of the total. Many of the GDR's leaders-to-be began their career as new teachers. Alongside such teacher training, faculties of education were established at universities and colleges.

The Ministry of National Education established when the GDR was set up in 1949, and the German Central Institute of Education (from 1970 the GDR Academy of Educational Sciences) created at the same time, ensured ideological unity in the curricula determining what was taught. After intense polemics directed against reformist German pedagogics Soviet educational ideas served as a "compass". Introduction of a polytechnic level in 1958 established a further emphasis. Here pupils in the 7th to 10th classes usually spent two to three hours a week on productive work preparing the way for a future job. That was an essential element within socialist restructuring of the school system. A crucial part was played by the "Law on Socialist Development of the GDR School System" (December 2, 1959) and later the "Law on a Unified Socialist Education System" (February 25, 1965). After 1959 the eight years of primary schooling were replaced by ten years with an emphasis on polytechnic education. The two-year extension of compulsory education was introduced in the sixties. With classes 11 and 12 the Expanded Upper School (EUS) led to the university entrance qualification (*Abitur*), but from 1982 there were no longer special preparatory classes at levels 9 and 10. From 1969 the three types of specialization were given up. In classes 11 and 12 the emphasis was on mathematics and the natural sciences, taught in accordance with a unified curriculum. During the sixties a particular attempt was made to link general and vocational education, and thus to take pupils at the same time up to a vocational qualification and university entrance. However, after a few years the EUS established itself as the normal way of gaining admission to university. Gaining that qualification in schools also offering vocational training took a year longer. For the highly gifted there were special schools (or classes) offering foreign languages, the natural sciences, mathematics, sport, and the arts.

Around 14 % of pupils continued to end their schooling after the eighth class – despite the regulation about ten years of compulsory schooling – and to start vocational training. Political and ideological assessments were as important as academic performance for moving on to the Extended Upper School. Objections by a school's FDJ ("Free German Youth") youth movement leaders were enough to block the way to university education even for pupils with very good grades. In reality there was a "selection process". The number of pupils admitted to Extended Upper Schools was determined by the places available for students at universities. That is why only about 12 % of an age-group gained the university entrance qualification. A rigidly directed "planned education system" thus prevailed in the GDR. All possibilities of schooling, studies, and vocational training beyond compulsory education in the GDR were assigned by the state. Oskar Anweiler remarked that this entailed "the most rigid selection system in all the socialist states including the Soviet Union". Teachers, who were themselves subject to special political supervision, were obliged to serve the construction of socialism, the "leading role of the Socialist Unity Party", and the educational objective of the "all-round and harmoniously developed socialist personality".

In the East too universities and colleges had largely been destroyed by 1945. External reconstruction was slow and laborious. After 1945 the influence of the Soviet occupying power ensured that in this zone the university system was restructured in accordance with Marxism-Leninism – despite considerable resistance by so-called bourgeois professors and students. That process was initially aided by celebrated scholars who had returned from exile (such as Ernst Bloch and Hans Mayer, who later had to leave the GDR).

From the start the aim of university policy was to train a "new socialist intelligensia". However, celebrated "bourgeois" scholars were long employed at universities, colleges, and research institutes. Up to 1961 conflicts with the SED (Socialist Unity Party) led around 2,700 university teachers and 35,000 students and sixth-formers to flee to the West. Some 1,200 students, including Wolfgang Natonek, chairman of the Leipzig students council, were arrested. University policy during the post-war period was characterized by the FDJ youth movement slogan: "Storm the Fortress of Scholarship". In 1946 preliminary classes – later known as Workers and Farmers Faculties – were established at universities. These were intended to open up universities to a wider range of students, especially workers and farmers, and to eliminate the monopoly of the *Abitur* in admissions. During the fifties there were times when up to a quarter of the students employed this approach. In 1962 the Workers and Farmers Faculties were dissolved since by then schools carried out an equivalent social and political selection process.

After 1946 the entire university system was step-by-step restructured in accordance with Marxism-Leninism. Social studies faculties were established at universities as centres of this ideology. In 1946 the SED set up the Karl Marx party college. Over the course of about five years

Marxism-Leninism became a compulsory subject in all curricula. Studies were strictly organized from 1951 and divided into study-years rather than semesters. University teachers and students increasingly came under rigid ideological control. Cases of conflict with the SED proliferated among students and sixth-formers in connection with the events of June 17, 1953. After the Berlin Wall was put up in 1961 the possibility of "flight from the Republic" was almost blocked in crisis situations.

During the fifties and sixties some developments in the GDR were of relevance for educational discussions in the West, serving as "precursors" for such developments as the replacement of tiny rural schools by central schools serving larger catchment areas, development of alternative forms of university admission, introduction of student grants (the Honnef Model in 1957), implementation of work studies (alongside polytechnic training), and extension of compulsory schooling. On the other hand, the GDR "unified school" was generally viewed negatively in discussions of comprehensive schools during the sixties and seventies.

1.4 Educational Reforms and Planning in the West

Since the mid-fifties the education system in the West has step-by-step become an integral component within the social and economic order of a welfare state. The debate on educational reform got under way in 1959 with the "Outline Plan on Restructuring and Unifying the General State School System" on which the German Commission for Education and Training had been working since 1953. International comparisons by the Council of Europe, the OECD, and the European Community strengthened the idea that the German school system was not capable of keeping up with developments within society. In 1957 the Science Council was established and this body's recommendations and evaluations regarding expansion and development of universities became increasingly important.

The necessity of long-term, comprehensive, and nationwide educational planning first became apparent to the general public when in February 1962 the Conference of Laender Ministers of Education published a report on the Washington OECD conference that had taken place the previous October. This report was entitled "Economic Growth and Expansion of the Education System", and included a thesis that Ralf Dahrendorf was later to take up and popularize: "Access to education and training will increasingly be viewed as a general right". In 1965 Dahrendorf summed that up in the catchy slogan "The Right to Education". One important outcome of the OECD conference involved acceptance of the view that expansion of education in the sixties should concentrate on high schools and universities. A broad-based strategy within educational planning and policy was devoted to tapping "reserves of talent", improving "selection procedures" during the transition from primary to intermediate and high schools, and increasing the availability of such schools. In 1963 the then Federal Chancellor, Ludwig Erhard, declared that the German people must become aware that the tasks facing education and research are as important for our time as alleviation of social problems was for the 19th century. In March 1963 the Conference of Laender Ministers of Education brought out a comprehensive survey of basic needs within the school system, teacher training, scholarship and research, art and culture for the period up to 1970. At first discussions of reform were limited to specialists, but that changed at the start of 1964. There was an unusually far-reaching response to Georg Picht's series of articles (in "Christ und Welt", a protestant and conservative weekly) headlined "The German Educational Catastrophe". According to Picht, only radical restructuring of the German education system would provide sufficient teachers for the additional two million pupils expected by 1970. The number of youngsters taking the *Abitur* should thus be at least doubled within a decade – and that actually happened.

The call for extensive reform of the education system was taken up by all political forces. In March 1964 the Conference of Laender Ministers of Education took its 100th plenary session as the occasion for a critical interim stock-taking. The Conference drew on international experience in concisely outlining the long-term objectives of educational reform in the Federal Republic of Germany:

- "Raising the overall level of training for young people through increasing and improving all kinds of schooling
- Increasing the number of youngsters completing higher levels of schooling
- Training every individual to the highest degree of his or her capacity for achievement
- Offering training possibilities better adapted to individual capacity. Measures for placing pupils in appropriate courses (e.g. observation levels)
- Increasing transferability between all existing schools (i.e. horizontally rather than vertically structured organization)
- Creating new forms of secondary education".

That constituted the basic consensus – beyond party allegiance – at the time.

The German Education Council came into existence in 1965 as the successor to the German Commission for Education and Training. Working closely together with the Max Planck Institute of Educational Research, established at Berlin under Hellmut Becker in 1963, the Education Council pronounced on educational developments in many recommendations and assessments up to 1975. An important contribution to pedagogic theory was also made by Heinrich Roth, the reform-oriented Göttingen educationist, who as early as the fifties, when working at the College of International Educational Research at Frankfurt/Main, had advocated mixed-ability classes (*Förderstufe*). "Begabung und Lernen", the anthology of views he published in 1969, gave rise to general discussion.

The comprehensive educational reforms discussed in that book were introduced at this time. All levels of the school system, from the primary school to the sixth form and vocational training, were "reformed", and new types of school (such as technical secondary schools) and a new type of college (the degree-granting college of higher education) as well as correspondence courses were created. Small universities with a long tradition turned into featureless mass institutions with tens of thousands of students. Between 1960 and 1980 24 new universities were set up in the Federal Republic, including for the first time an Open University (at Hagen in 1975). Expansion of all universities and far-reaching reforms made this part of the system an experimental arena, especially from the mid-sixties to the mid-seventies.

1.5 Student Movement and University Reform

In the sixties the student protest movement was an international phenomenon from San Francisco by way of Paris to Berlin. The German 68 movement indisputably had consequences, but how this attempt at a "cultural revolution" is ultimately to be evaluated remains open. The leftist student protest movement, consisting of many different groups, began its "march through the institutions" at that time. From 1965 to mid-1967 it was mainly restricted to Berlin's Free University. It first attracted widespread public attention through militant demonstrations following the death of Benno Ohnesorg during the Shah's June 1967 visit to Berlin. The student movement's highpoint was during the period of the Grand Coalition between the CDU/CSU (Christian Democrat Party / Christian Social Party) and SPD (Social Democrat Party) (1966-69). A broad-based "Extra-Parliamentary Opposition" developed at that time during the discussions about emergency laws and the Vietnam war. Even though the majority of students rejected radical political groupings, they allowed such groups great freedom by not participating in student elections. Student – and often anarchist – activism soon spread at many West German universities. Strikes, demonstrations, occupations of institutes and administrations, and disruptions of teaching by way of Teach-Ins and Sit-Ins were a daily occurrence. Demonstrations not infrequently led to clashes with the police, similar to civil wars. The student movement wanted to "undermine the establishment" and did not shrink from psycho-terror. Universities were basically intended to become a vehicle for revolutionizing society. These "system-surmounting", often highly crude efforts towards reforming society were also directed against the Basic Law whose free democratic order was mocked. However, such playing with revolution did not attract support among the general public. The 68 movement thus remained in the student ghetto. Just a few radicals drifted off to the terrorist scene, for years challenging the state as the "Red Army Faction".

Even one of the most influential of teachers, Frankfurt philosopher Theodor W. Adorno, was not spared these upheavals. Some students miscomprehended his neo-marxist theoretical models as a guide to action. Shortly before his death Adorno criticized the "fatal model of pseudo-activity". "We older representatives ... have recently been widely accused of resignation. We are said to have developed elements in a critical theory of society, but to have avoided drawing the practical consequences". Jürgen Habermas, who strove to make clear to students the difficult relationship between theory and practice, warned against "playing with terror (and its fascist implications)".

A quarter of a century later, one of the protagonists of the student protest movement – Klaus Rainer Röhl, at that time editor of the radical leftist student magazine "Konkret" and for a time married to the terrorist-to-be Ulrike Meinhof – saw things differently: "The movement generated aberrations and confusion, damage, and loss for both individuals and society as a whole". Berlin political scientist Gesine Schwan has remarked that "convinced sixty-eighters believe, on the contrary, that the rebellion at that time in fact established and impelled what there is in the way of democracy in Germany today". According to Schwan an "objective" answer is not possible. "The phenomenon of 68 was much too complex, and the causes much too entangled for a responsible and clear-cut statement to be possible".

The 68 movement did exert an impact on universities. Nevertheless, Hermann Lübbe says the belief that the student movement brought about university reforms is a "myth". These were already under way when students proclaimed their own ideas. Lübbe stresses: "The student protest movement did not develop in response to the pressure of stagnation but rather amid a highly dynamic policy of university reforms whose effective beginnings dated back to at least ten years earlier".

Until 1969 the Laender were responsible for education in the West. In May of that year the Grand Coalition changed the Basic Law in conjunction with extensive financial reforms. The objective was to involve the federal authorities in the financial burden of university expansion and to secure a unified educational system called in question by contrary reforms. These changes to the Basic Law also created the preconditions for intensified federal involvement in educational planning. In autumn 1969 the Social Democrat / Liberal coalition established the Federal Ministry of Education and Science. The Federal-Laender Commission for Educational Planning and Advancement of Research was then set up in 1970 as a discussion forum for all issues affecting both federal authorities and the Laender.

1.6 Federal Involvement in Structural Reforms

In his October 1969 government statement Federal Chancellor Willy Brandt put education policy at the top of his list of reforms. What was often retrospectively viewed as a striking sign of a new, future-oriented federal policy at the time seemed more like a late response to reforms the Laender had been pursuing for a decade. The federal authorities succeeded in passing several relevant laws: on vocational training (1969), assistance for university construction (1969), educational grants (1971), and after years of struggle the University Outline Law (1976).

Those educational reforms introduced by the federal government and social democrat administrations in the Laender dedicated to social change led to mounting political polarization. Years of close co-operation between educational policy-makers of all political parties during the sixties were succeeded by a phase of confrontation. That was particularly apparent during preparation of the "Overall Education Plan" passed in 1973. There were differences of opinion over the mixed-ability level, integrated comprehensive schools, and graduated teacher training. Continuation of this Plan had to be renounced in 1982 because consensus could no longer be achieved on its financing.

The comprehensive school was and remains a particular source of controversy. When at the end of the sixties the Conference of Laender Ministers of Education failed to reach agreement on important structural issues in school organization, the two big political parties came to an understanding about an experimental programme, especially with regard to comprehensives. That was founded on the view that the accompanying scholarly research could lead to results which would make political decisions easier. That overestimated what was possible for scholarship. Two decades later Ludwig von Friedeburg also declared: "Structural issues within school and society cannot be solved by educationists; if not already determined by the constitution they must be decided by parliament". Of the educational reforms he helped inaugurate Friedeburg remarked: "With these reforms were linked far-reaching hopes of changing society through its schools, of implementing more democracy. There schools exceeded their traditional limits". The attempt to implement social reforms by way of educational reforms demanded too much of the education system. A 1982 resolution of the Conference of Laender Ministers of Education brought to an end the experimental phase for comprehensive schooling whose qualifications were mutually recognized. In Laender governed by the social democrats comprehensives became the normal form of schooling, but the controversy over whether the hierarchical school system or the comprehensive achieves more persists.

1.7 Educational Objectives – Consensus and Dissent

During the initial post-war period in the West a wide-ranging consensus covering Christian, liberal, and socialist convictions regarding educational objectives received expression in constitutions and laws on schooling. Hesse and Bavaria provide examples of that. In article 56 the Hesse constitution (1.12.1946), considerably shaped by Minister of Education and constitutional lawyer Erwin Stein, states:

"Tolerance must be the basic principle in any teaching. In every subject the teacher must take into account the religious and ideological sensitivities of all pupils ... The objective of education is to fashion youngsters as moral personalities, preparing the way for vocational competence and political responsibility with autonomous and trustworthy service of the nation and humanity through reverence and neighbourly love, respect and tolerance, honesty and truthfulness. History lessons must be directed towards faithful, unfalsified depiction of the past. The emphasis must be put on the great benefactors of humanity and the development of state, economy, civilization, and culture rather than generals, wars, and battles. Views that endanger the foundations of the democratic state are not to be tolerated".

In the Bavarian constitution (2.12.1946) article 131 runs:

"Schools should not only mediate knowledge and skills but should also shape heart and character. The supreme educational objectives are reverence before God, respect for religious convictions and human dignity, self-mastery, sense of and delight in responsibility, readiness to help, openness to everything true, good, and beautiful ... Pupils should be educated in the spirit of democracy, love of their Bavarian homeland and the German people, and reconciliation with other nations".

Similar requirements, all dedicated to the idea of tolerance, are to be found in other Laender constitutions and school laws. It is not easy to transmit these objectives to each young generation, but whether, and the degree to which, that is successful is crucial for the future of Germany. That is why, right from the start, great emphasis was put on intensification of political education, particularly in order to prevent any recurrence of nationalistic tendencies. The quotation from the Hesse constitution makes clear what objectives have been served by history lessons since 1946. The restructuring of such classes during the post-war period was taken very seriously, as can be seen in the multitude of history books and curricula. The claim that the "student revolt" of the sixties led to a fundamental change in this sphere is not true.

Ever since the sixties the values outlined in Laender constitutions and school laws have often been called in question. The great movement towards secularization, which reached first the Protestant and later the Catholic church, both largely dissolved traditional religious ties and called traditional values into question. From the mid-sixties advocates of reform urged that teaching's highest objective should be emancipation of pupils. Concepts of emancipatory education exerted a considerable impact in the student movement. The term "emancipation" is, however, open to diverse interpretation, so it was sometimes comprehended as involving radically anti-authoritarian or "system-surmounting" education. Many supposedly socially critical or emancipatory concepts were discussed in the wake of Marxism, neo-Marxism, and psychoanalysis. Such criticism focused on the traditional comprehension of achievement, the school system, and teacher training.

Organisational restructuring of schools was supposed to be complemented by internal reforms. A concept for "curricular reform" was first put forward for discussion in 1967 by Saul B. Robinsohn of the Berlin-based Max Planck Institute of Educational Research. His brochure "Educational Reform as Curricular Revision" launched several years of debate and initiated such reform in Hesse. That concept, also favoured by other Laender, ultimately turned out to be impractical. In Hesse from spring 1968 a commission headed by Wolfgang Klafki (Marburg University) carried out further preliminary work. Commissions of experts developed guidelines for different levels of schooling and learning objectives. These discussions reached their peak when in 1972/3, during Ludwig von Friedeburg's period of office as Hesse's Minister of Education, guidelines for the teaching of German and social studies were produced, deriving from emancipatory and critical theories of socialization and communication. Many parental groups opposed this. Disturbed by the "calling into question" of "High German", Golo Mann criticized "the total breach with schools' past". In the meantime the importance of education in binding values has long become apparent once again, but individual teachers are free to choose how to present the values outlined in Laender constitutions and school laws.

1.7.1 Environmental Education

Another source of controversy concerned the importance to be assigned to environmental education in the seventies, particularly under the impact of the 1973 oil crisis. On 17.10.1980 the Conference of Laender Ministers of Education passed a fundamental resolution on "Environment and Teaching" (resolution no. 669) where the following words are to be found: "The school should mediate insight into complex interrelationships in our environment, revealing the problems arising out of change ... An attempt should be made through such insights to develop environmental awareness". That can take place in several subjects or in inter-disciplinary teaching. Environmental education thus involves an inter-disciplinary principle within teaching. Long-established reformist practices, such as the establishment of school gardens, once again became topical. Introduction of environmental studies as a special subject was turned down, but by now environmental education is largely an established element at school. The Conference of Laender Ministers of Education published its first detailed report on 12.12.1986. In the same year the Federal-Laender Commission on Educational Planning and Advancement of Research decided to make environmental issues a new focus of assistance and since then has provided considerable funds for pilot projects. In 1987 the Federal Ministry of Education and Science outlined an "Environmental Education" work programme, and in the following year published a report ("Environmental Education – Task for the Future") on the current situation and future perspectives. All this shows that environmental education has gained in importance. The Conference of Laender Ministers of Education 200 plus page report (8/9.10.1992) on "Environmental Education in German Schools" demonstrates to what extent that is currently the case. But back to the seventies.

1.7.2 Decoupling the "Education System" from the "Employment System"

At the start of the seventies people debated the decoupling of education and employment as proposed by Georg Picht in 1973. For Picht the basic mistake in Germany's supposedly bureaucratic education system involved the inescapability of viewing life-opportunities exclusively in terms of chances of working one's way upwards. "Advancement" was said to be a concept deriving from the bourgeois class society, "so a society that calls for equality of educational opportunities must demand expansion of freedom for individual development. It must open up for everyone the possibility of compensating in later phases of life for an unfavourable start. That can be achieved if (1) the education system is decoupled from careers, and (2) bureaucratic regimentation of education, justified only in terms of the system of qualifications, is abolished ..."

Were not those proposals utopian? Were not educational realities ignored here? Anyone who wants to do away with legitimation and separate education from employment must both clearly say what he will replace this with and also who has to bear the consequences of a "deregulated" system. One of the most incisive critics of such concepts of educational reform, Heinz-Dietrich Ortlieb, at that time director of the Hamburg-based Archive of the World Economy, wrote as early as 1971: "Anyone who at present propagates education as the be-all and end-all must expect to be told that he represents a new ideology which can at best only favour a privileged group of intellectuals and semi-intellectuals for whom others must make sacrifices. Today and in the foreseeable future we are still far from a society of such affluence that it no longer needs to pay heed to the individual and social cost-utility ratio in investment in education – in other words, the price paid by such expansion". What is needed is an education system "that is geared, absolutely consistently, to untiringly facing up to reality anew rather than cultivating utopias".

Wolfgang Jäger retrospectively stated: "The intensive debate on education, penetrating all spheres of human existence, was an impressive exercise in finding the self and discovering a way on the part of a society whose culture had reached a state of crisis. This was an exciting and often also fanatically conducted struggle. Seldom has there been a political concern that mobilized so much intellectual and at the same time emotionally raging involvement".

1.8 Corrections of Course in the West

The problematic political and social side-effects of educational reform were obvious. The first oil crisis in 1973 brought about a start in rethinking of educational policy. Ecological issues took on greater importance in schools and universities. Up to that time discussion of reforms took place against a background of mounting economic growth and continuing full employment. Widespread "educational euphoria" then gave way to a profound sobering-up. The oil crisis brought about structural unemployment, which affected young graduates too, especially teachers. The Club of Rome's report on "The Limits to Growth" also contributed towards a rethinking of educational policy. Karl Steinbuch called for a "change of course" rather than disoriented progress, writing: "We affirm the achievement-principle ... Freedom of research, teaching, and study must not become an unrestricted arena for revolutionary activities".

Public discussion of this "change of direction" characterized the intellectual situation in the Federal Republic during the seventies. This also involved the problematic political and social consequences of educational reform. The nine theses in the "Affirmation of Education" forum (9/10.1.1978) and the Tübingen counter-declaration by members of the German Society of Educational Science demonstrate what controversy was provoked by basic issues in education and training. The "Affirmation of Education" forum theses – signed by such celebrated scholars and makers of educational policy as Hermann Lübbe, Golo Mann, Robert Spaemann, Hans Bausch, Wilhelm Hahn, and Nikolaus Lobkowicz – attracted a considerable response.

The already mentioned 1976 University Outline Law ended a ten-year phase of experimentation in new university structures. Judgements by the federal constitutional court played a large part in this law. They accorded primacy to professors in decisions about new appointments and research. The influence of university teachers was thus once again increased at the "group university". In some respects that amounted to a considerable correction of course.

However, the increase in the number of those taking the *Abitur* and becoming students was not to be reversed. During the seventies the number of students doubled (from 510,000 in 1970 to 1,044,000 ten years later), and – despite contrary forecasts by the Science Council – rose further to 1.52 million by 1990. From 1972 the *Numerus clausus* selection procedure was established for many courses of study. In order to cope with this increase without adding to restrictions on admission the Laender Prime Ministers in 1977 agreed on an "opening" which remains in force up to the present day. What was known as the universities' "overload programme" became normality.

What remained of the educational reforms of the sixties and seventies? Hellmut Becker, for many years director of Berlin's Max Planck Institute of Educational Research, held the view that the reforms advocated by the German Commission for Education and Training and the German Education Council slowly infiltrated our education system: "Reform did not fail; it sometimes encountered unanticipated problems, but it increasingly determines our entire education system. Many things do not happen as quickly as had been hoped". That is correct, but what infiltrates also seeps away, and much of that flood of reforms on paper has long been forgotten.

1.9 German Unity and European Union

The great new challenge in the realm of education from 1990 has been German reunification. After decades of separation, patience is required for regaining "inner unity" within federal diversity. In 1968 the GDR presumed to eliminate the concept of "the German nation" from its constitution, but at the same time started putting greater emphasis on integrating in its historical depiction of the "socialist nation" the "national cultural legacy" from Luther to Thomas Mann, inclusive of German classicism and even the "progressive aspects" of Frederick the Great and Bismarck. Nevertheless, this schizophrenic relationship to the nation could not destroy awareness of national unity among the people of the GDR. That was demonstrated by the appeal of the slogan "We Are One People" in 1989/90. Once again there began a painful phase of coming to terms with history, which is still not concluded today.

In 1990 the GDR disposed over 54 institutes of higher education in 25 locations, offering courses in 270 specializations. There were three types of institution: universities, technical universities, and technical colleges, plus special colleges usually only offering a single subject (which had only recently been elevated to the status of higher education). There was nothing equivalent to degree-granting colleges of higher education (*Fachhochschule*) in the GDR. For training around 130,000 students there were about 7,000 university teachers (professors and lecturers) and 5,400 assistant lecturers on short-term contracts and over 12,000 on unlimited contracts. Staff-pupil ratios were much more favourable than in the West, but there was a great need to catch up in buildings and such facilities as research equipment, computers, and books.

Between the "changeover" in autumn 1989 and reunification in October 1990 initial changes took place in schools and universities, which began reforms on their own initiative. Those mainly affected the political climate. Hitherto prevalent ideological links were abrogated. There were signs of an autonomy not previously usual. The problems and limits involved in ideological self-purification quickly became apparent in connection with dissolving ("winding up") or restructuring ideologically particularly contaminated spheres of study at universities. When Leipzig historian Karl Czok states in his "History of Saxony", published just before the 1989 changeover, with regard to educational policy in the post-war period: "Every revolutionary upheaval exerts a profound impact on intellectual and cultural life", this is also true for the period after 1989. This declaration, which served to justify Marxism-Leninism's "seizure of power" in higher education after 1945, also applies to its surmounting. As is well known, every revolution is followed by a change of personnel.

Even though trends in university expansion moved in different directions in the two German states, the significance of the *Abitur*, determining university admission, was shared by the two education systems. All-German educational traditions received strongest expression here and in the dual system of vocational training on the job linked with trade schools.

With the end of the GDR the extensive socialist education system was also open to reform. Nevertheless, quite a few people in the East think that some elements – particularly such welfare components as a dense network of kindergartens and after-school facilities, scholarships and hostels for students, and holiday-care for school-children, etc – should be preserved, overlooking the fact that this abundance of provisions had greatly contributed towards the country's economic and financial ruin.

A new phase of educational policy got under way with the restructuring of the Laender by way of the GDR law dated June 22, 1990, regulating their introduction. The first Laender elections on October 14, 1990, decided the balance of power of political forces. The territorial re-ordering took up the Laender structures dissolved in 1952 – apart from a few regional changes. Like all other branches of bureaucracy, the education administration also had to be completely reshaped. Many experts from the West helped in that process. The new Laender were also integrated in all the institutions (developed in the former Federal Republic during recent decades) where the federal and regional authorities co-ordinate education policy. In December 1990 their Ministers of Education became members of the Conference of Laender Ministers of Education. The same applies to participation of the New Laender in the Federal-Laender Commission for Educational Planning and Advancement of Research, and the Science Council. The West German Rectors Conference, established in 1949, turned into the University Rectors Conference after rectors of the New Laender had become members. The federal University Outline Law and the law relating to assistance for university construction also apply to the New Laender.

Such fundamental restructuring was a great political and organizational achievement. The hitherto strictly centralized GDR school and university system was replaced by hierarchically-structured schooling, and the entire university set-up was reorganized with help from the Science Council. New universities were established at Potsdam, Frankfurt/Oder, and Erfurt; new technical universities at Cottbus and Chemnitz; and more than 30 degree-granting colleges of higher education set up.

With reunification the question of the role of national identity in education and training was raised anew. It should be remembered that in 1994 around 1.1 million foreign pupils attended general and vocational schools, amounting to an average of 9 % of the total number of children attending school. In addition there are 134,000 foreign students in Germany. Outbreaks of xenophobia, long thought to have been left behind, made clear that education in tolerance and non-violence is and remains one of the most urgent tasks in making young Germans into Europeans.

Decades of protection of the Federal Republic by the Western Alliance had cut off Germans from responsibilities within world politics, resulting in an all too cosily idyllic self-preoccupation. That came to an end with reunification and the regaining of full sovereignty. Apart from German unity there is also European Union. Increasing economic and political integration face schools and universities with new tasks. Foreign languages lessons for, if possible, all pupils will become indispensible. Far-reaching agreement will have to be reached over qualifications at the secondary and university levels. "Educational equivalents" are becoming an increasingly important topic. National and European objectives are overlapping more and more.

2 The Federal Structure

2.1 Area, Population, and Economic Structure

2.1.1 National Statistics

The Federal Republic of Germany was established in 1949 and is a federal state. Until 1990 it comprised eleven Laender: Baden-Württemberg, Bavaria, Bremen, Hamburg, Hesse, Lower Saxony, North Rhine-Westphalia, Rhineland-Palatinate, Saarland, and Schleswig-Holstein plus West Berlin. Following the treaty on German unification, on October 3, 1990 Brandenburg, Mecklenburg-Western Pomerania, Saxony, Saxony-Anhalt, and Thuringia also became Laender within the Federal Republic of Germany. The following table lists Laender areas and populations (as of 31.12.1993):

Area and Population according to Laender

31.12.1993

Federal State	Area	Population	Population Density
	sq. km	thousands	per sq. km
Baden-Württemberg	35,751.39	10,234.0	286
Bavaria	70,547.44	11,863.3	168
Berlin	889.11	3,475.4	3,909
Brandenburg	29,481.22	2,537.7	86
Bremen	404.23	683.1	1,690
Hamburg	755.33	1,702.9	2,254
Hesse	21,114.25	5,967.3	283
Mecklenburg-Western Pomerania	23,169.47	1,843.5	80
Lower Saxony	47,605.91	7,648.0	161
North Rhine-Westphalia	34,071.50	17,759.3	521
Rhineland-Palatinate	19,845.38	3,925.9	198
Saarland	2,570.02	1,084.5	422
Saxony	18,408.61	4,607.7	250
Saxony-Anhalt	20,445.85	2,777.9	136
Schleswig-Holstein	15,738.68	2,694.9	171
Thuringia	16,175.15	2,532.8	157
Germany	356,973.54	81,338.1	228

Source: Statistisches Jahrbuch für BRD 1995, p. 48.

In 1990 the old Federal Republic covered an area of 248,707.6 sq. km. The average density of population was 245 per sq. km. (figures for 1985). After reunification added five New Laender the federal area grew to 356,973.54 sq. km. The additional Laender are less densely populated so the average density of population dropped to 228 inhabitants per sq. km. Nevertheless, the Federal Republic with 81.3 million inhabitants is one of the most densely populated European states.

In 1994 15,537,000 Germans lived in the New Laender. Between 1989 and 1993 the birthrate went down there by over 50 % (1989: 198,922; 1993: 80,532). This figure reflects both economic uncertainty during reconstruction and adaptation to the Western pattern of starting a family later in life. Over the medium term births are expected to rise again in the New Laender. The present fall in the birthrate faces the school system there with particular problems. In the old Federal Republic the number of births has remained relatively constant (1993: 717,915). In later discussion of individual aspects of the education system reference will be repeatedly made to the great importance of demographic factors in the development of educational policy.

2.1.2 Foreigners and Foreign Pupils

The total population of 81.3 million (1993) includes 6.78 million people of foreign origin with 1.9 million Turks, 1.2 million Yugoslavs, 563,000 Italians, 352,000 Greeks, 133,000 Spaniards, and 105,000 Portuguese. The number of asylum-seekers reached a peak in 1992 with 438,191, but dropped to 127,210 by 1994. The number of immigrants of German origin from Eastern Europe and the Balkans went down from 397,000 (1990) to 222,600 (1994). Immigration is thus beginning to tail off. Three quarters of all foreigners live in Bavaria, North Rhine-Westphalia, Baden-Württemberg, and Hesse. The cities with the greatest numbers of foreigners are Frankfurt/Main (29 %), Stuttgart (23.6 %), and Munich (22.7 %).

In 1994/95 1,122,100 foreign pupils attended general and vocational schools: 79.1 % (887,200) at the former and 20.9 % (234,900) at the latter. Compared with the previous year the number increased slightly by around 24,500 – from 9 to 9.2 % of the total number of pupils. Most of these pupils come from Turkey (42 %), former Yugoslavia (17 %), Italy (8 %), Greece, Spain, and Portugal.

In 1994 these pupils were distributed as follows between the different kinds of school:

Grundschule (Primary Schools)	39.0 %
Hauptschule (Secondary Moderns)	24.2 %
Realschule (Intermediate Schools)	8.7 %
Gymnasium (Grammar Schools)	9.5 %
Gesamtschule (Comprehensive Schools)	6.6 %
Sonderschule (Special Schools)	6.6 %
Other Schools	6.1 %

In the same year the proportion of foreign pupils was highest (26 %) in evening classes at the secondary modern and intermediate levels, followed by Secondary Modern schools (19.2 %), Special Schools for pupils with learning difficulties (16.6 %), Comprehensives (11.6 %), other Special Schools (10.6 %), Primary Schools (9.7 %), Intermediate Schools (6.7 %), and Grammar Schools (3.9 %). Information about the distribution of foreign pupils in vocational schools can be found in section 10.3.

The percentage of foreign children among the total number of pupils varies according to Land. The average figure of 9.2 % is exceeded quite significantly in general schools at Hamburg (18.8 %), Bremen (16.8 %), Hesse

(15.1 %), Baden-Württemberg (14.2 %), North Rhine-Westphalia (13.6 %), and Berlin (11.6 %).

In 1994 80,700 foreign pupils left school. They achieved:

Secondary Modern Leaving Certificate	43.6 %
Intermediate School Leaving Certificate (and equivalents)	26.6 %
Qualification for University Admission	8.8 %
Qualification for admission to Polytechnics	0.7 %
No formal qualification at 16	15.8 %

Since 1985 there has been a clear-cut increase in higher qualifications. Intermediate School certificates have risen from 18.6 % to 26.6 %, and entrance qualifications for polytechnics and universities from 5.6 % to 9.5 %.

2.1.3 Economic Framework

As the table on page 29 shows, there are considerable differences between the federal states in terms of area and population. The same is true of economic development and tax income. Since 1990 the socialist centralized economy has been replaced in the five New Laender by a social market economy with high public investment.

The Federal Republic possesses relatively few raw materials and is a highly developed and export-oriented industrial state. There are great differences in gross domestic product between the Old and the New Laender. The gross figure per head of population in the West in 1994 was on average 40,700 DM compared with only 17,000 DM in the East. In the same year 36 % of the working population were in manufacturing industry, just under 20 % in trade and transportation, 21 % in service enterprises, 15 % in the state sector, somewhat under 3 % in agriculture, forestry, and fisheries. The service industry has been growing for decades while employment in agriculture and manufacturing has declined.

Since the seventies there has been relatively high structural unemployment. In September 1994 2.6 million people in the old Federal Republic and 1.1 million in the New Laender were out of work. Unemployment topped 9.2 % in the West and 16 % in the East. At the start of 1996 unemployment figures rose to a record 4.3 million.

2.2 National and Regional Co-Ordination of Educational Policies: Distribution of Power and Co-Operation

Educational and cultural policy in a federal state requires close co-operation between individual federal states and the federal authorities. When the Federal Republic of Germany was established in 1949 education remained a

Laender responsibility. Laender control over education is still the key aspect within regional autonomy. The Basic Law, the federal German constitution, did not accord the federal authorities any powers of jurisdiction over education. There were several decisive reasons for that. Laender constitutions, inclusive of laws regulating schools and universities, had been in force since 1946. That involved a clear-cut wish to avoid any renewal of centralization as practiced under Nazi rule between 1934 and 1945 with enforcement of ideological conformism by the Reich Ministry of Science, Education, and Public Enlightenment.

Development of the Federal Republic of Germany deliberately built on old German federalist traditions of autonomy for member states. For centuries up to 1934 the territorial states constituting Germany had been responsible for education. The Weimar Constitution of 1919 basically changed nothing, even though article 10 of the Constitution entrusted the Reich with legislating on basic issues regarding schools and universities. Up to the start of National Socialist dictatorship "cultural federalism" was viewed as a well-tried way of balancing religious differences between Protestant and Catholic territories, characterizing German history and the country's approach to education.

It was thus logical that the 1949 Basic Law does not contain any comprehensive regulation of the education system. Just a few fundamental issues are uniformly regulated for the whole of the Federal Republic, following articles 5 and 7 of the 1919 Weimar Constitution – such as freedom for art and science, research and teaching, state inspection of schools, religious education as a general subject at school, and guarantees of freedom for private schools. The Basic Law incorporates the education system in a democratic welfare state founded on the rule of law. However, it remains open whether a basic right to education can be derived from articles 1 to 19 of the Basic Law – in terms of the state's obligation to eliminate social and educational disadvantages, and to guarantee the greatest possible degree of equality of opportunity for all. Article 20, paragraph 1 of the Basic Law nevertheless explicitly states that the Federal Republic of Germany is "a democratic federal welfare state".

During the fifties and sixties the federal authorities seldom intervened in educational politics. However, the cultural section of the Federal Ministry of the Interior, initially headed by Erich Wende (retired state secretary in the Lower Saxony Ministry of Education, who before 1933 had worked in the Prussian Ministry of Education and Culture), helped implement co-operation between federal and Laender authorities in establishing the German Commission for Education and Culture (1953) and setting up the Science Council (1957). On 13.10.1967 Chancellor Kiesinger's Federal Government presented its first comprehensive report on measures taken in the sphere of educational planning (Bundestagsdrucksache V/2166). This "1967 Education

Report" contains contributions by both the federal authorities and the Laender, and throws much light on co-operative federalism. Among the Report's classic wrong forecasts was a prediction that between 1 and 1.2 million children would be born during the decade ahead. In fact use of the contraceptive pill halved annual birth rates.

The Laender thus had sole responsibility for the education system for two decades, up to 1969. Only then, in the course of financial reforms, did the federal authorities receive limited powers, such as the right to enact outline legislation with regard to the general principles involved in the university system, and the right to influence educational planning (see section 2.4). The federal authorities were not granted any right to produce guidelines for the school system. There thus does not exist any school legislation applying to the whole of the Federal Republic.

The administration of schools and universities is a Laender responsibility (see section 2.8). However, since articles 11 and 12 of the Basic Law guarantee to all Germans freedom of movement, choice of job, and choice of place of training throughout the entire country, the Laender are obliged to co-operate with one another and with the federal authorities – particularly with regard to implementing federal guidelines as Land legislation, as with the law concerning universities.

2.3 Standing Conference of Laender Ministers of Education and Cultural Affairs

The Standing Conference of Laender Ministers of Education and Cultural Affairs has been the most important instrument for autonomous co-ordination of educational policies since 1948. The Ministers of Education from the four zones of occupation met for the first time after the second world war on February 19/20, 1948 in Stuttgart-Hohenheim. This gathering was initiated by Adolf Grimme (SPD), the last Prussian and first Lower Saxony Minister of Education, and Theodor Bäuerle, the independent Württemberg-Baden Minister of Education. It was not to be foreseen at that time that this marked the beginning of a lasting and (despite occasional setbacks) successful working group for autonomous co-ordination of federal educational and cultural policy. By the end of 1995 there had been a total of 274 plenary sessions of Laender Ministers and Senators. Nevertheless, after the all-German beginning in February 1948, the Cold War prevented ongoing co-operation between East and West. That was only re-established after reunification. The Conference gained in importance when joined by ministers of education from the five New Laender at the 251st plenary session on December 6/7, 1990. It thereafter served a key function in all-German educational co-operation with preparation and implementation of joint reforms.

Since the Conference's modest beginnings around 150 ministers have belonged to this assembly. Among its leading lights have been very few but always important women, including Christine Teusch and Hanna Renate Laurien (both CDU) and Vera Rüdiger (SPD). Among the men involved in the immediate post-war phase of reconstruction were Theodor Heuß (FDP, the later Federal President who held office in Württemberg-Baden in 1945/46 and was among those who inspired establishment of the Conference, but was not himself a member because he resigned before it was set up), Alois Hundhammer (CSU), Joachim Tiburtius (CDU), Heinrich Landahl (SPD), Erwin Stein (CDU), and Adolf Grimme (SPD). During the fifties the Conference welcomed Willy Dehnkamp (SPD, later Mayor of Bremen), Hans Wenke (CDU), Ludwig Metzger (SPD), Eduard Orth (CDU), and Edo Osterloh (CDU). Wilhelm Hahn (CDU), Carl-Heinz Evers (SPD), Moritz Thape (SPD), Ernst Schütte (SPD), Ludwig von Friedeburg (SPD), Paul Mikat (CDU), Bernhard Vogel (CDU, who was later for many years Prime Minister of Rhineland-Palatinate and then Thuringia), Werner Scherer (CDU), and Hans Maier (CSU) were among those who made a name for themselves during the era of educational reforms.

The Conference's statutes define its task as involving discussion of "all matters of educational policy of national relevance with the objective of achieving common objectives and representing common aims". Conference resolutions and recommendations demand unanimity on the part of all the Laender ministers of education. Resolutions are documented in constantly updated loose-leaf volumes, providing information about the results achieved. Conference resolutions constitute recommendations to the federal states and only become binding when promulgated in the form of laws, decrees, and regulations. Conference agreements are prepared by specialized committees, sub-committees, standing commissions, and other bodies in conjunction with the organization's secretariat. There are four specialized committees, dealing with schooling, universities, the arts, and further education. Since 1990 the committee on German schools abroad has been a sub-committee within the set-up concerned with general schooling. In fact, all the other committees have sub-committees, such as a body dealing with student affairs in conjunction with the universities committee. Standing commissions exist for European affairs, university admission, and curricular reforms.

The Conference's most important bodies are the plenary assembly, its elected executive board with the president changing annually, and the senior officials. The Conference secretariat – a department of the Berlin administration since the early sixties – deals with co-ordination, headed by a secretary-general. Continuity has been assured by the fact that there have only been two secretary-generals during the past four decades. Kurt Frey, previously a leading figure in student administration and the German UNESCO commission, held office from 1955 to 1975. His thoughts on cultural and educational policy, published in 1976 as “Konstruktiver Föderalismus” (“Constructive Federalism”), offer excellent insights into policies at that time. Joachim Schulz-Hardt, previously an educational administrator in Schleswig-Holstein, has headed the secretariat since 1975. Linked with the secretariat are the Educational Exchange Service, the Central Office for Education Abroad, and the Central Office for Standardization and Educational Economics (successor to the former Laender Institute for School Construction). The Central Office for Education Abroad, which evaluates the equivalence of foreign school and university qualifications, is becoming increasingly important with the growth of international links.

The unanimity demanded of Conference resolutions entails great pressure towards compromise and demands of all the Laender a sense of national responsibility and renunciation of “self-assertion”. As long as the education system developed comparatively slowly during the post-world war II phase of reconstruction and was not the focus of political controversy, the co-ordination implemented by the Conference achieved considerable success. Until the mid-sixties the Conference succeeded in maintaining a balance between step-by-step reforms and a high degree of uniformity in development and expansion of the education system. The Conference also played a decisive part in preparing the way for three agreements reached by the Prime Ministers, unifying various aspects of the school system: the Düsseldorf Agreement (17.2.1955) on standardization in schools, its revision (Hamburg Agreement, 28.10.1964 – most recently amended on 14.10.1971), and the agreement on standardization of degree-granting colleges of higher education (31.10.1968) introducing this new type of college and providing for complete re-organization of this level of education (see section 15.8.6). The Hamburg Agreement was extended by later Conference changes, regulating reciprocal recognition of examinations and certificates (i.e. qualifications gained at comprehensive schools) and overall duration of schooling up to the *Abitur* (see sections 9.5 and 14.1). The Conference also reached agreement on additional common aspects within schooling and reciprocal recognition of qualifications gained at general and vocational schools in all the Laender.

The Düsseldorf and Hamburg Agreements relate to general rather than vocational schools. They contain regulations on length of holidays, staggering of the summer vacation, unified nomenclature relating to schools, recognition of examinations, and terminology relating to grades. In 1964 nomenclature and forms of organization in general schools, and the order in which foreign languages are taught, were newly regulated. The limitations imposed by the Düsseldorf Agreement on the progression of foreign language teaching at *Gymnasium* were eased. The 1963 Franco-German Treaty of Friendship exerted an influence there with French accepted instead of English or Latin as the first foreign language from class 5 – but that was only implemented to a limited extent. The way was also opened for establishment of special and observational levels in classes 5 and 6, and for organizational separation between the *Grundschule* and *Hauptschule*. Compulsory full-time education was unified at nine years, and the trend towards prolongation of schooling received expression in a regulation allowing for a tenth year at *Hauptschule*. The Düsseldorf Agreement's restrictions on possibilities of experimentation at school were considerably alleviated. These possibilities of experimentation have increasingly been made use of in the course of the past decades. The Hamburg Agreement also brought to an end years of controversy by laying down that the school year should start in the autumn rather than as previously – except in Bavaria – at Easter. The Hamburg regulations were thus more flexible than their precursors, guaranteeing the necessary freedom for new developments. That helps explain why they have now been in force for over three decades. The 1964 Agreement also applied to the New Laender after reunification in 1990, so it remains supremely important for general schooling in Germany up to the present day – despite individual deviations. By regulating certain aspects of the education system the Agreement almost assumes the status of what in centralized states would be a national law regulating school organization.

Co-operation and autonomous co-ordination among the Laender became more difficult during the second half of the sixties when educational structures were increasingly subjected to partial reform. Leading political figures from all the main parties were convinced that there should be greater educational uniformity and overall comprehensibility, and that the federal authorities should be accorded a say in educational policy. The emphasis was on federal involvement in the financing of university expansion. In May 1969, after years of debate on establishment of a “Federal Ministry of Education”, particularly advocated by the FDP, a constitutional change was finally agreed under the Kiesinger/Brandt Grand Coalition between CDU/CSU and SPD, creating the preconditions for increased federal involvement in educational policy. Only since 1969 do the federal government and parliament have limited powers within education (see section 2.4).

This development had consequences for the Conference of Ministers of Education. When the Federal-Laender Commission for Educational Planning (see section 2.5) was set up in 1970 under the SPD/FDP federal government, the Conference moved somewhat into the background as far as educational policy was concerned. The situation changed again at the end of the seventies when it became apparent that national educational planning was not feasible over the longer term.

The Standing Conference of Ministers of Education met in Bonn on February 19, 1988 to mark 40 years of existence. Erwin Stein, former Hesse Minister of Education and one of the few surviving participants from the first gathering in 1948, looked back on the Conference's beginnings: "The Conference succeeded in integrating the necessary minimum of educational uniformity within the federal constitutional structure and in preserving Germany's intellectual unity. Within this process of co-ordination it takes into account the cultural characteristics of each federal state, bringing about a degree of compatibility. Its activities throw light on the achievements and possibilities of constructive federalism ... By implementing democratic federalism the Conference has upheld wide-ranging political life and a developing political will founded on solidarity, while cultivating cultural diversity which was and remains characteristic of Germany and the wealth of its history. Today cultural autonomy has become a corner-stone in the Laender's federalist self-image".

Stein recollected the Conference's Bernkastel resolution (No. 20 dated 18.10.1949) as being a kind of "cultural and educational declaration of faith". That resolution says:

"1. The Standing Conference of Ministers of Education states that the Bonn Basic Law recognizes Laender cultural autonomy within the Federal Republic of Germany.

2. The Standing Conference of Ministers of Education is convinced that the totalitarian and centralized cultural policy of the recent past contributed towards fateful confusion and oppression of the spirit, and to many Germans' susceptibility to that evil.

The Conference thus views obligations involving local and historical autonomy and social diversity as a guarantee of the German people's inner regeneration and of a self-generated culture's organic growth ... "

Stein concluded his retrospective survey with some critical remarks:

"The Basic Law of 1988 is no longer the same as the law of 1949. The 36 additions and changes may offer the Basic Law as a strong foundation, but they clearly reveal a shift of emphasis between the central authorities and the Laender. Traditional federalism has developed into co-operative federalism and voluntary functions preserving balance have been replaced by legally assigned communal tasks (as laid down in articles 91a and 91b). Here – and particularly by way of the great budgetary and financial reforms of 1969, forms of mixed administration reducing Laender parliamentary autonomy, and centralized planning – a process of political emaciation of state powers becomes very apparent. Divergent convictions about educational policy and conflicting political allegiances in and between individual Laender also make it more difficult to remove this area of conflict between the federal authorities and the Laender".

No-one at the anniversary meeting in 1988 could anticipate that just two and a half years later the Conference would be put to a great test during the process of German reunification when the Ministers of Education from the five New Laender returned to the Conference (on 6/7.12.1990) after an absence of 42 years. The 252nd plenary session took place on 21/22.2.1991 at Stuttgart-Hohenheim, the historic site of its first gathering. Here the Hohenheim Memorandum on education, science, and cultural issues in a unified Germany was passed. The Ministers of Education of all the Laender viewed their primary task as involving contributing towards a growing together of education, scholarship, culture, and sport in hitherto separated parts of Germany, and supporting the development of new structures and conservation of cultural substance. Particular emphasis was put on commitment to Europe and greater co-operation with the states of Central and Eastern Europe.

During the years that followed, the Conference passed a number of important resolutions in the spirit of the Hohenheim Memorandum, including a “Common Framework for all Types of School and Courses in Secondary Sphere I” (2/3.12.1991 – Beschlußsammlung no. 102), regulations on the recognition and equivalence of qualifications, and an agreement on acceptance and integration of teacher training programmes from the former GDR (Beschlußsammlung nos. 438 and 719). All these measures (later to be described in context) serve the objective of securing “inner unity” within the German education system. The Conference's main task thus continues to entail co-ordinating development of the Laender education systems, particularly with regard to structures, curricula, and qualifications. That includes the previously mentioned agreement (concluded at the end of 1993) on types of schools and courses in secondary level I (Beschlußsammlung no. 102), the 1994 recommendations on primary schools, support for special education, and general agreements on vocational schooling, to which we will return later. Alongside work on national issues the Conference contributes towards EU developments as shaped by the Maastricht Treaty (see also section 18).

Over the decades there has also been much criticism of the Conference's activities. Some resolutions and recommendations were viewed as empty compromises and masterpieces of verbal evasion. Quite a few commentators believed in the seventies that the Conference was close to its end. However, the Conference has turned out to be indispensable, particularly at times of educational crisis, even though it may not always succeed in achieving the unity striven for.

2.4 Federal Ministry of Education, Science, Research, and Technology

The Federal Ministries of Education and Science and of Research and Technology were merged in cabinet reforms at the start of the 1994/98 legislative period. The former had been in existence since autumn 1969. The social-liberal coalition – at that time the Brandt/Scheel cabinet – thereby demonstrated that it wanted to make full use of the powers over educational policy accorded to the federal authorities in May of that year with changes to the Basic Law. The Ministry (in both its former and present form) thus oversees federal responsibilities in the educational sphere, apart from cultural policy abroad, which is still the responsibility of the Foreign Office. The Ministry of Education, Science, Research, and Technology is in charge of the following:

- Educational planning and research
- Financial assistance for training (educational grants) and young scholars
- Vocational training inclusive of assistance
- General university legislation, university expansion, and the promotion of scholarship.

Federal powers affect the following aspects of education:

a) *Concurrent Legislation*

- Non-school vocational training and further training (Basic Law, art. 74, nos. 11 & 12)
- Regulation of educational grants for school pupils, apprentices, and students (Basic Law, art. 74, no. 13)
- Assistance for scholarly research (Basic Law, art. 74, no. 13)
- Regulation of pay and welfare for public service employees inclusive of teachers and university lecturers (Basic Law, art. 74a)

b) *Outline Legislation*

- General principles for the university system (Basic Law, art. 75, no. 1a)

c) *Shared Functions*

- University expansion and building including university clinics (Basic Law, art. 91a)
- The federal authorities' right to involvement (so far as feasible) in educational planning and the promotion of scholarly institutions and research projects of national significance (Basic Law, art. 91b)

Since 1969 the federal authorities have succeeded in implementing six laws affecting educational policy: the University Building Assistance Law (see section 2.6), the University Outline Law (see section 15), a law providing protection for participants in correspondence courses (see section 17.2), the Vocational Training Law, the Training Assistance Law (see section 10.3), and the Federal Law on Educational Grants (see section 15.2). All these federal laws regulate aspects of the education system and have in the meantime been amended several times.

Administrative responsibility for non-school vocational training is jointly shared by the Federal Ministries of Education and Research, Economics, Labour and Social Affairs, and Food, Agriculture, and Forestry.

As previously mentioned, the Federal Ministry of Scientific Research was replaced in autumn 1969 by the Federal Ministry of Education and Science. The first Federal Minister of Education was Professor Hans Leussink (1969-72), a man free of any party allegiance. He had made a name for himself as rector of the Karlsruhe Technical University, president of the West German Rectors Conference, and member/chairman of the Science Council. Leussink was assisted by his secretary of state, Hildegard Hamm-Brücher who in the same capacity at the Hesse Ministry of Education (1967-69) had previously vigorously advocated educational reform. She was the main force behind the "Bildungsbericht '70", which in June 1970 outlined the federal government's first concept for educational policy – in many respects based on the "Educational Structure Plan" published by the German Education Council in February 1970. Its main educational objectives included re-organization of pre-schooling, development of an integrated and differentiated comprehensive school and university system, and replacement of teacher training for specific schools by a graduated system. The euphoria exemplified in this first "Educational Report" was highly unrealistic. For instance, it was hoped that by 1980 all youngsters would gain an initial secondary qualification (*Abitur* I) after ten years of schooling, and also that half the pupils within an age-group would get the *Abitur* II qualification, granting university admission. In that year 16.5 % of pupils passed the *Abitur*, while the number of students had doubled (from 510,000 to 1,044,000) in the previous decade. In 1977 Wilhelm A. Kewenig, chairman of the Science Council, had already spoken about universities being "in danger of drowning".

Leussink was succeeded by his ministry's former parliamentary secretary of state Klaus von Dohnanyi (SPD, 1972-74), who launched the first comprehensive plan for education (to be discussed in the next section). In 1976 his successor Helmut Rohde (SPD) succeeded in getting the University Outline Law through parliament. He was then followed by Jürgen Schmude (SPD, 1978-81) and Björn Engholm (SPD, 1981-2). After the social-liberal coalition was followed by a CDU-CSU-FDP coalition with Helmut Kohl as Chancellor, Dorothee Wilms (CDU) became the first woman to head the Federal Ministry of Education and Science. She, unlike her predecessors, remained in office for a long period (1982-87), ensuring consolidation of federal educational policy. The 1985 amendments to the University Outline Law brought important changes of course. Between 1987 and 1991 her dynamic successor Jürgen W. Möllemann (FDP) implemented several special university programmes and was closely involved in restructuring the university set-up in the New Laender (see sections 15.4 and 15.5). The next minister, Rainer Ortleb (FDP), was one of the first federal ministers from the East. From January 1991 to February 1994 he was a calm and thoughtful mediator between East and West Germans until forced to resign for health reasons. The period up to the autumn 1994 elections was filled by Karl-Hans Laermann, an expert with years of experience. Fritz Schaumann, secretary of state for education since 1988, made a particularly important contribution to redeveloping the system in the New Laender. Since autumn 1994 the restructured ministry has been headed by Jürgen Rüttgers (CDU), often called "Minister for the Future". Rüttgers is especially interested in new multi-media technologies and is planning, together with German Telecom, to establish internet links for schools. He aims to link up 10,000 German schools within a short period. The idea is that they should have free access to the German Scientific Network for several years. At the opening of the CeBit '96 international exhibition at Hanover in March 1996, Rüttgers declared: "We shall also establish a German 'education server' that the schools involved can use as a platform for information and communication. We shall set up a public body furthering such links for schools ... They should have a chance of involvement in current online multi-media. They should get to know about the media future rather than learning computer history".

The Conference of Ministers of Education discussed that initiative in June 1996 and approved a draft constitution for the planned public body.

The "Minister for the Future" may perhaps overestimate the importance of modern technology for schools and education. Even in the years ahead teachers and pupils, rather than computers, will remain the focus of teaching. Teaching involves the mediation and appropriation of subject-matter. To date rapid changes in technology have also led to ever-faster "obsolescence". Experience shows that superseded teaching technologies quickly accumulate in school storage areas.

2.5 Federal-Laender Commission for Educational Planning and Advancement of Research

Since 1969 the federal authorities have had a right to a say in educational planning – as laid down in article 91b of the Basic Law. The details were regulated in the administrative agreement between federation and Laender (25.6.1970, revised 17/21.12.1990) on establishment of the Federal-Laender Commission for Educational Planning and the Advancement of Research. Promotion of research was added to the Commission's sphere of work on 28.11.1975 and the organization has its present name since 5.4.1976. The outline agreement (7.5.1971, revised 17/21.12.1990) on co-ordinated preparation, implementation, and scholarly evaluation of educational pilot projects provides the foundation for the Commission's activities. The New Laender joined this set-up with effect from 1.1.1991.

The Conference of Ministers of Education serves co-ordination of educational policy among the Laender whereas the Federal-Laender Commission is a standing forum for all the issues in education and promotion of research that jointly affect the federal authorities and the Laender. Representatives of the Science Council, the chief local authority organizations, and members of the Federal Institute for Vocational Training attend Commission meetings in an advisory capacity. The chairmanship of the Commission alternates annually between a representative of the federal or the Laender governments. The Commission is headed by a secretary-general and based in Bonn. That position has been filled by such outstandingly experienced experts in educational administration as Karl-Gotthart Hasemann (1970-75), Kurt Kreuser (1976-86), Marianne Tidick (1987-88), and Jürgen Schlegel (since 1990). Commission staff do the groundwork for meetings of the main body, its committees, and study-groups. The Commission is a government body and works closely together with the Laender conferences of specialist ministers, particularly the Conference of Ministers of Education.

For its work on educational planning, the Commission consists of eight representatives of the federal government and one representative from each of the Laender governments. The federal representatives have 16 votes, cast uniformly, while the Laender have one vote each. Votes are thus equally balanced (16:16). Passing a resolution requires the agreement of at least 13 heads of government, and this is only binding on those that voted for it. More simplified procedures apply to voting on "assistance for research".

The Commission puts forward recommendations which are presented to the heads of government for their consideration and approval. Two committees have been established for preparation of such resolutions, covering educational planning and assistance for research.

The "educational innovation" project-group, which prepares decisions in accordance with the "pilot projects" outline agreement, is linked with the educational planning committee. So too are the following groups:

- Special commission for correspondence courses
- Editorial conference for the brochure "Choosing Degree Courses and Professions"
- Study-group on "Documentation of Qualifications in Secondary Level II".

The committee on assistance for research also includes:

- the "German Research Association / Max Planck Society" study- group
- the "Blue List" and "Information and Documentation" study-group.

The following belong to both committees:

- the "University Special Programme" study-group
- the "University Renewal Programme" study-group
- the "Assistance for Women Scholars" study-group.

The Commission's main task in the seventies was preparation of the Comprehensive Education Plan. This first plan to be jointly devised by the federal and Laender authorities was approved after long and tough negotiations in 1973. The Plan contained guidelines for educational development up to 1985, but it was not possible to reach unanimous agreement on far-reaching structural changes within the education system. CDU- and CSU-ruled Laender differed with regard to the orientation level, the integrated comprehensive school, and teacher training. Dissent over educational policy could not be bridged. Even though the overall plan was not implemented with regard to controversial aspects of co-ordinated structural development throughout the Federal Republic, it was nonetheless very useful as a means of planning quantitative targets such as teacher-pupil ratios. Increasing divergences over educational policy led in 1982 to the breakdown of the already largely agreed continuation of the Comprehensive Education Plan until 1995. Viewed superficially, this was the outcome of disputes over the costs involved in education, but the deeper reason lay in some Laender efforts to avoid restriction of their freedom of action. They feared imposition of majority decisions by the federation and other Laender. The Commission differs from the Conference of Ministers of Education in that there is less pressure towards showing partner-like harmony. Unanimity is not required, so the majority can enforce their wishes on a minority.

Since 1989 the Federal-Laender Commission has been charged with implementing the two University Special Programmes, and since 1991 also the federal University Renewal Programme providing financial assistance for redevelopment of the university system in the New Laender (see sections 15.4 and 15.5).

The Commission has always made a particularly important contribution to assisting and supervising educational pilot projects. There it works closely together with representatives of schools, scholarship, and research. These pilot projects are intended to yield new impulses for developments in schools, training, universities, and adult education. The Commission has published numerous reports on evaluation and implementation of such activities (most recently "Successful Pilot Projects. 2nd Report on Implementation in the Education System", 1995). This also promotes exchanges of experience. At present there are seven spheres where pilot projects are assisted:

- Vocational Training
- Universities
- New information and communication technologies
- Integration of environmental issues
- Education in the fine arts
- Girls and women in education
- Differentiated support for special groups.

Pilot projects are also deployed for solving current problems arising out of such urgent educational issues as media education, European studies, relevance of schooling, and behaviour inside and outside school. Between 1971 and 1995 both the federal authorities and the Laender made 1.8 billion DM available for pilot projects. The Commission several times devoted investigations to the impact of new media and technologies in schools and universities, and assisted computer investment programmes with considerable amounts of money.

One of the Federal-Laender Commission's main tasks is the monitoring of long-term staffing developments in the education system. Using projections the Commission in 1994 produced a report on trends up to the year 2010. Similar work in the university sphere was concluded in 1995 (see section 18).

Structural problems in the relationship between education and employment continue to occupy the Commission. These mainly involve the impact of structural changes (plus technological and economic innovations) on educational qualifications. On 12.12.1994 the Commission approved a report on employment prospects for school-leavers. This study comes to the conclusion that demand for higher qualifications will increase and people without such formal qualifications will continue to constitute the greatest problem. Considerable efforts will be necessary to help such people acquire the necessary qualifications.

On the other hand, university graduates will in future be faced with greater difficulties when trying to find employment. Jobs that previously went to people with middle-level qualifications are now being taken by university graduates and those who have completed a course at some other degree-granting college of higher education. Special recommendations are designed to solve problems arising when making the transition from education to employment. That issue is not just being discussed by specialists; it is also being studied by a high-level working group and raised by Laender heads of government in meetings with the Federal Chancellor.

In 1995 there appeared the 25th edition of "Chosing Degree Courses and Professions", an informative brochure which has been jointly published by the Commission and the Federal Labour Office since 1971, providing orientation about the many possibilities available in university studies and vocational training in business and administration. This publication underlies the work of university counselling offices and employment exchange career advice centres. Each edition has a print-run of around 600,000 copies (see also sections 14 and 15).

To summarize, it should be stressed that even though the Commission has not been able since 1982 to fully implement the task of comprehensive educational planning originally entrusted to it, its activities, producing recommendations on school, university, and research policy, have paved the way for the federal and Laender authorities. That is also true of European issues in educational policy and of all measures intended to increase Germany's attractiveness as a "centre of scholarship". The work done by the Commission is thus indispensable for the education policy of the federal authorities and the Laender.

On 26.6.1995 the Commission met in Bonn to celebrate 25 years of existence. The Thuringian Prime Minister Bernhard Vogel, who as the Rhineland-Palatinate Minister of Education had been the organization's chairman in the early seventies, stressed the rightness of the Federal-Laender Commission now limiting itself to essentials rather than getting involved in inflated comprehensive plans. Vogel called the Commission a living proof of the viability of co-operative educational federalism.

2.6 Planning Committee for University Construction

Until the end of the sixties the Laender were for the most part solely responsible for reconstruction and expansion of the university system. One of the most important reasons for implementation of article 91a in the Basic Law was to bring about federal participation and thereby relieve the Laender financially. This article lays down that the expansion and development of universities inclusive of medical clinics is a task for which the federal and Laender authorities are jointly responsible. The Planning Committee for University Construction was legally established in the law regulating assistance for university construction (1.9.1969, most recently revised in accordance with the Treaty of Unification, 31.8.1990 and the Treaty of Unification Law, 23.9.1990, Bundesgesetzblatt 1990 II, p. 885, 1130). The Committee has the task of drawing up a four-year outline plan for the federation and Laender. Responsibilities were increased with reconstruction of the university system in the New Laender from 1990.

Between 1970 and 1994 the federal and Laender authorities devoted 66.226 billion DM to university construction – with the federal share 29.898 billion and the Laender 36.328 billion. Both parties are jointly charged with enabling the universities to provide a sufficient, adequately qualified, and regionally balanced supply of places for study and research, and with making suitable buildings available. The targets for expansion decided on by heads of government in 1977 and 1989 still hold good today for the Western Laender: 850,000 study-places and an additional 50,000 at degree-granting colleges of higher education. In its 1993 ten theses on university policy (see section 3) the Science Council recommended a target of 1.25 million study-places for the entire country. That would include some 250,000 places in the New Laender and a total of around 350,000 in degree-granting colleges.

Two federal ministers and a minister from each of the Laender belong to this Committee with parity of voting (16:16). The Federal Minister of

Education, Science, Research, and Technology is the body's standing chairman and runs the Committee's business. Plans are always co-ordinated with the Science Council. The 25th outline plan for the period from 1996 to 1999 was approved on 14.9.1995. This provides for 3,689 projects with a total cost of 29.2 billion DM. Between 1970 and 1994 516,500 extra student-places were created and large numbers of existing buildings modernized. Yet universities are overcrowded because there are twice as many people studying as places available (in 1994 1,783,697 students and 986,820 places). In April 1996 the federal and Laender authorities reached agreement on a leasing procedure for university construction. In future private investors will share the costs of university building. Only when buildings are used will there be more extensive costs for the federation and Laender.

2.7 Constitutional and Administrative Jurisdiction in Education

Discussion of the "Crucifix Judgement" (16.5.1995) demonstrates how great the journalistic and educational impact of rulings by the federal constitutional court can be. The point of dispute was a Bavarian school ordinance laying down that crucifixes should be put up in all classrooms. A married couple objected to that. The constitutional court's ruling stated:

"1. The state regulation laying down that a cross or crucifix must be put up in classrooms in a state school, which is not a denominational school, infringes article 4, paragraph 1 of the Basic Law.
2. Section 13, paragraph 1, sentence 3 of regulations for primary schools in Bavaria is irreconcileable with article 4, paragraph 1 of the Basic Law and thus invalid".

Surveying the journalistic and legal consequences of this judgement would go too far, but this example shows that overall educational law is subject to the legal control of independent courts. Decisions by the constitutional and administrative courts have become of increasing significance for educational policy. The task of constitutional jurisdiction also involves instituting or assuring balance between state sovereignty over schools, parental rights, and educational freedom for teachers. Alongside reconstruction of the Eastern Laender, reunification also brought re-establishment of administrative and constitutional courts. Revealingly such courts did not exist in the GDR under Socialist Unity Party dictatorship.

In recent decades the federal constitutional court has reached landmark judgements on such matters as university legislature, the regulation of university admission, sex education at schools, and the previously mentioned "crucifix verdict".

Judgements by the Hesse state court concerned reforms of the upper level at *Gymnasium* and the mixed-ability level; and decisions by the Hesse administrative court affected transition from primary school to secondary education. In its judgement of 14.7.1978, the federal administrative court pointed out that legislators are obliged to take essential decisions rather than leaving them to school administrations. A decision by the supreme courts' joint senate covers vocational training.

Public discussion of "over-legalization" of the education system documents tension between administration of justice on the one hand and school and university legislation on the other. The term "over-legalization" involves a considerable degree of criticism – for instance of legal regulation increasingly restricting teachers' educational freedom. The 1976 German Lawyers Convention produced lively discussion of what legal principles should underlie state schooling. In 1981 the school law commission of the German Lawyers Convention presented comprehensive suggestions for fundamental new regulations. Amendments to Laender school laws during the past decade and a half – in Bavaria (1982 and 1994), Rhineland-Palatinate (1984 and 1994), and Hesse (1992) – took into account current legal decisions and made laws more relevant. The Bavarian constitutional court thus ruled in 1980 that the demands made on legal regulation of school organization had fundamentally changed during the two previous decades, making necessary new laws. The Hesse school law dated 30.6.1992 co-ordinated the eight laws that had previously regulated the school system and offered a systematic new approach that, for instance, took into account the basic principle of enlarging freedom of action for individual schools. This is not the place for an account of amendments to Laender school and university laws. Comprehensive information on that subject is contained in the publication entitled "Recht der Jugend und des Bildungswesens" ("Legislation on Youth and Education"). The question of whether very detailed legal regulations, which can only be corrected with difficulty, or more flexible administrative procedures that can be adapted more easily to current developments, are more practical for the school system remains unresolved.

2.8 Administration and Finance

The division of powers laid down in the Basic Law gives the Laender comprehensive responsibility for organization of education. Constitutional regulations, laws, and decrees of the individual Laender were and are decisive in that context. They determine the objectives of education, and regulate compulsory schooling, establishment and maintenance of schools, local control of schools, all levels of teacher training, supervision of schools, school administration, co-operation between parents, teachers, and pupils on the organization of work and play at school, pupil-status, free schooling and teaching aids, and assistance for education.

In the university sphere powers have been divided since 1969. The federal authorities are responsible for outline legislation and the Laender for everything else (see section 15). The Laender have autonomous powers over the establishment and organization of universities, legal jurisdiction, finances, and staffing policy. The individual universities are self-administering while implementing state policy on personnel, budget and finances, etc.

The responsibility for administration of schools and universities within a single Land devolves on a specific member of government. Until the sixties a single minister – the Minister of Education – was usually responsible, except in the city-states of Hamburg and Berlin. In the past two decades that responsibility has increasingly been shared – except in Bavaria and the Saarland. Even Bavaria split up the ministry into “Education and Culture” and “Science and Art” between 1986 and 1989, but then reunited those spheres. Administrative cutbacks and savings mean that only one ministry is responsible for education and science in Bremen, Mecklenburg-Western Pomerania, Rhineland-Palatinate, Saarland, and Schleswig-Holstein. In the other Laender schools and universities are administered by different ministries (details and addresses are to be found in appendix 27).

The tasks undertaken by the Federal Minister of Education, Science, Research, and Technology have already been outlined in section 2.4. To avoid misunderstandings, it must be stressed here that not one school or university is directly answerable to the federal ministry with its limited powers in specific spheres. The administration of schools and universities is a Laender responsibility. The Laender parliaments – and the federal parliament with regard to state responsibilities – are of decisive importance in organization of the education system and keeping a watch over government activities. Laender and federal parliamentary debates on education are very informative with regard to current developments.

Paragraph 1, article 7 of the Basic Law lays down that the school system as a whole is subject to state supervision. Inspection and administration of schools are a Laender reponsibility and in the large states are usually organized in a three-tiered system:

- lower level schools inspectorates on the municipal and communal level (state school authority)
- middle-level schools inspectorates at the district level with larger government administrative areas
- higher level schools inspectorates: the state ministries with responsibility for schools and senators for education in the city-states.

Private schools (see section 13) are also subject to state supervision. Federally-supported technical schools, degree-granting colleges of higher education, and universities (i.e. Army universities) are liable to legal supervision by the Land administration responsible.

The number of people involved in educational administration has increased considerably in order to cope effectively with the abundance of tasks facing federal, Laender, and local authorities as a result of expansion of the education system in recent decades. Relatively small Ministries of Education expanded greatly from the mid-sixties. Special departments or sections were created for such new tasks as educational planning, media education, etc. In Bavaria, for instance, ministerial appointees with responsibility for intermediate, grammar, and technical secondary schools are in charge of intensification of inspection and advisory facilities. The structures of school administration are also subjected to ongoing change.

In 1994 7.1 % of the overall education budget in the Federal Republic of Germany was met by the federal authorities, 72.2 % by the Laender, and 20.7 % by local authorities and support groups. In that year those three categories jointly provided a total of 164.4 billion DM for the education system. In addition private industry supplied an estimated 116.7 billion DM for vocational training, research, and development, and a further 19.9 billion DM was made available for training by the Federal Labour Office.

The state school system is jointly maintained by the Laender, local authorities, and municipal administrations. Expenditure on teachers is usually met by the Laender while costs of materials (plus office and maintenance staff) are mainly covered by local authorities. The German Cities Convention's schools committee facilitates exchanges of experience between the local authority departments concerned with schools, particularly in large cities.

Private schools are also eligible for Laender subsidies if they operate for the public good and replace state schools (see section 13).

Staffing costs at universities (apart from endowed professorships) are completely met by the Laender – except in the case of private colleges, church colleges, and institutions fully maintained by the federal authorities (see sections 15.7, 15.8.8, and 15.8.9). At present only about 150 of the 36,000 or so full professorships are financed by industry – including 40 by the Donors Association for German Science.

In 1989 and 1991 the federal authorities provided strong support for university expansion (Möllemann special university programmes I and II, named after the federal minister). Programme I entailed 300 million DM annually – half from the Laender and half from the federal authorities – from a total fund of 2.1 billion DM. The "Overloading Programme" was intended to improve teaching conditions, but the constitution did not permit federal financing of new staff at universities. However, the federal authorities helped the Laender in building projects so that increased Land funds became available for boosting the number of teachers.

At the beginning of September 1996 Federal Chancellor Kohl appended his signature to University Special Programme III, totalling 3.6 billion DM (with over two million provided by the federation – see section 15.6).

Experience has long shown that Finance Ministers are the 'real Ministers of Education', so it would seem apposite to outline the influence exerted by the Conference of Laender Finance Ministers on educational policy. However, that is not possible within the confines of this survey.

2.9 Education and Society

Somme educational issues are never-ending – such as reform of the final years at *Gymnasium*, the importance of the *Abitur* with regard to university entrance, and reduction of the time spent studying. It constantly becomes apparent how closely education and society are related. There was particularly lively public participation in the great debates on educational reform during the sixties and seventies. Beyond Laender and federal parliaments parents and parental associations, teachers and teachers' organizations, political parties, churches, employers' groupings and trade unions, and industrial circles and research institutes devoted attention to educational issues at that time. Their opinions were widely reported in the media. Today the political emphasis is on such topics as overcoming unemployment, environmental problems, and European unification.

2.9.1 School and Parents

Parental participation in education finds expression in a large number of legal regulations. The Basic Law lays down that bringing up children is the natural right and highest obligation of all parents (art. 6, para. 2). The state's duty to provide education has the same status as parental rights within the school system. In its judgement on sex education, the federal constitutional court ruled (21.12.1977) that the state has the indisputable right and duty to determine curricula, learning objectives and contents, whilst taking parental rights into account. The state was also held to be obliged to pay heed in schools to parents' responsibility for their children's overall upbringing, and to be open to the diversity of views on educational issues to the degree that is compatible with an orderly state school system. The previously mentioned dispute over the federal constitutional court's "crucifix judgement" (16.5.1995) makes clear that parents can get the country's highest court to reach binding decisions on aspects of educational policy.

The co-operation of schools and parents is regulated in detailed Laender legislation. All the parents of children in a specific class elect a parents council, and all such class councils constitute the school parents council, which together with other such bodies provides delegates for similar institutions at the local, district, and regional levels. Regional or national councils have differing participatory rights, and their advice is sought in basic issues within school policy such as the planning of curricula. The Hesse constitution (art. 56, para. 6) even accords the Land parents council a right to co-determination. At the start of the seventies, the dispute over new curricula (such as the Hesse guidelines for German and social studies), the introduction of mixed-ability levels, and the establishment of integrated comprehensives resulted in unusual mobilization of parents. Both the advocates and opponents of integrated comprehensives formed parental associations. There are also church parental organizations. The National Parents Council links Laender associations at the federal level.

When in 1977/78 the North Rhine-Westphalia Land government attempted to replace the tripartite school system by a comprehensive-style co-operative school with an earlier orientation level, "A Civic Action Group for a Referendum against the Co-operative School" was established. This campaign attracted an astonishing response. 3.63 million people – almost 30 % of those entitled to vote – supported a cause where 20 % would have been sufficient. The Land government and parliament in North Rhine-Westphalia then amended the disputed law on school administration, paying heed to popular wishes. This demonstrates the extent to which parents can be mobilized in response to educational developments, and how they can gain influence over school legislation and administration by way of the limited possibilities offered on the various levels of parental organization. In other Laender too, referenda have been employed by oppositions to correct or block governmental decisions on school policy.

2.9.2 Political Parties and Education

The political parties are of crucial importance in the organization and further development of the education system. Article 21 of the Basic Law says that the political parties should assist the development of the nation's political will. The constitution mainly assigns the power to take political decisions about education to parliaments in the Laender and city-states. However, debates on educational policy also occur in the federal parliament and the upper house to the extent that their sphere of competence is involved. Since 1969 the federal authorities have taken on greater powers in educational policy. Local, town, and district councils reach educational decisions within their spheres of reference.

The six parties at present represented in the federal and Laender parliaments – SPD, CDU, CSU, FDP, Alliance 90 / The Greens, and the PDS – have differing and sometimes antagonistic views about the structure and organization of the education system, despite often similar objectives with regard to European unification, integration of foreigners, and some other aspects of education. The often tough struggle over the course taken by education makes clear that such issues are also questions of power, which must be determined by political means. The parties each have their own policy commissions and study groups, determining an educational programme. The viewpoints of the six parties can only be considered very briefly here.

Particularly disputed is the organization of secondary level I inclusive of the orientation (mixed-ability) level. The CDU/CSU advocates a humanistic and achievement-oriented school system which differentiates according to ability. The intention is to implement the highest possible degree of equality of opportunity. In such a structured system each school type serves a particular educational purpose and should thus develop an autonomous profile. Only in such a system do parents retain a clear-cut right to co-determination of their children's progress at school. A pupil's abilities and parental expectations rather than state planning are thus seen as the decisive factor in decisions about the education a child receives. When in early 1996 the CDU group in the Saarland parliament went against party policy and expressed support for a SPD initiative to abolish secondary moderns and, in order to do so, change the Saarland constitution, Kurt Reumann (writing in the daily “Frankfurter Allgemeine Zeitung”, 24.1.1996) sarcastically remarked: “The SPD has failed in its policy of having comprehensives swallow up all types of school, including grammar schools. The CDU is equally stranded and now lacks any clear-cut policy”.

The SPD has a long tradition of commitment to education. Mention need only be made of the 1891 Erfurt Programme and the first large-scale schools programme at the 1906 Mannheim party conference. Since its 1964 policy guidelines the SPD views “educational policy as the most important shared task facing our people”, and has called for merging individual school types as within the organizational unity of the comprehensive school. A recently published SPD pamphlet, “Education 2000”, states: “We want the younger generation to have an education system implementing the right to the best possible education and training while taking into account social demands”. Objectives include increasing all-day schooling and further development of vocational training.

As early as the fifties the FDP advocated federal responsibilities within education – as were partially implemented in 1969. In the seventies the FDP also supported comprehensives as an “open school”, usually conceived as involving all-day activities. Even in the sixties liberal education policy proclaimed "the right to education" and that objective is still asserted. Liberals call for greater emphasis on values with training in tolerance and humanity, capacity for coping with conflict, and readiness for non-violent solution of discord. The FDP would also like to improve possibilities of taking the *Abitur* after twelve years at school. In recent years the demand for an "open school" has strikingly diminished. Today the emphasis is on assistance for anyone of ability and on compensating for social disadvantages. The party declares that only early assistance for socially deprived children makes achievement possible. Outstandingly able children, no matter what their social background, should therefore receive differentiated and additional support. Unhindered development of personal potential is ultimately best assisted by a wide range of educational opportunities. What is needed – believes the FDP – is free competition between ideas, diversity of types of school, more opportunities for independent sources of education, and the provision of competition by private colleges.

Alliance 90 / The Greens see their main task as involving reform of schools from within. They want to make schools places of real life experience and ecological learning. They oppose the pressure of grades, competition, and general stress at school. They fear that current school and university education promote conformist citizens and therefore advocate equivalence between all schools (particularly between state and alternative schools), unified and integrated schooling up to the tenth class, and education in ecologically aware social and democratic behaviour. Special schools for children with learning problems are thought unnecessary.

The educational policies of the PDS (Democratic Socialist Party) postulate integrated comprehensives and all-day schooling. The tripartite school system should be abolished. The party advocates amendment of the University Outline Law with the objective of parity of co-determination for all groups represented. Democratic processes within the public education system are to be extended.

2.9.3 The Churches and Education

The Protestant Church in Germany has around 28.5 million members (c. 35 % of the total population), and the Roman Catholic Church 28 million (c. 34.4 %). Ongoing secularization has led to a decline in those numbers from year to year – particularly in big cities. Today's Germany also has 370,000 adherents of the Christian Orthodox faith, some 200,000 members of Evangelical churches, around 50,000 in Jewish communities, and some 2.3 million Muslims, mainly of Turkish origin.

The Basic Law retains the 1919 Weimar Constitution's separation of church and state but took into account specific historical developments. In both Protestant and Catholic territories the education system was mainly in the hands of the church until the 19th century and only largely came under the state during the past hundred years. It was not until the 1960s that the remaining denominational distinctions among primary schools were abandoned. So close traditional links exist between the education system and the churches. The churches have a special say in the organization of religious teaching, which – in accordance with art. 7, para. 3 of the Basic Law – is a regular subject at general schools (except for a few non-denominational schools) with pupils free to participate or not. They also influence appointments to chairs of theology at universities and colleges.

Religion is taught at the great majority of schools in accordance with the basic principles of the churches, which take responsibility for seeing that content and presentation accord with their dispensations. In order to guarantee such uniformity, churches are allowed to inspect religious teaching, but their powers vary from Land to Land. Unfortunately in recent decades religious instruction has often become a form of "social studies". But anyone who wants to bring up young Germans as Europeans must impart basic knowledge about religion and its history, necessary for understanding German and European history and the present day.

The voluntary nature of participation in religious education is ensured by the fact that art. 7, para. 2 of the Basic Law accords parents the right to determine whether children participate or not. They can thus also withdraw their children from such classes. From the age of 14 pupils have a right to decide for themselves – as laid down in the Reich's law on religious education for children (15.7.1921). The Standing Conference of Ministers of Education report dated 7/8.5.1992 provides information about "The Situation facing Protestant and Catholic Religious Education" in the old Federal Republic.

Religious instruction has been the subject of fierce discussions during restructuring of the school system in the five New Laender after 1990. Religious teaching was banned in schools after 1945 in the Soviet occupied zone and later in the GDR. The churches organized denominational instruction on a voluntary basis, but that only reached a few per cent of school pupils, exposed as they were to the anti-church pressure of the ruling Socialist Unity Party. The reintroduction – with adoption of the Basic Law – of religious instruction as a "normal subject" at state schools in the majority of the New Laender was met with widespread incomprehension and even rejection. Here it becomes apparent that secularization in the former GDR (as the outcome of totalitarian rule and atheistic upbringing of the young since 1933) went much further than in the West. In 1950 92 % of the population in the East still belonged to a Church, but today in the New

Laender, traditionally predominantly Protestant, only 25 % still belong to the Protestant Church and 3 % to the Catholic Church. (In the old Federal Republic around 39 % of school pupils are Protestant, 41 % Catholic, and some 5 % Muslim). The social preconditions for (voluntary) religious instruction at state schools are thus completely different in the East.

There has been much discussion about whether the "Bremen Clause" (in article 141 of the Basic Law) is applicable in the New Laender. This runs: "Article 7, paragraph 3, clause 1 is not applicable in a Land where another legal regulation applied on January 1, 1949". This only refers to Bremen and Berlin where the churches and other religious communities are themselves responsible for the provision of religious instruction at schools. The Bremen Clause does not apply to the New Laender. Different regulations applied on January 1, 1949, in Brandenburg, Mecklenburg, Saxony, Saxony-Anhalt, and Thuringia – but the New Laender established in summer 1990 on the basis of GDR law are not identical with the territories existing at that time.

The reintroduction of religious instruction at state schools already faces difficulties because of lack of teachers. School laws lay down that religious instruction or ethics (for pupils who do not take part in religious instruction) is an obligatory subject. Only Brandenburg has introduced "Life-Choices, Ethics, Religious Studies" as a school subject, but that concept was rejected by the Protestant and Catholic Churches. A constitutional court judgement on the acceptability of this Brandenburg initiative is awaited. The triumphant headline of the pro-PDS "Neues Deutschland" (which used to be the main SED newspaper) on 29.3.1996, after the new Brandenburg school law had got through parliament, revealingly ran: "End to Biblical Omnipotence". In Brandenburg religious instruction can now only be provided by the Church.

Church study centres, offices, and commissions for religious education develop curricula and provide further training for teachers. The churches also run free schools (private schools – see section 13), colleges and polytechnics (see section 15.8.9) where theologians, teachers of religion, educationists, and social workers receive training.

The church academies play an important part in public discussion and adult education. Church synods time and again express views on educational issues. Relations between church and state are partly regulated by way of concordats (with the Catholic Church) and partly by treaty (with the Protestant Churches). In the sixties in Laender where denominationally separated primary and secondary schools existed, discussions with the Churches led to establishment of the legal preconditions for transforming these into mixed-community schools as had long been the rule elsewhere. Denominational teacher training for state schools was also abandoned at that time.

After a pause of eight years, discussion of issues in Protestant and Catholic teaching took place at Mainz (on 30.11.1995) between the executive board of the Conference of Ministers of Education, the German Protestant Churches Council, and the German Bishops Conference. The Churches were concerned about lack of expert delineation of the tasks involved in religious teaching within the Conference's guidelines on work in primary schools, the status of religious studies at the senior level in *Gymnasium*, and religious instruction at vocational schools. Church representatives stressed: "Provision with religious instruction as laid down in article 7 of the Basic Law is not guaranteed in all Laender for various reasons. The training of teachers of religion should be assured by the state with the necessary nationwide provisions". Reports by Ministers of Education, particularly from the New Laender, showed increases in participation in religious instruction and ethics lessons, but that only involves a minority of pupils.

The Churches presented a memorandum on religious education to the Conference. This stated: "The constitutionally assured status of religious instruction as an established subject signifies that the religious education thus mediated is an element within the general education offered in school under state supervision. It is therefore part of general basic education and also of more advanced general education and specialization". Harald Kästner, the Conference's schools expert, recently commented critically: "The outsider-role of religious instruction in the Conference resolutions on school types, courses, and qualifications ... clearly shows ... that there is a danger of treating religious education as something unimportant and turning it into an 'incidental' subject".

2.9.4 Industrial Associations, Trade Unions, Media

There also exists a broad spectrum of non-parliamentary social forces, which make an intensive contribution to discussion of educational policy. Teachers' associations thus play an active part in the shaping of public opinion about educational policy, and also provide further training for their members. The large majority of teachers are organized in one of the three big associations:

- the Education and Science Union (GEW with Land branches: 307,000 members – 230,000 teachers including 16,000 unemployed or retired)
- the German Teachers Association (DL with some 160,000 members)
- the Education and Training Association (VBE with over 140,000 members).

Affiliated to the German Teachers Association are the German Philologists Association, the Federal Association of Teachers at Vocational Schools, the Business Teachers Association, the Association of German Intermediate School Teachers, and the Saxony Teachers Association. The long-established German Philologists Association (with branches in the Laender) and the Federal Association of Grammar School Headmasters are very influential at upper school – and the same is true of the Association of German Intermediate School Teachers for that type of school.

The GEW and other associations publish a large number of professional journals, organize conferences and gatherings, and thereby influence public opinion. Among such publications mention should be made of "Die Grundschule", "Realschule in Deutschland", "Profil" (previously "Die Höhere Schule"), "Wirtschaft und Erziehung", "Die berufliche Schule", and (principally in the New Laender) "Die deutsche Lehrerzeitung". The Laender associations also have their own publications, such as "Das Gymnasium in Rheinland-Pfalz" (produced by the Rhineland-Palatinate Philologists Association). After reunification in 1990 teachers associations played an important part in the integration of teachers in the New Laender.

The German Society for Education, founded in 1963, serves the advancement of scholarly pedagogics by way of co-operation and exchanges of ideas among its members. It also cultivates contacts with other branches of scholarship and with educationists in other countries. This society comprises 17 commissions, covering such spheres as empirical educational research, economics and vocational pedagogics, adult education, recreational education, history of education, and comparative education. It has a membership of around 1,500 scholars. The bi-annual congresses constitute an important forum for meetings between people involved in educational scholarship and educational policy. That was also demonstrated by Federal President Roman Herzog's speech (quoted at the beginning of this book) at the 15th congress, held at Halle / Saale, in March 1996.

The German Society for the Administration of Education has since 1979 brought together administrative specialists and scholars. This organization views itself as an independent and interdisciplinary forum for issues within the administration of education. Current problems are discussed in the Society's "Zeitschrift für Bildungsverwaltung".

The Society for the Advancement of Educational Research (founded in 1950) works together with the German Institute for International Educational Research (Frankfurt / Main) on intensification of communication between teachers, policy-makers, and researchers. The Society also exerts an influence beyond the confines of academia through its "Discussions on Educational Policy", jointly organized with radio stations.

In the sphere of higher education the German University Association re-established in 1950 (following on from the organization disbanded by the Nazis in 1934) represents the interests of university teachers in independent and interdisciplinary fashion. It has a membership of around 16,000, and exerts an influence on educational policy with a great variety of reports and annual congresses. The Association's bulletin, now in its 43rd year, has also documented developments in higher education in recent decades. The Federation for Freedom of Scholarship has been in existence since 1970 and now has around 2,500 members. It was founded to defend freedom of research against student groups and political circles that had different ideas. Those times are fortunately past. Today scholarly freedom is no longer endangered by leftist political ideas. Now the Association works on behalf of qualitative improvements in the education system, stressing comparability of achievement rather than institutional uniformity.

Employers associations and trade unions express their views on educational problems in policy declarations. The German Trade Union Federation (DGB) thus called for legal establishment of a compulsory tenth year of general schooling and introduction of the all-day integrated comprehensive. The Congress of Industry and Trade has also often expressed its views on policies affecting education and vocational training. The Federal Union of German Employers Associations has organized educational gatherings together with teachers associations – for instance with the Association of German Intermediate School Teachers in the case of the September 1994 Cologne meeting on “Successful Diversity: Intermediate Schools in the Federal German Education System”. Co-operation between industry, schools (particularly vocational schools), and universities happens on many levels, including the development of curricula and courses of study and assistance for research programmes. In 1993 the Donors Association for German Science made available 119 million DM in support of scholarship and research. The number of foundations administered by this organization has risen to over 200 with capital of over one billion DM. The Donors Association's assistance programme is mainly concerned with structural and organizational issues. A special programme finances over 22 professorships at universities in the New Laender. Current problems are discussed at annual meetings and in the “Villa Hügel Discussions”. The “Wirtschaft und Wissenschaft” quarterly covers the Association's work.

The wide range of social forces influencing education cannot be adequately covered here. The activities of school-pupil and student associations are worthy of mention alongside the work of television, radio, and the press.

3 Advisory Bodies on Educational Policy

The fact that decisions in educational policy are reached on the basis of consultations with scholars, representatives of public life, and other experts is not a recent development. Mention need only be made here of the Prussian school conferences of 1849, 1874, 1890, and 1900, and of the 1920 Reich school conference.

Two recent examples from North Rhine-Westphalia show how stimulating and exciting studies or evaluations of educational policy can be. Both the 1991 study published by the Kienbaum Institute of Economic Research, and "Future of Education – Schools of the Future", a study of reorganization of the education system produced in 1995 by the "NRW Education Commission" for Prime Minister Johannes Rau, created quite a stir.

The Kienbaum study threw light on economic aspects of problems facing schools in North Rhine-Westphalia and attempted to harmonize educational requirements and financial capacity. Suggested measures for reducing expenditure included larger classes, longer working hours for teachers, reduction of further training for teachers, reduction of age-related bonuses, curtailment of the time devoted to experimentation with new structures, and procedures for cutting the number of cancelled lessons. Such measures are also being discussed in other Laender.

The 1995 memorandum produced by the North Rhine-Westphalia Education Commission sets out to initiate discussion of future developments in education policy. The Commission is working on a concept regarding schools as "a place for learning and living". "In future individual schools with specific educational objectives should define the overall 'image' to a greater extent than differentiation in terms of different types of school. ... The emphasis should shift from general systemic issues to the development of individual schools and the totality of what is on offer at the community and regional levels". The aim is therefore a partly autonomous school (see also section 18.1). This discussion has not yet been concluded and it remains to be seen what proposals are administratively implemented.

During the post-war period special advisory bodies on educational policy were established, following the English model of Royal Commissions. A distinction has to be made here between national consultative institutions and advisory bodies in individual Laender. In the spheres of schooling, teacher training, and adult education there were two experiments in comprehensive national consultation between 1953 and 1975:

- the German Committee for Education and Training (1953-1965) and
- the German Education Council (1965-1975).

Both institutions closed down after their initiators, the federal and Laender authorities, made clear that their task was viewed as having been completed. No successor organization has existed since 1975. Attention has been drawn to this lack several times during the past two decades, but there is as yet no sign of any new concept. The situation is different for universities, libraries, and research institutes. The Science Council established in 1957 is still at work and has exerted considerable influence on university policy with its many recommendations, declarations, and evaluations. However, we must return here to the sphere of general schooling.

3.1 German Committee for Education and Training (1953-65)

At the start of the fifties, the diversity of developments in the West German school system led to sharp criticism of educational federalism, and there was public demand for a "Federal Ministry of Education" or at least a "Federal Advisory Board", ensuring a greater degree of uniformity. Erich Wende – previously state secretary in the Hanover-based Lower Saxony Ministry of Education and then responsible for developing the education section in Bonn's Ministry of the Interior from 1950 – prepared an agreement with the Conference of Ministers of Education on establishment of the German Committee for Education and Training, which was inaugurated on September 21, 1953, in the presence of Federal President Theodor Heuß. The German Committee had the task of observing the development of education and training, and of promoting this through the provision of advice and recommendations. It was not a planning body but existed – independant of any influence by the authorities – in the political territory separating the federal and the Laender authorities. The Committee consisted of some 20 persons, around half of them educationists and the rest well-known scholars and experts from industry. The composition of the Committee reflected the diversity of views on intellectual and cultural policy prevalent at that time in discussions on education in the Federal Republic. While in existence (up to

1965) the German Committee produced 29 recommendations and evaluations amounting to a total of over a thousand pages. Particular interest was aroused by the outline plan for reorganization and standardization of the general school system (1959), the recommendations for expansion of secondary moderns (1964), and the report on vocational training and schooling (1964). The lack of organizational and institutional backing turned out to be a disadvantage. There was, for instance, no ongoing co-operation with the Conference of Ministers of Education, the Laender ministries, and with federal ministries. Even though the German Committee did not succeed in implementing the comprehensive educational reforms it advocated, its reports and recommendations did nevertheless provide important impulses towards such aspects as reform of the upper level at *Gymnasium* (Conference of Ministers of Education Saarbrücken Outline Agreement, 1960), the 1961 Conference of Ministers of Education resolution on "Transferring from One Kind of School to Another", and the introduction of orientation levels in several Laender.

3.2 German Education Council (1965–75)

At the start of the sixties it became apparent that the German Committee viewed its task as having been completed, and a debate on restructuring consultation on educational policy got under way, extending over several years. In 1961 the then SPD chairman in Bavaria, Waldemar von Knoeringen, proposed conclusion of a state agreement on a "Cultural Council", intended to co-ordinate policy. The Baden-Württemberg Minister of Education, Dr. Storz (CDU), countered by advocating establishment of an Education Council modelled on the Science Council. That was the direction taken by further discussions in the Conference of Ministers of Education, which in October 1964 recommended that the Laender Prime Ministers should conclude an administrative agreement between the federal and Laender authorities. That agreement on the setting up of a German Education Council for an initial five years was concluded on 15.7.1965, assuring close co-operation with the Science Council.

The German Education Council consisted of an education commission and a government commission. The latter was composed of the ministers or senators responsible for education in the eleven Laender, four state secretaries from the federal government, and the three chief executives from the leading local authority organizations, representing cities, rural districts, and smaller communities. The education commission consisted of eighteen noted scholars with a variety of specializations, and of leading figures in public life. Its tasks included drawing up plans for meeting educational requirements and developments in accordance with the demands of cultural, economic, and social life. It also had to put forward suggestions regarding educational structures, calculate financial needs, and make recommendations on long-term planning in the various levels ranging from pre-schooling to adult education.

In order to avoid the fate of the German Committee and ensure that sufficient attention was devoted to the political and practical possibilities of implementation of these recommendations and proposals, the agreement laid down that the education commission's plans, suggestions, etc, could only be presented to the federal and Laender authorities after consultation with the government commission. The same objective was served by the involvement of representatives of educational administrations on the education commission's committees. Numerous experts were involved in evaluations. The Education Council's publications document the far-reaching nature of discussions about educational theory and policy, covering such themes as ability and learning, performance at school and its assessment, and the issues involved in integration of special schools and the experimental introduction of comprehensives.

The German Education Council's structure plan (1970) was its main contribution towards preparing the way for the Federal-Laender Commission for Educational Planning's 1973 all-inclusive education plan (see section 2.5). This structure plan attempted to adapt education in the Federal Republic to international developments. Its proposals extended from pre-schooling to further education, and also covered vocational schooling, teacher training, and the administration and financing of education. Suggestions for reform included the introduction of an orientation level (between the primary level and secondary level I). Plans for secondary level I included replacement of the unconnected parallel existence of secondary modern, intermediate, and grammar schools by various forms of interlinking (school centres and co-operative systems), and an experimental programme for trying out comprehensive schools. In 1975 the education commission also advocated trials with comprehensives as the norm in large catchment areas.

The agreement providing for the German Education Council was extended for a further five years in 1970, but support for the comprehensive option almost inevitably provoked opposition to the Council's work. Controversy was also aroused by recommendations on reform of educational organization and administration, aimed at greater autonomy for schools and more participation by teachers, pupils, and parents (1973). Increasing polarization on educational policy between the SPD/FDP on the one hand and the CDU/CSU on the other exerted a persistent influence from the early seventies. Divergent assessments of the Education Council's work thus resulted in failure to reach agreement on extension of its existence beyond 1975.

Before its dissolution the Council's education commission published the "75 Report" (3.7.1975), which followed the theoretical and practical principles put forward in the 1970 structure plan, and outlined educational developments between 1965 and 1975. The report took up recommendations by the education commission as providing a foundation for change, reform, and longer perspectives. The commission's last report thus attempted to provide an analysis of the state of education in the first half of the seventies. A national advisory body's opportunities and limitations were once again clearly demonstrated.

If one looks back today at the long series of Education Council reports and recommendations, it becomes obvious how quickly developments in educational policy overtook the positions represented there. And yet the 1973 recommendation on participation by teachers, pupils, and parents remains topical within discussions of increased autonomy for schools.

Several times during the past 20 years an attempt has been made at launching another nationwide advisory body on education policy. That has remained a perceptible lack since dissolution of the German Education Council in 1975. Despite some problematic experiences there exists a need for ongoing advisory service even in the school sphere. Individual Laender have attempted to fill that gap – as with North Rhine-Westphalia's "Education Commission". However, there is still no national advisory body concerned with schools and teacher training. The example of the Science Council shows that such an institution can be successful and fruitful over the longer term.

3.3 Science Council

When in the mid-fifties, after years of discussion, schooling was unified by way of the Düsseldorf Agreement (see section 2.3), makers of education policy sought a solution for the much-needed co-ordination of science and research at the federal and Laender levels. The concept of a Science Council was prepared by such people as Gerhard Hess (then president of the German Research Association), Kurt Zierold (the Association's secretary-general), Waldemar von Knoeringen (the educationally committed SPD leader in the Bavarian parliament), Kurt Frey (secretary-general of the Conference of Ministers of Education, highly sensitive and helpful in all matters involving co-operation on educational policy), and Hans von Heppe (head of the higher education section in the North Rhine-Westphalia Ministry of Education). The question of increased financial assistance for science by way of federal subsidies also played a part. After long consultations involving Laender Ministers of Education and Prime Ministers, the Science Council was established in an agreement (5.9.1957) between the federation and the

Laender. The constituent assembly was held in Bonn University's main hall on 6.2.1958.

The agreement initially provided for a three-year period, but that was extended several times and increased to five years – most recently in 1995 covering up to the year 2000. The Science Council has the task of drawing up an overall plan for promotion of the sciences, basing its work on individual plans put forward by the federal and Laender authorities within their spheres of competence. It has to co-ordinate these individual plans, designating emphases and degrees of urgency. The Council is obliged to produce an annual programme indicating priorities, and to provide recommendations on utilization of the funds available in the federal and Laender budgets for the advancement of science. Since 1970 the expansion and development of universities (inclusive of medical clinics) have been the joint responsibility of the federal and Laender authorities – as provided for in article 91a of the Basic Law, amended in the law relating to construction of universities (see section 2.6). The Science Council issues recommendations on medium-term outline planning by April 15 every year.

The latest changes to the agreement underpinning the Science Council date from February 28, 1991. This revision takes into account unification of the two German states and accession of the five New Laender. The Science Council has produced many recommendations on university studies and structural development, scholarship, and research. These recommendations include consideration of means of implementation, and of the quantitative and financial impact.

The Science Council also has the task of evaluating issues within the development of universities, scholarship, and research if so requested by a Land, the federal authorities, the Federal-Laender Commission for Educational Planning and Advancement of Research, or the Conference of Ministers of Education. The federal and Laender governments endeavour to take Science Council recommendations into account when drawing up their budgets.

Until 1990 the Science Council consisted of 39 members. With accession of the New Laender that number was increased to 54 – consisting of scientists, leading figures in public life, or people whose job is closely associated with the promotion of science. The Science Council meets either as a full assembly or in the form of commissions. The science commission has 32 members appointed (initially for 3 years) by the Federal President (re-appointment is permitted): 24 on the joint recommendation of the German Research Association, the Max Planck Society, the University Rectors Conference, and the Association of National Research Centres (today Hermann von Helmholtz Association of German Research Centres) – and 8 on the joint recommendation of the federal and Laender governments. The 22 members of the administrative commission are delegated by the federal and Laender governments (six by the federal government and one each by the Laender governments). Resolutions by the full assembly and the commissions require a majority of two thirds of the votes cast. Other procedures are regulated in the Council's standing orders as amended on 5.7.1991.

The long list of members of the Science Council over almost four decades reads like a "role of honour" for German science, but only four women have been members to date. The annually elected chairman (who can be re-elected) comes from the science commission, is a university professor or director of a research institute, and has been granted leave of absence from other responsibilities. Dieter Simon, director of the Frankfurt-based Max Planck Institute of European Legal History, was chairman at the beginning of the nineties and made a name for himself when the Science Council played an important part in redevelopment of the university system in the New Laender. In 1996 a woman became chair-person for the first time: Dagmar Schipanski, rector of the Ilmenau technical university in Thuringia. That is also the first time that the Council has been headed by a member from the former East Germany.

The Science Council office in Cologne is headed by a secretary-general with around 20 specialists and 35 other staff. These secretary-generals have previously held top positions in research or university administration. It is largely thanks to them that the Council and its limited staff (one is inclined to talk of "German science's general staff") produce such generally recognized work. In the initial years that office was held by Friedrich Schneider (1958-66), followed by Karl-Gotthart Hasemann (who moved on to the Federal-Laender Commission in 1971), Joachim Peter Kreyenberg (1971-88), and Winfried Benz (from 1989).

The following recommendations played an important part in restructuring the university system between 1960 and 1970:

- Recommendations on expansion of science facilities (1960)
- Suggestions on the structuring of new universities (1962)
- Recommendations on re-organization of the teaching staff at universities (1965)
- Recommendations on re-organization of courses of study at universities (1966)
- Recommendations on the structure and expansion of university education after 1970 (3 volumes, 1970).

Since 1972 the Science Council's recommendations and evaluations have been published in annual volumes. Its most enduring successes have included the previously mentioned 1960 recommendations on expansion of scientific facilities, known as the "Blue Bible" after the colour of the binding.

During the past two decades the Science Council has produced an abundance of detailed positions on, for instance, assistance for empirical social research, the establishment and maintenance of additional spheres of special research, the expansion of polytechnics and universities, co-operation between universities and industry, and support for young scholars. On 20.5.1988 the Council approved recommendations on opportunities for universities in the nineties, covering research, teaching, studies, young scholars, university staffing, and, above all, finance. On 16.11.1990 followed recommendations on the development of polytechnics over the same period. Two decades after establishment of these institutions their development was surveyed and an attempt made at sketching perspectives for the future (see section 15.4).

The Science Council was faced with its biggest challenge ever when in 1990 the federal and Laender authorities requested that it should draw up recommendations on the future structure of universities in the New Laender and East Berlin. A multitude of assessments and recommendations were presented in five volumes, covering such issues as teacher training, the establishment of new universities, and the setting up of polytechnics (see section 15.5). Ten further volumes present recommendations on non-university research facilities in the former GDR.

In January 1993 the Science Council agreed on ten theses about university policy. These sparked off wide-ranging discussion about the future structure of university studies and the organization of universities. Only two of those theses can be presented here:

"*Thesis 1*: The younger generation's interest in university studies has constantly risen and will continue to rise. The economy and society will in future need more, not less, well-trained young people. It would be wrong to restrict possibilities of study and to counter the long-term increasing demand for study-places.

Thesis 2: High-quality university training for 30 % or more of an age-group demands corresponding expansion of universities and adaptations in the structuring of courses to cope with changing numbers. The Science Council recommends well-focused expansion of polytechnics and changes in the structuring of university courses".

With those theses the Science Council advocated intensified expansion of the university system. However, the question is whether the "limits to growth" may not long have been reached as is demonstrated by problems in financing universities and mounting unemployment among graduates. Forecasts by the Science Council have not always been accurate (see sections 15.4 and 18). At the beginning of the eighties it anticipated a decline in student numbers during the following decade. That was a wrong forecast.

As early as 1974 Rolf Berger was critical of the Council in his publication "Zur Stellung des Wissenschaftsrates bei der wissenschaftspolitischen Beratung von Bund und Ländern" ("The Role of the Science Council in Advising Federal and Laender Authorities"; Baden-Baden: Nomos). He maintained that the Council's way of working was largely unscientific. He claimed that the procedures for making appointments to the Council and its operations were impenetrable, inaccessible to the public, and beyond effective control. The combination of provision of advice and decision-making was said to result in many cases in a non-legitimated transfer of political responsibility from the executive charged with political decisions to the Science Council. In recent years the Council's recommendations for winding up GDR research institutes were particularly criticized, but no-one disputes the importance of its contribution to redevelopment of the university system in the five New Laender.

The Science Council's achievements have often received public praise. Karl Carstens, the former Federal President, spoke as follows during a ceremony – at Schloß Bellevue in Berlin on 27.1.1983 – marking the Council's 25th anniversary:

"The Science Council has now been in existence for 25 years. Those were eventful years, particularly for the universities ... The Council accompanied those developments, providing advice and making suggestions in accordance with its mandate. I should like to proclaim my respect for that work ... Many of its ideas were taken over by the Ministries of Education and the universities. They led to good results". However, Carstens was not uncritical at times: "We must also observe that another aspect of these reforms did not stand the test. It cannot be disputed that the Council's scientific and administrative commissions put forward a number of recommendations which the light of experience shows to have been misguided".

In the course of almost forty years of existence the Science Council has gained public recognition for the fruitfulness of its activities. Its structure and working methods have stood the test of the mounting demands made of scholarly advisors on educational policy. In brief, the Council has become an established institution, bringing together scholars and politicians in extensive co-operation. The first comprehensive attempt at assessment of its work is presented in Hans Christian Röhl's revised Heidelberg dissertation: "Der Wissenschaftsrat. Kooperation zwischen Wissenschaft, Bund und Ländern und ihre rechtlichen Determinanten" ("The Science Council. Co-Operation between Science, Federal and Laender Authorities and its Legal Determinants"; Baden-Baden: Nomos 1994).

3.4 German Federal Parliament's Commission of Enquiry (1987–90)

In December 1987 the German federal parliament established a commission of enquiry on the initiative of the SPD and the Green Party. This was intended to help activate federal educational policy – and in autumn 1990 a report was published, entitled "Educational Policy for the Future – Education

2000". "For two and a half years eight scholarly experts and nine members of parliament representing all parties ... have devoted all their efforts to the question of the future course of federal educational policy". With those words Eckart Kuhlwein (SPD), the chairman of this commission of enquiry, opened its final report – and he continued: "We were concerned with the question of how forthcoming challenges, associated with the new millenium, could be mastered by way of educational policy". The commission also discussed issues arising in a reunited Germany. Nevertheless, during a presentation in the federal parliament on October 26, 1990, Kuhlwein had to concede: "The Commission did not feel able to make long-term declarations about any growing together of the two German education systems". In another central issue Kuhlwein's position was contradictory. On the one hand, he praises the "degree of reconciliation" between the political parties as "a step away from earlier ideologically and tactically determined trench warfare in educational policy" (p. 13), presenting Commission consensus in seven areas – while, on the other, he recommends that "Educational policy – unlike other spheres of politics – must once again take greater pleasure in conflict" (p. 18).

This final report extends over some 300 pages, describes the Commission's brief and how this was implemented, and presents the basic challenges and possible orientations in future educational policy – with majority and minority votes. Findings and recommendations on such issues as vocational training, further education, university development, and education in Europe are briefly sketched. The accompanying volume of appendices offers summaries of the 18 evaluations sought by the Commission, assessments of hearings and discussions, the concluding recommendation, and the response by the federal parliament's education and science committee to the Commission's interim report, and an extract from the minutes of the parliamentary session (26.10.1996) discussing the final report. It is difficult to respond here in greater detail to the wide range of issues raised by this report since almost everything that has been kicked around in public during the past decade reappears. The attempt at mastering this sphere by way of a commission of enquiry obviously did not work out. That was presumably taken to heart by the federal parliament since it did not seek to establish another commission a little later. If the outcome of the first venture had been more convincing, the federal parliament would probably long ago have set up a similar enquiry with regard to redevelopment of the education system in the New Laender and the objective of "inner reunification".

3.5 Hamburg Parliamentary Commission of Enquiry into "Schools Policy" (1992/3)

Brief mention should also be made of the report (13.5.1993) produced by the Hamburg "Parliamentary Commission of Enquiry into Schools Policy", surveying demographic and structural developments, the demand for workers, European connections, the legal framework, and financial requirements. Recommendations were made regarding the structure of the Hamburg school system, greater autonomy for individual schools, and increased funding. The report concludes with five theses on schools policy, characterizing big city problems but not presenting anything new.

4 Educational Research

Educational research is a recent discipline, even though it has long been implemented in Germany under other names. It is fundamentally interdisciplinary, linking pedagogic, psychological, sociological, and economic aspects of research with legal and administrative concerns. There is always an empirical focus. In the Federal Republic such research was developed in the fifties following American, French, Swedish, and English models. Establishment at Frankfurt/Main of the College of International Educational Research (from 1964 the German Institute for International Educational Research) marks an important turning-point.

4.1 Objectives and Conditions

The objective of educational research is to analyze relevant national and international developments, thereby assisting policy-making. The degree to which educational research really can make such a contribution remains unresolved. During the years of the great debates about educational reform, in the sixties and early seventies, the potential of educational research was much overestimated – at least among the public. On the other hand, some highly important decisions within educational policy – such as the introduction of polytechnics or of comprehensive schools – went ahead irrespective of the virtual absence of extensive research.

In 1969, for instance, the German Education Council's education commission proposed that an "experimental programme" of at least pilot projects involving comprehensive schools should be established, accompanied by ongoing scholarly assessment. The findings thus made were to serve as the basis for later decisions on education policy. The Conference of Ministers of Education accepted this recommendation and on 27.11.1969 reached agreement on implementation and scholarly evaluation of such experiments with comprehensive schools (Beschlußsammlung No. 473.1). That course turned out to be unviable. Here the role of scholarly research was overrated. The idea that accompanying research could ease clear-cut political decisions was not confirmed. No matter how scholars evaluate school experiments, their criteria will be politically disputable. Experience shows that decisions on educational policy usually follow political trends in the area of organized interests.

During the period of educational reforms up to the mid-seventies, research enjoyed a boom. Public opinion took note of research and its expansion was promoted. Organizations like the VW Foundation generously financed research projects. Even though the number of big projects has certainly declined and staffing levels have long been at a standstill, the multitude of annual publications documents undiminished intensity and constant endeavours towards doing justice to research and international exchanges of experience. Approaches to research and thematic emphases rapidly change in our politically agitated age. The main foci of activities at research institutes thus by no means develop in protected zones remote from politics.

The research into education and vocational training that receives financial assistance from the Federal Ministry of Education, Science, Research, and Technology mainly serves such tasks as promotion of pilot projects and encouraging further development in schools, training, universities, and further education. Mention could be made of pilot projects in new information and communication technology, integration of environmental issues in education, lessons in the arts and culture, and the role of girls and women in education. The Federal-Laender Commission for Educational Planning and Advancement of Research is responsible for such ventures.

Educational research is pursued at universities, polytechnics, and colleges of education as pedagogic, psychological, or sociological research. Bochum university's Research Centre for Comparative Educational Studies (with an emphasis on the GDR and Eastern Europe), for decades headed by Oskar Anweiler, was unfortunately subjected to considerable cutbacks after his retirement in 1992. A similar set-up at Marburg university, built up since the sixties by Leonhard Froese, is carrying on after its founder's death in 1994. Marburg has devoted particular attention to European developments and Makarenko's research. Both centres also kept a close watch on what was happening in the GDR.

At other universities there are also long-established emphases, often assisted by the German Research Association in special areas of research. Since such research is usually conducted in close conjunction with involvement in teaching, and research capacity is limited, several national and regional institutes have been set up in recent decades.

4.2 National Research Institutes

4.2.1 German Institute of International Educational Research

The German Institute of International Educational Research (DIPF) at Frankfurt/Main was established as a public institution in 1951 on the instigation of the Hesse Land government. Up to 1964 this foundation was financed solely by Hesse, and then from 1964 to 1976 jointly by the eleven Laender on the basis of the Königstein agreement. Since 1977 the institute has been financed in accordance with the outline agreement on assistance for research concluded between the federal and Laender authorities.

The DIPF is the oldest national research institute in the sphere of non-university educational research in the Federal Republic of Germany. The co-operation of educationists, psychologists, legal experts, economists, sociologists, and historians paved the way for other developments. Research is concerned with the legal, administrative, economic, social, psychological, and historical aspects of education and training. The institute is divided into research and service spheres. The research sphere comprises five sections: general and comparative educational science, economics, psychology, law and administration, and sociology. That departmental structure is complemented by the Berlin research centre which is mainly concerned with historical aspects of education.

DIPF research focuses on four areas and an interdisciplinary approach:

- Management problems in the education system
- Migration and acculturation as a challenge to education and training
- Education policy and conflict-prevention in multi-cultural societies
- The relationship between general education and vocational training viewed historically and comparatively.

Those emphases are complemented by four long-term projects:

- Research into the history of education
- Health education
- Transformation processes in education and training in Central and Eastern Europe
- Current issues in Japanese education and training.

At the beginning of 1992 as part of German unification – and on the recommendation of the Federal-Laender Institute for Educational Planning and Advancement of Research and the Science Council – the German Institute of International Educational Research took over the long-established East Berlin Central Educational Library, which was part of the former GDR Academy of Educational Sciences. This library was founded in 1875 as the German Teachers Library and assimilated by the Academy in 1971. It has now become the Library for Research into the History of Education as part of the DIPF. Most of the staff in the library and at the Berlin Research Centre were formerly employed in a scholarly capacity by the Academy.

The DIPF is simultaneously intensifying its activities in the spheres of information and documentation. These form part of the service facilities which have become more important since 1992. The research library at Frankfurt/Main specializes in interdisciplinary educational research. The previously mentioned Berlin library contains over 700,000 books as one of Europe's largest collections devoted to research into educational history. It is also linked with an extensive archive in Berlin and the Leipzig library devoted to the study of deafness and linguistic impediments. The information and documentation department at Frankfurt/Main concentrates on registration and dissemination of writings on development of education in the Federal Republic of Germany, the European Union, and Central and Eastern Europe, as well as on migration and media education. The Education Information System at Eschborn co-ordinates the activities of the most important German and Austrian documentation centres devoted to education and training, and makes available joint information products – such as CD ROM, and printed bibliographies.

The German Institute works together with ministries, universities, research institutes, and schools in Germany and other countries, and publishes a magazine and several series of books. An agreement on co-operation with Frankfurt's Johann Wolfgang Goethe University was concluded in 1993, and this serves such activities as exchanges of scholarly experience, implementation of joint research projects, and the advancement of young scholars. The agreement also makes possible the joint appointment of professors. In the German Institute there are 62 established posts including 39 for scholars – and in the service facilities 54 with around 20 for scholars.

4.2.2 Max Planck Institute of Educational Research

During preparation of educational reforms in the sixties it became apparent that more research capacity was needed, so the Max Planck Institute for Educational Research was set up at West Berlin in 1963, headed by Hellmut Becker, who died in 1994 at a ripe old age. Since his retirement in 1981 the Institute has been jointly directed. Educational, psychological, sociological, and interdisciplinary issues are investigated in four spheres of research:

- Education, work, and social development
- Development and socialization
- Psychology and human development
- School and teaching.

"Education, work, and social development" involves empirical and theoretical research into the structure and changes in the education system's relations with other social spheres. One current emphasis is devoted to "Life-developments and historical change in the former GDR". This mainly concerns the importance of "personal networks" – social relations inside and outside the family with colleagues at work, friends, and neighbours in conjunction with the changes of recent years. The lives of around 2,300 people born between 1929 and 1961 have thus been surveyed.

Between 1965 and 1975 the Institute worked closely together with the German Education Council, supporting its work with many investigations and evaluations. In 1980 an Institute project-group published a comprehensive two-volume report on "Education in the Federal Republic of Germany. Data and Analyses" (Stuttgart: Klett/Cotta). This group has published four revised and expanded editions – most recently in 1994 – of "The Education System in the Federal Republic of Germany. A Survey of Structures and Developments" (Rowohlt-Sachbuch 9193, Reinbek near Hamburg). Earlier editions were translated into English, French, Spanish, Chinese, and Japanese.

In 1995 the Institute had a staff of 196 including 54 scholars. 20 stipendees and 11 guest scholars were also working there.

4.2.3 Federal Institute of Vocational Training

The Federal Institute for Research into Vocational Training was set up in 1970 on the basis of the 1969 law regulating such activities. After the 1976 law covering assistance for training places came into effect, this set-up was re-structured as the Federal Institute of Vocational Training (BIBB). Four of its main departments are based in Berlin and two in Bonn. Its present legal basis is the law for assistance of vocational training through planning and research (23.12.1981) as revised on 12.1.1994. The Institute is thus a completely federal organization subject to legal supervision by the Federal Ministry of Education, Science, Research, and Technology. It is not a purely research set-up, but is also charged with advisory functions and the provision of service facilities. The BIBB structure comprises a main committee, a standing committee, and a secretary-general. The main committee, grouping representatives of employers, trade unions, federal authorities, and the Laender, determines its activities. A secretary-general directs the Institute whose task – within the guidelines established by the federal government's educational policy – is to investigate the impact of the world of work on vocational training and to examine the structures and content of the different levels of training. The objective is to improve the implementation of vocational training. The Institute thus conducts research into the nature and objectives of vocational training, and its adaptation to technical, economic, and social developments. Above all, the Institute advises the federal government on basic issues in vocational training, watches over pilot projects, supports the planning, establishment, and further development of vocational training centres, and assists training technology. Another important task entails involvement in the preparation of annual reports on vocational training (see section 10.3). The Institute also works on preparation of training regulations and publishes a register of recognized occupations. In addition it evaluates media-backed correspondence courses in vocational training before transmission is permitted in terms of the law regulating such courses (see section 17.2). The Institute now has a staff of around 380 in Berlin and Bonn. The annual budget in 1996 amounted to 48.5 million DM of which 38.4 million was accounted for by staffing costs.

4.3 Regional Institutes of Educational Research

In the sixties and seventies a variety of federal and Laender institutes were established at Bad Kreuznach, West Berlin, Bremen, Dudweiler, Hildesheim, Kiel, Munich, Soest, Stuttgart, and Wiesbaden so as to intensify educational research in all Laender (except Hamburg). After 1990 such institutes were also set up in the New Laender at Arnstadt, Halle, Ludwigsfelde, Radebeul, and Schwerin (for addresses see appendix 29). These institutes, which are mostly under Ministries of Education, are mainly concerned with the following spheres:

1. Basic research on learning and ability
2. Evaluatory work on pilot projects, particularly comprehensives
3. Curriculum research and development
4. Research into socialization
5. Surveys in conjunction with educational planning, i.e. changes in demand for education, cost structures and changes linked with structural changes, and analyses of international developments.

These institutes have the task of putting the results of educational research and practice into effect at schools. For instance, the Bad Kreuznach Regional Educational Centre develops models of co-operation between various types of schools and also between schools and partners from outside the system. The centre mediates between school practice and educational planning, between teachers and scholars, and between schools, parents, and relevant political and economic institutions. It co-ordinates curriculum development and implementation of curricula in didactic teaching models. The Educational Centre has 20 full-time staff and 80 teachers are involved part-time.

The Centre for Educational Technology set up at Wiesbaden in 1971 was transformed four years later into the Hesse Institute of Educational Planning and School Development. Its tasks include co-ordination of work on curricular development, pilot projects, and school implementation of information and documentation systems. The Institute, which is not subject to directives but instead takes on commissioned work, thus mediates between scholarship, administration, and school practice. It employs 50 full-time and 120 part-time experts. At present the Institute is mainly working on implementation of the reforms contained in the new 1992 Hesse school law, calling for increased decentralization and school autonomy.

North Rhine-Westphalia's Soest Institute for Schooling and Further Education is charged with supporting schools' activities and assisting further education. All of the Land's guidelines and curricula are developed here. Concepts within advanced training for teachers are developed and tested out before being implemented regionally. That also includes specialist assistance for adult education through further training for instructors in that sphere. The Soest institute with its additional responsibility for curriculum development and advanced teacher training therefore enjoys a special status among state educational institutes since it serves both schools and adult education. Its extensive range of operations and location in the most densely populated of the Laender also explains its size and a permanent staff of around 200.

The state institutes integrated in Munich's Educational Research Centre support the advancement of Bavaria's education system through practice-oriented research and development. The Centre unites the institutes of school pedagogics and educational research, university research and planning, and early education and family research.

The Bavarian State Institute for Educational Research and Planning, set up in 1966, was closed down in 1983. That is the only such institute to have suffered this fate to date – after the death of its meritorious founder and director, Alfons Otto Schorb. The closure came as a complete surprise to the public, especially as the establishment's achievements were widely recognized.

4.4 Other Educational Research Institutes

Educational research has also been considerably assisted in recent decades by the funds made available by foundations. Initiatives by the Volkswagen Foundation led to the establishment of such well-known institutions as Kiel's

Institute for the Pedagogics of the Natural Sciences, Tübingen's German Institute for Correspondence Courses, and the Hanover-based university information system. Support from the Volkswagen Foundation was also involved in the 1973 start on development at Bielefeld University of an Institute for the Didactics of Mathematics. The Fritz Thyssen and Werner Reimers Foundations have provided ongoing backing for research into the history of education, and the Donors Association for German Science has made a great contribution to university research.

Finally, two institutions of educational research principally supported by the Churches: the Protestant Comenius Institute at Münster, and the non-denominational German Institute for Education and Knowledge at Paderborn. These small institutes (in terms of staffing) have with the part-time involvement of well-known experts made important contributions to recent educational research through publications and convening gatherings of experts. The Catholic Münster-based German Institute for Scientific Pedagogics was closed down in 1980 because of differences between German bishops and the scholars involved.

4.5 The Current Situation

We have attempted here to provide a brief introduction to the most important institutions involved in educational research in Germany, outlining their spheres of activity. Some readers may have got the impression that educational research on an unusually large scale and with high levels of staffing has developed here within the past decade. That is not the case. In terms of the area covered by research, the financial and personal resources devoted to this sphere should rather be seen as quite modest with hardly any increase during that period. The total sum made available annually from public funds for educational research (as narrowly defined) has been around 130 million DM.

5 Structural Outline of the Education System

5.1 Compulsory Schooling

Compulsory schooling begins for all children when they are six and usually lasts until they are eighteen. Full-time schooling is for nine years in most Laender – ten in Berlin, Bremen, North Rhine-Westphalia, and the Saarland; and then children who do not continue with such schooling have three years of part-time attendance (compulsory vocational schooling). Even those who have taken the *Abitur* have to attend vocational school if they are involved in an apprenticeship.

5.2 Elementary Sphere

There is no compulsory attendance at pre-school level. Nursery schools for three- to six-year-olds are usually not directly linked with the school system. Even though attendance is voluntary, efforts are made to provide as many children as possible with a kindergarten place close at hand.

5.3 Primary Level

The *Grundschule* (primary school) is the basic level within the education system, attended by all children. This lasts for four years – six in Berlin and Brandenburg. Children who have reached school-age but are not yet ready to attend are provided for in school kindergartens (pre-classes) as far as possible.

5.4 Secondary Level I

Shared primary schooling provides the foundation upon which the differentiated secondary education system is based. Secondary level I usually comprises the orientation level, the *Hauptschule* (secondary modern), the *Realschule* (intermediate school), the *Gymnasium* (grammar school), and the *Gesamtschule* (comprehensive school). In the New Laender provision is made for the *Hauptschule* qualification but there do not exist any autonomous schools in this category. They only existed up to 1996 in Mecklenburg-Western Pomerania where they were generally replaced by interlinked secondary moderns and intermediate schools. Alongside grammar schools and comprehensives in the East there exists the *Sekundarschule* (Saxony-Anhalt), *Mittelschule* (Saxony), *Regelschule* (Thuringia), and the *Verbundene Haupt- und Realschule* (Mecklenburg-Western Pomerania), which lead to the *Hauptschule* or *Realschule* qualification. These comprise class levels 5-10.

Co-ordinated outline curricula permit a high degree of transferability between the different types of school. None of these schools constitutes a "cul de sac". A differentiated secondary level I offers many possibilities of transfer, allowing each pupil to follow inclinations and talents.

Orientation Level: Classes 5 and 6 usually form the orientation (mixed-ability) level, serving the task of helping all pupils find their way within the possibilities offered by different types of school, keeping options open until the end of the sixth class. This orientation level can be established within the existing school organization or as an autonomous level regardless of the type of school involved.

Hauptschule: Where the *Hauptschule* exists, it is compulsory for all pupils after primary school or the orientation level who do not go on to a *Realschule*, *Gymnasium*, comprehensive, or another secondary school. It offers a basic general education and creates the preconditions for finding a job and qualified vocational training. The possibilities opened up by the *Hauptschule* are outlined in section 9.2.

The *Hauptschule* usually comprises five age-groups (classes 5-9) – but six in North Rhine-Westphalia (classes 5-10), three in Laender with autonomous orientation / mixed-ability levels (Lower Saxony and parts of Hesse: classes 7-9), and four in Berlin and Bremen (classes 7-10). Able pupils can gain the middle school qualification at the end of the 10th class. In the Saarland the *Hauptschule* will no longer exist from 1997 and is being replaced by the "Expanded Intermediate School".

In some Laender qualified children can move on to an extension *Gymnasium* after completion of the sixth, seventh, or (in rare cases) eighth class. A tenth voluntary year of schooling is experimentally available wherever this is not obligatory.

Realschule: The normal form of *Realschule* takes six or four years, comprising classes 5 or 7 to 10. The four-year form is mainly to be found in Berlin, Bremen, Hamburg, Lower Saxony, and Bavaria. In some Laender there are also three-class continuation forms for *Hauptschule* pupils, starting with the 8th school year.

The *Realschule* provides a general education preparing the way for employment, situated between what is on offer at the *Hauptschule* and *Gymnasium*. It leads to an intermediate qualification, which is the precondition for a variety of vocational courses and for attending the *Fachoberschule* (technical secondary school). Talented children who complete the *Realschule* course can transfer to the upper level at *Gymnasium*.

Gymnasium: The *Gymnasium* is the only kind of school that includes both secondary level I and II. Attendance usually lasts nine or seven years (classes 5 to 12 or 13, or 7 or 8 to 12 or 13). Transfer to the eleventh class is equivalent to completion of intermediate school. The *Gymnasium* offers more profound general education. This is the precondition for university studies, and also makes possible non-university vocational training.

Comprehensive School: Integrated or co-operative comprehensives usually comprise classes 5 or 7 to 10. Comprehensives for the most part provide joint instruction for secondary level I pupils integrated and differentiated in a variety of ways, or integrate the three traditional forms of school (*Hauptschule*, *Realschule*, and *Gymnasium*). Comprehensives lead to the same qualifications as the other schools in secondary level I.

5.5 Secondary Level II

Secondary level II comprises general and vocational schools between secondary level I and higher education. This entails classes 10 to 12, 11 and 12, or 11 to 13.

After completion of *Hauptschule*, *Realschule*, or the corresponding year-levels at a comprehensive or *Gymnasium*, most pupils start vocational training or get a job. *Vocational training* can occur in two ways. Either through the dual system of co-operation between firm and part-time vocational school (*Berufsschule*), or through full-time vocational school (*Berufsfachschule*) which mediates knowledge about a broader range of possibilities (i.e. commercial or trade schools) before starting work. Both ways can lead on to vocational extension school, technical secondary school, or sixth-form college, which provide the qualification for entrance to polytechnics or other institutions of higher education.

Vocational Schooling: This is highly differentiated and builds on from secondary level I schooling in accordance with the qualifications required.

This part of the system includes part- and full-time vocational schools (the former compulsory), vocational extension schools, technical secondary schools, technical schools, and special forms that do not exist in all the Laender: vocational grammar schools, vocational secondary schools, vocational sixth-form colleges, and non-university vocational academies.

Upper Level at Gymnasium: This comprises classes 11 to 12 or 13, concluding with the *Abitur* examination. In Mecklenburg-Western Pomerania, Saxony-Anhalt, Saxony, and Thuringia the *Abitur* is at present taken after the twelfth year at school. Saxony-Anhalt and Mecklenburg-Western Pomerania are considering introduction of a 13th year at some later date (in the latter case from the year 2000).

Alternative Form of University Admission (Zweiter Bildungsweg): This enables young people and adults who did not complete courses at *Realschule* or gain the university entrance qualification at general or vocational schools to make good that lack. The institutions providing this second chance include vocational extension schools, evening versions of the *Realschule* and *Gymnasium*, and sixth-form colleges.

Special Schools: These exist at all levels of the education system for physically or mentally handicapped children who cannot participate in general lessons.

5.6 Tertiary Sphere

The university system is structured as follows:
- Universities, technical colleges/universities, comprehensive colleges, specialized colleges (such as medical, sports, theological, and church colleges), and colleges of education
- Colleges of art and music
- Polytechnics
- Vocational academies (only in a few Laender).

As far as admission is concerned, a distinction must be made between
- Polytechnics where the necessary qualification is gained at technical secondary schools after 12 years of schooling
- Universities and other scholarly institutions where the *Abitur* is required for admission.

5.7 Quarternary Sphere

Institutions of adult education and further training, particularly evening classes and media-backed correspondence courses.

6 General Aspects of the School System

6.1 School Year

In the 1964 Hamburg Agreement on standardization of the school system the Laender Prime Ministers laid down that the school year throughout the Federal Republic should begin on August 1. In fact the start of the school year varies since summer holidays are staggered from Land to Land, ending between the beginning of August and the beginning of September.

6.2 Holidays

The total length of holidays was also fixed in the 1964 Hamburg Agreement, amounting to 75 working days. The start and finish of the summer holidays are staggered so as to avoid excessive road and rail traffic. The Conference of Ministers of Education determines dates for summer holidays well in advance. These holidays, which usually last for six to seven weeks, start at the end of June in some Laender, and end at the beginning of September in the areas that began last. The other longer holiday periods are around Christmas and Easter. In some Laender there are Whitsun and autumn holidays.

6.3 Free Schooling and Learning Aids; Travel Subsidies

Attendance at state schools is free in all of the Laender. Learning aids are also basically free, but there are differences in the range of materials involved. Most Laender provide textbooks without charge. Transport costs to centrally-situated rural primary, secondary modern, and special schools, and to schools within secondary levels I and II, are generally paid for out of public funds so as to balance educational opportunities between town and country areas.

6.4 Educational Grants

A federal law (*Bundesausbildungsförderungsgesetz*) regulates assistance from the 10th class onwards for pupils in need who no longer live at home because the requisite schooling does not exist in their locality. Special regulations apply to those working towards extra-school acquisition of the university entrance qualification.

6.5 Age-Levels (Classes)

Apart from levels 11-13 at *Gymnasium*, teaching takes place in classes, which are numbered upwards from the first year at primary school. These classes are organized in accordance with age. The term "class" thus refers to both the individual school class, and also to the entire year-level, which is now the more usual term so as to avoid misunderstandings.

6.6 Assessment of Achievement and Promotion

Pupils' achievements in the subjects taught are expressed in grades. A points system is used at the upper level of *Gymnasium*. The degrees of achievement were laid down in paragraph 19 of the Hamburg Agreement (28.10.1964), and grades were defined by the Conference of Ministers of Education on 3.10.1968 (Beschlußsammlung No. 675) as follows:

"*Very Good* (1): This grade is to be awarded if the performance is well above the required standard.

Good (2): Awarded for a performance that fully meets the required standard.

Satisfactory (3): Awarded for a performance that on the whole meets the required standard.

Adequate (4): Awarded for a performance which, though showing deficiencies, on the whole meets the required standard.

Poor (5): This grade is to be awarded for a performance that does not meet the required standard but indicates that the necessary basic knowledge exists and that the deficiencies could be overcome within a foreseeable period.

Unsatisfactory (6): To be awarded for a performance that does not meet the required standard and indicates that even the basic knowledge is so fragmentary that the deficiencies could not be overcome within a foreseeable period".

As grading is the outcome of subjective evaluations where the class average also plays a part, different assessment of similar performances cannot be excluded. An attempt is being made to ensure greater objectivity through utilization of standardized work and school tests. During the first years at primary school reports on learning behaviour and standard of achievement have often replaced the previous grades. The intention is that children starting school should be spared pressure towards achievement.

Transfer from one age-level (class) to the next is termed "promotion". The Conference of Ministers of Education has agreed on the principles regulating such promotion. There are no examinations before promotion to the next class, but results in written work during the school year exert considerable influence on evaluation of achievement. In some Laender pupils who do not move up to the next class have an opportunity of re-examination after the summer holidays. If it becomes apparent that a pupil has caught up again with the class's level of achievement, he or she does not need to repeat that year. In general a pupil at *Realschule* or *Gymnasium* is not permitted to fail promotion more than twice. If that happens, he or she must transfer to another kind of school – i.e. from *Gymnasium* to *Realschule*, or from *Realschule* to *Hauptschule*. New forms of individualizing the tempo of learning are also being implemented at comprehensives.

6.7 Final Examinations

These are generally conducted by the school itself – insofar as such final assessments occur at all in general or vocational schooling. The nature of written work is usually laid down by the schools inspectorate. Both young people and adults can acquire the qualification for completion of all levels of schooling and vocational training by way of external examinations. Decisions about promotions and examinations can be contested in the administrative courts.

6.8 Educational Qualifications

Greater detail is presented in the descriptions of individual forms of school and the university system. This is just a brief outline.

1. *Hauptschule* leaving certificate after the 9th or 10th class (depending on length of compulsory schooling in the Land concerned). Special achievements are specifically recognized in some Laender.
2. *Realschule* leaving certificate after the 10th class. A comparable qualification can be gained at *Hauptschule*, *Gymnasium*, comprehensive, and at vocational schools. This allows admission to technical secondary school (*Fachoberschule*).
3. *Fachoberschule* leaving certificate at a technical secondary school or comparable institution after the 12th class. This admits to the *Fachhochschule* (polytechnic).
4. The *Abitur* after the 12th or 13th class.
5. Master's degree, diploma, or first degree examination after university studies of usually at least eight semesters.

6.9 Teaching Time

Teaching normally takes place in the mornings from Monday to Friday (the five-day week).

6.10 All-Day Schools

The number of all-day schools where pupils are cared for and provided with educational activities once lessons are over is still relatively small but constantly increasing, especially in socially volatile areas. The following data for 1977 and 1988 apply to the Western Federal Laender.

In 1977 there were around 600 all-day state schools (including 380 special schools, 82 comprehensives, and 33 grammar schools) and 210 such private schools (112 special schools and 56 grammar schools).

In 1988 there were 800 all-day state schools (484 special schools, 44 primary schools, 33 secondary moderns, 16 combined primary/secondary moderns, 15 intermediate schools, 75 grammar schools, 118 comprehensives, and 17 other schools) and 534 private schools (including 288 special schools and 105 grammar schools).

In 1995 in the whole of Germany (excluding special schools) there were 992 all-day institutions (680 state and 312 private). They are headed by comprehensives with 320 schools including 7 private ones, followed by 231 grammar schools (124 private). Of the 96 all-day intermediate schools 69 are private, and of the 226 combined primary/secondary moderns 38 are private. 23 business and technical secondary schools (19 private) are part of vocational schooling.

In its report on "All-Day Care for School-Children" (5.2.1993), the Conference of Ministers of Education stated that parents' attitude to all-day schools has changed because of different family structures and mothers going out to work. It is now a social duty – rather than a matter of welfare policy – to create more all-day facilities. That, of course, will be difficult in the present budgetary situation and demands a transformation in teachers' mentality. One of their traditional privileges is the usually "free" afternoon, and renunciation would almost be "revolutionary". Hesse's Minister of Education, Hartmut Holzapfel (SPD), recently advocated a new "rhythm" for schools (from 9 to 3.30) with teaching, independent work, and a midday meal.

6.11 Teaching Hours

The number of hours prescribed for lessons per week depends on a pupil's age. Children starting school begin with about 20 lessons a week, and the total gradually increases to a maximum of 30. A lesson usually lasts 45 minutes. At many schools two lessons are often amalgamated to form units lasting between 80 and 90 minutes. There are short breaks between lessons, and these add up to about 40 minutes in a morning of five lessons. For years the public has complained about the cancellation of many lessons. That state of affairs is mainly the outcome of budgetary shortfalls in the Laender, leading to cutbacks in teachers.

6.12 Obligatory Work-Load for Teachers

The obligatory number of hours taught depends on the teacher's status and varies slightly between Laender. The Hesse guidelines dated 17. 7. 1995 serve as an example:

Teachers at	Weekly obligatory hours
1. Primary Schools	27
2. Special Schools	27
3. Secondary Modern & Intermediate (+ offshoots), Co-operative Comprehensives, Mixed-Ability Levels	26
4. Integrated Comprehensives	
a) with at least 8 hours a week in the *Gymnasium* upper level	24
b) other	25

5.	*Gymnasia* + offshoots Co-operative Comprehensives	
	a) with at least 8 hours a week in the *Gymnasium* upper level	24
	b) other	25
6.	Adult Schools	
	a) with at least 8 hours a week at Evening *Gymnasium* or Hesse College	23
	b) other	25
7.	Vocational Schools	24

At secondary level I this regulation in places increased the (previously slightly reduced) number of obligatory hours by one. Bavaria, Berlin, and the Saarland have similar regulations. The number of lessons taught is reduced for teachers with special responsibilities (administration and teacher training) and for people aged over 55. Some teachers also only work part-time – at their own request or for lack of staffing vacancies.

Teachers associations have long criticized the fact that the obligatory number of hours taught has only minimally declined in recent decades, whilst in other public service occupations weekly hours of work have gone down from 48 to 38.5 since 1957. The associations and the Education and Science trade union are pushing for similar reductions for teachers. The Conference of Ministers of Education decided (on 23/24.6.1988) that teachers should also benefit from such reductions, but in recent years the trend has been in the other direction. Even where this has not yet happened, there is discussion of increasing teachers' work-load by an hour a week so as to counter the loss of lessons resulting from budgetary cuts.

7 Elementary Sphere: Pre-Schooling and Nursery Schools

The elementary level includes all provision for children from their third birthday until they begin school. Administrative responsibility normally lies with the Ministries of Youth and Social Affairs. Only in Bavaria do both kindergartens and schools come under the Ministry of Education. Pre-schooling has a long tradition in Germany as the land where the kindergarten originated, but was only included at a late stage in discussions about reforming the education system because it takes place *before* compulsory schooling gets under way. The German Education Council's recommendations on nursery schools in the 1970 "Structure Plan for Education" played a decisive part there. Since then it has been accepted that kindergartens are a preliminary stage in education.

Nursery schools have the task of complementing upbringing and training in the family, and of holistically supporting children's development through play without pre-empting formal learning or introducing reading and writing. A kindergarten's task does not involve early practice of primary school subjects. An effort is made to pay individual attention to each child within groups of 20 to 25. It would be desirable to reduce the size of groups as much as possible since childhood is the time of key experiences forming the personality. Fortunately, there are also nursery schools with groups of between 10 and 15 children.

First some statistics: In 1960 the old Federal Republic had 12,290 kindergartens offering 817,200 places. By 1970 that had already risen to 17,493 nursery schools with 1,160,700 places; by 1980 23,938 kindergartens with 1,392,500 places; and by 1990 around 25,000 nursery schools with 1,525,000 places. So between 1960 and 1990 the number of kindergartens and places almost doubled. At the end of the eighties some 75 % of three-year-olds and over 80 % of five-year-olds attended a kindergarten. By now nursery schools are so widespread that they are to be found almost everywhere. And yet the demand for kindergarten places continues to exceed the supply – mainly because of the increased number of working mothers.

There were more kindergartens and day nurseries in the GDR than in the West. What was only gradually established in the old Federal Republic existed in the GDR as early as the fifties. Young working mothers were considered a "socialist achievement". In the GDR by 1970 there were already 13,100 kindergartens and day nurseries providing care for 654,700 children. The number of such facilities only increased slightly up to 1989: 13,452 with 747,100 children. Many works nurseries and equivalent communal facilities were closed down during the course of reunification and the great difficulties involved in the changeover from a socialist economy to new social market structures. By the end of 1991 there were clearly fewer kindergarten places in the New Laender (a total of 557,920) than two years previously. That led to a nationwide debate. When in 1993 the federal parliament revised the abortion law, paragraph 24 of the amended law on assistance for children and young people included the legal right to a kindergarten place by 1.1.1996. Such a regulation is something new in the Federal Republic. For the first time there exists a legally enforceable claim to a place at nursery school. Establishing a date galvanized public activity – despite all the controversy about such a right. Since 1990 55,000 new kindergarten places have been created in Lower Saxony, around 30,000 in Hesse, over 40,000 in Baden-Württemberg, and over 51,000 in Bavaria. The German Cities Convention estimates that there has been an increase of 400,000 kindergarten places across the country. Nevertheless, there are still not places close at hand for all children.

Attendance at nursery school is voluntary. Such facilities are established in accordance with the principle of subsidiarity. Over 70 % of kindergartens are dependent on private backing – mainly from the Churches, and to a lesser extent from workers welfare organizations, firms, and individuals. Around a quarter of all kindergartens are supported by local authorities. Private nursery schools are also subject to state supervision, and receive financial support from the Laender and local authorities. Despite considerable subsidies from public funds (and from church taxes in the case of church kindergartens), the parents of children at nursery school must make a financial contribution – varying in amount and sometimes graduated in accordance with income. These charges, which are sometimes considerable, vary between Laender and sometimes even within a Land. The Youth Office pays for the children of low-income parents. So, unlike schools and universities, pre-schooling is not free even today. A further worsening in the financing of kindergartens is feared when the Laender and local authorities are faced with a difficult financial situation. That would exert a deleterious impact on educational possibilities throughout pre-schooling.

Until the seventies it was mainly women who worked in kindergartens, but then an attempt was made to attract more men. Such nursery school teachers and social workers generally have three years of training at vocational schools (in Bavaria Academies of Social Work) or polytechnics for which the precondition is completion of *Realschule* (for the former) or the entrance qualification for polytechnics (for the latter) as well as a period of practical training. Nursery school teachers are supported by trained assistants.

In previous decades there was a great debate about the extent to which compensatory measures for children from socially and culturally deprived backgrounds could improve educational opportunities when those youngsters entered primary school – and also about whether it was expedient to advance the start of compulsory education from six to five. At that time the federal and Laender authorities conducted a comprehensive programme of pilot projects and scholarly evaluations. That did not, however, lead to any clear-cut conclusions with regard to reorganization of this sphere. The start of school attendance was not put forward by a year. Today there are also many pilot projects, for instance serving shared schooling for handicapped and non-disadvantaged children. Wherever possible individual assistance is given to both handicapped children and those whom medical assessment shows to be at risk. To some extent this happens in set-ups preparing the way for schooling.

Many newly-developed learning materials and new educational methods are tested in pilot projects. The emphasis is not just on mediation of knowledge. The child's emotional world also has to be taken into account and social learning promoted by way, for instance, of involvement in sport and the arts, and imagination and pleasure in play stimulated and security mediated. Radio and television devote attention to elementary schooling within children's programmes. The German version of “Sesame Street” had a particularly far-reaching impact. Such story programmes as the “Augsburger Puppenkiste” are popular too, and daily TV series and videos offer a rich range of experience.

8 Primary Level

The primary sphere takes in primary schools, school kindergartens (pre-classes), and school admission levels.

8.1 Grundschule (Primary School)

The aim of the primary school is to provide all pupils with the foundations for further education at secondary schools. Such a school thus endeavours to promote a many-sided unfolding of the child's personality, to awaken interests and abilities such as imagination, initiative, self-reliance, and social co-operation, and to increase joy in learning. Individual character and differences in learning speeds, attitudes to work, and the child's everyday background are taken into account as far as possible. The teaching thus builds on a child's experiences, incorporates them in school learning, and mediates basic skills in reading, writing, and arithmetic. A particular effort is made to promote children's creative powers, and capacity for perception and expression through arts subjects and sports. The first class usually starts with 20 lessons a week and gradually increases to between 27 and 29.

In 1994 there were 17,895 primary schools with 3,553,400 pupils, taught by 171,705 full-time teachers, mainly women. The number of children of primary school age in integrated comprehensives (inclusive of Steiner schools) was relatively low (49,300).

In most Laender the primary school involves classes 1 to 4, and constitutes the shared school for six- to ten-year-olds. In Berlin and Brandenburg classes 5 and 6 (11- and 12-year-olds) are also part of the *Grundschule*.

It can be presumed that the falling birth-rate in the Federal Republic since the mid-sixties is sufficiently known (see section 2.1.1). There were considerable consequences for primary schools. In 1972 4.15 million children still attended such schools, but by 1994 the number had fallen to only 2.8 million in the area previously forming the Federal Republic. However, recently the number of pupils has slightly increased again, while in the five New Laender the decline in the number of births is particularly pronounced. Between 1991 and 1994 primary school pupils declined from 823,600 to 736,500. That creates many problems. There is a danger that primary schools may have to be closed for lack of pupils. In the West, on the other hand, attendance in this sphere will probably continue to rise. Around 20 % more pupils are expected by the end of the decade. Experts are thus concerned about the reluctance of Ministries of Education to take on more teachers – because of the financial constrictions affecting Laender governments.

In Germany children who have reached the age of six by June 30 of the current year have to attend school. The school year begins after the summer holidays. Children who become six between that date and the end of the year can also be accepted at primary school if the head approves the parental application. All children are examined by the school doctor. If a child is not yet sufficiently mentally and physically developed, entry can be delayed for a year. If there is a school kindergarten (pre-class) in the locality, the child can instead attend that (see section 8.2). The average age for entering primary school is 6.7 years which contributes towards extending what is already a long time at school in Germany, providing considerable cause for concern. In recent years there has been an increase in the number of children who have had to wait before starting schooling (on average 8 to 12 %), so the Conference of Ministers of Education has commissioned a survey of the situation. Its schools committee is also to make suggestions about regulating school-entry differently.

During the first two years at school, teaching is largely carried out by a single person, the class teacher. That makes it easier for children to get used to school. They can concentrate on a single person rather than several different specialized teachers. The class teacher principle is intended to guarantee unity of character-training and teaching, ongoing educational advancement, and differentiated responsiveness to the needs of individual pupils. Teaching methods vary with individual-, partner-, and group-work applied as required. From class 3 onwards, pupils are increasingly taught by specialists and thus prepared for transition to the secondary sphere where such specialization predominates. An example of a timetable is contained in appendix 18.

In Bavaria, for example, German, mathematics, local history and geography, music and movement, and art are incorporated in a block of 15 or 16 hours of teaching weekly. In this "basic teaching" character-training is given precedence over transmission of knowledge. The teacher does not mediate specific subjects according to a timetable but rather changes between them in shorter units. The first graded reports come at the end of the second year.

All of the Laender endeavour to attain such individualization of teaching. Attempts are made at providing additional assistance for children with considerable long-term problems in picking up reading and writing. In North Rhine-Westphalia daily homework must not take longer than at most 30 minutes for the first two years. For the next two classes the limit is 60 minutes. Teaching is often enlivened by investigations in the locality – such as carrying out a survey at the post office or the fire station. Hiking or longer stays in school or youth hostels lead to direct contact with nature or encounters with historic sites. Visits to zoos or museums are popular. Today's primary school is thus anything but dry "book-learning".

Anyone visiting a German primary school nowadays usually sees happy children's faces, free from excessive demands. Colourfully-dressed girls and boys romp around modern classrooms which they have often arranged themselves. Their pictures are on the walls or hanging on lines, and cosy corners add to modern school furniture.

The *Grundschule* celebrated its 75th anniversary at the end of April 1995. Despite that respectable age, the German primary school is nevertheless a "young" school. It is the first school children encounter, which has to adapt to each new generation of pupils and their problems. The Weimar Reich constitution, dated 11.8.1919, stated in article 146: "The intermediate and secondary school system is founded on the *Grundschule*, common to all". This primary school was part of the "school compromise" which had to be reached to make approval of the Weimar constitution possible. This compromise was supported by the Social Democrats, the (liberal) German Democrats, and the (Catholic) Centre. The length of time spent at primary school was disputed. Details were left to the Reich Primary School Act. This law was well-prepared by the Reich and the Laender, and approved by the national assembly after a third reading on 19.4.1920. The (conservative) German National Peoples Party voted against it. The law was signed by Reich President Friedrich Ebert on 28.4.1920. This was the last great legislative achievement of the national assembly which then dissolved itself. Reformist forces emerged weakened after the parliamentary elections that followed. The law regulating primary education would no longer have gained a parliamentary majority. The fact that it was approved by the national assembly has lost none of its epoch-making significance up to the present day.

That law was therefore a compromise. At that time many of the forces pressing for reform – such as the German Teachers Association, champions of "unified schooling" – would have liked a statutory six years of primary school while many supporters of the *Gymnasium* preferred three. In the Kaiser's Reich – at least in much of Northern Germany – , children wanting to attend a higher school from their first year went to a public or private "feeder school" preparing pupils for secondary education. The young Weimar Republic eliminated that early class distinction from the first day of school, which constituted the first decisive step towards democratization of education. In Southern Germany, on the other hand, the majority of subsequent secondary school pupils first attended a *Volksschule* (elementary school) for four years. To that extent the situation in the South of Germany was "more democratic" than in the largely Prussian North. State feeder schools were phased out by the mid-twenties, but the closing down of their private counterparts dragged out until the end of the Weimar Republic.

Many people nowadays are no longer aware that only since the introduction of the four-year primary school in Germany has there been thirteen years of schooling leading to the *Abitur*. In Prussia at least, pupils usually only spent three years at pre-school and nine years at a higher school if they wanted to gain the university entrance qualification (3 + 9 = 12).

The six-year primary school was introduced in Hamburg, Berlin, and Bremen after 1945 – thanks to the influence of the SPD. This played a crucial part in the 1953 elections to the Hamburg city parliament. The SPD lost the election and the non-socialist coalition brought back the four-year primary school. This was the only time – before the 1987 Hesse dispute over the mixed-ability level – that a school issue decisively influenced the outcome of a Laender parliamentary election in the Federal Republic. Today six-year primary schools are only to be found in Berlin and Brandenburg.

At the end of the sixties the emphasis was put on subject-related teaching of an academic nature. There was an extensive public debate on the "New Mathematics" (set theory) which caused confusion among parents. People feared children would be overtaxed. They complained about a decline in character-training, and that soon led to a change of course. During the seventies, recommendations in the German Education Council's structure plan led to an attempt to advance compulsory school attendance by a year through including five-year-olds in the primary sector. The "entry-level project", tested out in numerous pilot schemes, could not be implemented nationwide, and only survives as a standard form in some 50 schools in Hesse.

Until the sixties the primary school remained part of the elementary school. In order to overcome the differences between town and country, a reorganization of the rural school system was launched in the post-war period. That meant that the idyllic period of the single-room village school was over. Larger schools, centrally located in an extensive catchment area, were established, making possible teaching in year-groups. The long distances sometimes involved were bridged with school buses. Only in the course of this reform did the *Grundschule* become an autonomous form of school. Paragraph 4 of the Hamburg Agreement, reached by Laender Prime Ministers in 1964, succinctly states: "The lower level common to all pupils will bear the designation 'primary school'".

In the eighties there was a change of direction in rural areas. Parents again called for village schools so as to avoid transport problems. In Baden-Württemberg in particular, small local primary schools were opened, sparing country children long journeys. In the core subjects of mathematics and German the combined classes are taught in separate age-groups as far as possible. Only teachers especially equipped and expressly ready for such a task are employed in such small village schools. In Rhineland-Palatinate too, smaller primary schools have been kept (despite low numbers of pupils) if other organizational solutions are not possible within an acceptable distance from pupils' homes. At the beginning of 1996, Dieter Wunder, chairman of the Education and Science trade union, called for the retention of small primary schools in the New Laender where a decline in pupil numbers makes closures necessary. Wunder recommended new forms of teaching and joint lessons during the first four years (a solution that the union had fought against three decades earlier).

The primary school was reformed during the seventies, following the "Recommendations on Work in Primary Schools" (Beschlußsammlung No. 130.2), approved by the Conference of Ministers of Education on 2.7.1970. During the run-up to the 75th anniversary the Conference agreed on new resolutions (6.5.1994) since "the social and educational circumstances of school and teaching" have in the meantime changed. The new recommendations reflect many of the experiences of recent decades when family structure changed rapidly through increases in the number of single mothers or fathers and one-child families. The foreword states: "The change in family structures, a varied spectrum of life-forms and educational ideas combined with greater parental involvement, the co-existence of people from different cultures, growing awareness of ecological issues, the influence of the media – all that faces the *Grundschule* with new tasks and calls for mounting readiness, within the realms of possibility, to teach pupils with special educational needs". The 20-page text has the following sections:

1. Basic education in the primary school
2. Entering the primary school and initial lessons
3. Transfer to secondary schools
4. Complementary and extended teaching measures.

The first section is the most important. Here one would expect that the objectives of basic education, due to be achieved by the end of the fourth class, are binding for all Laender. However, that is not the case. They are referred to somewhat obliquely. Completely in the spirit of the original twenties objective, the text states: "The main emphasis at primary school must be on the advancement of all pupils, holistically embracing all the senses. Laying educational foundations likewise requires the subject-related acquisition of basic knowledge". The subjects named are German, mathematics, practical studies, art, music, sport, and – in most Laender – religion. The reference to language studies is of central significance: "Language is of great importance as the key to understanding oneself and the world".

The emphasis on "media education" is something new. Pupils "are to be prepared for critical and circumspect dealings with the media. They should gain experience which calls in question the apparent objectivity of the media and reveals their limitations". That is of course an ambitious aim, difficult to achieve, when one considers how many "television-addicted" children spend countless hours in front of the "goggle-box" nowadays. It is justifiably asserted: "Reading and writing play a minor part in many families today. By now many children watch television more than they play, do things, experiment, and explore. Television and computer games are replacing personal adventure. Unprocessed television experiences cause lack of concentration and loss of reality".

Local studies, which were formerly a constitutive element in primary education, are now linked with openness to the world: "Attachment to one's homeland and membership of a social group shape personality and engender trust in one's own actions. In our world understanding for other ways of life, tolerance, and capacity for dialogue are particularly important. In that context the European idea acquires particular significance for education in the primary school".

A correction of course becomes apparent with regard to reading and writing. People now talk of "acquisition of written language". In that connection we read: "In the first two years of schooling this is one of the crucial tasks in teaching. ... The primary school must open up access to the primary culture of the written word". Criticism is often expressed about pupils completing primary school not having mastered reading and writing. One aspect here involves the fact that many foreign children, sometimes lacking knowledge of German, enter primary school and need special assistance. In 1994 there were 330,000 foreign pupils in primary schools. That represents an average of 9.7 % of total numbers at the *Grundschule* – and the percentage is often considerably higher in densely populated areas.

The "encounter with foreign languages" is a new objective which is gaining in importance. Here the Conference of Ministers of Education recommendations state:

"Pupils experience foreign languages through the media, travel, and dealings with fellow pupils from other countries. That – alongside the linguistic demands of a united Europe – is why children of primary school age should already be offered the possibility of encountering a foreign language. ... The mediation of foreign languages in classes 3 and 4 at primary school requires a special didactic approach, characterized by playful forms of learning and working which make possible individual progress, participation by all pupils, and renunciation of grading. Alongside the language-encounter concept, in some Laender there exist projects which foresee more systematic dealings with a foreign language from the third class".

First steps towards learning a foreign language from the third year onwards have long existed in some Laender. In Hesse in particular, extensive experience has been assembled under Professor G. Gompf from Frankfurt. In 1995 39,500 pupils from the third and fourth classes attended English lessons (i.e. over a third of that age-group), and almost 3,000 (2.5 %) were learning French. In some Laender Italian lessons are also available. However, experts still do not agree about the long-term advantages for pupils who make an early start on language lessons, or whether all the expense is worthwhile.

Some particularly attractively designed periodicals – for instance "Grundschule", "Grund-Schulmagazin", and "Die Grundschulzeitschrift" – serve the exchange of experiences and discussion. In 1969 the Primary School Study Group (Arbeitskreis Grundschule, D-60486 Frankfurt a.M., Schloßstraße 29) was established, and this now involves over 15,000 primary school teachers and scholars. This organization has produced many publications on reforms in the *Grundschule*. Teachers associations such as the Education and Science trade union and the Education and Training Association, which bring together people from all kinds of schools, also work together with the Primary School Study Group. At the end of 1994 and in December 1995 they jointly agreed on a list of demands, calling for:

- more primary schools with fixed hours (in Hesse there are already 144 such schools open until around 1 p.m.)

- an increase in child-care facilities and co-operation with non-school organizations
- local primary schools for all children
- further implementation of joint lessons for handicapped and non-handicapped children.

In December 1995 the teachers associations complained about the bad situation in primary schools with large classes. The outcome is more frontal teaching and too little social learning. They reached agreement on the 1995 Berlin Memorandum: "A Future for Children – Primary School 2000". There they call for the six-year primary school, playful learning of a foreign language, and an introduction to dealings with the modern media. Such reforms would, however, demand increased investment. Only with more teachers will it be possible to continue reform of the *Grundschule.*

The demand for introduction of the six-year primary school is problematic as educational history shows – both in 1920 when the *Grundschule* was introduced and after 1945 during reconstruction of the school system when the four-year model made its way or was confirmed. Once again calling those decisions in question does not lead further, but instead entails an attempt at launching a structural discussion that centrally affects secondary level I, unleashing a "carousel" of changes without any gain.

8.2 Transition from the Primary School to Secondary Level I

The transition from a primary school to the orientation (mixed-ability) level, secondary modern, or comprehensive school does not involve any admission procedure. Such special procedures usually apply when transferring to an intermediate school or *Gymnasium.* Parents and school are jointly involved in the decision over pupils' school careers. An evaluation by the primary school plays an important part – alongside parental wishes – in pupils' transfer to secondary education. Schools organize special events to try and help parents decide on their children's school career, offering information about different kinds of school and what they have to offer. In some Laender pupils who do not fulfil specific minimum demands and have been advised against higher education are required to take an entrance examination (or undergo a trial period) at *Realschule* or *Gymnasium.*

The transfer procedure from primary school to secondary education has time and again been the object of political and legal disputes – as in Hesse in 1992. This involved the question of whether too much is being asked of primary schools by expecting them to provide a recommendation, or whether parental wishes should be decisive with regard to transfers. The latter has been the case ever since the new Hesse school law dating from 1992. But does not such a regulation – as by now also exists in other Laender – in turn demand too much of parents? Are parents capable of assessing their child's abilities objectively? Reaching a balanced solution to the question of transfers requires close co-operation between school and parents.

8.3 School Kindergartens and Pre-Classes

School kindergartens (pre-classes) have been established for children old enough to enter school whose admission has been delayed. Unlike nursery schools these are state institutions which are completely integrated in the education system (also outside Bavaria) and form part of the primary school. School kindergartens mainly exist in big cities. Attendance is voluntary and without charge. Such kindergartens have also been established at special schools in some cities so as to provide care for handicapped children as early as possible. In 1960 only 3,100 children attended school kindergartens but by 1986 the figure had risen to 36,800. In 1994 there were 2,747 school kindergartens with 44,500 pupils. Reception classes (pre-classes) also accept children who are capable of starting school even though they have not reached the requisite age. In 1994 there were 1,423 such classes with 42,000 children.

9 Secondary Level I (Lower Level)

Secondary level I has been a disputed area of educational policy for three decades now. Discussions have revolved around the issues of appropriate differentiation and assistance for pupils in accordance with their ability and achievement. Should the tripartite system (*Hauptschule*, *Realschule*, *Gymnasium*) be retained, or instead be complemented or replaced by a comprehensive system? Is external differentiation involving different types of school, or inner differentiation within the comprehensive school, a more convincing solution educationally and organizationally? Alongside integrated comprehensive schools there exists the co-operative form (in Bremen school centres) where the three school types work under joint headship. "Regional schools" have existed in Rhineland-Palatinate since 1992, bringing together *Hauptschule* and *Realschule* courses. By now 20 schools are participating in this experiment in inner differentiation. In the Saarland there has been a similar linkage since 1992 in what is known as the "Secondary School", and by 1995 there were 29 such schools.

Since the SPD's original aim of replacing the tripartite system with comprehensive schools could not be achieved, in some places the outcome has been introduction of a four-part system, bringing greater diversity rather than the intended unification.

At present several Laender are introducing structural reforms within secondary level I. That occurs as part of new school laws or amendments in Mecklenburg-Western Pomerania (15.5.1996), Saarland (21.8.1996), and Saxony-Anhalt (27.8.1996).

After reunification only Mecklenburg-Western Pomerania (up to 1996) took over the tripartite system. The other New Laender – largely inspired by West German educational consultants – have a predominantly bipartite system, structured as follows: secondary schools and grammar schools in

Saxony-Anhalt; *Regelschule* ("norm school") and grammar schools in Thuringia; middle schools and grammar schools in Saxony; and comprehensives and grammar schools (complemented by *Realschule*) in Brandenburg. Right from the start no provision was made for the *Hauptschule* in those Laender. The new school law (15.5.1996) in Mecklenburg-Western Pomerania replaces separate secondary modern and intermediate schools by a "combined *Haupt-/Realschule*" – with the former now only exceptions requiring ministerial authorization. Those changes revived discussions about differentiation in the Old Laender. Saarland recently became the first Land to decide to do away with the *Hauptschule*, leaving only "Extended Intermediate Schools", grammar schools, and comprehensives. In Saxony-Anhalt the mixed-ability level has been introduced for all secondary schools and comprehensives. Grammar schools will in future start with class 7. All these innovations followed SPD educational initiatives.

Unlike the primary school, which brings together all pupils, secondary level I offers a differentiated range of teaching, which accords with the Land's educational tradition and – as the introduction of comprehensives shows – with the political situation there. Most pupils still attend secondary moderns, intermediate schools, and grammar schools. Only in Berlin, Brandenburg, Bremen, Hamburg, Hesse, and North Rhine-Westphalia is the number of children at comprehensives above the federal average of around 9 %.

In 1994 the average national distribution of pupils in the 8th class of secondary level I was as follows:

Type of school	1994	
	pupils	percentage
Hauptschulen	225,800	25.6
Integrated classes *Haupt-/Realschule*	60,600	6.9
Realschulen	234,400	26.5
Gymnasia	278,300	31.5
Integrated Comprehensives	79,700	9
Steiner Schools	4,800	0.5

Source: Conference of Ministers of Education documentation No. 134, November 1995.

The 8th class was taken as an example because transfers to other kinds of school have been completed by then in all Laender.

All schools within secondary level I offer a general education intended to enable pupils to enter vocational training or go on to higher education (secondary level II). In the majority of Laender the following schools belong to this category:

- *Hauptschule* (Secondary Modern)
  except for Saarland, parts of Hesse, and the New Laender
  (classes 5 - 9/10, or 7 - 9/10)
- *Realschule* (Intermediate School)
  (classes 5/7 - 10)
- *Gymnasium* (Grammar school)
  (classes 5/7 - 10, i.e. lower and middle level)
- Integrated (or Co-operative) Comprehensive, sometimes including Mixed-Ability Level
  (classes 5/7 - 10)
- Special Schools (for physically handicapped children or pupils with learning difficulties, see section 12)

The following secondary level I school types exist in specific Laender:

- *Förderstufe* (Mixed-Ability Level – Hesse)
  Orientierungsstufe (Orientation Level – Lower Saxony)
- *Schulzentrum* (School Centre – Bremen)
- *Mittelschule* (Middle School – Saxony
  Regelschule ("Norm School" – Thuringia)
  Sekundarschule with *Förderstufe* ("Secondary School" including Mixed-Ability Level – Saxony-Anhalt)
  Integrierte Haupt- und Realschule (Integrated Secondary Modern and Intermediate School – Hamburg)
  Verbundene Haupt- und Realschule (Combined Secondary Modern and Intermediate School – Mecklenburg-Western Pomerania)
  Regionale Schule (Regional School – Rhineland-Palatinate)
  Erweiterte Realschule (Extended Intermediate School – Saarland)
  Wirtschaftsschule (Trade School – Bavaria, see section 10.3.2)

This diversity is not completely covered by the Hamburg Agreement. However, the possibility of transfer between different types of school has been much improved. In addition, Hesse has prescribed shared curricula for classes 5 to 10 (see appendix 22). That does, of course, lead to a reduction of schools' individual characteristics. In most Laender there are extension classes opening up admission to the *Realschule* or *Gymnasium* which *Hauptschule* pupils can join after completion of years 6, 7, or 8. Extension *Gymnasia* lead to the university entrance qualification after six or seven years. If they provide for boarders, special attention is devoted to the visual arts, music, sport, and the natural sciences.

In the seventies the number of pupils at secondary level I rose from 4.3 to 5.3 million, but during the following decade the decline in birth-rate exerted a particularly striking impact. Between 1980 and 1990 the number of pupils in the Old Laender declined from 5.313 to 3.442 million. The reduction in numbers of teachers was not so drastic, falling from 266,700 to 228,750 between 1980 and 1989. Endeavours by Ministers of Education to maintain the number of teachers at the highest possible level led to reduction of the pupil-teacher ratio from 19.9 (1980) to 14.7 (1989). Since then that figure has been climbing again. It should be stressed that these figures relate to the national average. Developments in different kinds of schools will be considered separately at a later stage.

These few figures express a basic aspect of developments in the eighties. The Ministers of Education strove to profit from declining numbers of pupils at secondary level I for reduction of the size of classes and improvement of the teaching on offer. The Conference of Ministers of Education Agreement dated 16.6.1978 on an outline curriculum for pupils in levels 7 to 10 at general schools also paved the way (Beschlußsammlung No. 121). It contained regulations on obligatory subjects and minimum numbers of lessons for pupils' timetables at all general schools (except certain special schools). The 1978 agreement was superseded by the "Agreement on School Types and Courses at Secondary Level I" (Conference resolution 3.12.1993, Beschlußsammlung No. 102). This new agreement outlines school types and courses at secondary level I, and also takes into account development in the New Laender. It includes a shared structure for the lessons taught and the qualifications gained. Section 3.1 describes the general characteristics of secondary level I as follows:

"The organization of schools and curricula at secondary level I is based on the principle of providing a general education with individual specialization and appropriate backing. That is sought by:

- Encouragement of the intellectual, emotional, and physical development of all pupils; and by training in self-reliance, capacity to take decisions, and personal, social, and political responsibility
- Guaranteeing teaching, based on the current state of knowledge, that in its structure and demands takes into account pupils' age-related capacity for understanding
- Step-by-step increases in specialization, taking up pupils' individual abilities and interests
- Assuring flexibility, which after an orientation phase opens up possibilities of changing course".

Those are certainly ambitious aims and difficult to implement in an everyday school environment. Existence of the previously mentioned 15 different kinds of school at secondary level I makes the 1964 Hamburg Agreement's strivings towards standardization appear increasingly illusory.

At this point it should merely be stated that nearly all pupils at secondary level I are taught English at different levels – and some French, particularly in the Western border areas. The development of foreign language teaching will be discussed in greater detail in section 18 (see also appendices 8 and 9).

In its resolution dated 11/12.5.1995, the Conference of Ministers of Education established standards for middle-level school learning qualifications. That complemented the agreement on school types and courses at secondary level I (Conference of Ministers of Education resolution dated 3.12.1993, Beschlußsammlung No. 102), outlining obligatory standards in German, mathematics, and the first foreign language in order to ensure compatibility. However, Laender can still set particular emphases. It remains to be seen whether the 1995 resolution can assure unified standards. The Conference of Ministers of Education is obviously more concerned about comparability within a differentiated system of qualifications and structures than about standardization of types of school. Harald Kästner has said of the current situation: "Knowledge will no longer be identified in terms of the type of school attended but instead in relation to the course completed and the qualification gained. ... The Laender will have to decide what is functional or dysfunctional about that. Critical parents and teachers may have to seek publicity for their case".

The Conference of Ministers of Education has published a survey of the qualifications available at secondary level I. This 176-page document demonstrates what a range of qualifications can be gained (as of 16.12.1994).

According to a supposedly "representative" survey of public opinion, conducted in November 1995 by Dortmund University's Institute for Research into School Development, 49 % of parents would like their children to gain the *Abitur*, 45 % a middle-level qualification, and only 6 % the secondary modern leaving certificate. But was this survey conducted correctly? Was it not akin to asking: "Would you like your grown-up child to drive a small car or a Mercedes; to rent accomodation or own a home?" It should also be asked whether parents can correctly assess their child's (especially a single child's) abilities. For years people have tried to put such surveys to political use. They serve the strategy of getting rid of the *Hauptschule* and promoting comprehensives.

The Association of German Intermediate Teachers – and especially its chairman Walter Trapp – criticize the fact that there are still no standardized criteria for achieving the *Realschule* qualification. It is still left to the Laender to establish degrees of difficulty in each subject. Standardization can only be achieved by introducing final examinations based on unified criteria. Those should apply to any middle-level qualification no matter where it was acquired – at *Hauptschule*, *Realschule*, *Gymnasium*, comprehensive, or vocational school. That is particularly important since many people see this qualification as a norm within general education – especially those who want to get rid of the secondary modern qualification or do not find it attractive.

The middle-level qualification opens up access to vocational training courses and – in special cases – to secondary level II schools leading to admission to polytechnics or university. The standards reached by, say, pupils at *Gymnasium* or *Realschule* at the end of the 10th class may be comparable but are quite varied. Recent surveys maintain that between 10 and 25 % of those completing *Realschule* achieve better results than the average grades of pupils in the same class at *Gymnasium*. That finding was presented in the 1995 final report by the special commission on "Further Development of the Principles involved in Upper Level at *Gymnasium* and the *Abitur*", appointed by the Conference of Ministers of Education.

Most pupils who complete secondary level I start training in the dual system, so industry's expectations are of relevance here.

What school achieves has long been a source of controversy. Employers who provide training expect that school-leavers will possess the foundations for a stable personality, team spirit, and readiness to learn and achieve. Their minimum requirements include a command of written and spoken German, simple mathematics, basic scientific knowledge, the fundaments of economics, and the basics of English.

9.1 Orientation Level (Mixed-Ability and Observation Levels)

Years 5 and 6 in all types of schools constitute a phase of special support, assessment, and orientation with regard to further schooling. As the heading indicates, there is no standardized terminology for this phase. In Berlin and Brandenburg, for instance, years 5 and 6 are part of primary education and there is no separate orientation level since assessments take place in primary school. Orientation levels independent of the kind of school involved exist in Bremen, Lower Saxony, and parts of Hesse, but in other Laender they are integrated in a specific form of secondary level I school.

In 1994 there were 2,362 independent orientation levels, attended by 374,900 pupils. In the Old Laender that number has only risen minimally. Apart from the demographic factors involved, that is also an outcome of the fact that independent orientation levels have not been able to gain additional support as part of school policy. The great majority of pupils in this age-group thus attend secondary moderns, intermediate schools, grammar schools, and comprehensives.

The mixed-ability level is a continuation of primary schooling and allows pupils to stay together for two additional years. The decision about further schooling is kept open until the end of the sixth class. Mathematics and English are taught as courses in streamed groups according to achievement, ability, and interest. Teachers, parents, and pupils decide in a school meeting whether German should also be offered in similar fashion from the second half of year 5 or from year 6, or whether it should continue to be part of the core programme. At the end of year 6 pupils move on to class 7 at a *Hauptschule*, *Realschule*, *Gymnasium*, or comprehensive.

The objectives in the orientation level are:

- Promotion of the individual pupil's readiness and ability to learn
- Orientation in terms of his or her talents, abilities, and achievements
- Improvement of decisions about the next step in schooling
- Compensation for social differences affecting education.

Teachers from all types of school in secondary level I give lessons in orientation levels, but *Hauptschule* and *Realschule* teachers predominate. Appendix 19 presents a typical timetable.

In Lower Saxony individual schools can choose between a general and an alternative timetable. The latter serves to give schools greater organizational freedom, encourages interdisciplinary teaching and projects, relaxes adherence to the 45 minutes rhythm of lessons, and reduces excessive diversity of subjects. English is a compulsory foreign language, but Latin or French can also be studied provided at least 15 pupils wish to do so.

Discussion of the orientation level since the fifties can be briefly summarized as follows. The outline plan for reshaping and standardizing the general state school system, produced in 1959 by the German Committee for Education and Training, envisaged four years of primary schooling followed by a two-year mixed-ability level within the *Hauptschule*. That was intended to serve the streaming of ability by way of differentiation between core classes and optional courses. The German Committee was influenced here by school pilot projects already under way in Lower Saxony and Hesse.

The Laender Prime Ministers' Hamburg Agreement on standardization in the school system (28.10.1964) expressly permitted orientation or observation levels in the 5th and 6th school years. The German Education Council also advocated establishment of an orientation level in its 1970 education structure plan. In the 1973 comprehensive education plan, the then federal government and the SPD-ruled Laender called for the setting up of "independent" orientation levels. In a special vote the CDU- and CSU-governed Laender spoke in favour of both possibilities being retained. Those reservations were the outcome of doubts about reducing courses at *Gymnasia* (and in some Laender also at the *Realschule*) by the two lowest classes.

The orientation (mixed-ability) level is a disputed aspect of school policy up to the present day. Ultimate acceptance in Hesse and Lower Saxony is briefly presented in what follows. When in 1976 the CDU took over political control from the SPD in Lower Saxony, it inherited an extensive independent orientation level and retained this with certain modifications. In 1990 the SPD again took over responsibility for government there. Remarkably, the CDU – going against its own educational policy – did not do away with the orientation level during the period when it was in political charge of Lower Saxony and Hesse. The mixed-ability level had also been disputed in Hesse for decades. This had been launched by the SPD with 12 pilot projects in the 1961/62 school year. By 1968 there were already 60 such projects, attended by 11.2 % of all pupils in classes 5 and 6 in Hesse. In the following year the mixed-ability level was established as the norm. By 1973/74 their number had risen to 216 (44.1 % of the age-groups). A decade later (1984/85) 317 mixed-ability levels covered around two thirds of the pupils eligible. Just before participation in mixed-ability levels was due to be made compulsory throughout Hesse, there was a Land election with this theme playing a prominent part. The SPD lost the election. Prime Minister Walter Wallmann's CDU-FDP coalition established a new emphasis in education policy with a law for re-establishment of free choice of schooling in Hesse (2.6.1987). The obligation to attend the mixed-ability level in classes 5 and 6 was abolished, once again giving parents the right to choose between *Hauptschule*, *Realschule*, and *Gymnasium* after pupils had spent four years at *Grundschule*. Or they can decide in favour of an integrated comprehensive or a mixed-ability level. Freedom of choice following primary school was re-established on 1.8.1988. However, in some areas not all forms of secondary school are available because where comprehensives predominate there are usually no secondary moderns. Since that time Hesse has settled for a compromise in its school policy. When the CDU-FDP coalition was succeeded in 1991 by a coalition between the SPD and the GREENS , existing solutions were largely retained. Parents have freedom of choice between a voluntary mixed-ability level, what is available within a vertically-structured school system, and comprehensive schools with local differences of availability.

9.2 Hauptschule (Secondary Modern)

The *Hauptschule* provides its pupils with a basic general education which will enable them to go on to vocational training or further education, depending on their achievements and interests. The number of pupils at *Hauptschule* is declining because of rising demand for longer, more qualified further education. In 1980 1.9 million children attended this form of school; in 1985 the figure was down to 1.3 million, and in 1990 to 1.05 million. In 1994 1,112,800 pupils attended the *Hauptschule*: 1,081,200 in the Old and 31,600 in the New Laender. They were taught by 76,103 teachers. The average number of children per class was 21.8, and the pupil-teacher ratio 14.6.

The Saarland changed its constitution in spring 1996 and decided to let the *Hauptschule* run down in 1997 with pupils transferred to an "extended intermediate school". Since then this decision has been widely discussed on television and in newspapers and magazines. The Saarland development must be seen in conjunction with decades of discussion about the *Hauptschule* as a place for "left-overs" – to which we will return later. Interestingly, in reconstructing their education system after 1990, the New Laender (except for Mecklenburg-Western Pomerania) from the start favoured a bipartite system at secondary level I. The *Hauptschule* was not established since this was considered a "discontinued model". Even in Mecklenburg-Western Pomerania there will in future usually only be "combined" secondary moderns and intermediate schools. The Saarland decision marks the first instance of school policy in a New Land being taken over by an Old Land. Strictly speaking, these regulations were not in line with the Hamburg Agreement (28.10.1964) which applies to both Old and New Laender.

In most of the Old Laender the *Hauptschule* comprises five years of schooling (5-9), but there are six (5-10) in North Rhine-Westphalia since the law dated 4.7.1979, three (7-9) in Laender with autonomous orientation (mixed-ability) levels (e.g. Hesse and Lower Saxony), and four (7-10) in Berlin and Bremen. Examples of timetables are to be found in appendices 20, 22, and 23.

During the sixties the *Hauptschule* succeeded the traditional *Volksschule* (elementary school). For the most part it incorporated the primary school and the upper level of the *Volksschule* in a single building. The upper level, usually involving classes 5 to 8, was later extended by a ninth year. Paragraph 9 of the 1964 Hamburg Agreement states: "The *Hauptschule* follows the *Grundschule* and ends with the 9th class. A tenth year is permissable. From year 5 a foreign language is taught, usually English". Compulsory full-time schooling for 10 years at present exists in Berlin, Bremen, and North Rhine-Westphalia. The latter offers class 10 in two forms. The precondition for attending type A is successful completion of class 9. Anyone who then completes class 10 can gain admission to a technical secondary school (*Fachoberschule*) by way of completed training and high grades at part-time vocational school. The precondition for attending type B is good grades in German, mathematics, and English. Successful completion of type B qualifies for admission to a *Fachoberschule* after the 10th class or (if grades are good enough) to the *Gymnasium* upper level. Completion of type B is comparable with the *Realschule* qualification.

Several Laender offer voluntary attendance of a tenth year at *Hauptschule.* In Hesse those who complete the 10th year receive a final certificate and can gain the *Realschule* qualification by taking a special examination. Even though that tenth year is voluntary in Hesse, youngsters who do not stay at school or start vocational training after finishing class 9 have compulsory full-time schooling extended by a year. This extra year can be spent either at class 10 of a *Hauptschule* or comprehensive, or in a preparatory or foundation year at a part-time vocational school. The tenth year of *Hauptschule* is also voluntary in Schleswig-Holstein. Successful completion of that year can meet the educational qualifications for acceptance in a technical secondary school or a technical school.

Successful completion of the voluntary tenth year in Rhineland-Palatinate opens up the possibility of attending more advanced forms of vocational schooling (two-year upper levels at full-time vocational school, vocational *Gymnasium,* after vocational experience the technical secondary school, and after conclusion of initial vocational training and a practical the technical school). A pupil with a special recommendation can even transfer to class 11 of *Gymnasium.*

In earlier times almost every village used to have its own elementary school. Until the sixties in thinly-populated areas there existed a small number of single-class elementary schools grouping pupils of all ages. These were often disparagingly called “dwarf schools”. The restructuring of rural elementary schooling got under way in the fifties. Hesse developed the concept of “central schools” and Lower Saxony called them “community schools”. These gradually made their way nationally, from the start established as multi-level schools, usually, as in Hesse, combining a *Haupt-* and *Realschule.* These schools were financed by the communities involved setting up special school associations. The Laender assisted the construction of modern schools and covered the costs of bussing pupils. During the sixties an aspect of schools policy from the 1919 Weimar constitution was implemented as part of these changes without, however, attracting much public attention. The compromise reached at that time envisaged the introduction of community schools bringing together the different denominations. That now happened in Laender where elementary schooling had been denominationally segregated since the war.

When the closing down of thousands of small elementary schools in favour of central, multi-level secondary moderns had been largely completed, the Conference of Ministers of Education agreed (3.7.1969) on "Recommendations regarding the *Hauptschule*" (Beschlußsammlung No. 130.1), mainly concerned with internal reforms. The objectives were defined as follows: "The *Hauptschule* should enable pupils to find access to cultural life, to achieve integration in political and social life, and to participate in working life in accordance with their abilities". The educational standards were considerably higher than in the upper level at elementary schools. That objective was mainly served by the introduction of a compulsory foreign language (usually English but sometimes French in areas bordering on France). The launching of English had got under way (initially on a voluntary basis) in some Laender two decades earlier but only approached full implementation in the seventies.

The introduction of "work studies" was new too, but had been foreshadowed by "polytechnic education" in the GDR. "Work Studies" were intended to transmit insight, knowledge, and skills in the technical, industrial, social, and political spheres, and to provide assistance in choice of a job. In Rhineland-Palatinate such a course is obligatory for every pupil at *Hauptschule* from the 7th class onwards, but different emphases are available:

- Study area I: technology, business studies, vocational studies, information technology
- Study area II: domestic science, business studies, vocational studies, information technology
- Study area III: business and administration, information technology.

In the 7th class all pupils are given an introduction to those areas of study before making an individual choice from class 8 onwards.

The teaching of foreign languages, mathematics, and, if possible, German, physics, and chemistry is generally differentiated in accordance with pupils' ability. Special lessons are available for children who require extra help. The curricula presented in appendices 20 and 23 show the lessons taught at *Hauptschule.*

For decades discussions of educational policy have been concerned with the danger that the *Hauptschule* might develop into a place for "left-overs" as an increasing number of pupils move after primary school to a *Realschule, Gymnasium,* or comprehensive. In 1986 the federal average for attendance at class 8 of *Hauptschule* was 38 % – compared with 29.2 % at *Realschule,* 27.6 % at *Gymnasium,* and 5.2 % at integrated comprehensives. By 1994 the figure for *Hauptschule* attendance had dropped to 25.6 %. 6.9 % were at integrated *Haupt-/Realschule* classes, but only a few of those would have come from a secondary modern. By that time the *Realschule* accounted for 26.5 %, the *Gymnasium* 31.5 %, and integrated comprehensives (inclusive of Steiner schools) 9.5 %.

Considering the situation in individual Laender rather than the federal average, the outcome is as follows. In Berlin, Bremen, Hamburg, Hesse, and the Saarland, the number of children attending a *Hauptschule* is significantly lower than the federal average, whereas in Baden-Württemberg, Bavaria, North Rhine-Westphalia, and Rhineland-Palatinate it is considerably higher. There are various reasons for those differences. The city-states and large conurbations offer a wider range of attractive secondary schools. In addition the *Hauptschule* there takes on the function of integrating the children of foreign workers and settlers from Eastern Europe, which discourages German parents from sending their children. Where relatively many comprehensives exist, as in Hesse, they take the place of the *Hauptschule.*

Attempts are often made at persuading the public that the *Hauptschule* has no future. However, general elimination of the *Hauptschule* in favour of a bipartite secondary system – mainly with the *Realschule*, *Gymnasium*, and comprehensive – would not be any solution. That would merely displace the organizational and educational problems. As happened in the GDR, parents would be led to believe that every child could gain a middle-level qualification after ten years at school. But even in the GDR, about 14 % of the pupils in the ten years of polytechnic education left after class 8 and began vocational training. In addition, the slogan about "left-overs" is educational defeatism because *Hauptschule* children are then from the start declared to be supposedly incapable of "advancing through education".

The former upper level of elementary schooling was a "dead-end" in organizational terms, since pupils could only transfer to part-time vocational schools but not to the kind of secondary education that opened up further possibilities. That is not, however, true of the *Hauptschule* as reformed in the sixties. Such Laender as Bavaria, Baden-Württemberg, North Rhine-Westphalia, and Rhineland-Palatinate wanted to create a good image for the *Hauptschule* and designed an education programme that included practical experience. In Bavaria, for instance, all pupils in years 8 or 9 have to attend two weeks of work experience, which is intended to make their choice of job easier. Computer studies have been introduced into the curriculum as an option and the teaching of English intensified. Baden-Württemberg also focused on advancement of the *Hauptschule*, and pupils are offered the option of an "extended education programme", involving study-groups and projects giving pupils insight into their local environment, institutions, and associations.

In Bremen, Hamburg, Hesse, Lower Saxony, Schleswig-Holstein, and more recently Saarland and Mecklenburg-Western Pomerania the

Hauptschule is usually coupled with the *Realschule.* In Rhineland-Palatinate, as previously mentioned, there are now 20 regional schools.

Differentiation in classes 7 to 10 takes the following forms:

- according to grades in some subjects at specific levels,
- in terms of preparing for the final *Hauptschule* qualification or *Realschule* equivalent,
- combination of the two types.

The first form is viewed as taking precedence. The other two can be introduced after consultation with the school's parents association. In the former (classes 7–10) courses are established for two levels of achievement:

- from class 7 in the first foreign language (usually English) and mathematics,
- from class 8 in German,
- from class 9 in physics and chemistry.

The courses come to an end no later than class 9. Up to that point pupils stay together in the same class. Class 10 prepares for the *Realschule* qualification.

An initial general certificate can be gained at the end of class 9 in all Laender. In most of them it is termed the *Hauptschule* leaving certificate - but in Brandenburg and Rhineland-Palatinate other terms are used, indicating readiness for vocational training. This is granted when performances in all subjects were at least adequate.

This *Hauptschule* certificate opens up the way to

- practical vocational training (e.g. apprenticeship in a craft trade, commerce, industry, or administration accompanied by attendance at a vocational school),
- a career at the lower and middle levels of public service with part-time attendance at vocational school,
- attendance at vocational schools for specific professions.

In cases of exceptional achievement, pupils in Bavaria, Lower Saxony, Saxony, Saxony-Anhalt, and Thuringia obtain a special ("qualified") leaving certificate. Able pupils who complete *Hauptschule* can gain the qualification for entering a polytechnic by attending a vocational extension or technical secondary school, or for university admission by way of a sixth-form college or evening classes.

In most Laender no special examinations are taken to complete education at the *Hauptschule.* Only Baden-Württemberg has introduced a centralized final examination for all pupils at this level – in connection with the Land government's efforts to upgrade the *Hauptschule* final certificate. Able pupils who complete a training in child care can then also qualify as nursery school teachers. Introduction of a foundation year also gives suitable candidates a chance of moving on to a career at the middle levels of public service.

In 1994 165,829 pupils gained the *Hauptschule* leaving certificate, and 30,635 achieved an intermediate qualification. However, the total number of secondary level I leavers with the *Hauptschule* qualification amounted to 222,181: 12,863 at the integrated *Haupt-* and *Realschule*, 9,142 at the *Realschule*, 19,471 at integrated comprehensives, 3,033 at *Gymnasia*, and 7,633 at special schools. 2,699 gained an external qualification – a small number at evening classes and Steiner schools. In that year 74,200 pupils left secondary level I, including 30,000 from special schools, without the *Hauptschule* certificate. The statistics do not show clearly how many of the 44,200 pupils (8.7 %) did not gain the *Hauptschule* qualification. However, it is clear that this certificate makes demands and that not all pupils are capable of achieving them. The dilemma facing the *Hauptschule* is revealed by the broad range of achievements in Laender that have split up this qualification.

Pupils who leave the *Hauptschule* without a qualification cannot easily find training. However, should they complete vocational school successfully, they will receive a belated *Hauptschule* certificate. In Berlin, Bremen, Hamburg, Hesse, and the Saarland, there exist a few evening *Hauptschulen* where this qualification can still be acquired. In 1994 they were attended by 1,200 pupils across the country.

Most of those who have completed *Hauptschule* then receive training in a firm. The improved introduction to the world of work and employment provided by the *Hauptschule* establishes crucial preconditions for appropriate vocational training. Chambers of industry and commerce have welcomed the more recent development of greater autonomy at the *Hauptschule.* A large percentage of trainees still come from the *Hauptschule*, and over half of school-leavers are trained in manual work.

One key issue within the hierarchical school system concerns the future of the *Realschule* certificate. Will that become the minimum educational norm demanded by society? Introduction of the 10th school year strengthens the trend in this direction. If both *Hauptschule* and *Realschule* involve a similar length of course everywhere, the question of differentiation of qualifications arises. There is a danger of devaluation of the *Realschule* final qualification through the integration of *Haupt-* and *Realschule* (with shared final certificates). And what will happen in future with pupils who even today have great difficulty, or do not succeed, in gaining the *Hauptschule* qualification? Are not vocational training and a job more meaningful for such pupils than another year at school?

9.3 Realschule (Intermediate School)

The *Realschule* differs from the *Hauptschule* in offering an extended general education, which enables pupils to specialize according to achievement and interests, and to continue their schooling in vocational courses or gain university entrance qualifications. Compared with the *Gymnasium*, the course is more practical and geared towards vocational training.

The spread of the *Realschule* is one of the great post-war political achievements in the Laender. Schleswig-Holstein, Lower Saxony, North Rhine-Westphalia, and parts of Hesse were able to build on the middle school system started during the Prussian period. Southern German Laender – Bavaria, Baden-Württemberg, and Rhineland-Palatinate – for the most part only started setting up the *Realschule* system in the fifties. A research project on general school attendance carried out by Professor Friedrich Edding of the Frankfurt/M.-based College (from 1964 the German Institute) of International Educational Research made headlines in March 1962. At that time availability of intermediate schools varied considerably. Edding asked why only 4 % of pupils in Saarland achieved intermediate qualifications compared to 24 % in Schleswig-Holstein. Making known that discrepancy in development of the *Realschule* created a political sensation. Only with the great expansion of the sixties did access to such schooling become more equal.

The success of the *Realschule* – also acknowledged by public opinion – largely occurred in the slipstream of school politics. Rarely did such schools hit the headlines. Their spread across the country and the rapid increase in pupils went largely unnoticed. Numbers of pupils increased from around 235,000 (1950) to 430,700 (1960), 863,500 (1970), and even 1,351,100 (1980). This figure fell again to 857,800 (1989) because of low birthrates, but started rising again from the early nineties. In 1994 there were 972,100 pupils in the Old Laender and 169,300 in the New Laender, making a total of 1,141,400 with 66,062 teachers. The average number of pupils per class was 24.9 with a pupil-teacher ratio of 17.3.

Over the longer term the growing numbers of pupils also result from the fact that the *Realschule* offers opportunities to many pupils from social backgrounds cut off from the *Gymnasium* and university education. So the *Realschule*, particularly in rural areas, serves the function of opening up reserves of talent. Research has shown that the *Realschule* contains a balanced cross-section of the social classes, and that no other school type in secondary level I so closely corresponds to the overall social structure.

The *Realschule* comprises years 5-10 or 7-10. The four-class form is found in the three city-states (Berlin, Hamburg, Bremen), Bavaria, and where the orientation level is autonomously organized, as in Lower Saxony and parts of Hesse. These schools are usually self-determining. In Berlin, Hamburg, Bremen, Hesse, Lower Saxony, North Rhine-Westphalia, Schleswig-Holstein, and soon in Mecklenburg-Western Pomerania, intermediate schools are often linked with secondary moderns or integrated in co-operative comprehensives or school centres. Saarland will introduce "Extended Intermediate Schools" from 1997 when the *Hauptschule* comes to an end.

There are a limited number of three-class continuation forms for secondary modern pupils who transfer after year 7, and also aspects of the *Realschule* in special schools. The Rhineland-Palatinate experiment with "regional schools" was discussed in section 9.2.

Autonomous intermediate schools have only been established in two of the New Laender: Mecklenburg-Western Pomerania (until 1996) and Brandenburg. In Mecklenburg-Western Pomerania the number of pupils at the *Realschule* increased from 47,413 (1991) to 78,074 (1994), while those who attended integrated classes declined between 1992 and 1994 from 19,285 to 2,006. This model will nevertheless become standard practice. Among the New Laender Mecklenburg-Western Pomerania has the highest attendance at *Realschule*. In Brandenburg (where this kind of school covers classes 7-10) there were 20,756 pupils in 1994 with numbers more than doubling since 1991. Integrated classes for *Hauptschule/ Realschule* pupils are called *Mittelschule* (Middle School) in Saxony, *Sekundarschule* (Secondary School) in Saxony-Anhalt, and *Regelschule* (Norm School) in Thuringia. In 1994 these were attended by 142,778 pupils in Saxony and 77,852 pupils in Thuringia. *Realschule* courses in Saxony-Anhalt's secondary schools were attended by 69,846 pupils in that year.

The *Realschule* is not biased towards either preparing pupils for university studies or vocational training, and thus offers a dual perspective. On the one hand, pupils are prepared for practical functions, especially professional, economic, and social responsibilities (related to middle-level jobs). On the other, they can move on to more advanced vocational or general schooling, such as upper level at *Gymnasium*. The *Realschule* differs from the *Hauptschule* in offering a greater range of subjects, for instance in foreign languages with English as a compulsory subject and French as an option. Normally the *Realschule* course takes a year longer – except in Berlin, Bremen, and North Rhine-Westphalia, which have introduced a tenth year at *Hauptschule*.

The term *Realschule* was first generally introduced in 1964 with the Hamburg Agreement. Until then such an institution was usually known as a *Mittelschule* (Middle School). This older expression, which indicates the bridging function served by this kind of school's autonomous educational aims, was expounded by the Conference of Ministers of Education (17.12.1953) in their declaration on the "Function of the Middle School in the School System" (Beschlußsammlung No. 150). This resolution demonstrates the consensus on education policy between the main political parties at that time. For instance, in Hesse in the fifties it was the SPD which succeeded in establishing the *Realschule* extensively through its programme for "nodal schools". In its 1953 resolution the Conference of Ministers of Education declared: "The Middle School meets an urgent need on the part of German education and business life... . It caters for acquisition of theoretical knowledge by able children combining practical inclinations and considerable capacity". Other recommendations were concerned with the various types of Middle School, the curriculum, transfers to other schools, teacher training, and final qualifications.

The Middle School system did not play a prominent part in the great debate on educational reform which got under way in 1959 with the German Commission for Education and Training's outline plan. The German Commission wanted to preserve the *Realschule* with an additional eleventh year. That never happened. One of the Commission's main theses maintained that the tripartite school system was a relic of the 19th century. However, one can only speak of a tripartite set-up since the fifties. Commission members intent on introducing reforms either did not see, or repressed the fact, that the *Realschule* played a central part in post-war modernization of secondary level I.

About a quarter of a century ago the German Education Council approved its "Structure Plan for the Education System". That became the basis for the then social-liberal federal government's "1970 Education Report" and for the first "Comprehensive Plan for Education" prepared by the Federal-Laender Commission in 1973. At that time the Education Council and the Federal Government wanted to restructure secondary level I, introducing "*Abitur* I" as an initial qualification for *all* pupils after ten years of schooling. What at first sight appeared to raise standards and increase the status of middle-level qualifications would probably have led to a levelling down. However, the Education Council thought differently. "Basic education concludes with *Abitur* I which opens up the way for further training. As a high-level qualification it is superior to current completion of *Hauptschule* and middle-level certificates. Compared with today's situation, individual pupils gain greater freedom through no longer being bound by a rigidly determined path through education".

The education offered by the *Realschule* is largely accepted and respected by the population as a whole. Without that consensus between school and economic and social expectations the *Realschule* would never have made its way. Doris André acknowledged that during the September 1994 Cologne educational forum of the German Intermediate Teachers

Association and the Confederation of German Industry: "The *Realschule* is especially suited to combination of theory and practice, making applied learning possible. It stands between the *Hauptschule* and the *Gymnasium*, but is particularly geared towards vocational training and preparation for employment". The *Realschule* would not have spread if it had not proved to be such an attractive and modern type of school, meeting a wide range of needs.

The timetables in appendices 21 and 24 provide an overview of what is taught at the *Realschule*. All pupils learn English and almost a third as a second language French (280,104 in 1993) or – mainly in the New Laender – Russian (1993: 81,435). In years 5 and 6 teaching usually involves the whole class. From year 7 (year 8 in Bavaria) differentiation in terms of subject-specialization increases. This was introduced in Bavaria as early as 1949, resulting in compulsory choice between three possibilities:

- Group I with an emphasis on mathematics, the natural sciences, and technology with more lessons in mathematics, physics, and technical drawing. These subjects mainly prepare the way for a technical career.
- Group II with an emphasis on business and economics offers more lessons in economics and law, accountancy, shorthand, and typing, helping towards careers in business and administration, but can also lead to professions requiring technical skills.
- Group III includes various emphases in the creative and artistic spheres, domestic science, and social studies. Many choices are possible in this group.

Not every school can offer all combinations of subjects. French and computing are additional compulsory subjects. French is mainly taken by pupils who want to transfer to upper level at *Gymnasium* or a language school and have to demonstrate their knowledge of a second language. Around 50 % of boys choose Group I and two thirds of girls Group II, while Group III is the choice of 13 % of the boys and around 28 % of the girls.

In Rhineland-Palatinate differentiation begins in year 7. Each pupil chooses weekly lessons that strengthen compulsory subjects or add new subjects, which could be a second language (usually French), mathematics and natural sciences, business and social studies, or social welfare. In North Rhine-Westphalia differentiation also begins at that level. Here three to four lessons a week offer a choice between a second foreign language, social studies, and technology in levels 7 and 8. In classes 9 and 10 differentiation is based on interest in foreign languages, natural sciences, social studies, technology, etc, plus an additional compulsory subject (2-3 lessons weekly). Every school offers several such possibilities (domestic science, information technology). In Baden-Württemberg from year 7 pupils choose between domestic science/textiles, environment and technology, and a second language (usually French). Basic training in information technology is included in mathematics lessons from year 8.

The *Realschule* leaving certificate opens up access to:

- on-the-job training accompanied by attendance at a part-time vocational school,
- employment in the middle and higher levels of public service with attendance at a part-time vocational school
- schools in secondary level II (full-time vocational school, technical secondary school, technical *Gymnasium*),
- technical schools (e.g. for domestic science or social welfare) whereby an eighteen-month or two-year practical or vocational must usually be first completed.

The *Realschule* qualification thus opens the way for a broad spectrum of possibilities in further education or careers. The majority of school-leavers find employment in the commercial and service sectors. In Bavaria the special tenth classes are highly popular. They enable gifted *Hauptschule* leavers to gain the *Realschule* certificate without any loss of time.

The achievements of the *Realschule* are recognized by industry, skilled professions, commerce, and administration. That was also acknowledged at the previously mentioned Cologne educational forum (30.9.1994) organized by the German Intermediate Teachers Association and the Confederation of German Industry. Horst Wollenweber, a great expert on this type of school, emphasized that the *Realschule* needed to strengthen its autonomy and defend itself aginst a tendency towards levelling down, resulting in lower achievement. He believed that could be done through unified Laender final examinations as only exist in Bavaria and Baden-Württemberg to date.

9.4 Gymnasium (Grammar School)

The *Gymnasium* provides the advanced general education necessary for both university studies and access to vocational training for non-scholarly professions making considerable educational demands. The terms '*Gymnasium*' and '*Abitur*' are almost synonymous in Germany. When people talk about the *Gymnasium*, they are usually concerned about the *Abitur*. Education is after all directed towards the *Abitur* qualification (allowing admission to university) at the 13th year in the Former Federal Laender, and in the New Laender (except Brandenburg) after the 12th year.

The *Gymnasium* is the only kind of school providing general education that incorporates secondary levels I and II. The normal form of *Gymnasium* – in the Old Laender and Brandenburg – has nine or seven classes, and comprises years 5-13 or 7-13, depending on the number of years at primary school or autonomous orientation/mixed-ability level. In Mecklenburg-Western Pomerania, Saxony, and Thuringia the *Gymnasium* comprises years 5-12, in Saxony-Anhalt years 7-12. The 13th year is to be introduced in Mecklenburg-Western Pomerania from the year 2000, and that is also being discussed in Saxony-Anhalt.

There are a small number of continuation grammar schools, adapted for acceptance of *Hauptschule* pupils not later than the 7th class or the 10th class for holders of the *Realschule* qualification and youngsters who have been attending full-time vocational school. The *Gymnasium* should be seen as a single unit within secondary levels I and II, but it is convenient here to first describe it with regard to level I.

In 1960 641,700 pupils attended classes 5 to 10 at *Gymnasium*. During the second half of the sixties in particular the debate on educational reform resulted in the greatest expansion ever in the history of the *Gymnasium*. By 1970 the number of pupils had risen to 1,062,100, and by 1980 to 1,495,500. There was a decline to 1,011,100 up to 1988 because of the falling birth-rate, but then numbers started to rise again. In 1994 *Gymnasium* classes 5-10 were attended by 1,181,700 pupils in the Old Laender and 356,900 in the New Laender. The total of 1,538,600 was a new record for Germany.

Developments were similar for full-time teachers. The total number of *Gymnasium* teachers (including those at level II) rose from 46,000 (1960) to 69,700 (1970), 115,800 (1980), and peaked in 1985 with 126,000. After that came a slight fall to 121,200 (1990) in the Old Laender.

If the figures relating to *Gymnasium* teachers in secondary level I over the past 20 years are examined more closely, one sees that there were 64,259 teachers in 1975 and 73,526 in 1980. That was followed by a gradual decline down to 65,345 in 1985 and 64,190 two years later. That was a turning-point, followed by an increase to 69,018 in 1990. If the teachers working at this level in both the Old and the New Laender are added together, there were 92,587 in 1992 and 91,888 in 1994, balancing out at around 92,000.

Looking now at the pupil-teacher ratio, the average for classes 5-10 in 1975 was 21.7, in 1980 20.4, in 1985 17, and in 1990 15.3. That was followed by a slight increase up to 16.7 in 1994. During the past decade the average number of pupils per class in secondary level I was between 25 and 26.

Expansion of the *Gymnasium* was a great challenge for all those responsible for financing schools, particularly cities and local authorities.

Around 500 new grammar schools were built between 1964 and 1970 alone. In 1960 there were 1,823 *Gymnasia* in the Federal Republic, in 1970 2,311, in 1980 2,477, in 1985 2,486, in 1990 2,441, and in 1994 2,504 plus another 648 in the New Laender making a total of 3,152.

Those few figures reveal the unusual density of the network of such schools. In the sixties and seventies *Gymnasia* were mainly constructed in previously neglected rural areas. Nevertheless, considerable regional differences within the individual Laender still remain. Hardly were the buildings finished than they frequently turned out to be too small despite being supposedly planned on a generous scale. During the phase of expansion many schools were overcrowded, and had to cope with twice as many pupils as intended with even basement rooms used for classes. That gave rise to the much-lamented "mammoth schools". Today these schools are far from the manageable "norm" laid down by the Prussian School Conference in 1890 whereby a higher school should never have more than 400 pupils. Even at that time educationists wanted to avoid impersonal mass operations. They aimed at numbers that would allow a head teacher to know each pupil more personally. However, those were times when the *Gymnasium* was an "elite" school, only catering for a small percentage of an age-group.

In the middle of our century an average of 4 - 5 % of pupils of the same age gained the qualification for university admission. By 1963 that was 7.4 %, in 1970 11.1 %, in 1980 16 %, at present around 25 %, and in big cities often more than 30 %. The *Gymnasium* has transformed itself from an educationally elitist school with relatively stringent selection and ongoing assessment to an institution for pupils from all sections of the population, willing and able to gain the university entrance qualification. Internal selection, resulting in pupils leaving the *Gymnasium* prematurely, has declined since the sixties. With over 30 % of primary school pupils transferring to *Gymnasium*, teaching methods and educational concepts inevitably have to be different from those of five decades ago. The spread of abilities and inclinations is greater today, the learning tempo more diverse, so greater individual assistance for pupils is indispensable. It is disputed whether already in secondary level I at *Gymnasium* education should be geared to the upper level and preparation for university. That has repercussions on the canon of subjects taught. Reforms of the upper level in 1960 and 1972 – the latter have been amended several times in recent years (see section 10.1) – also affected lower and middle levels at *Gymnasium*.

Up to that time *Gymnasia* were usually structured as institutions with particular specializations: classics, modern languages, or mathematics and the natural sciences. In 1972 such structuring was abandoned at the upper level, but remains for secondary level I in *Gymnasia* – even though in most Laender that does not receive expression in the school's designation. Today's *Gymnasium* is usually a combination of schools specializing in modern languages and mathematics/natural sciences.

The sequence of language-teaching was regulated in the 1964 Hamburg Agreement (see section 2.3). Modern language and mathematics/natural sciences *Gymnasia* usually start with English (or French). The second foreign language from class 7 is normally Latin, French, or English. A third option is possible from the 9th class – one of the previously mentioned languages, or Russian, Spanish, etc. The mathematics/natural sciences *Gymnasium* as a rule presents the same sequence of foreign languages, but intensified teaching of mathematics and science replaces the possibility of learning a third language. The classics *Gymnasium* as a rule starts with Latin as the first foreign language in year 5, followed by English or French in class 7 and Classical Greek in year 9. So in the classics *Gymnasium* three languages are obligatory, and in all other forms of this school two. In secondary level I, where a distinction is usually made between lower (classes 5-7) and middle (classes 8-10) levels, the curriculum is largely unified and the broad-based general education differs only in terms of the sequence of language-teaching. In several Laender – including Bavaria, Baden-Württemberg, and Rhineland-Palatinate – it is possible in schools specializing in classics or modern languages to follow the sequence: Latin, English, French (instead of Greek). An attempt is made at taking into account differing abilities and interests among pupils through a diversity of emphases and sequences of language-teaching. In some Laender there also exist a few *Gymnasia* specializing in foreign languages, economics, the arts, or sport (for special forms of the *Gymnasium* at secondary level II see sections 10.2 and 10.3.5).

Let us take Bavaria as an example. Only here is the term “Humanistic *Gymnasium*” still officially used. At this form of school understanding of European culture and thought is founded on study of classical antiquity and its languages (Latin from class 5 and Greek from class 9 – plus English from class 7). The modern languages *Gymnasium* focuses on English and French and the cultures of those countries. Latin can also be chosen as the main language with English from class 7 and French from class 9. Italian, Russian, or Spanish are possible as a third language. The mathematics/natural sciences *Gymnasium* provides an intensified introduction to those subjects with English from class 5, and Latin or French from class 7.

Alongside those traditional forms Bavaria also offers:

- Arts *Gymnasia* with an emphasis on German, music, and art. Latin is taught from class 5 and English from class 7.
- Economics *Gymnasia* with an emphasis on economics, law, and accountancy (English from class 5 and French from class 7).
- Social science *Gymnasia* with special preparation for tasks in the family and society, and English from class 5 and Latin or French from class 7.

(Further information on timetables is to be found in appendix 25.)

Up to 1900 the classics *Gymnasium* was the only school in Germany that mediated the full qualification for university admission. Anyone completing a *Realgymnasium* or *Oberrealschule* who wanted to study medicine, law, etc, had to take an additional examination in Latin and Greek. The classics *Gymnasium* then lost its monopoly over university entrance and the *Realgymnasium* (today's modern language *Gymnasium*) became the most widespread type of high school with its precursor becoming increasingly peripheral. After the 1955 Düsseldorf Agreement all general schools leading to acquisition of the university entrance qualification were given the traditional designation "*Gymnasium*" – a considerable upgrading in the light of educational history, alongside the fact that ever fewer pupils learn the traditional core humanist subjects of Latin and Greek. In 1970 41,400 pupils still learned Greek (= c. 3 %), in 1985 23,000, and in 1994 in both the Old and New Laender combined only 15,000 (in secondary levels I and II). The teaching of Latin has much deeper roots. 571,300 pupils in secondary levels I and II attended classes in 1993. However, it should be born in mind that this mostly involves first steps in Latin with only 131,778 pupils introduced to Cicero, Horace, and Tacitus. Nevertheless, Latin is the third most popular language, preceded by English, which all pupils learn, and French with 622,280 pupils at secondary level I in 1993. The teaching of Latin to some extent still links the traditions of the *Gymnasium* with those of the Latin Schools of early modern times. In Berlin – Germany's capital with almost four million inhabitants – only four *Gymnasia* still specialize in the classics. The spiritual legacy of modern humanism, where Latin and Greek ruled 19th century higher education after Wilhelm von Humboldt's school reforms around 1810, is today imparted to at most 1 % of *Gymnasium* pupils. A "breach in tradition" has taken place here, step by step, in the course of our century while the "*Gymnasium*" has constantly expanded.

Participation in foreign language lessons is shown in tables 8 and 9 in the appendix. Section 19.3 provides more detail about bilingual courses. The schools with a special emphasis on foreign languages include the Franco-German *Gymnasia* at Freiburg/Breisgau and Saarbrücken, and the long-established French *Gymnasium* in Berlin. At these schools some other lessons are given in French. At the French *Gymnasium* German and French pupils are taught together, and the final examination is taken at the end of year 12. Bilingual elements (German-French and German-English) are also to be found in Hesse *Gymnasia*. In Bavaria five *Gymnasia* have been participating in a "European *Gymnasium*" experiment since the 1992/93 school year. This project involves three obligatory foreign languages (starting in classes 5, 6, and 9), greater stress on the natural sciences than in modern languages *Gymnasia*, and an emphasis on the arts. Schools in Berlin, Hamburg, Hesse, Lower Saxony, North Rhine-Westphalia, and Rhineland-Palatinate are participating in a nationwide pilot project with "Japanese as a third foreign language". In Hamburg French, Spanish, Russian, Latin, Chinese, Japanese, Arabic, Portuguese, and Italian are offered at several schools as optional third foreign languages. In Bavaria Italian and Spanish are available at six *Gymnasia*, and Russian at four as third languages.

All *Gymnasia* have computer facilities and the intention is that every pupil should receive basic training in information technology.

It was often maintained during the great sixties debate on educational reform that the *Gymnasium* is "out of date", and its status was much contested in some Laender when comprehensive schools were introduced, but determination to preserve this form of school remained strong among much of the population. Despite all the reforms, the *Gymnasium* – whose educational contents have by now developed far beyond its classical precursor from which the name derives – is still viewed as an embodiment of the German education system's humanist tradition that many parents would like to see maintained for their children.

For pupils who leave *Gymnasium* with the *Realschule* qualification after class 10 in order to start an apprenticeship accompanied by part-time vocational school, the *Gymnasium* serves the same function as the *Realschule* with regard to educational objectives.

The objectives of a broad general education, qualification for university entrance, and capacity for studies are closely linked, and do not involve some special task merely for the upper level at *Gymnasium*. If the *Gymnasium* course is deprived of classes 5 and 6, and secondary level II is decoupled, then it is no longer a continuum. If that unity vanishes, the *Gymnasium* loses its image and will only be a shadow of the school once honoured across the world. This inner distinctiveness in turn very much depends on the way subjects are structured. The core subjects, upheld for almost two centuries despite many interventions and changes, are now in danger of being called in question by the demands of politics and business, science and society, and of being supplanted by new areas of teaching.

9.5 Gesamtschule (Comprehensive School)

Comprehensives usually comprise classes 5 or 7 - 10. Not all such schools are linked with a *Gymnasium* upper level. A basic distinction must be made between two main forms: co-operative and integrated comprehensives.

The *co-operative* comprehensive (called a school centre in Bremen) combines the *Hauptschule*, *Realschule*, and *Gymnasium* both organizationally and educationally. The curricula and teaching structures of those three forms of school are co-ordinated so as to permit a high degree of transferability between them. According to the Comprehensives Association at present there are 200 co-operative comprehensives. They are not to be found in all Laender, but are particularly numerous in Hesse (122 schools), Bremen (38), and Lower Saxony (27). It is difficult to monitor their development since these schools are not included in national school statistics.

The *integrated* comprehensive is unified both educationally and organizationally, and leads to the three secondary level I qualifications irrespective of the number of graduations within differentiation of subjects.

The integrated comprehensive is viewed as an alternative to selective education, but is faced with the problem of combining integration with differentiation. Individual Laender have found different solutions, sometimes varying from school to school. The different types of teaching are :

Core lessons: Pupils differing in ability are taught as a class in such subjects as social studies, work studies, religion, music, and art. However, distinctions are still made within these classes so as to do justice to pupils' different needs.

Differentiated achievement courses: Mathematics, English, German, and to some extent natural sciences are taught at different levels (at least two), depending on pupils' abilities.

Compulsory options: In years 7 and 8 pupils have to choose a weekly four-lesson course (e.g. a second foreign language) or two two-lesson courses; and in years 9 and 10 a six-lesson course (or a four- and a two-lesson course).

Options: Additional subject-related, multi-disciplinary, or independent areas of study are on offer on a voluntary basis.

Special needs: Additional help is available for pupils who have difficulties in individual subjects.

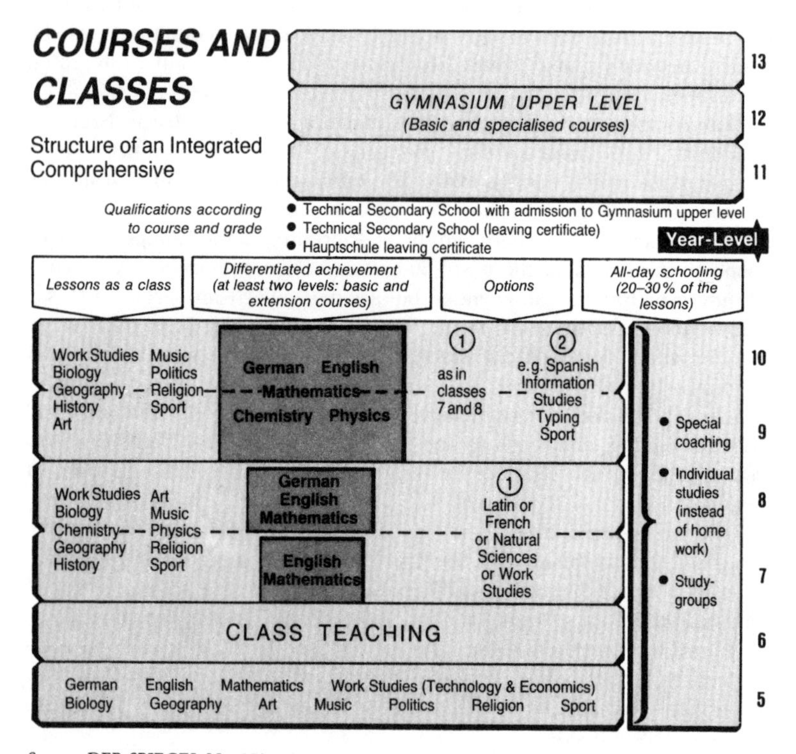

Source: DER SPIEGEL No. 27/1988, p. 29.

Three other characteristics should be mentioned :

1. Integrated comprehensives mainly provide all-day schooling and extra-curricular activities on at least four days a week. On those days pupils are usually in school from 8 a.m. to 4 p.m.
2. Comprehensive schools usually have between four and eight parallel classes per age-group. However, there are also smaller schools with only three parallel classes. In Brandenburg almost half the comprehensives only have one or two classes per age-group.
3. Not all integrated comprehensives have the equivalent of a *Gymnasium* upper level. However, there is a growing tendency towards establishing integrated secondary levels II with general and vocational courses.

The number of integrated comprehensives (including independent Steiner Schools) was 216 in 1975, 255 in 1980, 314 in 1985, and then doubled in the Old Laender to 638 in 1994 (figures from *Grund- und Strukturdaten* 1995/96). In the New Laender there were 330 such schools in 1992, and then the number declined slightly to 319 in 1994. In that year there thus existed 957 integrated comprehensives (157 private institutions) with 450,400 pupils (351,400 in the Old and 99,000 in the New Laender). 33,907 teachers were at work in these schools (including Steiner Schools) in classes 5 to 10. The average figure of 25.6 pupils per class is only slightly lower than in *Gymnasium*, whereas the pupil-teacher ratio of 13.3 is significantly better than 16.7 in *Gymnasium* (1994). That may partly be due to all-day schooling but indicates better staffing at comprehensives.

Figures presented in the 1995/96 Basic Structural Data and in a 1996 survey by the Comprehensives Association do not tally. The Association reports on 765 state integrated comprehensives and the Data on 957 (inclusive of Steiner Schools). The 765 are distributed between Laender as follows :

Baden-Württemberg	3	special forms mixing integrated & co-operative
Bavaria	1	special form
Berlin	65	
Brandenburg	286	
Bremen	10	
Hamburg	36	
Hesse	81	
Lower Saxony	24	
Mecklenburg-W. Pomerania	16	
N. Rhine-Westphalia	198	
Rhineland-Palatinate	9	
Saarland	14	

Saxony	–
Saxony-Anhalt	2
Schleswig-Holstein	19
Thuringia	3

The number of integrated comprehensives is thus relatively modest in terms of the number of selective schools in secondary level I. Those figures are sobering, considering the vehemence with which, three decades ago, the SPD and the Education and Science trade union (GEW) declared the integrated comprehensive to be the "school of the future". Between 1965 and 1982 the controversy over the comprehensive school sometimes took on the character of a "religious struggle" or a "cultural war", determined by opposing objectives within social policy. At that time the SPD and GEW declared that the integrated comprehensive would implement equality of opportunity for children from deprived backgrounds and cut off from higher education better than schools within a selective system. The CDU/CSU made themselves the spokesman for traditional schools and advocated further development of the *Hauptschule*, *Realschule*, and *Gymnasium*, autonomously adapting to changing educational circumstances. Nevertheless, the CDU/CSU were also open to experiments with co-operative and integrated comprehensives.

North Rhine-Westphalia's experimental school at Bielefeld University is an integrated comprehensive. This "*Laborschule*" was established in 1974 in accordance with the ideas of educationist Hartmut von Hentig. The intention was that it should work together with the university's education faculty on the development of new forms of teaching, learning, and school life. The work of the "model school" and the "*Laborschule* Research Institute" are closely linked. Hartmut von Hentig was himself in charge of the school until 1987. The school comprises eleven year-groups (0-10), each with sixty pupils. Schooling begins at the age of five, pupils do not have to repeat classes, and teaching takes place in mixed-ability groups. Learning difficulties are attended to by way of children working in small groups, receiving individual attention, and confronting a wide range of material. As a living environment offering experience, the school should not just be a place where teaching takes place. Provision of stimulating surroundings enables pupils to create their own experiences. There are a library and media rooms, wood and metal workshops, a music room and dark room, a kitchen, a painting area, a theatre space, the zoo, the garden, an adventure playground, science laboratories, and sports halls. Twice a year pupils receive progress reports which are collected in a file. These inform parents about the contents and objectives of lessons, the child's behaviour and development inclusive of attitudes to learning. During the tenth year (or at the end of year 9 if so wished) pupils also get graded reports since those are needed when applying for a job. At the end of year 10 the *Laborschule* issues the standard qualifications.

Recently disputes about comprehensives have quietened down, but that does not exclude intermittent revival of old upheavals. That was mainly made possible by the Conference of Ministers of Education's outline agreement (27/28.5.1982) on reciprocal recognition of qualifications at integrated comprehensives (Beschlußsammlung No. 473.4). In Hesse co-operative comprehensives became established in law as early as the late sixties, whereas in most Laender integrated comprehensives were still viewed as experiments until the start of the eighties. Their legal status was only secured in the Laender after the 1982 agreement. Since then both types of comprehensives have been an accepted part of multiply-structured schooling at secondary level I.

Let us recall the way leading to such acceptance. In the mid-sixties mainly SPD-governed Laender, such as Hesse and the three city-states, launched the first experiments with comprehensive schools. In 1969 the German Education Council's education commission proposed that at least 40 comprehensive projects should be established, and that these experiments be accompanied by scholarly assessments. The outcome was intended to serve as the basis for later decisions on the general re-organization of secondary level I. The Conference of Ministers of Education took up this recommendation and reached agreement (on 27.11.1969) on implementation of pilot projects (Beschlußsammlung No. 473.1). The ministers also committed themselves to subjecting each of these experiments to evaluatory research. The Conference secretariat took on the responsibility of keeping the Laender in touch with what was happening and supplying them with ongoing documentation. That was the task of the Conference working party on "The experimental programme for comprehensives and all-day schools".

Four years later, in 1973, the federal government and the SPD-governed Laender urged introduction of the integrated comprehensive within the overall education plan. The CDU/CSU-ruled Laender responded by referring to the current pilot projects, arguing that only when the planned evaluation of the entire programme had been completed and scholarly findings were available could a decision be taken about which secondary level I system offered most advantages or whether the different systems should operate alongside one another. Since 1971 the federal authorities have provided financial backing for many pilot projects on the basis of an outline agreement with the Laender. The Federal-Laender Commission for Educational Planning and the Advancement of Research produced several comprehensive reports on these experiments. In the early eighties a report by the Commission's "comprehensive school project group" on 129 such experiments signalled the end of the developmental phase in the majority of Laender where integrated comprehensives were not legally established (Modellversuche mit Gesamtschulen. Auswertungsbericht der Projektgruppe Gesamtschule. Bühl/Baden 1982). That report paved the way for the previously mentioned Conference of Ministers of Education's outline agreement in 1982.

Baden-Württemberg, Lower Saxony, and Rhineland-Palatinate also brought out their own reports, comparing pupils' performance at comprehensives and selective schools. In his 1987 "Schulvergleich in der Diskussion" ("School Comparisons under Discussion"), Freiburg educationist Kurt Aurin presented a critical interim stock-taking of scholarly discussion of such comparative surveys in the German Federal Republic. The accompanying research brought people down to earth. The Federal-Laender Commission's overall assessment had not produced any convincing demonstration of general differences, and Aurin also came to the conclusion that the accompanying research did not provide a clear-cut answer. Obviously comparative investigations can only cover certain aspects of teaching and education in individual schools or the system as a whole. They contributed towards putting an emphasis on achievements, limitations, and problems within both integrated comprehensives and the hierarchical system.

In autumn 1994 the comprehensive school made the headlines again when the integrated form celebrated 25 years of existence. Criticism was not lacking when developments were reviewed. An account by Ulrich Sprenger of the many years he had spent as director of studies at a Ruhr comprehensive and as head of a *Gymnasium* upper school attracted much response. He argued that many comprehensives no longer had sufficient pupils from the upper half of the range of ability because more gifted children did not receive sufficient support. So many parents preferred to send more able children to *Realschule* or *Gymnasium*. Comprehensives are thus increasingly becoming extremely expensive all-day secondary moderns (*Hauptschule*). According to a 1991 report by Kienbaum management consultants, in North Rhine-Westphalia the comprehensive had expanded at the expense of the *Hauptschule*. Classes at comprehensives were unruly because pupils only received a maximum of six to eight hours a week of class teaching. Streaming and the associated fragmentation of classes thus got in the way of looking after pupils. At the time of widespread reluctance to send more able children to a *Realschule* or *Gymnasium*, the integrated comprehensive helped open up reserves of talent. Such problems – says the report – no longer exist, so the current structure of the integrated comprehensive no longer meets today's needs.

These critical comments were even taken up by *Die Zeit*, the Hamburg weekly, which had long supported integrated comprehensives.

Articles had such headlines as "Disappointed Teachers Pass Dismissive Verdict" or "Comprehensive on Its Way Out", and even (unsuccessfully) called for far-reaching reforms (17.2.1995).

By now discussion of the comprehensive school has faded away again. However, it is still being debated whether integrated and co-operative comprehensives are "superior" to selective schools – in terms of objective decisions about school courses, pupils' achievements, increasing motivation to achieve, children's satisfaction with school, social integration, and support for children from the lower classes. In assessments of opportunities at the two forms of comprehensive school, educational viewpoints are to some extent influenced by political ideologies. Comprehensives suffered during the reform phase from additional problems, such as demands for curriculum reform, which made experimentation more difficult. The fact that some of the schools in such pilot projects were extremely large, with between two and three thousand pupils, created social and psychological problems.

Termination of the experimental phase by the Conference of Ministers of Education's May 1982 agreement should have resulted in reduction of the financial and staffing advantages enjoyed by comprehensives compared with selective schools. In 1991 the previously mentioned Kienbaum report on school organization (commissioned by the Ministry of Education in North Rhine-Westphalia) stated that the pupil-teacher ratio at comprehensives was considerably better than at the *Hauptschule, Realschule,* and *Gymnasium.* There is no convincing reason why state comprehensives should be better off in that respect than schools in the tripartite system. In other words, a comprehensive should operate under the same conditions as the *Hauptschule, Realschule,* or *Gymnasium.*

10 Secondary Level II (Upper Level)

Secondary level II within general schooling comprises the upper level at *Gymnasium* and to some extent also at comprehensives, the broad spectrum of vocational schools, and sixth-form colleges in North Rhine-Westphalia.

People have long discussed whether general and vocational schools provide education of equal value. On 2.12.94 the Conference of Ministers of Education approved a declaration stating among other things:

"In Germany general and vocational education have developed their specific values and image. Both spheres mediate qualifications and issue certificates of achievement for particular courses. Division of function into general further education and vocational schooling accords with distinctions between subject-matter. In some spheres co-operation and integration of general and vocational education have also produced courses leading to dual qualifications. However, equivalence between general and vocational schooling must be further developed both educationally and socially with the aim of balancing out the public image of these two spheres and creating the necessary preconditions".

The outcome of that resolution is shown in section 10.3.1 with its description of the possibility of gaining a *Realschule* certificate at vocational schools. There are also plans for awarding the entrance qualification for polytechnics at these schools.

10.1 Upper Level at Gymnasium (Classes 11-13)

The rapid developments of recent decades are demonstrated in the following figures: In the former Federal Republic the numbers of pupils attending classes 11 to 13 rose from 211,700 in 1960 to 672,100 in 1982.

There was a decline to 482,200 by 1991 for demographic reasons, but that was followed in the Old Laender by a slight increase to 501,600 in 1994. In the New Laender the number of upper level pupils rose from 66,900 to 108,600 just between 1991 and 1994. Nationwide, 610,100 youngsters thus attended the *Gymnasium* upper level in 1994. They were taught by 53,998 teachers, so the pupil-teacher ratio was 11.3. A further 50,400 pupils attended secondary level II at integrated comprehensives (including Steiner Schools).

No other theme has been so discussed in recent years as the upper level at *Gymnasium* and university entrance qualifications. At the same time no other aspect of schooling has been so radically changed by reforms during the past three and a half decades. Even experts find it difficult to gain an overview of developments and the present situation. A distinction has to be made between three levels:

1. Outline agreements by the Conference of Ministers of Education
2. Laender regulations
3. Specific attempts at reform and educational emphases in individual schools.

Conference agreements create the framework for reforms which are implemented by the Laender in specific ways and then applied by individual schools in accordance with local initiatives and possibilities.

In this context only a brief outline of the Conference's trail-blazing agreements is possible. Developments in the Laender and in individual schools cannot be considered here. It is well known that the idea of reforming the upper level is as old as the *Gymnasium* itself. Reform of the *Gymnasium* usually starts at that level. Crucial impulses have always come from the universities, which demanded higher standards in the *Abitur* and improvements in first-year students' capacity for study. The "Tübingen Resolutions" at the "University and School" conference (30.9-1.10.1951) initiated the first national discussion. They already aimed at schools' restructuring of teaching, restriction of what was taught, limitation of the number of subjects examined in the *Abitur*, and abandonment of the principle of strict curricula. During the fifties the school committees of the Conference of Ministers of Education and the West German Rectors Conference many times deliberated on the university entrance qualification. The minimum requirements were outlined in the "Tutzing Canon of Maturity" (28-30.4.1958). A 1959 outline plan by the German Commission for Education and Training, concerned with restructuring and unifying state schools providing general education, developed a convincing concept for reform of the upper level at *Gymnasium*. The Conference of Ministers of Education took up some of these ideas and on 29.9.1960 approved an outline agreement regulating teaching in that sphere, named the Saarbrücken Outline Agreement after the place where the meeting was held. This reduced the number of compulsory subjects and aimed at intensification of teaching through concentration of subject-matter, promoting training of pupils in intellectual independence and responsibility. Some of the compulsory subjects could be completed by the end of the 10th or 11th class. History, geography, and social studies were amalgamated in classes 12 and 13 as "community studies". Such integration of subjects gave rise to much discussion. The agreement also contained additional recommendations on didactics and methods at the upper level, and laid down the available selection of subjects taught (Beschlußsammlung No. 175.1). This reform attracted a lively response, and by no means met with general approval. There was criticism, for instance, of reduction of the range of lessons in mathematics and the natural sciences, leading to protests by professional associations and university groupings.

In the sixties more and more youngsters attended *Gymnasium*, which progressively became a "mass school". Increasing the number of those qualified to enter university has been one of the main objectives of educational policy since the mid-sixties. In 1964 Georg Picht called for a doubling of the number of holders of the *Abitur*, evoking the threat of an "educational catastrophe". A year later sociologist Ralf Dahrendorf took the view that "increasing the number of pupils gaining the *Abitur* constitutes the most important criterion and the symbolic objective of any policy of expansion of education". That thesis attracted general acceptance among the public. This expansion of the *Gymnasium* at the same time intensified many pupils' "motivation crisis" which became evident in their lack of interest in what was taught at the upper level. Selective measures were progressively abandoned in the course of achieving the educational objective of doubling the number of pupils completing the *Abitur*, so school administrators increasingly had to seek new didactic methods for conveying upper level subject-matter to youngsters who could not easily cope with conventional expectations and showed little interest in traditional subjects.

After years of experiments at schools and negotiations with the West German Rectors Conference, the Ministers of Education approved (7.7.1972) the Bonn agreement on reorganization of the upper level at *Gymnasium* as secondary level II (Beschlußsammlung No. 175.3). This was thus a response to criticism of the 1960 Saarbrücken agreement, emphasized reform of the curriculum, and established the organizational preconditions for its implementation.

The objective was to individualize learning and increasingly adapt subject-matter and forms of teaching to university demands. Individualization was intended to motivate pupils to become more involved in their areas of interest. The backing of the German Education

Council was crucial – as the support of the German Commission had been for the Saarbrücken agreement. The Council called in the 1970 structure plan for "orientation towards science", but lack of space prevents discussion here. Also recommended were experiments in co-operation between general and vocational courses, as, for instance, happened in North Rhine-Westphalia's "sixth-form college". However, the objectives there extended far beyond reform of the upper level since an attempt was made to integrate the two kinds of course (further details in section 10.2).

Two innovations in the 1972 reforms particularly affected school organization. Since then the upper level has no longer been structured in terms of types of *Gymnasium* (classical, modern languages, mathematics/natural sciences); and classes 11-13 have been replaced by a system of basic and specialized courses. Teaching is organized by way of compulsory and optional classes in a ratio of around 2:1 with 30 lessons a week. A distinction is made in both spheres between basic and specialized courses depending on the subject. Basic courses should offer two to three lessons a week – in German and mathematics, and in foreign languages at least three lessons. Specialized courses are intended to provide deeper scholarly understanding and expanded knowledge with at least five and usually six lessons a week. There is no fundamental difference – merely a gradual transition in depth – between the two levels. The choice of main obligatory subjects includes German, foreign languages, art, music, philosophy, religion, community studies, history, geography, social studies, economics, mathematics, physics, chemistry, and biology. Optional courses take in the previously mentioned subjects plus education, psychology, sociology, law, geology, astronomy, technology, statistics, and data-processing.

The agreement lays down in detail how many lessons a week the pupil must attend in both compulsory and optional subjects at the upper level.

The reorganized upper level is basically a three-year course but the agreement does also provide for individualization of learning-speed. For the individual pupil the course can take a minimum of two years and a maximum of four. Able pupils are thus given the opportunity of taking the *Abitur* a year earlier than previously – after at least twelve years of education – but few actually do so. Achievements in the course of upper level at *Gymnasium* and in the actual *Abitur* examination are evaluated on the basis of a points system derived from the traditional grades 1-6 (see section 14).

From 1972 until the present the reforms briefly described here led to serious disputes in the spheres of educational policy, constitutional law, and the law as applying to schools. Experts question whether the 1972 reforms are in line with historical continuity. There is no doubt that the 1960 Saarbrücken outline agreement preserved this continuity. Its reformist concept of opening up the upper level was only implemented step by step after years of discussion and many pilot projects.

The 1972 reform may have shared the objective of further developing the upper level within a context of historical continuity, but in fact it intervened – without broad-based preliminary experimentation – much more profoundly in the *Gymnasium*'s traditional structure than was envisaged by the Saarbrücken agreement. Quite a few experts spoke of the most profound change ever within the *Gymnasium*'s history, and even of a break with tradition. Criticism was mainly directed towards the lack of staff and space for a course system. The reforms were, after all, carried out at the peak of school expansion in a time of overcrowded *Gymnasia*. Lack of teachers at that time often restricted the number and nature of courses possible. The situation was made even more difficult by the fact that educational and didactic issues were not resolved before the introduction of reforms, and the curricula necessary for such courses were also only developed as reforms proceeded. In addition the ending of age-group classes was viewed as problematic. Unusually great administrative efforts were called for in the preparation of six-month courses, assignment of teaching responsibilities, and the selection of subjects. Pupils continue to be confronted with difficult decisions when choosing their specializations. In earlier times they generally made a choice of profession after the *Abitur*, but now they must take later vocational interests into account as early as the start of upper level when selecting their specialized subjects. Diversity of regulations – from Land to Land, school to school – also increases the difficulty of changing schools. The objective in the upper level used to involve providing a broad general education and an overview of such spheres as history, literature, geography, at least two foreign languages, mathematics and natural sciences, the arts, and religion, but reforms led to premature specialization, even partially pre-empting university studies.

Ever since the seventies universities, in particular, have complained about disparities in basic knowledge and a decline in knowledge of history, foreign languages, the natural sciences, and mathematics. However, it should be remembered that even before the upper level was reformed people with the *Abitur* entered university with varying degrees of knowledge – but the degree of difference has increased since the seventies. Individualized courses of study increased specialization at upper level. University teachers criticize students' lack of ability to express themselves, give written expression to complex topics, or cope confidently with mathematical symbols and models. Unfortunately, there is a lack of more recent studies, devoting well-founded attention to such experiences and educational shortcomings.

Despite such criticism there has been no lack of positive experience with reform of the upper level. The advantages of pupils now being able to choose their own specializations without being restricted by the type of *Gymnasium* were recognized. Multiple possibilities of choice open up individualized courses of study offering an opportunity of exemplary in-depth absorption – as opposed to the previously often regretted over-abundance of subject-matter. Choosing specific specializations has today become more important for university admission than deciding on the type of *Gymnasium* attended used to be.

The West German Rectors Conference (since 1990 the University Rectors Conference) several time expressed critical views about reform of the upper level, warning against the danger of premature specialization. It advocated restriction of options in favour of broadly-based compulsory subjects. The rectors believe that German, mathematics, two foreign languages, two science subjects, and history should be compulsory throughout the upper level. That range of subjects is viewed as being an essential part of readiness for university studies.

Even before the 1977/78 reforms had been implemented in all the Laender – with Baden-Württemberg last of all – the Conference of Ministers of Education felt a need to reconsider them. Major and minor amendments to the 1972 upper level reforms were undertaken up to as recently as December 1995. In general it could be said that an attempt was made to preserve the basic structure, which consists of:

- an introductory phase and the time for gaining a qualification
- organization of teaching in basic and specialized courses
- co-ordination of subjects and areas of study
- availability of compulsory and optional courses, providing a possibility of individual specialization.

The other objective was to safeguard the quality of the general qualification for entrance to higher education in terms of basic competences. To satisfy that requirement German, a foreign language, and mathematics have to be taken throughout the qualifying phase (classes 12 and 13), whereby the foreign language can be taken up at the start of upper level provided it is taught to upper level standards.

Let us attempt to summarize the amendments of upper level reforms that have time and again been attempted since 1977. These mostly involved safeguarding an obligatory core. To exaggerate slightly, it could be said that this entails a step-by-step return to the Saarbrücken outline agreement of 1960. The most important stages were as follows.

The Conference of Ministers of Education's accord (2/3.6.1977) on unified implementation of the 1972 agreement made clear that its position on the importance of broad general education reflects that of the West German Rectors Conference. Its recommendations on work in the

Gymnasium upper level (Conference agreement, 2.12.1977 – Beschlußsammlung No. 175.4) elucidated the basic educational principles, outlined the main objectives of learning (self-reliant learning, scholarly studies, and character formation), and described teaching procedures, organization of social relations, and provision of advice.

Those recommendations, however, did not silence criticism. Public opinion, the Philologists Association, the West German Rectors Conference, university teachers, and makers of educational policy time and again demanded that the core subjects of German, foreign languages, mathematics, the natural sciences, history, and the arts should be taught continuously up to the *Abitur*. A ruling by the Hesse high court (30.12.1981) was of particular significance in that context. The judgement concerned the following main issues:

- the objectives of education as guaranteed in the constitution, especially assuring the broadest possible range of general knowledge
- ongoing teaching of German up to the *Abitur*
- the autonomy of history as a subject
- the role of the age-group class and the course system
- the thematic sequence followed by courses and subjects.

Hesse then changed the law regarding the upper level. The South German Laender, in particular, limited the freedom of choice allowing a degree of leeway under the terms of the Bonn agreement, and thereby gave rise to discrepancies between the Laender and further discussions. The Conference of Ministers of Education then revised (21.10.1983) the 1977 agreement on unified implementation of the 1972 accord (Beschlußsammlung No. 175.6). The points of discord in the following years were: extension of compulsory subjects to include German, a foreign language, mathematics, and a natural science; alteration of the weighting between specialized and basic courses; recognition of vocationally-oriented qualifying courses leading to general university admission; and continuation of unified examination demands. Those standardized demands, established in 1979, led to intensification of work on curriculas, exerting a positive impact on *Abitur* standards and the examination's reputation at university (Beschlußsammlung No. 195f.).

After three years of consultations agreement was reached in 1987 on revision of the *Abitur*. The "Agreement on continuation and unified implementation of accords on upper level at *Gymnasium*" was approved on 4.12.1987 by the Conference of Laender Ministers of Education. That served as the basis for acceptance (11.4.1988) of a new version of the 1972 agreement (Beschlußsammlung No. 176), which now regulates organization of the upper level. The preconditions have thus been established for unified nationwide agreements governing acquisition of the university entrance qualification. That is intended to ensure a broad general education and a varied spectrum of possible specializations. The minimum demands have been increased, and courses at specialized *Gymnasia* and vocationally-oriented training leading to a dual qualification (university entrance and a job qualification) have been recognized nationwide for the first time. That applies particularly to sixth-form colleges in North Rhine-Westphalia (see section 10.2). All pupils have to take at least two subjects – chosen from German, a foreign language, and mathematics – right up to the *Abitur*. That had long been the case in most Laender, but not in Hamburg where the greatest possible degree of choice had hitherto prevailed. The new regulation came into force there in 1996 after a transitional period. History and the natural sciences have been upgraded. In future German, a foreign language, or mathematics are prescribed for examination in the *Abitur*. The foreign language that can be presented must already have been taken by pupils at the intermediate level (but this regulation was modified in 1995). That involves a degree of restriction for pupils who transfer to the *Gymnasium* upper level from a *Hauptschule* or *Realschule*. Achievements contributing to the overall grade have been re-weighted. Basic courses have been up-graded, and specialized courses down-graded. Greater importance is thus now attributed to basic knowledge. New too is a regulation also permitting German to be chosen as the chief specialized subject, provided that mathematics or a foreign language is included among the four subjects examined for the *Abitur*. That agreement was only achieved after recognition of qualifications gained at sixth-form college and vocational *Gymnasium* was included as part of a compromise. Controversy over the sixth-form college blocked negotiations on revision of *Abitur* regulations for months. Agreement was also reached on continuation or completion of unified examination demands, which constitutes an essential aspect of the accord.

After reunification in 1990 the New Laender took over the basic elements in reform of the upper level when redeveloping the *Gymnasium*. The upper level there only takes two years (classes 11 and 12) – except for Brandenburg which introduced a three-year course. The introductory phase, which entails year 11 in the Old Laender, was advanced by a year in the East (again except for Brandenburg), followed by the two-year qualification level.

Criticism of the *Gymnasium* upper level and those completing the course has persisted. Universities and industry have spoken of a loss of substance in the education offered by *Gymnasia*, of a lack of achievement, and of failure to prepare would-be students adequately. University teachers have also complained that first-year students no longer possess the largely unified degree of knowledge that used to be the case. This great diversity is said to be due to individual specializations and combinations of subjects. Students are highly specialized in some areas but lack basic knowledge in others.

These arguments were taken up by the Conference of Ministers of Education in meetings at Loccum and Bonn, followed (on 25.2.1994) by a declaration on safeguarding the general university entrance qualification as school-leavers' certificate and guarantee of suitability for studies. It was agreed to retain the concept of a general university entrance qualification. Developments in individual Laender were intensively discussed in connection with previous Conference agreements. The Conference took up a suggestion by the president of the University Rectors Conference about establishing a discussion group with representatives of the two Conferences in order to safeguard quality. These experts went to work between March and October 1995 and in conjunction with the German University Association, the Confederation of German Industry, the University Rectors Conference, representatives of industry and trade unions, teachers and parents, pupils and students, and numerous other education experts published a 175-page final report entitled “Further Development of the Principles underlying Upper Level at *Gymnasium* and the *Abitur*” at the end of 1995. We cannot survey its recommendations in detail, but the commission came to the conclusion that the objectives and principles of upper level at *Gymnasium* should be further developed but were not in need of extensive revision. Significantly, the experts could not reach agreement on the issue of obligatory subjects in the *Abitur*. They saw a need for regulation of organization of the curriculum, forms of study at upper level, and the *Abitur* examination. The commission thus recommended that German, one foreign language, and mathematics should be taken throughout upper level and must be taken into account with all other courses in the final qualification. The experts also urged that achievements in inter-disciplinary activities should be treated exactly like other levels of performance in the overall qualification. Such demands with regard to the *Abitur* examination will be discussed in section 14.

Those proposals served as the basis – at a Conference of Laender Ministers of Education meeting at Mainz (30.11/1.12.1995) – for “Directives for Further Development of the Principles underlying Upper Level at *Gymnasium* and the *Abitur*”, affecting “specific arrangements in the introductory phase”, “spheres of competence”, and “testing of teaching methods and subject-matter”. Clause 4 of the directives reads:

“Three areas of competence are particularly important with regard to shaping study skills: linguistic ability, especially concise written presentation of thought-processes, understanding of complex texts in a foreign language, and competence in dealing with mathematical symbols and models. German, a foreign language, and mathematics have to be taken throughout the phase leading to the final qualification and be included in the actual qualification so as to ensure acquisition of those basic competences. The foreign language may be started on entry into the upper level provided it is taught at the appropriate standard. Acquisition of basic skills can only be ensured by all relevant subjects contributing towards that task. The Laender thus become responsible for the requisite development of curricula. If such basic skills are systematically mediated in other subjects, credits in up to four such courses can be taken into account in conjunction with the requirements of German, a foreign language, and mathematics".

Nevertheless, it must be added that the CDU- and CSU-governed Laender were not satisfied with the outcome of the Mainz plenary session whose dramatic course will enter the annals of the Conference of Laender Ministers of Education. The wording of the agreement leaves much leeway for interpretation. Some see "basic skills" as involving a further departure from a binding canon of specialized knowledge, which others wish to strengthen. The SPD-ruled Laender rejected the idea of an *Abitur* with five obligatory subjects, striven for by CDU-CSU Ministers of Education. *Gymnasium* education will continue to mean 13 years of schooling. Those Laender which wish to reduce schooling to 12 years have to provide the same number of lessons and fulfil the same conditions. Mecklenburg-Western Pomerania plans the introduction of class 13 from the year 2000, and Saxony-Anhalt is also considering an extension of upper level for one year. Saxony and Thuringia want to persist with 12 years of schooling. Four pilot projects with the *Abitur* after 12 years have been under way in Baden-Württemberg since 1991, and there are plans for including other schools.

The University Rectors Conference, which expressed its views on the *Abitur* in a paper in October 1995, was critical of the Ministers' decisions. In their paper, the rectors again emphasized the view that the *Abitur* failed to sufficiently fulfil claims to demonstration of general readiness for university studies. They maintained this was shown by ongoing university criticism of school-leavers' qualifications and readiness for studies. The Conference of Laender Ministers of Education 1988 agreement on restructuring the upper level at *Gymnasium* had obviously not led to lasting improvement. The University Rectors Conference put forward its "Demands of the *Abitur*", adapting the 1958 "Tutzing Canon of Maturity" to today's requirements. It said about "The Profile of the *Abitur*":

"The *Abitur* will only be able to meet demands for demonstration of general capacity for studies if core subjects are prescribed, and these are successfully pursued up to the *Abitur* examination by the entire class without specialization. Those core subjects are:

- mother tongue (German)
- mathematics
- a foreign language continued from secondary level I
- a science subject continued from secondary level I
- history (inclusive of contemporary history)."

German and mathematics should be compulsory in the final examination, plus a choice of at least one other subject from the five others taught throughout.

The CSU is considering introducing from 1997 an entrance examination for Bavarian universities for would-be students with an *Abitur* from other Laender, particularly those governed by the SPD. Pupils in Bavaria have to sit four written examinations in *Abitur* subjects, one more than elsewhere. The Bavarian *Abitur* is thus thought particularly difficult, and that is reflected in the number who gain this qualification: 20 % as compared with the federal average of 27 % (1994). In some Laender the figure rises to between 30 and 40 % of the relevant age-group.

Discussions about the "*Abitur*" will thus remain part of the educational agenda. It remains to be seen whether the Conference of Laender Ministers of Education compromise of December 1995 helps improve school-leavers' capacity for university studies and whether complaints will ease up.

10.2 Special Types of Gymnasium (Specialized Gymnasia and Sixth-Form Colleges)

These special forms involve all types of *Gymnasium* apart from those focusing on classics, modern languages, and mathematics plus natural sciences. Since the beginning of the fifties their number has constantly increased. Some were set up as pilot projects, and all of them lead to general university admission or a qualification for specific studies. Some of these schools are part of the general educational system, others of vocational education. They include *Gymnasia* specializing in economics, technology, domestic science and nutrition, agriculture, the arts, and textiles. They usually only comprise the upper level (classes 11-13).

A large number of these schools were closed down after the 1972 reform of the upper level since elimination of fragmentation of the *Gymnasium* into different types was a specific objective. The current version of the agreement on reorganization of the upper level, concluded by the Conference of Ministers of Education on 11.4.1988 (Beschluß-sammlung No. 176), lists such specialized *Gymnasia* – devoted to economics, technology, nutrition and domestic science, agriculture, and social education – leading to the general university entrance qualification (see section 10.3.5).

Most widespread are the economics *Gymnasia* (years 11-13). In all Laender a three-year course leads to the general university entrance qualification (except for Bavaria where only nine- or seven-class versions exist). Specializing in economics means that pupils renounce the possibility of choosing certain specialized courses and *Abitur* subjects, listed for upper level in the Conference of Laender Ministers of Education agreement. The main subjects are: economics, accountancy, law, and data-processing (information technology in business) – sometimes differently designated from Land to Land. Between 50,000 and 60,000 pupils attend the economics *Gymnasium*. In 1995 over 17,000 completed their education at such schools (8.6 % of all those who gained the university entrance qualification).

In Bavaria arts, economics, and social studies *Gymnasia* exist in nine- or seven-class versions. They are viewed as a standard form of school (see section 9.4). The arts *Gymnasium* focuses on German, music, and art; the economics *Gymnasium* on economics, law, and accountancy; and the social studies *Gymnasium* on social tasks in family and society.

After seven preparatory years, the sixth-form college (*Kolleg*) has existed in North Rhine-Westphalia since 1977. These schools investigate ways of overcoming the traditional separation of vocational training and general education. One objective is to provide pupils with both vocational qualifications and more advanced general education, allowing admission to polytechnics or universities (dual qualification). All courses are taught in an integrated way, i.e. general subjects contain vocational aspects while vocational subjects also put greater emphasis on general elements. There are six different kinds of course with the first three leading to the *Hauptschule* qualification or entrance to a technical secondary school (*Fachoberschule*), providing basic vocational training or completion of specific forms of apprenticeship. Various training programmes, lasting three or four years, lead to admission to a polytechnic and a vocational qualification, or the general university admission in conjunction with either a professional qualification or to such positions as technical assistant, a job combining social work and teaching, work in sport and leisure activities, and employment in home economics.

This project got under way with 13 schools. By 1990 their number had increased to 30, and by 1994 to 41 – where 19,200 pupils attended a *Kolleg* full-time and 60,400 part-time. Of the 29,057 who completed the course in 1994, 22,152 gained qualifications and 6,905 none. 2,664 graduated with dual qualifications: 154 gained both university admission and a vocational qualification, and 481 polytechnic admission plus vocational qualification; 237 received vocational school certificates and the possibility of attending a polytechnic; and 540 completed an apprenticeship and qualified for polytechnic. The majority of these school-leavers (19,488) left the *Kolleg* with a single qualification. 13,877 completed vocational training, 1,690 qualified to enter polytechnic, and 349 to enter university. 1,586 gained the technical school certificate. Reciprocal recognition of university entrance qualifications gained in *Kolleg* courses is linked with a number of conditions. North Rhine-Westphalia produced its most recent comprehensive report on this pilot project in 1992.

The upper level college at Bielefeld is another special institution. This was founded on the initiative of Hartmut von Hentig, who headed the college until his retirement in 1987. It tests new forms of university admission, based on four years of classes within a system of new types of schooling. The college, which is also a research institution, is testing out inner reform of the *Gymnasium* upper level and basic university studies. Its 800 or so pupils (around 200 in each age-group) are selected by means of a special procedure.

10.3 Vocational Schooling: the Dual System of Vocational Training

No other aspect of German education has attracted such international interest as the system of vocational training. For decades other countries have regarded that system as exemplary, but recently doubts have arisen in Germany itself. For instance, experts have asked whether the German form of vocational training needs to adjust more to accelerated change in industrial society. Increasing demand for retraining shows that initial training, intended to provide a job for life, seldom guarantees permanent employment.

The importance of Germany's dual form of vocational training is indisputable. European training policies, inaugurated by the European Commission after the Maastricht Treaty, are also becoming increasingly significant.

After full-time schooling in Germany most youngsters complete three to three and a half years of vocational training in the dual system, involving learning both on the job and in part-time vocational school. Every year over two thirds of general school-leavers (between 560,000 and 600,000 youngsters) begin their training in this system, emphasizing its importance within educational policy. In 1995 there were 450,128 apprentices in the Old Laender and 122,646 in the New, making a total of 572,274.

The highly-differentiated German system of vocational schooling is organized in a multiplicity of types of school and specializations that may at first seem confusing to the outsider:

- *Berufsschule* (Part-Time Vocational School)
- *Berufsfachschule* (Full-Time Vocational School)
- *Berufsaufbauschule* (Vocational Extension School)
- *Fachoberschule* (Technical Secondary School)
- *Berufliches Gymnasium / Fachgymnasium* (Specialized Grammar School)
- *Fachschule* (Technical School)

Table 6 in the appendix provides information about the distribution of pupils between these types of school.

These schools are by no means "relics" of a historical process. They should be comprehended as a flexible response to the changing demands of industry and society, and to new emphases in technical development. Even though vocational schooling is not organized as a completely hierarchical system, the Conference of Ministers of Education has nevertheless succeeded over the past three decades in largely co-ordinating this sphere and opening up possibilities of attainment of the qualifications for admission to a polytechnic or university.

The Laender are responsible for vocational training within schools, and the federal authorities for other sources of such training in firms. Training regulations apply nationwide. After some 50 years of effort, a vocational training law (*Berufsbildungsgesetz*) was approved on 14.8.1969, creating a country-wide foundation for such activities. This law accepts the dual system of training on the job and at vocational school. Responsibility for vocational school training was not included in the law for constitutional reasons. The law does, however, apply to all jobs and branches of industry (with the exception of training for the civil service and on board ships). Different levels of vocational training and retraining inclusive of correspondence courses and programmes for the disabled are regulated here. It is laid down that the trainee (this colourless term replaced the traditional and still commonly used "apprentice") should be provided with a broad basic knowledge and the specialized skills needed for practice of a qualified trade.

The law also led to the establishment at West Berlin in 1970 of the Federal Institute for Research into Vocational Training, which was later transformed into the Federal Institute for Vocational Training (see section 4.2.3) after the law for improvement of the supply of training places had been passed (7.9.1976). Its tasks are, for instance, to help in the preparation of training regulations, support the establishment and further development of regional training centres, compile and publish (annually) the register of recognized training courses, and evaluate correspondence courses in the vocational sphere. The main objective of the 1976 law is to counter unemployment among young people and to ensure the necessary training-places for the younger generation.

The vocational training law of 14.8.1969 was the outcome of compromise between the CDU/CSU and the SPD in the Grand Coalition. The most recent amendment dates from 26.5.1994. The SPD/FDP federal government, which succeeded the Grand Coalition shortly after the original law was passed, soon planned a new version. This received the approval of the Lower House but failed to get through the Upper Chamber where the CDU/CSU-governed Laender had a majority at that time. The main source of dispute was the financing of vocational training. The Social Democrats and allied trade unions called for a "contribution towards training" from all firms for financing the costs incurred by companies actually providing training. That contribution was supposed to replace financing by individual firms – and similar demands were repeatedly put forward at the start of the nineties. There were also many calls for nationalization of all vocational training. Critics objected to in-firm training being administered by industry rather than the state. It was and remains questionable whether nationalization would ultimately benefit young people.

In view of such criticism national and international praise for the vocational training law on its 25th "anniversary" in 1994 came as a surprise. The Federal Institute for Vocational Training emphasized that this law is much discussed – from the Chinese People's Republic by way of Central and Eastern European states to the USA – and some elements have even been taken over by other countries. Since the amended law was not approved in the seventies, the federal parliament passed a new law for improvement of the supply of training places (*Ausbildungs–platzförderungsgesetz*, 7.9.1976), but the federal constitutional court declared this null and void on 10.12.1980 in response to Bavaria's complaint that this law required approval from the Upper House. A new law (23.12.1981) for assisting vocational training through planning and research (*Berufsbildungsförderungsgesetz*), which largely retained the regulations in the previous legislation – except for the financial regulations –, took into account the federal court's criticism of unconstitutional directives. This still applies today with amendments dating from 12.1. and 26.4. 1994.

Since 1977 the federal government has published an annual report on vocational training, rendering an account of developments. Reports since then offer a comprehensive survey of supply and demand with regard to training places, general perspectives, regional developments, organization of specific forms of training, further training, vocational training for young foreigners, and the costs and assistance involved in such activities.

The latest reports (1995 and 1996) are each over 200 pages. The number of new training contracts in Germany amounted in 1994 to 567,840 and in 1995 to 572,800. Supply and demand were statistically in balance. Also in the New Laender almost all young people found training. In 1994 the number of training contracts in the public sector declined in all Laender except Saxony by an average of 25 %. That is partly the outcome of privatization of German Rail and the German Post Office. The number of new training contracts also went down in commerce and industry compared with the previous year whereas the overall importance of skilled trades increased. At the start of the nineties there was a shortage of training-places for skilled trades in the New Laender while in the Old Laender supply exceeded demand. In the former GDR skilled trades had been of limited importance, but after 1990 many new firms were established. That was accompanied by an increase in training-places from around 32,000 (1990) to some 47,000 (1994). In the same year 52,800 training vacancies remained unfilled in the Old Laender, but that figure sank considerably in the following year. The most popular traineeships are in organization, administration, and clerical work, as metal workers, construction and related jobs, electricians, carpenters, and staff in service industries.

In summer 1996 there was extensive discussion of the lack of training-places. The extent of this shortage was and still is disputed. In July of that year 120,000 youngsters were said to be still seeking training even though representatives of industry had in 1995 told the Federal Chancellor that there would be a 10 % increase in openings in 1996. In fact many firms, especially large companies, have recently reduced their work-force. Training apprentices puts firms under considerable financial pressure (on average 30,000 DM annually per place), so they suggested a reduction of trainees' pay (on average about 1,000 DM a month). The SPD countered by demanding that firms which do not adequately participate in training schemes should be legally obliged to pay a training-place tax. By now the discussion has faded away again, and Federal Chancellor Helmut Kohl has taken on the problem. It was to be expected that, as in previous years, sufficient training-places would be created, even if belatedly and without every youngster being able to prepare for the job of their dreams.

In recent decades educational standards and trainees' age have changed. In 1970 around 80 % of applicants for traineeships aged between 15 and 17 still came from the *Hauptschule*, but by 1993 the figure was down to 34.2 %. 35.8 % of would-be trainees had completed *Realschule* or an equivalent, and 13.7 % had the university entrance qualification. In 1993 one in six trainees in the Old Laender and almost one in ten in the New Laender had the *Abitur*. A total of 216,000 youngsters with the *Abitur* were in training that year, and on completion a large part will move on to higher education. Between 1970 and 1993 the average age of trainees rose by almost two and a half years from 16.6 to 19, and three out of four trainees are older than 18.

The regulations governing in-firm training are issued as ordinances by the relevant ministries with the agreement of the Federal Ministry of Education, Science, Research, and Technology. Co-ordination of on-the-job and school training is necessary in the dual system, so the federal government and the Laender Ministers of Education reached agreement in 1972 on a procedure serving the standardization of ordinances and outline curricula. Such harmonization is regulated by a co-ordinating committee grouping officials from the Federal Ministry of Education, Science, Research, and Technology, other federal ministries responsible for specific aspects of vocational training, and all the Laender Ministries of Education. Regulations are drawn up by groups of experts appointed by the Federal Ministry of Education in conjunction with the other specialized ministries involved. The outline curricula for teaching of individual subjects at vocational schools are developed by study-groups appointed by the Conference of Ministers of Education. The Federal Institute of Vocational Training also plays a part in the co-ordination of Laender training regulations and school outline curricula. The Federal Ministry of Education, Science, Research, and Technology publishes an annual register of recognized forms of training with the accompanying ordinances.

Since the 1969 vocational training law came into force, the number of recognized forms of training has declined considerably. In 1971 there were still 606 jobs for which training regulations existed, but in 1994 there were only 373 – 256 of which had been regulated anew. The Federal Institute of Vocational Training is at present revising a further 90 or so categories. This simultaneously demonstrates that the state and industry are endeavouring to take account of rapid technological developments and increase the vocational mobility of young people whose opportunities on the labour market would be restricted by narrowly defined forms of training. During the past quarter century existing training regulations have been modernized, new ordinances have been developed, and outdated jobs have been abandoned.

The vocational training system has been comprehensively regulated by the Laender Ministries of Education in laws, decrees, and ordinances. Vocational schools have a long tradition in Germany, experiencing rapid growth in the 19th century. State vocational schools sometimes developed out of church Sunday schools which served general education. A differentiated vocational system came into existence, but it was long before participation was generally obligatory. In 1873 Saxony became the first state to establish a compulsory three years of further training for boys. Article 145 of the 1919 Weimar constitution provided for compulsory schooling until completion of the 18th year, basically involving attendance at elementary school followed by a *Fortbildungsschule* (school of further education). The latter expression shows that this form of school was originally intended to extend elementary education. The 1920 Reich school conference recommended that this designation should be replaced by the term *Berufsschule* (vocational school), which more accurately expressed the autonomous objectives and special tasks involved. Attempts to pass a law regulating such schools failed during the Weimar Republic for political and financial reasons. A general obligation for both boys and girls to attend vocational school was, nevertheless, largely established. The first nationwide unified ordinance (6.7.1938) came with a law regulating compulsory school attendance.

Since 1948 the Conference of Ministers of Education has expressly sought to achieve far-reaching unification of the diversity of vocational training. That endeavour is demonstrated in an abundance of agreements. The Ministers have several times clarified the terminology employed in vocational schooling (most recently on 8.12.1975, Beschlußsammlung No. 319). The Conference defined the following terms, elucidated below: *Berufsschule, Berufsfachschule, Berufsaufbauschule, Fachoberschule,* and *Fachschule.* The agreements of the Conference of Ministers of Education allow the Laender a certain amount of leeway in order to accomodate new developments. For example, the curricula of the vocational schools reveal differences from Land to Land. Important impulses towards the reform of vocational training came from the German Committee for Education and Training, which in 1964 published an assessment of vocational training and schooling past and present. The concept of the "dual system" used there to designate simultaneous training on-the-job and at vocational school – as had existed in fact if not in name for over a century – became general usage.

Federal regulations (Vocational Training Law and Skilled Trades Ordinance) apply to initial in-firm training. This is based on a civil law contract signed between the trainee and the firm, covering all essential aspects such as training objectives, duration, daily hours, and payment. Trainees have free periods so that they can attend vocational school. Both firms and schools together fulfil the educational objectives of a dual system. Traineeships conclude with a final examination in two parts (practical/oral and theoretical/written). These assessments are conducted by representatives from firms, employees, and vocational school teachers. Successful trainees receive certificates testifying to competence in different spheres. In 1994 there were around 1.7 million youngsters undergoing dual training in industry, the public sector, the free professions, and private households. 564,000 (36 %) of the total of 1.6 million firms provided training for young people. 90 % of such firms have fewer than 50 employees. Their expenditure on training amounts to around 30 billion DM annually plus an additional 16.6 billion for further in-firm training.

Public funds are available for supporting the training of youngsters with learning difficulties and foreigners with insufficient knowledge of German. In the 1994/95 school year 234,900 foreign pupils attended vocational schools: 65 % part-time vocational schools, 16 % full-time vocational schools, 11.5 % a vocational foundation course, 2.5 % technical secondary schools, 2.5 % technical *Gymnasia*, and 2 % technical schools. Young foreigners train for just a few jobs. Girls prefer to learn to become hairdressers or doctors' assistants, and boys motor mechanics or electrical fitters. In 1994 around 9 % of students at vocational schools were foreigners.

Local vocational training centres provide back-up for in-firm training since the availability of modern technical equipment opens up possibilities not available to smaller firms lacking capital or capacity. According to the 1995 vocational training report, 616 such centres with 78,456 places (54,440 in skilled trades) existed in the Old Laender.

In the New Laender serious economic problems during reconstruction resulted in some youngsters being unable to find training-places. Some gained job qualifications in separate training centres receiving assistance from a special Federal/Laender programme and from the European social fund. In-firm training is provided in workshops and offices. Work experience guarantees awareness of the way firms operate in practice. There are 173 such centres in the New Laender with a total of 32,609 workshop places. The emphasis here – as compared with the Old Laender – is on industry and commerce.

10.3.1 Berufsschule (Part-Time Vocational School) and the Year of Basic Vocational Training

In 1994 there existed 1,774 part-time vocational schools, attended by 1,563,900 pupils. Attendance at such a school is compulsory for all young people who have completed full-time schooling at secondary level I and are either receiving initial vocational training or have a job. Attendance at a *Berufsschule* usually lasts three years – up to the age of 18, or in some Laender until completion of vocational training.

The organizational form of the *Berufsschule* depends on the economic structure and the population density of the area served. During the past two decades many less-structured schools were merged to form larger and more efficient systems. In large cities schools for different trades predominate. Five main vocational courses are to be found in the Laender: industry, commerce, home economics, agriculture, and mixed. The Laender, district, and local authorities have done much to adapt the vocational school system to economic and social developments. Today many such schools are exemplary and visited by foreign guests.

Young people have up to 12 lessons weekly (over one or two days) at *Berufsschule* alongside three or four days training in firms or their jobs. The basic idea behind the dual system is that really valid vocational training requires an introduction to both practice and theory.

Two factors distinguish the *Berufsschule* from other vocational training. It is usually a part-time school and fulfils its function in co-operation with firms' training facilities. Teaching at such schools can be provided in blocks of lessons rather than in once or a twice a week classes. Blocks extending over several weeks at school then alternate with periods when young people spend all their time receiving in-firm training. The prevalence of block-teaching is increasing, especially in North Rhine-Westphalia and Rhineland-Palatinate. Experiences with such a block system vary. It has long been practiced in jobs with a very small number of trainees (known as "splinter" jobs). Centralized Land *Berufsschulen* then provide instruction, sometimes inclusive of boarding facilities.

The aim of the *Berufsschule* – as laid down in the Conference of Ministers of Education agreement dated 14/15.3.1991 (Beschlußsammlung No. 323) – is:

- "to provide vocational capacity linking specific competence with general human and social abilities,
- to develop flexibility for coping with changing demands in work and society with regard to a Europe that is growing closer together,
- to awaken a readiness for further training and education,
- to increase readiness and ability for responsible action in private and public situations".

Specialized instruction, which accounts for about 60 % of the teaching, takes into account the training regulations for different trades. The remaining 40 % of the teaching covers general subjects such as German, community studies, social studies, economics, religion, and sport. Provision is also usually made for teaching a foreign language.

As a general principle teaching involves specialized classes based on a particular trade (or related trades). Pupils at such a school generally devote the first year to basic studies and the following years to specialization. At the initial level a general introduction to working life is presented. In the second and third years pupils are prepared for the final examination in their specific trade. The *Berufsschule* concludes with an independent vocational and general qualification.

The Conference of Ministers of Education reached agreement on this issue on 1.6.1979. An amendment dated 29.9.1995 (Beschlußsammlung No. 324) regulates reciprocal recognition of *Berufsschule* certificates. The agreement lays down that a certificate will be issued if a pupil after regular attendance at a *Berufsschule* attains the course objective by demonstrating at least adequate achievement in all the subjects taught. The possibility of making up for unsatisfactory performance in individual subjects is dependent on Laender regulations. It is up to the Laender to decide whether a pupil who attends a *Berufsschule* until the age of 18 but does not achieve a satisfactory standard may be allowed to acquire this certificate at a later date. Successful completion of such a school is viewed as being equivalent to finishing the *Hauptschule* course for youngsters who had previously failed to do so.

In individual Laender completion of *Berufsschule* (with average grades of 3 – or 2.5 in Bavaria and Saxony) can be viewed as equivalent to the *Realschule* qualification if a foreign language has been studied for at least five years. This possibility of gaining a *Realschule* qualification in conjunction with completion of basic vocational training is linked with considerations of "equivalence between general and vocational education" (as mentioned at the start of section 10). Regulations differ.

In Hesse a qualification comparable to completion of *Realschule* can be gained in certain circumstances (additional lessons, achievement of specific requirements). The same applies in Baden-Württemberg when completion of *Hauptschule* and *Berufsschule* is linked with specific vocational qualifications. Bavaria has also introduced a special *Berufsschule* qualification in recognition of good achievements at school and in vocational training.

During the past decade the *Berufsschule* certificate has thus been upgraded in several Laender. The leaver's certificate – in conjunction with proof of successful vocational training (i.e. certificate of proficiency or articles) – permits entry to technical schools.

Year of Basic Vocational Training

Some Laender refer to basic vocational schooling. The outline agreement reached by the Conference of Ministers of Education (19.5.1978, Beschlußsammlung No. 321) lays down that the function served by this year entails mediation of general and broad-based theoretical and practical subject-matter as basic vocational training. This year of basic vocational training was introduced at the start of the seventies. In 1971/72 only 4,000 pupils attended such a school, but by 1994 34,900 attended full-time and 63,200 part-time. This system is more extensively developed in Bavaria, Hesse, Lower Saxony, and North Rhine-Westphalia than in other Laender.

The full-time year of basic vocational training usually replaces the first year of in-firm training. Thirteen spheres of employment are at present involved. Crediting this year within the total length of training is regulated in a decree by the Federal Ministry of Economics. Vocationally-oriented teaching usually amounts to 26 lessons a week. The co-operative form, involving both firm and school, provides for between two and two and a half days of teaching per week. In both forms the training objectives, and the practical and theoretical subject-matter, are concerned with large-scale aspects of work (i.e. industry and administration, metallurgy, electrical engineering, and civil engineering) rather than a specific trade.

Young people are accepted for this year of basic vocational training after completion of the nine or ten years of compulsory full-time schooling. Youngsters who left *Hauptschule* without achieving the final qualification can make up for that by successfully completing the training year. A certificate testifies that this corresponds to completion of *Hauptschule.* Pupils who leave a general school after at least nine years of education but for a variety of reasons cannot immediately begin training or a job, or participate in some youth employment scheme, are obliged to attend a special preparatory form of this year of basic vocational training. This is especially intended for youngsters who leave a *Hauptschule* without qualification and was attended by 51,700 pupils in 1994.

10.3.2 Berufsfachschule (Full-Time Vocational School)

The fact that these are full-time schools means that they cannot be attended alongside in-firm training. The mounting importance of *Berufsfachschulen* is expressed in the great increase in numbers of schools and pupils. In 1960 there were 1,636 such schools; in 1994 2,408 in the Old Laender and 315 in the New Laender, making a total of 2,723. There are relatively many private schools – 545 in 1994. Numbers of pupils were as follows: 1950 88,000, 1960 125,700, 1970 182,700, and 1980 325,600. By 1990 the figure had fallen to 245,600 for demographic reasons. In 1994 249,600 pupils attended full-time vocational schools in the Old Laender and 34,500 in the New Laender, totalling 284,100 throughout Germany.

Various institutions are subsumed under the designation of *Berufsfachschule,* differing with regard to conditions of admission, range of training objectives, and length of training. Admission is dependent on completion of either *Hauptschule* or *Realschule* (or an educational equivalent) depending on the school's objectives. Courses last at least one year and at most three years. The Conference of Ministers of Education regulated full-time vocational schooling in a resolution dated 3.11.1971 (Beschlußsammlung No. 401). A distinction was made between three types of school:

1. Schools with a final qualification in a recognized trained skill
2. Schools where attendance is credited towards training in recognized skills
3. Schools leading to a vocational qualification only obtainable through attending such a school.

The majority of *Berufsfachschulen* belong to the second type. In its recommendation (14.10.1977, Beschlußsammlung No. 402) on the organization of basic training at these schools, the Conference provided guidelines for the development of such courses.

Berufsfachschulen provide both more extended general education and basic vocational training of a specific nature. Schools thus specialize in commerce, technical trades, home economics, tourism, and social welfare. The one-year course complements the dual system since in some trades it is meaningful to leave training to the school during the first year. Vehicle mechanics, for instance, often spend the first year of apprenticeship in such one-year schools. The two-year form offers basic vocational training and leads to an educational qualification comparable to the *Realschule*. The two-year *Berufsfachschulen* specializing in child-care train state-recognized nurses. A similar institution devoted to secretaries with foreign languages was established in Hesse in the eighties, concluding with an examination. These schools must be distinguished from the two-year higher *Berufsfachschule* (belonging to the third type), which is for youngsters who have a *Realschule* certificate. These institutions offer training for technical assistants working in biology, chemistry, physics, domestic science, commerce, and information studies.

The Bavarian *Wirtschaftsschule* (commercial school) constitutes a special form. In 1994 there were 67 schools with 18,267 pupils. This kind of school follows on from classes 6 or 7 at *Hauptschule* and leads in three or four years to the *Realschule* leaving certificate. It furthers general education and offers basic vocational training in economics and administration. There are two emphases in courses. In one the focus is on accountancy, organization of a firm, and data-processing. This prepares for a business career and employment in industry and administration. In the second type the stress is on commercial subjects and mathematics, particularly the use of mathematics in economics and physics. This course thus prepares the way for further training and extends over four years. This qualification is credited with a year off the training period for commercial employment. Its holders can also move on to a technical secondary school, a transitional class leading to a *Gymnasium* specializing in economics, or – after training – to a higher commercial school or academy.

10.3.3 Berufsaufbauschule (Vocational Extension School)

Vocational extension schools were developed in the fifties and remained an important alternative means of access to university. Recently their numbers have declined. Outline agreements by the Conference of Ministers of Education in 1959 and 1965 assured unified organization of the basic aspects of these institutions – most recently revised on 25.6.1982 (Beschlußsammlung No. 415). These accords on education and assessment at such schools state that their objective is to expand and intensify general and vocational training before or during on-the-job instruction. Such courses lead to the qualification for acceptance at technical schools, which is equivalent to completion of *Realschule*. The length of training varies. In the full-time form it takes at least a year, and in the part-time form correspondingly longer. Transfers between the two forms are possible. The precondition for admission is completion of *Hauptschule* (in Bavaria the qualified form). Anyone who has completed at least two years of vocational training is admitted to the full-time form. Admission to the part-time form is open to anyone who has started on vocational training. The teaching amounts to at least 1,200 lessons – and at least half of those devoted to German, a foreign language, mathematics, and the natural sciences. Teaching of specialized courses must entail a minimum of 160 lessons.

These vocational extension schools are usually linked with part- or full-time vocational schools. Provision is made for four specialized courses: technology, economics, domestic science / social welfare, and agriculture. In Bavaria music is another possibility. The choice of course depends on previous vocational training. There were still over 50,000 pupils in 1965, but numbers declined to around 28,000 in 1975, and 9,700 in 1985. In 1994 4,500 attended the full-time vocational extension school, and 200 the part-time form. That is partly an outcome of greater possibilities of getting the *Realschule* certificate today compared with previous decades. Youngsters who complete the course at *Berufsaufbauschulen* are then qualified to enter technical secondary schools, technical schools, technical academies, upper vocational schools, and sixth-form colleges. This type of school does not exist in Berlin, North Rhine-Westphalia, or the New Laender.

10.3.4 Fachoberschule (Technical Secondary School)

This is the most recent type of school in the vocational system. It exists in all Laender except for Baden-Württemberg where there are *Berufsoberschulen* (vocational secondary schools). The *Fachoberschule* was created on the basis of the Conference of Ministers of Education outline agreement dated 6.2.1969. The current accord dates from 26.2.1982 (Beschlußsammlung No. 418). In 1970 this type of school attracted 50,000 pupils, in 1980 around 80,000, and in 1990 52,900 attended the full-time form and 21,600 the part-time school. A start has also been made on development of this type of school in the New Laender with some 9,000 pupils in 1994. In that year total attendance throughout Germany was 55,200 for the full-time form and 22,800 for the part-time form.

Two-year courses at a *Fachoberschule* lead to a qualification for admission to a *Fachhochschule* (polytechnic), mediating general and specialized knowledge and abilities, both practical and theoretical. The precondition for admission is completion of *Realschule* (or an educational equivalent). This type of school comprises classes 11 and 12, and is organized to specialize in engineering, economics, and in some cases agriculture, social studies, and design. Practical training in the student's specialization takes place in the 11th class, extending over at least four days a week. Up to half of this training can be given in either a firm's or the school's own workshops. Further practical training takes place in firms. The school lessons accompanying this practical training should if possible amount to twelve lessons a week – but at least eight. In the 12th class there are 30 compulsory lessons a week in general and specialized subjects at the full-time form. German, social studies, mathematics, natural sciences, a foreign language, and physical education are compulsory, accounting for at least three fifths of obligatory lessons. Applicants who have the *Realschule* qualification (or its equivalent) with completed vocational training can be accepted in the second year at *Fachoberschule*. Completion of a course, concluding with an examination, qualifies for admission to a polytechnic.

10.3.5 Berufliches / Fachgymnasium (Vocational Gymnasium)

These institutions are sometimes regarded as being part of general education and sometimes as part of vocational schooling. A number of special types of *Gymnasium* were already mentioned in section 10.2. These schools were not included in the "Terminology Applying to Organization of Vocational Schooling" agreed by the Conference of Ministers of Education (8.12.1975, Beschlußsammlung No. 319). They are for the most part relatively new types of school. The Conference reached initial agreement on these vocationally-oriented courses, leading to the general qualification for university entrance, on 11.4.1988 (Beschlußsammlung No. 176, appendices 1 & 2), assuring reciprocal recognition of *Abitur* results. These courses cover: economics, technology, nutrition, domestic science, and agriculture (appendix 1). Appendix 2 concerns social education, textile techniques, and design – with 12 schools in Baden-Württemberg, Lower Saxony, and North Rhine-Westphalia.

These vocational *Gymnasia* do not exist in all Laender. Terminology, structures, and qualifications are different too. They first entered school statistics in 1970 with 8,100 pupils. By 1980 numbers had increased to 54,500, in 1990 to 62,600, and in 1994 to 66,900. This type of school is also represented in the New Laender with a total of 19,100 pupils. Total nationwide attendance in 1994 was 85,900 (around a seventh of pupils at upper level). Unlike the *Gymnasium* with classes 5 or 7 to 12 or 13, the vocational model does not have any lower or intermediate level. In Lower Saxony these schools are called specialized *Gymnasia* and lead to the general qualification for university entrance. In Rhineland-Palatinate the vocational *Gymnasium* is integrated in the upper level as vocational specialization in economics or technology. During the introductory phase (class 11) teaching takes place in the class as a whole. During years 12 and 13 it is organized in terms of basic and specialized courses with additional options. Specialization in economics includes business studies, accountancy, and economics, and such options as law, management, data-processing, and a third language. Technological specialization includes metallurgy, electro-technics, and construction technology, and such options as applied science, information studies, and applied geometry. Other subjects accord with what is usually found at upper level in a *Gymnasium*. The *Abitur* provides the qualification for general university admission. Admission to the vocational *Gymnasium* is dependent on completion of the intermediate level with an average grade of at least "satisfactory" (completion of *Realschule*, of the voluntary tenth year at *Hauptschule*, of the 10th class at *Gymnasium*, of full-time vocational school with qualified secondary level I certificate, of vocational extension school, or of level I at the Open University [*Telekolleg* – see section 17.2]).

In Schleswig-Holstein vocational *Gymnasia* offer four specialized courses leading to the university entrance qualification: technology (construction, data-processing, electro-technology, and mechanical engineering), economics (theory and policy), social economics (nutrition and chemistry), and agriculture (agro-technology and biology). These courses can be completed after year 12 with the qualification for entering a polytechnic.

In Berlin vocationally-oriented centres for higher studies lead to the *Abitur*. They offer such courses as economics and administration, metallurgy, electro-technology, chemistry, physics, biology, nutrition, and home economics. The difference from the usual *Gymnasium* upper level – as with North Rhine-Westphalia's sixth-form colleges – lies in the fact that these centres do not just offer general subjects. The emphasis is also on specialized theoretical and practical instruction in such vocational areas as economics and business studies, and law and computer studies.

At Hamburg since 1986 there have been two technical *Gymnasia* in schools of commerce – alongside economics *Gymnasia* (nine schools mostly linked with state trade schools). Dual qualifications can be gained at four schools. The training in integrated courses provides both the full-time vocational school certificate and the entrance qualification for polytechnic or university (in conjunction with qualification as a technical assistant in the business world or the chemical industry). Baden-Württemberg's vocational *Gymnasia* have four main courses: technology, economics, domestic science and nutrition, and agriculture. Specific subjects are emphasized within particular courses, e.g. mechanical engineering, electrical engineering, and practical work in laboratories and workshops at the technical *Gymnasium*. At five economics *Gymnasia* there is also a six-year extension form for *Hauptschule* pupils. Baden-Württemberg's vocational *Gymnasia* lead to either the general or subject-specific university entrance qualification.

Saxony has vocational *Gymnasia* for agriculture, nutritional studies, technology (with specialization in mechanical engineering, electro-technology, and construction), and economics.

10.3.6 Fachschule (Technical School)

Further vocational education at a *Fachschule* aims at preparing skilled students with work experience for middle-level functions including independent management in their areas of specialization (e.g. agriculture and home economics), training of new staff, and other specialized tasks. Holders of the *Fachschule* qualification thus take on functions at a level between skilled workers and university graduates. The precondition for admission to such schools include completion of apprenticeship in a recognized trade and relevant work experience. Students at a *Fachschule* are aged over 18.

Attendance at technical schools declined for a while during the eighties for demographic reasons but has increased again since 1990. In 1994 there were 98,400 pupils in the Old Laender and 12,000 in the New, thus totalling 110,400 in full-time training. Another 48,000 attended part-time facilities. Courses at such schools take either one, two, or three years. The Conference of Ministers of Education approved an outline agreement on the two-year form on 12.6.1992 (Beschlußsammlung No. 429), regulating establishment, structure, training, and examinations in over 90 courses. The minimum admission requirements are completion of *Hauptschule* and *Berufsschule*, completion of a recognized training course, and two to three years of relevant work experience. Courses are directed towards specific jobs. Passing the final examination qualifies, for instance, as a technician, expert in business management, or optician. In Hesse a two-year course in the technology of environmental protection has existed since the eighties. The most frequent courses include electro-technology, mechanical engineering, business studies, civil engineering, and chemical technology. Schools specializing in social education offer a three-year state-approved course for educators in youth work (formerly nursery teachers at kindergarten).

10.3.7 Special Forms of Vocational Schooling

The following forms of vocational school exist in some Laender: *Berufsoberschule* (vocational upper school) / Baden-Württemberg and Bavaria, *Technische Oberschule* (technical upper school) / Baden-Württemberg, *Fachakademie* (technical academy) / Bavaria, and *Berufskolleg* (vocational college) / Baden-Württemberg. These designations also reflect different preconditions for admission, final qualifications, and forms of training (sometimes linked with vocational schooling, sometimes with the university system). (See section 15.8.7 on vocational academies.)

Technical academies only exist in Bavaria. They usually prepare students, who have experience of vocational training, for higher-level careers. 7,887 students attended such schools in 1994. Preconditions for admission are an intermediate school leaving certificate, initial vocational training, and practical work experience. Courses run for a minimum of two and a maximum of four years, depending on specializations. A final examination leads to a state-recognized profession, e.g. state-registered educator (comparable training is provided in technical schools in other Laender). Students who get an overall grade 1 ("very good") qualify for entrance to a polytechnic or a specific subject at university. Possible specializations in Bavaria include social education, jobs requiring foreign languages, music, domestic science, economics, remedial education, medical technology, ophthalmology, and a number of modular courses.

In 1994 1,082 students attended technical upper school in Baden-Württemberg, and 2,841 vocational upper school in Bavaria. The latter comprises two years of schooling, offering general and specialized education, and university entrance. It could also be viewed as part of alternative forms of access to university studies since it serves the educational objective of supporting a non-academic approach by way of *Hauptschule* and vocational training. The precondition for admission is completion of vocational training and *Realschule* (with an average grade of at least "satisfactory"). The *Berufsoberschule* offers four course specializations: technology, agriculture, economics, domestic science and social welfare. Instruction includes both general and more specialized subjects, concluding with subject-specific university entry. The general university entrance qualification can be gained by taking an additional examination in Latin or French.

The precondition for admission to Baden-Württemberg's vocational colleges is also completion of *Realschule*. The course takes between one and three years. Technical assistants, for instance, require two years of training, and graphic designers three. A three-year college operating a dual system is a special feature. Course participants spend two days a week at school and work in a firm for three. After three years they receive a state-recognized certificate of proficiency. The qualification for admission to a polytechnic can be gained by way of additional lessons during training and an examination. The dual form of vocational college exists for machine technology, civil engineering, electro-technology, and garment technology.

11 Alternative Forms of Access to University (Zweiter Bildungsweg)

It has long been possible in Germany for talented adults to gain admission to university studies even if they did not get the *Abitur* at school (see section 14.4). Hitherto this procedure was basically meant for special cases. In recent years, however, the Conference of Ministers of Education's objective of equal recognition of general and vocational education has led to intensified discussion of ways of enabling talented workers to study – e.g. opening up possibilities for nurses to study medicine. This will be discussed in section 14.

Since the fifties new possibilities have been established in both general and vocational schooling, enabling people with a job to gain the *Realschule* qualification and also access to higher education. In the fifties and sixties this "second way" particularly served the objective of correcting the social selection entailed in the *Gymnasium*, and of offering youngsters a chance of gaining university entrance at a time when the network of *Realschulen* and *Gymnasia* was not fully established. Vocational extension schools and sixth-form colleges were also added in the fifties, and the technical secondary school at the end of the sixties. As the previous section on vocational schooling showed, there now exists a variety of forms of admission to polytechnics and universities through such training.

In the sphere of general education, evening forms of the *Hauptschule*, *Realschule*, and *Gymnasium*, and sixth-form colleges must first be mentioned. These enable people with jobs to gain the relevant qualifications, but that is particularly difficult because of the double burden involved. In 1994 the evening *Hauptschule* (in Berlin, Bremen, Hamburg, and Hesse) was attended by around 1,150 students, the evening *Realschule* by 11,590, and the evening *Gymnasium* by 17,575. In

Rhineland-Palatinate and Thuringia there are no evening *Gymnasia*, and in Mecklenburg-Western Pomerania, Lower Saxony, Rhineland-Palatinate, and Thuringia no evening *Realschulen*.

The Conference of Ministers of Education reached agreement on the evening *Gymnasium* as early as 1957, and that was adapted to current developments in 1970 (Beschlußsammlung No. 240). The 7.7.1972 accord on reorganization of the *Gymnasium* upper level as secondary level II also made necessary a restructuring of the evening *Gymnasium*. That occurred in a Conference resolution dated 21.6.1979, revised on 10.11. 1989 (Beschlußsammlung No. 240.2). Training at evening *Gymnasium* is organized as an introductory phase followed by a course system and usually lasts three, or at most four, years. Admission is limited to applicants who are at least 19 and have either completed vocational training or at least three years of regular work. The student must also have a job while studying, except for the final three half-year periods. Applicants who do not have the *Realschule* certificate (or an equivalent) must attend a six-month preliminary course. The course system is modelled on the upper level at *Gymnasium* with certain modifications.

Evening *Gymnasia* continue to provide an autonomous, alternative possibility of gaining the university entrance qualification. Introduction of the course system demonstrated, however, the danger of students dissipating their energies, so these institutions endeavour to guarantee qualified training by way of concentration and intensification of work in basic and specialized courses, concluding with the *Abitur*. Two specialized subjects and two others are chosen by the student for examination. One must be a language and the other mathematics or a natural science. The Conference of Ministers of Education agreements on unified requirements in the *Abitur* examination also apply to the evening *Gymnasium*. The grades achieved are recognized by all of the German Laender.

The *Kolleg* (sixth-form college), formerly the Institute for Attainment of University Admission, is another important institution offering adults an opportunity of going to university. These colleges have been developed since the fifties, and the Conference of Ministers of Education has several times regulated their activities. Here too adaptation to the reorganized upper level at *Gymnasium* turned out to be necessary. The Conference thus reached agreement on reorganization of the sixth-form colleges on 21.6.1979, and that was amended on 2.2.1990 (Beschlußsammlung No. 248.1). The preconditions for admission are the same as at evening *Gymnasium*. An aptitude test or a preliminary course of at least six months are expressly required. The course generally lasts three, or at most four, years, concluding with the *Abitur* examination. An introductory phase of two half-year periods is followed by a course system.

There are sixth-form colleges in most Laender except for Bremen, Mecklenburg-Western Pomerania, and Schleswig-Holstein. In the New Laender their development began in 1991 in Brandenburg, Saxony, Saxony-Anhalt, and Thuringia. In 1994 these colleges were attended by a total of 14,082 students. Teaching styles at both evening *Gymnasia* and sixth-form colleges are adapted for adults. Unlike the evening *Gymnasium*, the colleges usually have boarding facilities. Students are not permitted to take employment and most of them receive state grants. These colleges are full-time schools.

12 Special Schools

Special schools (*Sonderschulen*), called *Förderschulen* in some Laender (e.g. Bavaria, Brandenburg, and Saxony), serve the upbringing and education of children and young people with physical, mental, psychological, or other disabilities preventing them attending, or receiving adequate assistance at, general or vocational schools. There are schools for children with learning difficulties, the blind and partially sighted, the deaf and hard of hearing, those with speech problems, the physically, mentally, and behaviourally handicapped, and the seriously ill (inclusive of home-teaching). Schools for the blind, deaf, physically disabled, hard of hearing, and the partially sighted normally comprise the primary sphere and secondary level I. Their curricula – except for children with learning difficulties and the mentally handicapped – are based on those for general schools. Teaching methods depend on the nature of pupils' disabilities. Qualifications and certificates for secondary levels I and II can be gained at special schools. Support programmes at vocational schools for students with specific disabilities lead to vocational qualifications at secondary level II. Pupils at special schools are also integrated in more advanced vocational education and retraining.

The organization of special schools depends on the nature of the disability and local conditions. The principle that disabled children are best assisted in institutions exclusively designed to meet their needs was established after world war II, but has increasingly been called in question in discussions of educational policy since the start of the seventies. Demands were raised – in connection with the establishment of comprehensives – for abandonment of special schools for retarded or maladjusted pupils so that these children could be integrated in the primary and secondary level I stages at general schools. An October 1973 recommendation by the German Education Council's education commission supported the principle of integration, and suggested that handicapped and non-handicapped children should in future be taught together so far as possible. In the Council's view, segregated teaching of pupils at special school should be ended, especially in the case of the educationally backward, who constitute by far the largest group of pupils at such schools. From the start of the seventies numerous pilot projects and research studies testing measures for integration of the disabled in general schools have been assisted by the federal and Laender authorities. In its recommendations on teaching in schools for the backward (17.11.1977, Beschlußsammlung No. 310), the Conference of Ministers of Education stressed: "Re-integration of pupils from schools for children with learning difficulties into primary schools and the *Hauptschule* is to be undertaken in all cases where there is a prospect of successful participation in lessons". Individualization in the classroom has improved general schools' ability to assist pupils with learning problems so that it is not absolutely necessary to transfer them to special schools. Greater efforts are being made towards integration of disabled children in general schools. Another possibility of supporting children through special teaching involves co-operation between general and special schools. Such measures open up access to different types of school and courses, easing the transfer of pupils from special to general schools. Special schools exist as part- or full-time institutions, inclusive of boarding schools and centrally-situated facilities for pupils with infrequent forms of disability. The long-established *Gymnasium* for the blind at Marburg is one such case.

In 1994 there were 382,265 pupils at special schools – 217,865 at schools for children with learning difficulties. The number of special schools in the Old Laender rose from 1,106 in 1960 to 2,856 in 1980, but then declined to 2,679 in 1991 and rose slightly to 2,715 in 1994. In the New Laender there were 676 such schools in 1994. The national total was thus 3,391. In the same year 26,006 teachers were employed at schools for children with learning difficulties and 31,098 at other special schools. In the former case the average number of pupils per class was 11.7, and in the latter 8.4 (with only minimal variations over the past decade). Such figures are self-evidently significantly lower than at other schools.

Special schools look back on a long tradition and often developed out of church initiatives. Even today the churches maintain many special schools – alongside the Laender and the district and local authorities. The Conference of Ministers of Education has devoted intensified attention to special schools since 1960 when it published an "Assessment of the Organization of Special Schooling". Looking retrospectively at the period of National Socialist rule, this report stated: "The German nation has a historical debt to pay with regard to people deprived as a result of suffering and infirmity. Such people must not be viewed or treated as less valuable. Germans must once again take seriously the task of making possible a meaningful existence for all children and young people who are unable to attend general schools with profit".

The Conference of Ministers of Education has constantly striven to boost the public image of special schools. The way forward in development of these schools was laid down in Conference recommendations dated 16.3.1972 and 6.5.1994 (Beschlußsammlung No. 301). The 1972 recommendation states that the task of such schools is to "implement the handicapped child's right to an education and upbringing in accordance with his or her ability and nature". The Conference approved thirteen highly detailed recommendations in the context of this reorganization (Beschlußsammlung Nos. 302-315). Those recommendations have since been superseded by new ones dated 6.5.1994, intended to outline a shared approach towards future developments and educational changes in the Old and New Laender:

"On the one hand, these recommendations on support for special schools in the Federal Republic of Germany take into account the educational implications of social changes and of alterations in living conditions and the circumstances underlying learning for children and young people in recent years. On the other, they accomodate a transformation in the way educationists view their task. Mounting diversity of forms of organization and ways of applying educational assistance, experiences of lessons shared between handicapped and non-handicapped children, pedagogic initiatives, and emphases within school policy in individual Laender have become increasingly synchronized in this day and age. They reveal more personal, individualized approaches in educational assistance rather than an emphasis on institutions. In this process the concept of 'need' has been increasingly augmented by that of 'support for special educational need' which is not restricted to special schools but can also be offered on a larger scale to general schools inclusive of vocational schools. The education of a disabled young person must be progressively seen as a shared task for all types of school". Attendance at state special schools is free of charge and travel costs are refunded. In the case of state-funded boarding schools, parents usually have to make a contribution towards the costs of upkeep. Foreign pupils are treated in exactly the same way as Germans. Political parties, the churches, and various social groupings make a considerable contribution towards assisting disabled children and young people. Over 100,000 parents and backers are organized in the nationwide "*Lebenshilfe*" ("Life Help") association, which is the largest parental body in the Federal Republic of Germany.

Handicapped young people have to attend vocational schools. There are special vocational schools and "workshops for the disabled" –

particularly in larger towns and cities – as well as individual classes at the usual institutions of vocational education. Special state ordinances promote integration of the handicapped in the world of work and assist their chances of advancement.

During the past decade particular attention has been devoted to special needs support from an early age, shown to be very effective if started in primary school with close co-operation between medical, educational, and psychological services. Discussion of integration has led to the appointment of additional special school teachers at general schools, offering practical help and extra lessons. Successful integration of handicapped and non-handicapped pupils provides particular educational benefit for children without disabilities.

13 Private Schools

Education is largely a state system in the Federal Republic but there is no state monopoly of schooling. In 1994 473,100 pupils attended 2,082 private schools offering a general education, an increase of around 10 % since 1990. The greatest number (209,700) went to *Gymnasium*, followed by 79,400 at *Realschule*, and 61,000 at Steiner schools. 48,300 attended special schools, 30,200 primary schools and 18,600 *Hauptschule*. In the same year there were 1,345 private vocational schools with 131,500 pupils: 49,300 at technical school, 38,800 at full-time vocational school, and 29,500 at part-time vocational school. There are also a great variety of private business and medical schools at different levels. In the New Laender private schooling is still obviously underdeveloped since it could only be launched after 1990. By 1994 only 114 private schools offering a general education (14,600 pupils) and 140 vocational schools (9,500 pupils) existed there with 21 *Gymnasia*, 16 Steiner schools, 48 special schools, 59 full-time vocational schools, and 59 technical schools.

Throughout the history of German education private schools have often served as pace-makers – as, for instance, in the education of girls, vocational training, and facilities for the disabled. State-recognized private schools award the same qualifications as their state counterparts. Apart from a few exceptions, private schools are not "elite schools", either in terms of their educational concept or of the pupils who attend them. Between 1960 and 1990 the number of pupils at private schools offering a general education more than doubled – from 200,100 to 420,700. The total of youngsters at private vocational schools did not increase quite so much (1960: 76,900; 1990: 118,300).

The high constitutional status enjoyed by privately-backed schools in the Federal Republic also receives expression in the fact that article 7 (paragraphs 4 and 5) of the Basic Law guarantees the right to establish private schools. Approval is made dependent on these schools attaining equivalent standards to state schools in terms of teaching objectives, facilities, and teachers' qualifications, and on their non-advocacy of segregation of pupils from rich families. Teachers' economic and legal status must also be sufficiently assured. Article 7 (paragraph 1) of the Basic Law states that the entire school system – i.e. inclusive of private schooling – is subject to state supervision. That is why the term "free schools" (as opposed to "private schools") which established itself in recent years is not completely accurate since even such institutions are not free of the state. They operate under state supervision and require authorization by the state. The details have been regulated in almost all the Laender by special laws on private schools. For instance, article 90 of the Bavarian education law of 7.7.1994 defines the task of such schools as follows: "Private schools serve to complete and enhance the state system. Subject to the law, they enjoy freedom of choice with regard to educational, religious, or ideological inclinations, methods of teaching and education, subject-matter, and forms of organization". Private schools are thus at liberty to develop and try out their own educational concepts. At the heart of that freedom is the opportunity for parents to send their children to non-state schools if they do not approve of the organization of, or what is taught at, public institutions.

A distinction is made in school law between "substitute" and "complementary" schools. Substitute schools are private institutions whose educational objectives accord with those of existing or planned state schools. Most private schools are of that nature. Complementary schools do not fulfil that requirement, but such an institution can receive state recognition (subject to withdrawal) if it provides training for a specific profession, offers instruction in accordance with a curriculum approved by the relevant Ministry of Education, and holds the final examination in accordance with ministerial regulations and under state supervision.

The Federal Association of German Private Schools questions whether the definition of "substitute school" in Laender laws still complies with the concept of independent organization and present circumstances. There is, for instance, the issue of maintenance of status if any form of state school is either modified or even abolished since the concept of the substitute school is founded on what exists in the state system. Today's understanding is that private schools have to be run as complementary schools if they plan a new course not provided in the Land but comparable to existing qualifications. This would mean that such courses could not receive public subsidies.

The fees usually paid for attending private schools cover only a small part of the overall costs involved. Private substitute schools can apply for state assistance in accordance with specific Laender regulations if they operate for the common good and relieve the state system. Laender subsidies for private schools take into account the costs incurred by state schools but non-state institutions receive only a percentage of that, varying from Land to Land. Private schools are thus less of a burden on Land budgets than their state counterparts. Years may often pass before state subsidies are granted.

In recent years subsidies to such schools were also cut to some extent because of the difficult financial situation facing the Laender. Parents and maintaining bodies then raised constitutional objections. The short-fall between state subsidies and actual costs is usually made good by the churches in the case of their schools, but elsewhere school fees have to serve that function. Subsidies are an explosive aspect of educational policy, time and again making the headlines. Disputes broke out in early 1996 when Hesse planned to cut staffing costs by 5 %. Hesse private schools thought their existence was threatened. They had already been affected by cuts in the state system since regular assistance for private schools is linked with the financing of state schools. The original plan for reductions was cut by half, but church schools still feared financial difficulties because of a decline in funds from church taxes, causing a gap which could not be closed by raising school fees.

In Germany around 6 % of all pupils attend private schools, a relatively low figure compared with France, Belgium, and Holland. That is the outcome of the way education has developed in this country. As already mentioned, Germany (except for the former GDR) did not experience the same radical separation of Church and state as France which established a secular school system in the 19th century. Even though "secular" schools, called for by Social Democrats in the 1891 Erfurt Programme, were tolerated in article 149 of the 1919 Weimar constitution, their number remained low at that time. With denominational religious education guaranteed by law in Germany (except for the GDR and with Brandenburg now a controversial exception, as mentioned in section 2.9), many parents who wanted an education founded on religion for their children were not forced to send them to private schools. The entire education system used to depend on the Churches, and they still support the great majority of private schools today. That is particularly true of the Catholic Church. In 1993 there were 1,184 independent Catholic schools with 302,965 pupils. Around half of those youngsters attended *Gymnasium*, 56,000 went to *Realschule*, 26,800 to *Hauptschule* or primary school, 6,700 to comprehensives, 19,000 to special schools, 21,000 to vocational schools, and around 18,000 to medical schools.

Catholic schools are particularly strongly represented in North Rhine-Westphalia (347), Bavaria (298), Baden-Württemberg (143), Rhineland-Palatinate (112), and Lower Saxony (108). 18 schools have been established in the New Laender in recent years.

Catholics view these institutions as being a part of church life rather than "private" schools. This is not the place to outline the great Catholic tradition of schooling and its diversity. Mention can merely be made of St. Blasien and Ettal as Jesuit and Benedictine monastery schools. Today such schools are by no means attended only by Catholic pupils. The percentage of non-Catholics is often between 10 and 20 %. There are around 500 boarding schools and school homes with places for 46,000 boys and girls. The Working Group for Independent Catholic Schools and the Bonn-based German Bishops Conference's education office foster co-operation between German Catholic schools.

Protestant involvement in private schools is equally diverse but numerically much weaker. That is historically conditioned and explicable in terms of Protestantism's association with state schooling. A large part of the state school system in fact derives from church initiatives in Protestant areas. According to the Siegen-based Association of Protestant School Federations, church-maintained schools are as follows. The Protestant Land churches and other institutions (such as the social welfare organization) maintain around 120 schools providing general education (mainly *Gymnasia*), 225 schools for the disabled (usually with boarding facilities), 290 vocational schools (including 130 full-time institutions), and 185 nursing schools. Around half of the *Gymnasia* and *Realschulen* have boarding facilities catering for the disabled, educationally disadvantaged, artistically talented, good athletes, and the highly gifted.

The German Christian Youth Village Association, established by Pastor Arnold Dannenmann in 1947, supports 10 Christopherus youth village schools, which are state-recognized *Gymnasia* – some linked with primary, secondary modern, intermediate, and vocational schools. Several are all-day institutions which also provide for boarders. Each of these schools serves an autonomous educational function. For instance, the Brunswick school tests ways of furthering the highly talented in classes 9 to 13. Other schools develop forms of therapy for psychologically-based disruptions of learning and performance, look after children and youngsters with diabetes, assist great musical talents, or teach top sportsmen from the German Skiing and Tobogganing Association. Refugees from crisis areas and late German emigrants from Eastern Europe are maintained in several schools. One was recently established at Droysig (Saxony-Anhalt) and another at Rostock (Mecklenburg-Western

Pomerania). These Christopherus youth village schools thus attempt to provide a practical response to current educational challenges.

Educational reformism exerted an influence on the Steiner schools, the *Landerziehungsheime* (private boarding schools), Montessori schools, and the Peter Petersen schools (6 in all, including Cologne and Frankfurt/Main). The 30 or so Montessori schools are partly Catholic-backed and partly state institutions. In 1994 about 61,000 pupils attended the 100 Steiner schools offering classes 1-13 and 60 others which do not yet cover the whole range. At present there are also 16 new schools in the New Laender and East Berlin (4 in Brandenburg, 3 each in Saxony and Thuringia, and 2 each in Berlin, Saxony-Anhalt, and Mecklenburg-Western Pomerania). Rudolf Steiner (1861-1925), editor of Goethe's scientific writings and a teacher at a workers school in Berlin, developed anthroposophical concepts based on Christianity. Steiner pedagogics differ fundamentally from state schools with regard to the teacher's role, the curriculum, the methods employed, the nature of reports, and the co-operation of parents which is greatly emphasized. The great majority of pupils attend these schools without having had any previous connection with anthroposophy. Ideological motives play little part in parents' decision to send their children to Steiner schools. They are basically attracted by the educational climate at the schools, which stress education in the arts. These schools are organized in accordance with local circumstances and differ in some respects. They generally have twelve co-educational classes. An additional 13th class is devoted to preparation for the *Abitur*. A kindergarten is attached to many of these schools, and sometimes also a special class for pupils with learning difficulties. All pupils are taught in age-groups and stay together – without any special selection or repetition of a year – until the end of the 12th class. Reports involve brief evaluations rather than grades. Steiner pedagogics also emphasize arts and crafts in all aspects of teaching. Openness to new developments is, for instance, demonstrated by the "practical development of upper level courses providing dual qualifications" pilot project at the Hibernia school in Wanne-Eickel, which sparked off similar experiments in North Rhine-Westphalia's state schools. The German Steiner schools are part of an international movement. Autonomous teacher seminaries exist in Stuttgart, Mannheim, and Witten.

The *Landerziehungsheime* (private boarding schools) arose towards the end of the 19th century within a reform movement critical of educational and cultural policy. The first, following English precedents, was developed at Ilsenburg/Harz by Hermannn Lietz (1868-1919). Today there are 20 such schools including two newly-opened in Thuringia. Many reforms in the state school system derive from this movement's initiatives. The Odenwald school at Oberhambach/Bergstraße, which was expanded into an integrated comprehensive, thus provided important impulses towards reform of the upper level at *Gymnasium* during the seventies. This had been a UNESCO model school from 1963 and since 1978 offers a possibility of “dual qualification” with both university entrance and state recognition as a chemist’s technical assistant.

The *Landerziehungsheime* are attended by around 3,000 boarders and some 2,000 day children. Among them is Schloß Salem, which was founded after world war one by Berlin educationist Kurt Hahn (1886-1974), who was later forced to emigrate by the National Socialists and then developed new schools in Great Britain.

Accomodation in boarding schools is expensive, but private institutions strive to avoid creating the impression that they are for “the poor children of rich parents”. The private boarding schools endeavour – for educational reasons – to achieve a socially balanced mix of pupils, offering scholarships for the children of less well-off families.

A number of “alternative” private schools arose out of the sixties and seventies debates on educational reform. They too are a token of criticism of the state system of education. Some are influenced by the Green Party's ideas about education.

Mention should also be made of the schools for national minorities (such as the Duborg schools for Danes in the north of Schleswig-Holstein) or foreigners (e.g. Greeks and Japanese). There are also Jewish private schools in Frankfurt/Main and Berlin.

14 General University Admission

Revision of the regulations governing university admission has been discussed several times in recent years. The main issue is whether university entrance examinations should be introduced in addition to the *Abitur*. German tradition sees the *Abitur* as part of the school rather than the university system.

The "Leipzig Declaration" – at a conference (22/23.6.1995) organized by Saxony's Minister of Science and the Arts, Hans Joachim Meyer, and the Gütersloh-based Centre for University Development – aims at reshaping the *Abitur* and university admission. Taking the *Abitur* as a foundation, universities themselves should select suitable candidates for their courses, using subject-specific criteria, application data, interviews, and aptitude tests. So far there is no sign of consensus on such university entrance examinations.

The traditional German *Abitur* extends back over 200 years. Its demands were and still are determined by regional Ministers of Education and the Conference to which they belong. Since 1948 the Conference of Ministers of Education has thus several times reached agreement on reciprocal recognition of grades permitting university entrance – most recently on 11.4.1988 and 30.11/1.12.1995.

The first such accord between the former states in the Imperial Reich was concluded as early as 1874 and later frequently amended – in 1909, 1922, 1931, and 1954. The latest currently valid regulation is the revised version (11.4.1988, Beschlußsammlung No. 176) of the 7.7.1972 accord on the reorganization of secondary level II at *Gymnasium*. Admission to university has therefore been the object of highly differentiated arrangements between the federal states for over a hundred years now. Basic issues pertaining to entrance requirements are not, however, decided by Ministries of Education without previous consultation with universities and colleges. In recent decades the Ministers' decisions were preceded by intensive discussion with the West German Rectors Conference (since 1990 the University Rectors Conference), grouping the heads of institutes of higher education. Time and again there has been public discussion of whether would-be students have been adequately prepared and how improvements could be made. That has also been a constant theme throughout the history of German education.

Since the sixties university expansion has not kept pace with the increase in the number of *Gymnasia*. The outcome was that places were not always immediately available in the courses people wanted to study. Up to that time almost every holder of the *Abitur* had pursued university studies. At the start of the seventies that was still the case for around 90 % of those qualified to do so. The short-fall in university places, forecasts of a surplus of graduates, the threat of unemployment among degree-holders, and mounting demand for holders of the *Abitur* in business and administration resulted, however, in an ongoing decline in the number of those who wanted to study immediately after leaving school: 72.7 % in 1977, 61.4 % in 1987, and 53.7 % in 1991. Today almost a quarter of those starting on their studies have previously completed post-*Abitur* vocational training. In-firm training is thus not viewed as an alternative to studies but rather as an initial practice-oriented aspect of training. In addition, the polytechnics are not just attracting people whose final school qualification limits them to that. More than half of those starting out on their studies at polytechnics are qualified to go to university.

In 1994 216,312 pupils gained the general qualification for university admission and 75,088 for studying at a polytechnic. Of the former 191,566 came from schools offering a general education: 175,311 from a *Gymnasium*, 6,653 from an integrated comprehensive, 3,350 from an evening *Gymnasium*, 4,018 from a sixth-form college, and 462 as external candidates for the *Abitur*. 24,746 gained the general university entrance qualification through vocational schooling: 20,300 from a technical *Gymnasium*, 2,149 from a vocational or technical secondary school, and 1,533 from a full-time vocational school. 68,781 qualified for polytechnic entrance in vocational schooling: 39,739 in technical secondary school, 19,527 in full-time vocational school, 4,775 in technical school, 798 in technical *Gymnasium*, 936 in a technical academy, and 3,006 in sixth-form college in North Rhine-Westphalia. 6,307 school-leavers had the polytechnic qualification from general schools, among them 4,128 from a *Gymnasium*. In 1994 young women accounted for 52.5 % of those gaining the university entrance qualification, and for 42.3 % of the polytechnic qualification.

The enormous increase in numbers of *Abitur*-holders led at the start of the seventies to introduction of nationwide restrictions on admissions to certain courses. Regulations for admissions to these subjects were drawn up by the Conference of Ministers of Education on 12.3.1970. The award of study-places was regulated by a state agreement concluded by the Laender on 20.10.1972. This provided the first unified regulation of application and admission procedures for university studies in courses where restrictions existed at all or a majority of colleges. On the basis of this agreement the Laender established a central admissions board at Dortmund. The board ascertains – on the basis of the applicant's papers and the relevant admission regulations – whether and at which college he or she can be accepted and assigns a place. This Laender agreement complied with a federal constitutional court judgement (18.7.1972), demanding that in situations of restricted access to courses of study decisions about admission should be made centrally in accordance with unified criteria, providing for full utilization of training capacity. The federal university outline law, which came into force on 30.1.1976, changed the law affecting admission in several respects. The 1972 regulations had to be adapted to the university outline law. The Conference of Ministers of Education then drew up a new draft state agreement which the Laender Prime Ministers signed on 23.6.1978. That also took into account judgements by the federal constitutional court including that of 8.2.1977 – laying down that applicants who have had to put up with an excessively long wait under the previous regulations must be accorded an opportunity of immediate admission. The possibility of offering places on the basis of a testing procedure was thus opened up. On 30.3.1979 the Conference of Ministers of Education approved a resolution on the introduction of tests in the reorganization of admission to university medical studies. These tests were utilised for the first time in the 1980/81 winter semester. The outcome led the Ministers of Education to reorganise (29/30.9.1983) the procedure regulating admission to medical studies, and that has been in force since the 1986/87 winter semester. 45 % of all study-places are allocated by way of a combination of *Abitur* grades and testing, 10 % on the basis of the test results alone, and the rest in accordance with differentiated procedures (interviews, length of time already waited, etc).

After reunification a revised version of the state agreement on distribution of study-places was passed by the Laender on 12.3.1992. Like the initial agreement concluded two decades earlier, the revised version also regulates the tasks of the central board, procedures for assessing capacity, establishment of admission figures, incorporation of study courses, procedural aspects, distribution, and selection. This is not the place for detailed description of the complicated procedures laid down by the state agreement. The applicant's qualifications and the time that has passed since gaining the qualification for a particular course of study play an important part. A distinction must be made between three procedures: the distribution procedure, and the general and special selection procedures. In the 1995/96 winter semester only the geology course was offered at North Rhine-Westphalia's universities under this distribution process, guaranteeing a place to all applicants. The central board merely determines whether a study-place can be offered at the preferred, or any other, university.

In the 1995/96 winter semester places at universities in all Laender were allocated according to the general selection procedure in the following courses: architecture, biology, business studies, the chemistry of nutrition, domestic science and nutrition, economics, forestry, law, pharmacy, and psychology. After quotas for special groups (cases of hardship, foreigners, and applicants for a second course of studies, etc) have been dealt with, the study-places still available are allocated: around 60 % in terms of qualifications and 40 % in accordance with the time already spent waiting for a place.

The special selection procedure applies to courses in medicine, veterinary science, and dentistry. This procedure also involves a special test which all applicants must take before seeking a place at university.

Selection involves the following quotas:

- around 10 % of the study-places go to special groups (cases of hardship, applicants for a second course of studies, foreigners)
- around 45 % are awarded on the basis of a combination of *Abitur* grades (55 % weighting) and the test result (45 %)
- around 10 % go to applicants with the best test results
- around 20 % are allocated in terms of the time already spent waiting for a university place
- around 15 % are allocated by universities on the basis of an interview. Those summoned for interview are drawn by lot from among applicants who did not gain a place in the other quotas. The success rate among these interviews is set at one in three.

The Conference of Ministers of Education decided in 1996 to abolish the special selection procedure for medical studies with effect from the 1998 summer semester since there has been a signicant decline in the number of applicants. Admission procedures will in future follow the rules applying to other courses where there are restrictions on admission.

Apart from such nationwide or Laender restrictions, there are also a number of local restrictions at individual universities. Information is available in the “Studien und Berufswahl” (“Choosing Degree Courses and Profession”) brochure jointly published by the Federal-Laender Commission for Educational Planning and the Advancement of Research and the Federal Labour Office (25th edition, 1995). This has been a valuable source of guidance for a quarter of a century now.

Distinctions must be made between the different qualifications granting access to higher education:

- *allgemeine Hochschulreife* (the general qualification for university entrance)
- *fachgebundene Hochschulreife* (the qualification for a specific university course)
- *Fachhochschulreife* (the qualification for attending a polytechnic).

14.1 Allgemeine Hochschulreife or Abitur (General Qualification for University Admission)

This qualification opens the way to all courses at all universities and institutes of higher learning. Art, music, and sports faculties also demand demonstration of ability in that particular subject – often in the form of an aptitude test. Technical courses stipulate several months of vocationally relevant practical work, usually before studies get under way. Under certain circumstances, anyone who has successfully completed the basic course at a polytechnic can be admitted to specific university courses.

The qualification for university entrance is generally gained at *Gymnasium* through the *Abitur*, concluding 13 years of schooling (or 12 still in the majority of New Laender). Similar qualifications can be gained in secondary level II of integrated comprehensives, technical *Gymnasia*, evening *Gymnasia*, sixth-form colleges, and external assessment.

The *Abitur* examination at *Gymnasium* consists of written and oral sections, and also practicals in the case of such subjects as physical education, music, art, and the natural sciences.

The pupil is examined in four subjects covering the three obligatory categories. Either German or a foreign language must be examined in arts subjects. The Laender can make provisions for inclusion of special achievements within a two-semester course in the overall number of points leading to the *Abitur*. Pupils may choose to offer this specialization in the final examination. It can constitute a fifth of the total number of points. The fourth subject is only examined orally.

A subject can only be offered for examination if it accords with the "Unified *Abitur* Regulations" drawn up by the Conference of Ministers of Education, and with the approved curriculum for classes 11-13. Religion or sport can also be offered for examination. The oral examination involves a science or arts subject – of the pupil's own choice – which was not previously the subject of written examination. The pupil's achievements in general and specialized courses in classes 12 and 13 and performance in the *Abitur* examination jointly provide the basis for assessing readiness for university studies. Those who do not pass have one more chance to retake the whole examination a year later.

To ensure comparability and standardization of *Abitur* assessments the Laender agreed on regular exchanges of the questions used in written examinations and the results in particular subjects. They also disclose criteria for evaluation of achievements and offer the possibility of reciprocal participation in oral examinations.

There are also plans for regularly commissioning independent research – from university and other organizations – on schools' standards of performance and the status of *Abitur* results.

Specific points were most recently regulated by the Conference of Ministers of Education in their agreement on the *Abitur* examination at the reorganized *Gymnasium* upper level dated 19.12.1988 (Beschlußsammlung No. 192). Those regulations were confirmed by the Conference on 30.11/1.12.1995.

Qualifications for university admission obtained in *Gymnasium* upper levels receive reciprocal recognition by the Laender if they comply with the agreement dated 19.12.1988 (Beschlußsammlung No. 179).

A survey of this complex issue is provided by "Studierfähigkeit konkret" ("A Practical Guide to Study Requirements") by Thomas Finkenstaedt and Werner Heldmann, published by the German University Association in 1989. It describes 36 courses and university expectations of students.

14.2 Fachgebundende Hochschulreife (Specialized Qualification for University Admission)

Extension forms of *Gymnasium*, leading to qualification for studying a specific subject at university, existed in most Laender until into the seventies. That qualification could be extended to general admission to university by taking an additional examination in a second foreign language. During the past decade and a half such *Gymnasia* have increasingly adapted to the Conference of Ministers of Education's regulations concerning the upper level. It seems that qualifications tied to a specific subject at university are rarely to be found in the Laender today (see section 10.3.5).

14.3 Fachhochschulreife (Qualification for Fachhochschule Admission)

This qualifies for studies at *Fachhochschulen* (degree-granting colleges of higher education). The qualification is usually gained through the final examination at technical secondary school (see section 10.3.4). It involves a written examination in four subjects (German, mathematics, a foreign language, plus one other subject). There are also orals in the subjects of the written examination and an additional vocationally-oriented subject. This qualification can also be gained at some two-year full-time vocational schools or at Baden-Württemberg's vocational colleges. The Conference of Ministers of Education reached agreement on special educational possibilities qualifying for entrance to *Fachhochschulen* on 14.7.1995 and 15.9.1995 (Beschlußsammlung No. 469). This provides for qualification without attending technical secondary school. There also exists an opportunity of gaining this qualification by taking an external examination. Special aptitudes in the specific subject must be demonstrated for art or design courses. In some cases preliminary practical studies, extending over several months, are a condition of acceptance at a *Fachhochschule.*

14.4 The Examination for Admission of Particularly Gifted People in Employment to Higher Education

Ever since the twenties, applicants who have outstanding ability in a particular sphere but lack the *Abitur* or polytechnic qualification can be admitted to higher education by way of a special examination procedure. The Conference of Ministers of Education has several times regulated this – most recently in the 6.4.1987 amendment of the 27/28.5.1982 resolution (Beschlußsammlung No. 298). Applicants with a job, qualified by ability, personality, and previous training for university education but lacking the general qualification, can take a special examination if they have acquired relevant knowledge and abilities after some years at work. Such people are relieved of having to pursue schooling or take the *Abitur*. They must be aged between 25 and 40. The examination must be taken in the Land where the applicant is mainly resident. Applicants who have already attempted but twice failed to pass the normal *Abitur* are not admitted to the examination. The evaluation is both written and oral. Further details are contained in the previously mentioned agreement. Understandably, only a few people undertake this way to university studies.

At present there is discussion of whether access to studies should in general be made easier for particularly able people in employment. It is, for instance, being considered whether nurses could be admitted to medical studies in certain circumstances. A comprehensive paper (November 1995) by the Conference of Ministers of Education describes the possibilities of admission to university studies in all Laender for people with vocational but not school qualifications.

15 Tertiary Level: The Higher Education System

In 1991 Dieter Simon, at that time chairman of the Science Council, declared that "the German university is ... rotten at heart. New orientation is required. We need a policy that replaces belief in growth – first in the universities and then in all other spheres of scholarship". Since then discussion has not ceased. Simon had provoked the spirit of the age. Up to the present day German educational policy has remained under the spell of growth-oriented thinking – as expressed in the "Concept for University Development in Germany" approved in 1992 by the University Rectors Conference. Planning is thus based on forecasts of numbers of new students over the next decades and the labour market's supposed demand for university-trained employees. The assumption is that in future over a third of any age-group will pass through higher education. However, it should be remembered that today approximately one in three students does not complete the course. Not all those have necessarily "failed" – some make an early transition to a job – , but the high numbers provide food for thought, suggesting that many students did not acquire the necessary degree of capacity for studying during their time at *Gymnasium*. There are also an increasing number of university graduates who do not find a job or employment compatible with their training. At present that affects 37 % of students of languages and culture, 30 % of graduates in economics and social studies, and even 10 % of medical and veterinary students.

Universities have been "under-financed" for two decades now. The University Rectors Conference ascertained that staffing levels have remained almost unchanged despite a 75 % rise in student numbers between 1977 (the year of the "opening" to which we shall return) and 1989. In his interesting publication "Rotten at Heart? High Noon in Germany's Universities" (Stuttgart, Spring 1996), Peter Glotz, formerly

Berlin senator for science and SPD parliamentary spokesman on education policy, demanded the reintroduction of student fees to compensate for the current deficit of around 4 billion DM. If the state and Laender provide colleges and universities with billions of DM, then students can also be expected to make a contribution (1,000 DM per semester). That suggestion encountered harsh criticism from within the ranks of his own party. Many SPD politicians view it as a “step backwards in educational policy”. After all, abolition of student fees during the first fifteen years of the post-war period was synonymous with democratization of the German university system. At that time Hesse as “a model of Social Democracy” made a name for itself as a pacemaker. If Peter Glotz's proposal were to be implemented, some 3.6 billion DM would become available annually with 1.8 million students paying 1,000 DM per semester. That would largely cover the financial deficit. In July 1996 the University Rectors Conference rejected the introduction of fees by a large majority, arguing that this would not be an appropriate way of helping universities out of their financial difficulties. The rectors considered the social implications and also expressed fears that if student fees were introduced state funds for universities would be correspondingly cut.

Nevertheless, it cannot be denied that Glotz and Simon are right to call for a change of course in university policy. That is urgently necessary.

Apart from the two great challenges of chronic overcrowding in the West and post-1990 reconstruction of the university system in the East, the European dimension is becoming increasingly important. European union faces Germany's universities with new tasks as part of intensified integration. To understand these developments within their overall context a retrosepctive look at the post-war period is necessary.

15.1 Reconstruction after 1945

In May 1945 Karl Jaspers wrote: “The future of our universities ... depends on renewal of their original spirit ... Universities have the task of seeking truth within the community of scholars and students”. Jaspers went on to say: “Outlining an idea of the university involves orientation towards an ideal that reality can only approximate”. There Jaspers followed in the footsteps of Wilhelm von Humboldt whose 1809 university principles were based on the universality and autonomy of scholarship and required small universities. Anyone who today rereads Jaspers' programmatic “The Idea of the University” (1946), cannot avoid asking: Did this “renewal” fail and have not Germany's universities increasingly moved away from the traditional German model founded on extensive autonomy? Where does there still exist a comprehensible "community of scholars and students"?

When the second world war came to an end in 1945 most German universities lay in ruins. The first steps towards reconstruction were taken under the supervision of the occupying powers. Despite agreement on denazification of university teachers and courses, and democratization of studies, there was no unified programme for reforming higher education. Many university teachers had to be dismissed temporarily or permanently because of their involvement in National Socialism. One third of the staff were affected at Frankfurt/Main university. University administrations in the newly-established Laender were faced with almost insoluble problems. The initial step involved removing all the "ruins" of the past, both material and spiritual. The first universities opened their doors at the end of 1945. A younger generation shaped by war began their studies. They were praised by Eduard Spranger (as already mentioned in the introduction).

University reforms even got under way amid the ruins. Mention should be made of the Marburg University Discussions (1946-48), the Schwalbach Guidelines (1947), and the 1948 Hamburg "Blue Report". This "Assessment of University Reform" was carried out by a studies commission appointed by the military governor of the British zone of occupation, consisting of German, British, and Swiss scholars and representatives of the churches and trade unions under the chairmanship of a unionist. An attempt was made at outlining a new status for German universities within intellectual life, state, and society. University autonomy was to be strengthened and a middle-level of lecturers and professors created. One central objective entailed opening up universities to all sections of the population. However, it was made clear that this was only possible if the numbers of overburdened staff were expanded. In the "Blue Report" the international study commission testified that "German universities embody an old and basically sound tradition". The task of reform was said to involve "devoting the healthy core of this tradition to service of contemporary needs". As early as 1945 Karl Jaspers had stressed: "In re-establishing the university the destiny of our intellectual and spiritual life depends on a return to our best traditions by way of contemporary re-creation".

In Frankfurt/Main too, Ernst Beutler, director of the Freies Hochstift and respected Goethe scholar, pointed out to American officers responsible for universities: "We still have a sound group of academically trained university teachers who would live up to the traditions of this country". In his history of Frankfurt university Notker Hammerstein observes: "The younger generation often gets the impression that 1945 brought a revival of conservative values rather than the revolutionary fresh start which was needed. Perhaps judgements are being passed too quickly here. Each age can only speak the language it understands and implement what is comprehended, desired, and accepted by the majority".

15.2 University Expansion and Reform

Political developments in the post-war period led in the West to the setting up of three universities: Mainz (1946), Saarbrücken (1948), and West Berlin's Free University (also 1948) with ongoing support from the occupying powers. The new foundations were particularly open to reformist ideas. The reconstruction phase lasted about fifteen years and was concluded around 1960. The fifties did not only involve the "economic miracle"; there was also a "university miracle". Celebrated emigrants returned including historian Hans Rothfels and philosophers Plessner, Löwith, Horkheimer, and Adorno. Notable scholars – such as Eduard Spranger, Martin Heidegger, Hans-Georg Gadamer, Wolfgang Schadewaldt, Helmut Thielicke, Romano Guardini, Rudolf Bultmann, Bruno Snell, Friedrich Meinecke, Gerhard Ritter, Franz Schnabel, Percy Ernst Schramm, Hermann Heimpel, Ernst Robert Curtius, Alfred Weber, Werner Heisenberg, Otto Hahn, Walter Hallstein, and Ludwig Raiser, to name only a few – exerted an influence in intellectual reconstruction far beyond the universities. However, events in the sixties were to show that this was a late and deceptive splendour, almost a pale reflection of the Wilhelminian and Weimar eras.

After 1945 the Laender had sole responsibility for the university system. From 1948 they co-ordinated their university policies in the Conference of Ministers of Education with the university commission, grouping Laender administrations and making an important contribution towards preparing agreements. The Science Council (see section 3) has acted in a consultative capacity for nationwide educational policy from 1957. Its 1960 recommendations on university expansion (known as the "Blue Bible") attracted particular attention. The establishment of new universities (as at Bochum, Bremen, Konstanz, and Bielefeld) led to widespread public discussion. Between 1960 and 1975 there occurred the greatest upsurge of university foundations in more recent German educational history. During that period 24 universities and comprehensive colleges were set up and the higher education "network" intensified. Expansion was also the outcome of regional planning since the new universities were mainly built in densely populated areas (in the Ruhr at Bochum, Essen, Dortmund, Duisburg, Wuppertal, and Hagen) or border areas (Bremen, Trier, Kaiserslautern, Passau, Bayreuth, Bamberg).

That was also the time of great structural changes in German universities and colleges of higher education. Two international trends are documented in the expansion of the German university system: democratization of secondary and higher education, and scientization of state, economy, and society. The former was assisted by supporting measures such as financial assistance for students from less well-off families ("Honnef Model" from 1957). Until 1971 it was mainly the Laender which provided funds for student grants and loans; since then the state has taken on this responsibility. The number of those taking the *Abitur* and becoming students doubled as early as the fifties, but during the following decade that increase became the most important criterion of educational progress.

German discussion of university reforms erupted again in the course of a worldwide debate, often accompanied by student unrest. Mention has already been made in the introduction (see section 1.5) on the connection between the student movement and university reforms. A large number of neo-Marxist university groups (particularly the Federation of German Socialist Students – SDS) played a considerable part in the wave of university reforms. Other proposals for change came from the Association of German Students and the Federal Conference of Junior Lecturers, linking middle-level academics who later merged with the Education and Science trade union. At that time two basic political trends – "democratization" of structures and university expansion – overlapped dangerously. A great impact was exerted by the student unrest which broke out in 1967/68. The Laender still had sole responsibility for the university system and regional parliaments started to implement university reforms and experiments. The student movement may have played an important part in discussions, but it was by no means the actual motor of reform. Such reforms had long been under way, and certainly no later than establishment of the Science Council in 1957. In fact, students were relatively late in making known their ideas in this sphere. The key political event for the 68 generation was the Vietnam war which was experienced daily on television. Radical discussion, critical of society, spread to schools and universities, state and society, aiming at changing society through educational reform, and led to street demonstrations, occupation of institutions, and boycotts of lectures.

In 1984 Helmut Thielicke, a well-known theologian, wrote retrospectively of Hamburg developments with their celebrated slogan "Beneath academic gowns a thousand years of mustiness":

"One of the saddest periods of my life began on November 9, 1967, in the Great Hall of Hamburg University ... This is where the student revolt broke out in a paroxysm of unleashed Happenings. Its depressing manifestations not only clouded the years that followed but also shook the structures of the German university to their very foundations ... This revolt constituted a historical turning-point initiating the downfall of the German university. I observed a worldwide loss of prestige for a once highly regarded institution".

The universities and politicians felt largely helpless and unsure. Debates on university policy in Land parliaments showed – as Walter Rüegg, rector of Frankfurt university, stated – "to what a frightening extent the university has become remote from the public". Only thus is the political readiness to throw overboard so relatively quickly and thoughtlessly German universities' traditional structures to be explained. The traditional German "professorial university" – where university teachers, and especially full professors, had a largely autonomous right of decision over research, teaching, and appointments provided these did not infringe the law of the Land – was succeeded by the "group university", rushed through in a series of often ill-founded political decisions by Laender parliaments. All the groups at work in universities – professors, lecturers, students, and other staff – thus became involved in decision-making, with variations from Land to Land. But that was not the only intervention. Long-established faculties were also dissolved. The usual four faculties were often replaced by more than 20 departments based on highly differentiated scholarly disciplines, largely following the Anglo-Saxon model. This development has led recently to intensification of a call for "interdisciplinary research", which used to be a matter of course in traditional faculties.

One of the most important innovations within university expansion at the end of the sixties was introduction of the *Fachhochschule* (degree-granting college of higher education / polytechnic) as a new kind of college. The Laender concluded an agreement (31.10.1968) on standardization of this sphere, raising the status of long-established schools of engineering and other colleges (for economics, social studies, textiles and design, agriculture, etc). The schools of engineering had previously been expanded on a large scale and courses unified, following plans laid down by the Conference of Ministers of Education.

15.3 Federal Involvement in the University Sector: the 1976 Hochschulrahmengesetz (University Outline Law)

Changes in the Basic Law, implemented in 1969, accorded the federal authorities responsibilities within the university system. The objective was to involve the state in the financing of expansion and to renew the unity that had been called in question by reforms. At that time the Grand Coalition of CDU/CSU and SPD granted the federal authorities powers for regulation of the university system, following financial reforms. They were also given the right to a say in educational planning and sole responsibility for students' grants. University expansion and the construction of new facilities (including university clinics) were declared to be a joint task for the state and Laender. Since that time the federal authorities have contributed half of the costs of university development. In recent years the state has established fresh emphases through stimulating special financial programmes. A planning committee concerned with university construction was set up in 1969 in accordance with the law regulating this sphere (see section 2.6).

After years of difficult negotiations the university outline law was passed on 26.1.1976. It must be stressed that the federal authorities are only responsible for general legislation while the Laender retain responsibility for establishment and organization, legal supervision, finances, and staffing. This 1976 law to some extent concluded around ten years of experimentation with new university structures. Judgements by the federal constitutional court at Karlsruhe paved the way for this, according precedence to professors in preparations for making high-level appointments and in research. The importance of university teachers in the “group university” was thus restored, entailing a considerable correction of course.

The university outline law is something new in the history of German education. It contains regulations about the tasks of a university, admission procedures, university members, staffing, organization and administration, and state recognition of facilities and qualifications. Basic principles and regulation of procedures within reform of studies were thus established. These were meant to lead to reorganization of the contents of studies and shortening of the excessive time spent at university. At the heart of the law are directives on the re-ordering of studies and examinations. The objective is that courses of study should be completed within fixed periods, which should only exceed four years in exceptional cases. Detailed regulations and course structures were devised for that purpose. However, the university outline law has not as yet achieved any far-reaching tightening up and shortening of studies.

The law also established degrees of participation of all university members in the most important administrative organs. The course of studies (in some Laender once again termed “Faculty”) became the basic organizational unit in universities. Professors had a majority in bodies with direct powers of decision over issues of scholarly relevance – in accordance with a decision by the federal constitutional court. To ensure more effective self-administration a choice had to be made between a rector or president, elected as a full-time administrator for at least two years in the former case and four years in the latter. This regulation replaced the traditional German system of an annual change of rector, which could only be maintained at smaller universities. A chancellor acted as head of the university administration. In recent decades what were originally small university administrations became large enterprises.

The Laender had to adapt their university laws to the federal law by the end of the seventies. Since this is an "outline law" the Laender retained a degree of latitude, which they have made use of in establishing different emphases. In the meantime there have been several amendments. The third such revision, introduced by the CDU/CSU-FDP coalition on 14.11.1985, dropped the comprehensive university as the envisaged unified organizational model, granted universities greater freedom in the autonomous organization of their courses, added the principle of subject-representation to group procedures, increased university teachers' responsibilities, and reorganized the staffing structure among middle-level academics. The coalition viewed the amendment as a correction of misguided developments. The currently valid version of the university outline law dates from 9.4.1987 (most recently amended on 20.5.1994).

The 1986 law on salaries for civil servants changed the standardized designation of university teachers ("Professor") following a judgement by the federal constitutional court. The official title at universities is now "university professor" while at other institutions of higher education this remains "professor".

Looking back at the seventies, it can be said that the situation at that time was still characterized by great politization and radicalization. The principle of co-determination time and again resulted in the foundations of freedom of teaching and research being threatened and endangered by political minorities. Conflict over university policy was to some extent institutionalized through the "group university" because radical political minorities entered committees where parity prevailed. In 1987 Franz Letzelter, the former secretary-general of the German Education Council and chancellor of Saarbrücken university, summarized developments: "Needless to say, politization went hand in hand with group consciousness. Coalitions of political groups took over from expertise in determining issues ... Political conflict over university issues only calmed down after the two judgements by the constitutional court and the economic and financial recession which got under way in 1974/75 ... Those factors made possible more objective discussions".

15.4 The 1977 Decision on Maintenance of Access to University and the Consequences

As was already mentioned in section 14 on university access, at the start of the seventies places in the preferred course of study were not always available for all applicants. In 1972, following a state agreement on assignment of university places, the Laender established a central admissions board at Dortmund. That agreement was amended within 6 years. In November 1977 the federal and Laender heads of government decided that access to university should be maintained for youngsters born in years with high birth-rates. That holds good up to the present day. Sufficient possibilities at university were thus to be assured in higher education despite restrictions on study-places. Existing capacities were to be fully exploited and admissions expanded through "overburdening quotas" and flexible restructuring of staffing levels to meet demands. This "overburdening" has in fact increased far more than expected, but more students were accepted without any intensification of restrictions on admission.

Predictions made during the eighties by the Conference of Ministers of Education and the Science Council demonstrate the unreliability of forecasts. It was assumed that the numbers of new students would decline considerably during the nineties to about the level of the mid-seventies. The call at that time was for "digging in". The Science Council forecast an end to university expansion during the nineties. What a tremendous miscalculation! As is now known, the opposite happened. The Council also ascertained in 1988 that total public expenditure on universities had declined by around 2.4 % in real terms since 1975 – despite the increase in numbers of students. It saw the main reason for overcrowding in the fact that university expansion had stagnated up to 1988 because of the anticipated decrease in student numbers. Lasting relief was expected from reduction of the time spent on studies. However, that hope has not been fulfilled either. As early as 1965 Hans Dichgans lamented: "We spend more time studying ... than any other country in the world". All measures for changing that have had little impact.

The slowing down in university expansion and financial stagnation indicate a decline in public interest. After the large-scale debate on educational reform other themes such as protection of the environment and combatting unemployment became political priorities from the mid-seventies. Education and university policy attracted little public interest. That changed in December 1988 when students at Berlin, Frankfurt/Main, and Munich took to the streets to demonstrate and draw attention to their difficult situation, poor facilities, and shortage of hostel accomodation. This time, unlike the sixties, these demonstrations were widely supported by the general public. The politicians responded immediately. Within a few days a special 2.1 billion DM expansion programme had been drawn up by the federal and Laender authorities. Following a proposal by the Federal Minister of Education and Science, Jürgen Möllemann (FDP), the University Special Programme I was agreed between the state and the Laender on 10.3.1989. Between 1989 and 1995 an additional 300 million DM for university expansion was made available annually with the state and Laender each providing half. Agreement was reached on 2.10.1990 on a further special programme, offering assistance to young scholars: four billion DM over ten years with 60 % coming from the federal authorities and 40 % from the Laender. These funds are available as grants towards qualifying for university teaching careers and doctorates, and for research studies abroad.

During the big public debates accompanying implementation of these programmes, prominent makers of educational policy openly conceded that they had miscalculated the growth in student numbers. Forecasts about the numbers starting studies had been particularly wrong. For years a demographically-induced decline had been expected, but students kept streaming into universities despite a clear-cut fall in birth-rates. Overcrowding at universities and polytechnics particularly affected courses in business studies, computer science, and engineering. Professor Hinrich Seidel, at that time president of the West German Rectors Conference, was of the opinion that German universities experienced a second qualitative leap-forward between 1987 and 1989. The first had been between 1964 and 1975. After 1988 the general public had realized the significance of universities as decisive national resources for education of the new generation of academics. In his opinion, the special programme was much too little but nevertheless marked a start.

So from December 1988 the state and the Laender endeavoured to make a crucial change of course in university policy. The Laender, which previously had mainly sought a way out of difficulties by "re-allocating" professors and lecturers (especially from the greatly reduced departments for teacher training), could not avoid fundamental adjustments to planning staffing. Once again it was assumed that student numbers would continue to rise. Demands for reform of courses were intensified so as to reduce the excessive time spent at university. The syllabus was to be reorganized to make possible completion of study courses in ten semesters as opposed to today's average of between 13 and 15 semesters.

The previously mentioned student protests signalled far-reaching dissatisfaction, particularly with the teaching. The current system of academic training was also fundamentally questioned with demands for greater adaptation to changes in professional life. A new element was introduced with discussion of women's role in research and scholarship and a call for greater opportunities in academic careers.

Recommendations on university perspectives in the nineties were agreed by the Science Council as early as 20.5.1988. These covered research, academic teaching and studies, the new generation of scholars, staffing, and, above all, finances. From a report of over 400 pages only the following can be quoted here:

"Introduction of the European single market from 1992 will result in almost total freedom of movement in Europe. That will bring a greater number of young academics onto the German labour market, competing for positions. This development not only requires an improvement in qualifications but will also lead to an opening up of new careers, quantitatively and qualitatively. Here universities are challenged to remain imaginative and inventive, and to demonstrate flexibility in adapting their courses to changing demands".

Shortly after re-unification, on 16.11.1990, the Science Council approved recommendations on the further development of degree-granting colleges of higher education in the nineties. Two decades after the establishment of such colleges, a stock-taking was implemented and an attempt made at sketching future perspectives. Among the Council's recommendations were:

- rapid expansion of *Fachhochschulen*
- broadening of the range of subjects offered, taking vocational demands into account, and development of new courses
- safeguarding the status of the *Fachhochschule* with emphasis on autonomous, practice-oriented training
- improvement of opportunities for transferring from the *Fachhochschule* to university.

As previously, studies at such colleges should not take longer than six semesters (plus at least one semester of in-service training), but *Fachhochschulen* were not spared extensions of study-periods.

15.5 Reorganization of the University System in the New Laender

The last GDR government and the federal and Laender governments invited the Science Council to evaluate plans for development of universities and degree-granting colleges of higher education/polytechnics, and the restructuring of teacher training and non-university research institutes, in the New Laender. Recommendations were immediately prepared in numerous Science Council study groups and committees with participation by experts from the New Laender and detailed on-the-spot consultations, and agreed in the course of 1991. They fill several fat volumes.

The establishment of *Fachhochschulen* (degree-granting colleges of higher education / polytechnics), which had not existed in the GDR, played a special part in reorganization of the university system there. Other Science Council recommendations involved the commissions concerned with university structures, appointments policy, renewal of teaching, and individual subjects, offering Land governments a basis for appropriate further development. Two key concepts determined the New Laender's university policy at the start of the nineties: "winding up" and "intermingling". "Winding up" mainly involved the disbanding of departments ideologically committed to Marxism-Leninism: social studies, law, and history. "Intermingling" gave many younger university teachers from the West career opportunities which they might not have had to the same extent in the Old Laender.

In the first half of 1991 the new university laws were approved by parliaments in the East, striving for consensus on education policy. They served renewal of the overall university system with the objective of comprehensively guaranteeing freedom of research and teaching. The 1976 federal university outline law and its amendments was the model for the new Laender university laws. East Berlin was incorporated in the area of application of the existing Berlin university law. Special regulations applied until 31.3.1994. The objective was development of an efficient university system.

The Science Council had recommended the establishment of 20 state *Fachhochschulen* with an initial 52,000 study-places. By the beginning of 1992 23 had already been set up. Brandenburg, which had previously had no comparable institutions, founded universities at Potsdam and Frankfurt/Oder and a technical university at Cottbus. Erfurt University (1392-1816), renowned during the age of humanism and the reformation, was re-established by Thuringia in 1994, but it will be some years before courses commence there. Nine of the ten colleges of education were largely integrated in universities, following the West German "model". Only the Erfurt college is still autonomous, and that will become part of the university in future.

The most important regulations in the New Laender university laws concern changes in staff. The treaty of unification stipulated that the situation of existing scholarly staff had to be clarified within three years. They could be given notice in cases of absence of demand, inadequate qualifications, or lack of personal integrity. Commissions concerned with staffing and subject-matter evaluated university personnel and made recommendations about the dismissal of professors or other scholars. All such activities led at times to considerable unrest and uncertainties at universities.

On 11.7.1991 the federal and Laender authorities reached agreement on a comprehensive "Renewal Programme for University and Research" to run for five years. The 1.76 billion DM available – 75 % from the state and 25 % from the New Laender – was available for:

1. New Professorships: Funds for 200 new professorships in university and college faculties in need of renewal and 100 inaugural professorships at degree-granting colleges of higher education were employed in accordance with the Science Council's recommendations. Assistance was, for instance, given for 35 professorships in legal studies, 43 in economics and business studies, 48 in education, and 53 in the humanities.
2. Guest scholars: Guest scholars assisted in reorganization of courses of study.
3. Assistance for young scholars: A large number of university teachers will reach retirement age during the nineties, so additional provision has been made for completion of doctorates and lectureship qualifications alongside establishment of post-graduate colleges. The Donors Association for German Science also provided funds for 22 professorships.

Thanks to great commitment on the part of all those involved, the Science Council's recommendations were largely implemented on schedule. The university renewal programme made possible a good start for university teaching and gave crucial support for establishment of the preconditions for a differentiated university system and speedy reorganization of staffing and study courses.

15.6 Recent Developments

In July 1992 the University Rectors Conference produced a "Concept for the Development of Universities in Germany". This outlines the current situation and measures for strengthening the university system: reform of studies, safeguarding university research, strengthening degree-granting colleges of higher education, and university expansion. This concept still holds good. The Science Council's 10 theses on university policy (see section 3.3) are similar in many respects.

As early as 1992 the Conferences of Ministers of Education and University Rectors set up two joint study-groups which prepared suggestions on reducing the length of studies and on university structures. Those received the approval of the two Conferences in July

1993 and formed the basis of a declaration on educational policy by the Laender heads of government on 29.10.1993, including the following:

"The Laender heads of government view education, training, science, and research as essential resources shaping the culture and economy of a federal Germany. They are of the opinion that far-reaching reforms are necessary so as to preserve university efficiency. The courses on offer at universities must distinguish between theoretical, vocationally-oriented studies, training for a new generation of scholars, and advanced academic training. Studies as a whole should once again be completed within a reasonable time. The heads of government agree that reform of study-courses, taking account of proposals made by the Science Council and the Conference of University Rectors, should be speedily implemented. The following measures are thought particularly urgent for achievement of reform:

- Norms for length of studies should be established by law or agreement ...
- The state and universities must ensure that studies can be completed within the norm established. It is thus necessary to limit what is studied and examined to essentials, making clear the standards expected. Binding upper limits to course requirements and examination demands must be determined by law or agreement".

It remains to be seen whether these objectives can be realized.

In summer 1996 the civil service law was changed in Bavaria on the initiative of Minister of Education Hans Zehetmair (CSU), creating a possibility of appointing professors for a limited six-year period. This "increase in flexibility" is intended to facilitate the offering of posts to up-and-coming young scholars. Full professors will continue to be appointed for life.

In 1996 there was animated discussion of the introduction of tuition fees. The situation calmed down again when the University Rectors Conference pronounced against this in July. Federal Chancellor Helmut Kohl opened up the way ahead in September by signing "University Special Programme III". This new programme unites its predecessor assisting young scholars and the university renovation project supporting development in the New Laender in recent years. University Special Programme III provides a total of 3.6 billion DM up to the year 2000 – around 2 billion from the federal authorities and the rest from the Laender. The emphasis is on improvement of study facilities, backing for university contacts in other countries, assistance for young scholars, and promotion of women in science and research. For instance, support will be given to the setting up of additional post-graduate colleges. 340 million DM will be spent on establishment of tutorships, intended to shorten the time spent on studies and reduce the number of people who leave university prematurely. The Federal Minister of Education Jürgen Rüttgers (CDU) rightly called this programme "a show of financial strength", which also opens up the way for structural reforms and amendment of the university outline law introduced twenty years ago.

15.7 The University System: Structure and Sources of Support

Anyone who wants to gain a clear picture of the German university system should consult the excellent publication “Universities in Germany” (in German and English, Munich and New York 1995) produced by Christian Bode, Werner Becker, and Rainer Klofat. Experts such as Walter Rüegg, Theodor Berchem, and Hans-Uwe Erichsen have contributed far-reaching articles and there are many illustrations.

Higher education in the Federal Republic of Germany mainly consists of public universities maintained by the Laender. In 1995 there were 325 universities with a total of 1.8 million students (inclusive of 65 small private universities with around 30,000 students), comprising:

- 88 universities (including colleges with similar status)
- 1 comprehensive university
- 6 colleges of education (see section 16)
- 17 theological colleges
- 46 colleges of art and music
- 136 degree-granting colleges of higher education / polytechnics
- 31 autonomous federal and Laender *Fachhochschulen* for the training of high-level administrative staff

The 65 non-state colleges comprise:

- 6 universities or colleges with equivalents to university courses (in human medicine, dentistry, economics)
- 17 theological colleges (church colleges)
- 40 *Fachhochschulen* (including 19 church-backed colleges for social work)
- 2 colleges of art and music.

During the past ten years the number of theological/church colleges and church-backed degree-granting institutions for social work has changed only minimally. The number of private *Fachhochschulen* concentrating on science and economics has, however, risen from 9 to 17. The funding of non-state colleges varies. Church colleges are financed from church funds, and other private institutions by foundations and business firms. Fees often have to be paid – unlike the situation at public universities. They range between 150 DM per semester (Bonn College of Library Studies) to 8,100 DM (European Business School at Oestrich-Winkel). A financial crisis at the Witten-Herdecke private university (established in 1982 with around 600 students) hit the headlines in 1996. This institution receives support from various foundations, but despite having access to its own capital required for the first time a 6 million DM subsidy from the authorities in North Rhine-Westphalia. Tuition fees for ten semesters of study are to be increased from the present 30,000 DM to 60,000 DM.

State universities are public corporations – institutions that, like communities and churches, have a right to self-administration within the established legal framework. Legal supervision is exercised by the Land concerned. The Land and university act conjointly in regulation of studies and examinations, the establishment and re-organization of courses and scholarly facilities, planning, and the appointment of professors. The universities' task is to further the development of the sciences and arts by way of research and teaching. The Basic Law in the Federal Republic of Germany expressly guarantees (in article 5, paragraph 3) the freedom of art and science, research and teaching, whereby freedom of teaching does not release from adherence to the constitution. Freedom of scholarship is also under state protection. The state thus guarantees freedom for teaching and research in which it is not allowed to intervene. The courses offered by universities and *Fachhochschulen* include many concluding with a first degree state examination, or a university examination leading to an M.A., diploma, or doctorate. There are state examinations, for instance, in the fields of medicine, education, law, pharmacy, and nutrition chemistry. Previously some courses of study concluded with a doctorate, but today a state or university examination must first be taken. M.A. and diploma examinations in the humanities – e.g. education – have for the most part only been introduced since 1960. For the numbers involved since 1965 see appendix 17.

The institutions of higher education have worked closely together in the West German Rectors Conference since 1949. That voluntary co-operation has been continued in the University Rectors Conference since 1990. Originally only universities and colleges with a rectorial constitution and the right to grant a doctor's degreee and post-doctoral teaching qualifications belonged to the organization. By now there are 240 member colleges in all 16 Laender. Universities and colleges with the right to accord doctorates continue to preponderate, but polytechnics and colleges of art and music are also represented. The Rectors Conference has produced many recommendations and statements on university development and policy, and on reform of the *Gymnasium*.

The tables in appendices 14-16 offer an overview of the growth in numbers of students and staff between 1960 and 1994/95.

The size of institutions of higher education varies considerably. Munich, for instance, is the home of the largest university in the Federal Republic (with around 60,000 students) and also one of the smallest colleges, the Film and Television College with scarcely more than 200 students. The largest universities after Munich are in Berlin, Cologne, Münster, Hamburg, and Frankfurt/Main. In 1993 Berlin's Free University was still attended by 59,600 students but numbers had dropped to 48,900 two years later. That is the outcome of a completely changed situation since the fall of the Wall. In recent years the Humboldt University has grown by more than a third, now totalling 23,000 students. Cologne has overtaken the Free University and with 55,000 students was in second place in 1995, followed by Hamburg (44,450), Münster (44,000), Hagen's Open University (39,500), the Berlin Technical University (37,300), and Frankfurt/Main (36,500). Werner Thieme recently wrote sarcastically: "Universities with more than 40,000 students and departments with over a thousand are contrary to all academic objectives. Humboldt envisaged smallness of scale at university".

There are similar variations in size at polytechnics. The three largest are at Cologne (18,000 students), Munich (16,300), and Hamburg (around 16,400). Most have considerably fewer students – between 1,000 and 3,000 in medium-sized colleges.

In 1992 123,052 foreign students participated in German higher education – 101,384 at universities and colleges of art and music, and 21,668 at polytechnics. The 1994 figure was 136,948, constituting around 7.5 % of the total number of students in the Federal Republic. Information about countries of origin is only available for 1992. Around 40 % of these students probably grew up in Germany and were educated there – particularly in the case of Turks, Italians, and Spaniards. In 1992 some 67,235 students came from other European states: 15,859 from Turkey, 7,167 from Greece, 5,772 from Austria, 4,733 from France, 4,207 from Italy, 3,112 from Spain, 2,750 from Great Britain, and 2,714 from Poland. From Africa came 10,245, from the USA 4,436, from Canada 440. There were 4,353 from South America and 34,100 from Asia, including 10,369 Iranians, 4,636 South Koreans, 2,125 Indonesians, and 5,752 Chinese from the People's Republic.

These initially impressive figures conceal the fact that the number of foreigners studying in Germany has stagnated recently. Since the end of 1995 there has been discussion of how to make "German education" more attractive for foreign students. The fact is that in 1995 over seven times as many Asian students (totalling 250,000) were at American rather than German universities. Germany will only be able to maintain its leading position in foreign trade if its educational image is improved. Widespread criticism within Germany of any "creation of an elite" has the undesirable side-effect of this country losing out in the competition for the best foreign students. Experts have therefore developed concepts intended to change that trend and make studies in Germany seem more worthwhile to foreigners – for instance, by offering higher grants, extension courses, and special programmes for the promotion of student exchanges. The German Academic Exchange Service has concentrated in recent years on development of new programmes for scholarly co-operation with Asia, but regrets that only half as many German students and scientists do research in Asia as Asians come to Germany. Exchange thus remains somewhat one-sided.

The precondition for studies is an educational qualification equivalent to the *Abitur* and sufficient knowledge of German. Anyone who lacks the educational qualification can take a two-semester preparatory course leading to the examination for ascertainment of the suitability of foreign applicants for admission to university or polytechnic studies. The Conference of Ministers of Education has laid down guidelines for foreigners' access to studies together with regulations for the preliminary course and the admission examination. A special quota for foreign applicants forms part of the selection procedure in courses where there are restrictions on admission. For other courses there are in principle no restrictions. Studies at state institutions of higher education are free for both German and foreign students. Around 8,000 of the latter receive German grants, mainly from the German Academic Exchange Service. Most foreign students must finance their own living expenses, and a residence permit is not granted unless that can be guaranteed.

15.8 An Overview of Universities, Colleges, and Degree-Granting Colleges of Higher Education

Reforms and the establishment of new universities, comprehensive colleges, and polytechnics during the past three decades have led to development of a diversity of forms hitherto unknown in the Federal German system of higher education.

15.8.1 Old Universities

Even though today very few differences still exist between "old" and "new" universities, the former will be mentioned first. They include the universities which already existed *before* 1960, mostly looking back on a long history. The oldest German university, the Ruprecht Karl University at Heidelberg, celebrated 600 years of existence in 1986. However, some of these institutions were set up in the immediate post-war years, including the Johann Gutenberg University at Mainz, Berlin's Free University, and the Saarland University at Saarbrücken. There are older universities at Berlin (Humboldt University), Bonn, Cologne, Erlangen-

Nuremberg, Frankfurt/Main, Freiburg, Gießen, Göttingen, Greifswald, Halle-Wittenberg, Hamburg, Hanover, Heidelberg, Jena, Kiel, Leipzig, Marburg, Munich, Münster, Rostock, Stuttgart, Tübingen, and Würzburg. They cover the whole range of disciplines from theology, the traditional humanities, the social sciences, to medicine and the natural sciences. That is not the case in all the new universities.

15.8.2 New Universities

The universities set up after 1960 regard themselves as institutions devoted to reform. Their establishment was preceded by long and comprehensive planning. Experienced scholars in special committees developed new concepts. Memoranda and counter-memoranda went the rounds. These universities either came into being as completely new institutions or were developed out of already existing colleges – such as Hohenheim university which arose out of an agricultural college or Mannheim from an economics college. The institutes in old universities are based in many buildings all over a town or city whereas the new foundations mostly involve great complexes of recent buildings on a campus.

Never before were so many universities literally conjured up in so short a time. Their numbers include: Augsburg, Bamberg, Bayreuth, Bielefeld, Bochum, Bremen, Dortmund, Düsseldorf, Erfurt (from 1997/98), Flensburg, Frankfurt/Oder, Hagen, Hildesheim, Hohenheim, Kaiserslautern, Koblenz-Landau, Konstanz, Lübeck's medical university, Lüneburg, Magdeburg, Mannheim, Oldenburg, Osnabrück, Passau, Potsdam, Regensburg, Trier, Ulm, and Vechta.

The colleges with university status are: the German Sports College at Cologne, the Hamburg College of Economics and Politics, the Hanover Medical College, the Hanover Veterinary College, the Speyer College of Administration, and the Weimar College of Architecture and Building.

Some of those colleges were also established long before 1960 but only attained university status later. A number of the new universities, such as Bamberg and Trier, had precursors dating back to the end of the 18th century.

The new concepts underlying the Ruhr University at Bochum (established in 1965), and the universities of Konstanz (1966) and Bremen (1971) were much discussed. Bochum was intended to unite the scholarly disciplines of the traditional university and the technical college. The expectation that discussion would be possible between the humanities and engineering at all levels of the university could only be implemented to a limited extent. Bochum was generously planned right from the start in terms of contemporary conditions. Calculations were for 15,000 students. Konstanz, on the other hand, was intended to be a small, more elitist, reformist university with 3,000 students. Today Bochum has 36,000 students and Konstanz 9,600. At Bochum the emphasis was supposed to be on interdisciplinary research, but it has scarcely been possible to maintain that concept either. Like Bochum, Bremen university unites technical and scientific disciplines with economics, the social sciences, the arts, and teacher training. Bremen saw itself as a highly politicized "counter-university". It was originally planned as a campus university integrating study facilities and student hostels, but that idea has been given up in the meantime. The organization of studies in terms of projects was also new at Bremen, but little of that remains now. In conclusion it should be remarked that high-flying plans for reform have long become part of university history.

15.8.3 Comprehensive Colleges / Universities

The *Gesamthochschulen* were also a reform concept of the sixties and seventies. They united in various ways the functions of universities, technical universities, colleges of education, polytechnics, and – to a limited extent – colleges of art and music. The university outline law of 26.1.1976 entertained the distant objective of expanding all colleges of higher education into comprehensive universities or of guaranteeing co-operation between the various forms of college by way of co-ordinating bodies. The 1985 third revision of the law expressly deleted that objective. For some years now the comprehensive colleges have also called themselves universities, indicating that their former designation is obsolete – to some extent a relic of superseded reforms. The first (and at present last) comprehensive college was set up at Kassel in 1971 when the existing colleges in the region were amalgamated and augmented. Most of these "universities / comprehensive colleges" are in North Rhine-Westphalia: Duisburg, Essen, Paderborn, Siegen, and Wuppertal. For the most part these also developed out of the merging of previously autonomous colleges and polytechnics.

15.8.4 Technical Universities and Colleges

Technical colleges, for the most part founded in the 19th century, have mostly been redesignated technical universities in recent decades with professorships and institutes in the humanities and social sciences newly established in some cases, frequently serving teaching training. The emphasis at technical universities continues to be on technology and the natural sciences. Their numbers include the technical colleges at Aachen and Darmstadt (retaining their traditional designations) and technical universities at Berlin, Brunswick, Chemnitz-Zwickau, Clausthal, Cottbus, Dresden, Freiberg (Mining Academy), Hamburg-Harburg, Ilmenau, Karlsruhe, and Munich. What used to be technical universities at Hanover and Stuttgart now simply call themselves universities.

15.8.5 Colleges of Art and Music

The 44 state (and 2 private) colleges of art and music cater for all kinds of artistic training: architecture, ceramics, church and school music, composition, conducting, dance, design, glass-work, work in gold, applied and free graphics, studies in individual instruments, interior design, musicology, painting, sculpture, song, and stage design. Teachers of art and music at general schools are also largely trained at these colleges.

15.8.6 Fachhochschulen (Polytechnics/Degree-Granting Colleges of Higher Education)

This form of college was first created in 1968 by way of an agreement between the Laender (see section 2.3). Schools of engineering and other advanced technical schools were then transformed into *Fachhochschulen*. Studies there differ from universities in being more oriented towards the requirements of everyday practice. They do not usually take so long and include longer periods of in-service training. Possibilities of continuing at universities or other degree-granting colleges are open to those who have completed studies at *Fachhochschulen*.

The university outline law also applies to *Fachhochschulen*, laying down that these have a status similar to public corporations while remaining state institutions. They are mostly financed by the Laender with the exception of the federal and private (largely church) foundations. Colleges specializing in social studies were in fact mostly established by the churches. 47 subjects were initially on offer at *Fachhochschulen* with a broad range of choice. That was reduced to 17 in accordance with an agreement (14.11.1980, revised 24.5.1991) by the Conference of Ministers of Education. Also included among such institutions are 31 autonomous federal and Laender colleges serving the training of future high-level administrators, particularly in technical spheres.

During the past two decades the number of *Fachhochschulen* in the Old Laender has increased from 97 (1975) to 134 (1994) with students increasing from 89,500 (1970), 202,000 (1980), 372,600 (1990), to 398,200 (1994). A start was made on construction of polytechnics in the New Laender in 1991. Their number grew from 17 (1991) to 33 (1994) inclusive of 7 specializing in administration studies. In 1994 Germany had a total of 136 general *Fachhochschulen* (including 40 private institutions) and 31 offering courses in administration with 420,000 students (52,300 at polytechnics offering administration courses). Those figures indicate the great attractiveness of polytechnic studies, and the Laender are responding to that trend with continuing expansion.

15.8.7 Vocational Academies

Vocational academies are a "successful model" from Baden-Württemberg and have now been adopted by Berlin and Saxony too. They also exist in Schleswig-Holstein, independent of other models.

This all began as an offshoot of the Baden-Württemberg Academy of Administration and Economics in 1972, and was taken up at Stuttgart and Mannheim in 1974. Such vocational academies were originally non-degree-granting institutions within the tertiary sphere of education outside the universities. They became established institutions by way of a Law dated 29.4.1982. Paragraph 1 of the current revision of that law (10.1.1995) states: "Vocational academies mediate training oriented towards both scholarship and practical experience. They also serve further education and can be involved in associated events ... Vocational academies are part of the tertiary sphere of education, and offer an alternative to studies at polytechnics and universities. They work together with colleges of higher education and other educational facilities. Successful completion after three years of training at the Baden-Württemberg *Berufsakademie* is equivalent to corresponding studies at a Land *Fachhochschule* and offers the same qualifications ...". The training concept was developed in close conjunction with such companies as Robert Bosch, Daimler-Benz, and Standard Elektrik Lorenz. This is characterized by close links between theory and practice within the dual system, alternating between in-service training and academic work. During their three years of training students have contractual links with a firm or welfare institution, switching between theoretical and practical phases of training every three months. A two-year version of the course (equivalent to full-time vocational schooling) offers qualifications as technical assistant or nursery school teacher. The three-year training ends with acquisition of a *Berufsakademie* diploma designating the specialization studied (i.e. engineering or business management).

The three spheres of training are economics, technology, and social studies. The nine vocational academies and two subsidiaries offer a total of 12,140 study-places. Following the Baden-Württemberg model, academies have existed since 1993 in Berlin (2,250 study-places) and Saxony (6 campuses and around 4,500 study-places). On 28/29.9.1995 the Conference of Ministers of Education reached agreement on recognition of their qualifications.

The Schleswig-Holstein vocational academy provides a practical alternative to university studies, leading to qualifications for high-level jobs in industrial management. Here too training is both theoretical and practice-oriented. The precondition for admission is the university entrance qualification and signing a training contract with a company. There are three-year courses in economics (inclusive of information studies) and four-year courses in technology (with an emphasis on engineering). There were 557 students at this institution in Schleswig-Holstein in 1994.

15.8.8 Army Universities

These were originally established as federal army colleges in 1973 and granted university status in 1980. They are the responsibility of the federal authorities and are not just intended to serve all levels of military training. Army colleges are primarily conceived as scholarly institutions that provide young officers with courses of study which assist both their military career and a civilian profession should they leave the forces. These studies are limited to three years of three terms each plus an examination semester which can be repeated if need be. The Hamburg *Bundeswehr* university provides courses in electrotechnology, mechanical engineering, education, economics, and business management. The Munich university is organized in faculties of civil engineering and surveying, electrotechnology, information studies, aero-space technology, education, political and social sciences, sport, and economics and business management. In addition, there are *Fachhochschule* courses in electrotechnology, business management, and mechanical engineering. In 1996 some 2,100 officers studied at Hamburg, 1,580 at Munich, and a further 500 at the *Bundeswehr* polytechnic.

15.8.9 Theological and Church Colleges

The majority of theologians and teachers of religion are instructed in the theological faculties of state universities, while around 40 % of all social workers and remedial teachers receive their training at church colleges of higher education (*Fachhochschulen*). Church colleges also serve the instruction of clergymen and religious teachers, and *Fachhochschulen* train staff for community welfare and educational services.

Church law, state law regarding churches, and state law as applicable to higher education overlap in these church colleges. For centuries the Catholic Church has maintained faculty-status seminaries for the training of priests alongside the theological faculties at universities. At present such theological colleges or faculties exist at Erfurt, Frankfurt/Main (St. Georgen), Fulda, Paderborn, and Trier; and there are monastic colleges for Capuchins and Franciscans at Münster, Jesuits at Munich, Pallotines at Vallendar and Untermerzbach, Redemptionists at Hennef/Sieg, Salesians at Benediktbeuern, and the Steyl Mission at St. Augustin. Church *Fachhochschulen*, usually for social studies and religious pedagogics, exist at Berlin, Cologne, Freiburg, Mainz, Munich, Osnabrück, and Saarbrücken. A Catholic university was established at Eichstätt in 1972. Like a comprehensive university, this incorporates *Fachhochschule* courses in religious pedagogics and social studies with the following faculties: Catholic theology, philosophy and education, linguistics and literature, history and social studies, mathematics and geography, and economics.

Apart from Bethel, which was founded as early as 1905, the Protestant church colleges (Wuppertal and Berlin) were set up in the thirties during the period of conflict between church and state before being soon closed down by the Nazis – and then re-established during the post-war period. There are also church colleges at Neuendettelsau (in conjunction with a *Fachhochschule*), Oberursel where the Independent Evangelical Lutheran Free Church has a theological college, and Friedensau which is supported by the community of the Seventh Day Adventists. Protestant *Fachhochschulen* for social and religious pedagogics exist at Berlin, Bochum, Darmstadt, Dresden, Freiburg, Hamburg, Hanover, Ludwigsburg, Ludwigshafen, Moritzburg, Nuremberg, and Reutlingen.

A College of Jewish Studies has been established at Heidelberg since 1979. This is maintained as a state-recognized private institution by the Central Council of Jews in Germany, and offers a Masters course for both Jewish and non-Jewish students. It now also has the right to grant doctorates.

15.9.1 Hagen Open University (Comprehensive College)

Forecasts made in the seventies were greatly exceeded by developments in Open University studies. University studies based on correspondence courses have only existed in the Federal Republic of Germany since 1974. It was then that the North Rhine-Westphalia parliament passed a law on establishment of an Open University, and this institution commenced operations at Hagen on 1.10.1975. This Open University is meant to provide relief for other institutions, not replace them. During the initial phase, courses were restricted to economics, mathematics, and related subjects in education. These pilot schemes received financial support from the Federal Ministry of Education and Science. By 1977 some 10,000 students had enrolled. By 1990 there were 41,200: around 5,000 full-time, 22,500 part-time, and 13,700 visiting students. In the 1995/96 winter semester the number had risen to 54,630, a third of them women: 8,773 (16.1 %) full-time, 30,491 (55.8 %) part-time, and the rest either visiting students or people taking a second course.

The Open University / Hagen Comprehensive College comprises the departments of mathematics, information studies, education, the humanities, social sciences, economics, electrotechnology, and law apart from the Central Institute for Research into Media-supported Correspondence Courses. Most participants study economics with education in second place. Study materials include course texts and multimedia teaching programmes. Personal contact is meant to facilitate individual questions about courses. Regional study centres constitute a complementary component within this system. Here students can get information and advice, work together on preparing for examinations, and borrow books. At present there are 29 study centres in North Rhine-Westphalia, 32 elsewhere in Germany, 3 in Austria, and one each in Hungary and Switzerland. Studies involve integrated courses at university and polytechnic level in economics, mathematics, electrotechnology, and information studies; M.A. courses with education and social sciences as the main subjects, and mathematics, economics, sociology, pedagogics, psychology, law, modern German literature, and philosophy as secondaries; and various supplementary courses – business management and economics for lawyers; business management for those holding a diploma in mathematics, engineers, and natural scientists; and advanced training for teaching staff in further education.

15.9.2 Studies for Senior Citizens

The number of older people, retired from the world of work, who attend lectures or study full-time is on the increase in the Federal Republic, but only rarely do they wish to gain an academic degree. The universities of Marburg, Dortmund, Oldenburg, Mannheim, Frankfurt/Main, and Bielefeld have introduced special courses for senior citizens. At Frankfurt, for instance, there is the "University of the Third Age". Munich is also testing out "Studies for Senior Citizens". These lectures, seminars, and discussions usually serve further education of a general nature. Over 10,000 senior citizens have made use of such opportunities.

15.9.3 Pilot Projects – particularly Post-Graduate Colleges

After implementation (7.5.1971) of the outline agreement on co-ordinated preparation, implementation, and scholarly guidance of educational pilot projects, the federal and Laender authorities have supported innumerable such ventures at colleges of higher education, mainly serving reform of studies, improving the efficiency of teaching, reducing the time spent on studies, development of post-graduate colleges, enhancement of course offers for foreign students (particularly from developing countries), and correspondence courses.

On 29.1.1988 the Science Council approved recommendations on furthering the concept of post-graduate colleges. Financial support came from the Fritz Thyssen and Volkswagen foundations while the state covered around 65 % of the costs. The Science Council viewed these measures for assisting up-and-coming scholars in conjunction with four objectives in research policy:

- the promotion of innovative research
- the intensification of interdisciplinary endeavours as a counterweight to extensive specialization
- co-operation with border disciplines
- joint planning of research projects and programmes.

The objective is to provide additional support for post-graduate students working on doctorates or qualifications for a university career, thereby improving assistance for young scholars. At present there are 262 post-graduate colleges. If all 60,000 PhD candidates are to receive the backing of such institutions, around 2,000 colleges would be needed. The number will be increased to 300 by the year 2000 under the previously mentioned University Special Programme III.

16 Teacher Training

Schools are as good as their teachers". That declaration by Adolf Diesterweg, one of the great 19th century educationists, still holds good and has not changed in our computer age. That is why a teacher's training in methods, didactics, and specialized knowledge is of great importance. Historical developments must be taken into account if the complex situation facing teacher training today is to be understood.

16.1 The History of Teacher Training

Until the twenties there were two standard forms of teacher training in Germany: by way of a seminary for teaching at elementary schools, and by way of academic training for posts at higher schools. To overcome that division elementary school teachers demanded a university education for all teachers as early as 1848. The Weimar constitution took account of those objectives in article 143, paragraph 2: "Teacher training must be uniformly regulated throughout the Reich in accordance with the basic principles which apply to higher education in general". But neither unified regulation nor upgrading of training were achieved during the Weimar Republic. The draft of a law on teacher training did not get further than the cabinet. The Reich Minister of Finance and his Land counterparts opposed any such unified reform of teacher training because of the anticipated increase in costs entailed in higher qualifications. At the end of the Weimar Republic the training of elementary school teachers was less unified than previously. Bavaria and Württemberg adhered to the old form of seminary; from the mid-twenties Prussia developed pedagogic academies following Minister of Education Carl Heinrich Becker's political concept; and Hamburg, Thuringia, Brunswick, Saxony, and Hesse variously incorporated such training in universities. After 1933 the National Socialists initially introduced colleges of teacher training, but from 1941 reconverted them into seminary-like institutions.

After 1945 the autonomous college of education, patterned on the original Prussian model, prevailed in all Laender except Hamburg, which again incorporated teacher training in the university. The basic principle of academic and scholarly training for elementary school teachers was scarcely disputed any longer, but the form such university training took certainly was. In an assessment dated 13.3.1958, the German Committee for Education and Training spoke in favour of autonomous colleges of education and advised against their incorporation in universities or concentration in university-linked institutions as planned and for a time implemented in Hesse.

In most Laender colleges of education were denominational in character until the sixties – i.e. Catholic, Protestant, and sometimes a combination (as in Prussia during the Weimar Republic). At the end of the fifties Bavaria and Hesse went against the Committee's advice and attached their colleges of education to universities – and most of the Laender also followed that solution. By the end of the eighties autonomous colleges of education only survived in Schleswig-Holstein, Rhineland-Palatinate, and Baden-Württemberg. In 1990 Rhineland-Palatinate turned its college of education into the university of Koblenz-Landau. The Flensburg college of education in Schleswig-Holstein gained university status in 1994. At both new universities further courses were set up. Today the only remaining colleges of education are in Baden-Württemberg (Freiburg, Heidelberg, Karlsruhe, Ludwigsburg, Schwäbisch-Gmünd, and Weingarten) and Thuringia (Erfurt which will be integrated in Erfurt university).

During the phase of expansion of general schooling from the mid-sixties, appropriate training for the necessary teachers was the key issue in educational policy. That is why Georg Picht in 1964 called for a doubling of the number of holders of the *Abitur* by 1970. Makers of educational policy were agreed that this involved quality as well as quantity. At that time there were great efforts to improve the level of training, making this publicly apparent by way of affiliation with or integration in universities. In 1971 the German Education Council published “Materials and Documents on Teacher Training”. In its structure plan the previous year the Council had already advocated far-reaching changes with graduated courses replacing different training for different types of school. It was also recommended that all academically-trained teachers (such as senior secondary school teachers – *Studienrat*) should be paid as higher civil servants. In autumn 1970 the Conference of Ministers of Education discussed the harmonization of teacher training and remuneration. The Ministers reached agreement on 8/9.10.1970 at Frankenthal/Palatinate over the basic elements in an outline accord providing for all teachers in future receiving six or eight semesters of academic training followed by eighteen months of preparatory service. After a transitional phase there were to be three streams within the teaching profession with graduated emphases for the primary, secondary I, and secondary II levels. On entering the profession all teachers at the upper level were to be equally paid. Never again were the Ministers from the SPD, CDU, and CSU to be so close on these issues. Shortly afterwards this compromise could no longer be implemented in a unified outline agreement. A storm of protests arose after the Ministers' Frankenthal discussions. The Philologists Association viewed them as a damaging compromise which levelled down all teaching posts in terms of length of training and salaries, undervaluing and discriminating against scholars. The Association primarily demanded that only teachers fully qualified in two subjects should give lessons in the upper level at *Gymnasium*. They wanted revocation of the possibility that a teacher with just six semesters of training in a single subject could in future also be employed in secondary level II. The philologists organized demonstrations and big rallies, impressing CDU and CSU Ministers of Education.

The Federal-Laender Commission for Educational Planning's 1973 comprehensive education plan may have taken over the basic elements of the Frankenthal solution, but the then CDU/CSU-governed Laender – Baden-Württemberg, Bavaria, Rhineland-Palatinate, Saarland, and Schleswig-Holstein – advocated (in a special vote) differentiated teacher training with different rates of pay. They thus upheld the organization of teacher training for specific types of school. However, Rhineland-Palatinate, Saarland, and Schleswig-Holstein have been ruled by SPD governments for some years now, so graduated training – as developed since the seventies in Hamburg, Bremen, North Rhine-Westphalia, and Hesse – now predominates in the Old Laender.

The trend towards transfer of teacher training to universities was largely the outcome of social ideology and vocational ambitions. Political majorities were of greater importance than professional considerations in deciding whether organization of teacher training should be graduated or relate directly to the type of school concerned. The rapid changes that occurred in the Laender cannot be described here. The laws relating to teacher training and examination regulations were often altered again within just a few years. Complete integration of teacher training in universities in many places fulfils the demand raised in 1848 by many elementary school teachers, but it remains uncertain whether today's mass university can really supply a grounding that is both scholarly and practical. There are frequent complaints of inadequate attention being paid to instruction in educational psychology, anthropology, educational theory, and the history of schooling.

16.2 Teacher Training in the Former GDR

At present some 160,000 teachers who were trained in the GDR before 1990 are employed in the New Laender and East Berlin, so a brief sketch of their background seems apposite. Under the GDR there were three levels of teacher training:

- Primary school teachers (for classes 1-4) were trained at institutes of teacher training akin to technical schools.
- Specialized teachers for classes 5-12 at the polytechnical or expanded upper school were trained at universities, technical colleges, and colleges of education. This training, concluding with a diploma, mainly took place at ten highly specialized colleges of education, concentrating on either mathematics and the natural sciences or social studies, history, philology, and the arts; or else at university level in faculties of education newly developed after 1945 and technical colleges.

An introduction to everyday practice at schools was integrated in this training. The didactics and methodology of teacher training in the GDR were viewed as being of great importance. The Marxist-Leninist ideological fixation of entire subjects – such as the training of teachers in "citizenship" – led after 1990 to extensive "winding up" of departments. Around 29,000 teachers lost their jobs in the New Laender up to 1993 because of budgetary difficulties. That led to hardship and provoked discussion.

The Conference of Ministers of Education reached agreement (7.5.1993) on recognition and re-assignment of former GDR teacher training courses so as to accord with established career patterns in the Federal Republic (Beschlußsammlung No. 719).

16.3 The Current Situation

Teachers for all kinds of schools – apart from staff at pre-schools and kindergartens, and technical instructors at general and vocational schools (e.g. for stenography and typing) – are trained at universities, technical universities and colleges, and colleges of education, art, and music. The precondition for admission to training is the *Abitur* (or equivalent).

Anyone who wants to study music, art, or sport must submit to an aptitude test. The usual requirement for teaching at vocational schools entails appropriate training or at least a year of relevant practical experience.

Two phases of training can be distinguished:

1. Studies, i.e. scholarly training in educational and social studies, in at least two of the subjects to be taught, and in didactics and practical application. This concludes with the first degree examination.
2. The introduction to school practice (on-the-job training). The Conference of Ministers of Education laid down a unified period of two years in its resolution dated 12.12.1986 (Beschlußsammlung No. 812). This phase comprises teaching practice at schools providing training, and complementary training at study seminars. In Schleswig-Holstein the Land Institute for School Practice and Theory is responsible for initiation into the profession. Training concludes in all Laender with part II of the degree examination.

The examinations for the teaching profession carried out by the Laender in accordance with the Conference of Ministers of Education recommendations are reciprocally recognized – following the Hamburg Agreement of 28.10.1964 (see section 2.3).

There have been attempts at merging those two phases of training (as in the former GDR) with initial practical experience incorporated in studies (as at the universities of Oldenburg and Osnabrück/Vechta from the mid-seventies), but those were abandoned in the eighties.

The present state of teacher training is briefly outlined in the following. In the majority of Laender teachers are usually trained for specific types of school. In North Rhine-Westphalia and Brandenburg such training is graduated in terms of different levels of specialization at school. In Berlin and Hamburg training for teaching in the primary and intermediate levels, and in the upper level at general schools, incorporates both different types and levels of schooling. In Bremen there is unified training for state schools, structured in terms of the different levels.

Training courses differ from Land to Land as is shown in the following survey. Greater standardization would be desirable. The Science Council, which in 1991 approved proposals for reorganization of teacher training in the New Laender, should take on this task. However, it seems as if standardization and reform of both phases of teacher training are not viewed as being urgent aspects of educational policy. Yet they are long overdue since the quality of teacher training suffers amid the many (and sometimes faltering) attempts at reform.

16.4 Teaching Careers

16.4.1 Primary and Secondary Modern Teachers (Primary and Secondary I Levels)

Apart from Baden-Württemberg and Thuringia where courses are provided by colleges of education, training for teaching in primary school and/or *Hauptschule* (secondary level I) is completely integrated in universities. In 11 Laender studies take at least six semesters, in Berlin and Lower Saxony seven, and in Bremen, Hamburg, and Mecklenburg-Western Pomerania eight. Such training includes several internships (during lecture-free periods) and practicals during semesters. Bavaria, Brandenburg, Hesse, North Rhine-Westphalia, Saarland, Saxony, Saxony-Anhalt, and Thuringia offer separate courses for primary and *Hauptschule* teachers. Instruction is provided in educational theory and subject-related didactics. Subject-combinations differ between Laender with one main and one or two subsidiary subjects.

16.4.2 Intermediate School Teachers (Secondary Level I)

Berlin, Brandenburg, Bremen, Hamburg, Hesse, Mecklenburg-Western Pomerania, North Rhine-Westphalia, Saarland (intermediate schools and comprehensives), Saxony (middle schools), Saxony-Anhalt (secondary schools), and Thuringia (norm schools) link courses for teaching in *Hauptschule* and *Realschule*, and secondary level I respectively. Separate courses for *Realschule* teachers exist in Baden-Württemberg, Bavaria, Lower Saxony, and Rhineland-Palatinate. The minimum study period is six semesters in Bavaria, Hesse, North Rhine-Westphalia, Rhineland-Palatinate, Saarland, and Schleswig-Holstein; seven in Baden-Württemberg, Saxony, Saxony-Anhalt, and Thuringia; eight in Bremen, Hamburg, Lower Saxony, and Mecklenburg-Western Pomerania; and nine in Berlin. After completion of training as a primary or *Hauptschule* teacher it is possible to gain the *Realschule* teacher qualification by taking an additional course. Training involves specific practical experience, and the course entails educational studies and subject-related didactics. Normally two subjects are prescribed, but combinations vary from Land to Land.

16.4.3 Gymnasium Teachers (Secondary Levels I and II)

Here too, apart from Baden-Württemberg, two periods of practical experience are prescribed. The course usually involves educational studies and the two subjects to be taught, which can be extended to three in some Laender. Subject combinations vary from Land to Land. In most Laender studies take at least eight semesters, but in Berlin, Saxony, and Saxony-Anhalt nine are prescribed, and in Lower Saxony ten.

16.4.4 Teachers at Vocational Schools (Secondary Level II)

Training in the various professional spheres reflects the diversity within vocational schooling. Specific connections between courses and subjects are laid down with normally two subjects prescribed. Options include metallurgy, electrotechnology, construction technology, and social work. The minimum training period for vocational school teachers is eight semesters in the majority of Laender, nine in Berlin, Saxony, and Saxony-Anhalt, and ten in Lower Saxony. The diploma course for teachers at trade schools involves at least eight semesters studying the didactics of economics and vocational training. Different combinations of commercial and technical studies are offered by the Laender, leading to qualification with a diploma in business teaching, vocational education, or part I of the state examination for teaching at vocational schools. In several Laender there are also courses in agriculture, home economics, and the food industry, concluding with part I of this state examination.

16.4.5 Teachers at Special Schools

In most Laender training takes the form of basic studies, but an additional course following on from qualification as a primary or *Hauptschule* teacher (or secondary level I) is sometimes also possible. During basic studies students are specifically prepared for working in special schools without having had any previous training as a teacher. Such a course is available in Baden-Württemberg, Bavaria, Berlin, Bremen, Hamburg, Hesse, Lower Saxony, Mecklenburg-Western Pomerania, North Rhine-Westphalia, Rhineland-Palatinate, Saxony, Saxony-Anhalt, and Schleswig-Holstein. Training as a special school teacher is highly differentiated, involving such specializations as the blind, the partially sighted, the deaf, the hard of hearing, the mentally handicapped, the physically disabled, and children with learning, speech, and behavioural difficulties. Studies usually comprise two specializations. The minimum training period is seven semesters in Saxony and Saxony-Anhalt, eight in the other Laender, and nine in Berlin. Supplementary and extension courses normally last four semesters in Baden-Württemberg, Brandenburg, Hesse, Rhineland-Palatinate, and Thuringia, and two in Schleswig-Holstein.

16.4.6 Technical Teaching Staff

The technical staff employed at vocational schools (e.g. teachers of stenography and typewriting) must have completed job training, an additional qualification at a technical school, and acquired basic educational skills in special courses.

16.5 Further Training for Teachers

In the years following reunification in 1990 further training for teachers was faced with great challenges. After all, teachers in the New Laender had to be prepared for new tasks within the tripartite school system. There was also a shortage of teachers, i.e. modern language teachers, especially for English and French. Completely new curricula had to be introduced in such ideologically contaminated subjects as history and politics. Experts from the Old Laender assisted the re-organization of further training for teachers.

In all of the Laender there are many opportunities for further and advanced training. This is intended to keep teachers up to date on developments in the pedagogics, psychology, sociology, and didactics of their subjects. In recent years projects involving the environment, media, and information studies have become more important. Alongside in-school and regional possibilities of further training, there are centralized courses at such places as the Reinhardswaldschule near Kassel, the Bavarian Centre for Advanced Teacher Training in Dillingen, the Rhineland-Palatinate State Institute of Advanced Teacher Training at Speyer, and the Brandenburg Institute for Further Training, School Practice, and Teaching Research at Ludwigsfelde. In addition, Protestant and Catholic academies, the church study centres for religious education, and the Land institutes and the Federal Centre for Political Education all offer a wide range of courses. Such advanced training usually takes place during teaching hours. Teachers are excused their school duties when they are taking part in such courses. A start has also been made on media-backed correspondence courses for teachers as, for instance, developed by the Tübingen-based German Institute for Correspondence Courses. The abundance of state and private backing for further and advanced training for teachers offers opportunities for a diversity of educational and didactic initiatives and methods. Increasing participation demonstrates that what is on offer attracts interest.

In-service training aids constant adaptation of the teacher's knowledge to developments in scholarship and educational policy. Further training is directed towards acquisition of additional qualifications, for instance preparing teachers for such new spheres of instruction as information theory and work studies. Statistically, every teacher participates in advanced training at least once a year, but some attend several courses and others none since such training is voluntary.

16.6 Shortage of Teachers, Unemployment, and Long-Term Developments

During the past five decades teacher training in the Federal Republic was both stimulated and restricted by phases of great shortage of teachers and high unemployment. Denazification programmes after 1945 led to the dismissal of many teachers who had been tainted by National Socialism. Relief was sought by calling in already retired teachers and organizing crash courses. Such courses also existed in the Soviet occupied zone for the training of new teachers. There was a particular shortage of teachers in the sixties during the years of accelerated educational expansion. Since the seventies, however, there has been a surplus. Many newly qualified teachers were unable to find employment. Training capacity at colleges and faculties of education was drastically reduced and many professorial posts reassigned.

The Conference of Ministers of Education has documented the development of unemployment among teachers on the basis of statistics provided by the Federal Labour Office. In 1987 22,981 fully trained teachers (15,580 of them women) were registered as unemployed. The number declined to 16,008 (10,935 women) by 1990. Figures remained roughly constant between 1991 and 1994 when they went down to 13,997 (9,499 women). These statistics refer only to the Old Laender.

In February 1995 the Conference of Ministers of Education published a special report on employment of teachers between 1980 and 1994, and some of the key data is presented here. In 1980 85.7 % (33,698) of the 39,329 applicants for a teaching job who had completed a probationary period were taken on. That percentage halved during the eighties, sinking to only 37.5 % in 1987. The following year only 6,400 applicants found a job. When the number of pupils started rising again from 1989, more young teachers were employed. 13,540 found work in the Old Laender in 1994; thus the number of teachers who found a job was 22.2 % higher than the number of teachers who had completed the probationary period that year (11,075). Unemployment among teachers peaked in 1985 with 25,012 and went down to 14,920 in 1993.

In the Old Laender the situation varies according to type of school. The number of teachers taken on in primary schools, *Hauptschule* (primary level), *Realschule* (secondary level I), and special schools was greater than the number of those who completed probationary training. The situation is the same at vocational schools. At *Gymnasium* (secondary level II) the opposite is the case. Here clearly more people are trained than find a job. In 1994 a total of 33,000 applicants (71 %) failed to find teaching posts in state schools – 19,600 of them would-be *Gymnasium* teachers.

The situation in the New Laender is very different. Introduction of the tripartite school system and application of the Old Laender's criteria for employment have led since 1990 to a considerable reduction in staffing. Nevertheless, there is a lack of teachers in individual subjects including English, French, Latin, the arts, and ethics. In 1994 only 1,340 new teachers were taken on at a time when 1,946 completed probationary training.

Calculations by the Federal-Laender Commission for Educational Planning and Advancement of Research indicate that over the medium- and long-term a clear-cut increase in staffing is necessary in order to maintain the provision of teaching at general schools. Employment opportunities will significantly improve in all kinds of schools from the mid-nineties. If bottlenecks in the availability of teachers are to be avoided in the years ahead, recent increases in the numbers of students undergoing teacher training must continue. However, offers of employment depend on the financial resources available to individual Laender where budgetary decisions are taken by Land parliaments.

17 Quaternary Sphere

17.1 Adult and Further Education

Adult and further education are not new developments in the realm of future-oriented German education policy. The abundance of sponsors and organizational forms involved in further education cannot be anywhere near completely outlined here. Anyone who wants to find out about the current situation in the 16 Laender should look at "Weiterbildung" ("Further Education"), the June 1994 report on the available literature and research, assembled by Hannelore Faulstich-Wieland, Ekkehard Nuissl, Horst Siebert, and Johannes Weinberg in conjunction with the German Adult Education Institute.

Adult education is a recent development in the history of education. During the 19th century urban reading circles and museum and literary societies flourished. There were religious associations such as the "Katholischer Gesellenverein" ("Association of Catholic Journeymen", Kolping-Verein) and Protestant attempts at encouraging education in rural areas. At the beginning of this century university teachers met for the first "Adult Education College Gatherings". Before the first world war Germany led the way in European mass education with some 8,000 educational groups. However, only during the Weimar Republic did the state begin to devote greater attention to "free popular education". Article 148 of the Weimar constitution stated that: "Popular education, inclusive of the colleges of adult education, should be supported by the Reich, Laender, and local communities". A new epoch in adult education got under way during the twenties, and in 1932 there were over 200 evening colleges in the German Reich. The period of National Socialist domination ended that era. Many adult education centres were closed down or forced to toe the party line. After the second world war adult education was built up anew and by 1956 there were already over a thousand centres. A large number of church educational centres were also established at that time, including the Protestant academies which were later to be joined by Catholic counterparts. A report (29.1.1960) by the German Education and Training Committee on "The situation and task of German adult education" was of great importance for educational policy. The Committee called on the state to recognize adult education as a free and indispensable part of the public education system, providing financial assistance and, when the time was right, a legal foundation. Further education was first integrated in overall planning in the German Education Council's 1970 structure plan. That declared:

"The concept of ongoing further education entails organized learning being extended to later phases of life, and attitudes towards education being fundamentally changed. ... It is necessary to establish institutionalized further education as a comprehensive and complementary post-school sphere of education. Further education as a continuation or resumption of earlier organized learning constitutes a connected whole in conjunction with the processes experienced during pre-schooling and normal schooling. Further education involves extended learning, retraining, and adult education. It complements conventional schooling and provides further training when schooling has been completed. At the same time it endeavours to relieve the educational system of the social pressure arising from unsatisfied educational needs and demands".

The 1973 comprehensive education plan called for expansion of further education to become a major element within the system. This – said the planners – could not be seen and treated as an arbitrary private matter or as a measure merely serving group interests. The comprehensive education plan took up the Education Council's ideas, viewing assistance for expansion of further education as a public responsibility, even though the individual had to develop the initiative for his or her personal development. Land laws, comprehensively regulating adult and further education, were passed in Schleswig-Holstein, Hesse, Bremen, Bavaria, North Rhine-Westphalia, Rhineland-Palatinate, and Baden-Württemberg during the years of the great debate on educational reform from the end of the sixties to the mid-seventies. Programmatic political declarations about the tasks and objectives of further education were accompanied by discussion of the conditions for state recognition of and assistance for the associated institutions. The ideas put forward in the structure and comprehensive education plans were largely taken on board so that further education became recognized as a fourth sphere of education and a public responsibility. The budgetary funds provided by federal, Laender, and local authorities more than tripled between 1975 and 1987, increasing from 1,054 million DM to 3,300 million DM. Ekkehard Nuissl has outlined the development of financing in "Adult Education in Germany". This reflects the great diversity of sponsors and organizational forms in this sphere, characteristic of the German situation, so finance comes from federal, Laender, and local authorities, private industry, the Federal Labour Office, and such sources of support as trade unions, churches, foundations, and associations.

Expenditure on Adult Education 1987[1], 1990, and 1992[5]

Source of Funds	Amount in million DM		
	1987	1990	1992
European Union	–	–	82[2]
Federal, Laender, & Local Authorities	3, 216	3, 217	3, 999
of which: Federation	769	657	956
Laender	1, 306	1, 224	1, 474
Local Authorities	1, 141	1, 337	1, 569
Federal Labour Office	5, 659	6, 324	18, 900[3]
Private Industry	10, 400	21, 000	36, 500[4]
Backer Organizations	110	130	130[2]

1. Only the Old Laender. Sources: Arbeitsgruppe Bildungsbericht 1990, p. 429; BMBW 1993, p. 262ff; DVV Pädagogische Arbeitsstelle, VHS-Statistik 1992
2. Estimate
3. According to information from the Federal Labour Office. The enormous increase between 1990 and 1992 is the outcome of expenditure on education in the New Laender. This will have fallen again by 1994.
4. Information from the Institute for German Industry
5. For 1993 the Federal Ministry of Education, Science, Research, and Technology estimates that the federal, Laender, and local authorities will spend 4,300 million DM on adult and further education throughout Germany (Grund- und Strukturdaten 1994/95). More recent figures are not yet available.

Source: Ekkehard Nuissl – Erwachsenenbildung in Deutschland, Frankfurt/Main 1995, p. 24.

If private expenditure is included, estimated at 6.5 billion DM for 1992, the total amount devoted to adult education that year amounted to 70.1 billion DM. During the past two decades public expenditure in this sphere may have increased more than in any other educational sector, but the sum involved is still modest in comparison with what is devoted to schools and universities. Contributions from the Federal Labour Office are for measures regulated by the work assistance law.

"Lifelong Learning for Everyone", a key demand in the Federal Ministry of Education and Science's 1985 "Theses on Further Education", is often cited up to the present day. This states that structural change in the economy, technology, and society can only be implemented if all citizens become increasingly qualified. The initial phase of training is no longer sufficient for that, and further training will become a necessary lifelong task for everyone. The highest possible degree of readiness for further training should therefore be aroused among the population. The foundations should already be established in school, college, and vocational training. However, further training cannot be planned, organized, and financed by the state to the extent possible with schools and universities. Moreover, the federal government believes that pluralism and openness within a diversity of tasks can best be guaranteed through competition between various sponsoring bodies.

At the start of the seventies the federal government still upheld the view that further education could be organized by the state through systematization and expansion of courses to cover all areas. A clear-cut change of direction occurred during that decade. The "Theses on Further Education" also stressed the mounting significance of further academic training, which was seen as an important task for universities. Courses of further study were therefore be developed beyond what was already available, and also opened up to qualified people with a job even if they did not have the *Abitur*.

Since reunification in 1990 the structures of further education in the GDR have largely vanished. New laws and regulations, following models in the Old Laender, were introduced. One example is the Brandenburg law (17.12.1993) which regulates and supports further education. Paragraph 2 views the right to further education as an element within the basic right to free development of personality. Paragraphs 5 and 6 are concerned with the basic provision of further education in the 14 new districts and four city authorities established in Brandenburg's territorial reforms at the end of 1993. Developments are co-ordinated by a regional further education council, and the Land government consults an advisory board on fundamental issues and the financing of this sphere. Initially 6.2 million DM were available annually for further education, and that rose to around 8.3 million DM from 1996. Brandenburg's low population density creates difficulties for the development of further education. Nevertheless, during the past four years a wide variety of courses have been developed at colleges of adult education, residential facilities, and rural centres.

Even though it is difficult to collect statistics on adult education, there do already exist 33 volumes of differentiated information on activities at colleges of adult education. The latest figures published by the Frankfurt-based German Institute of Adult Education (part of the German Association of Adult Education Colleges) cover 1994.

The *Volkshochschule* (College of Adult Education) is the furthest developed and most widespread institution in this sphere, usually financed by the local community or district. In 1994 there were 871 such colleges in the Old Laender and 160 in the New Laender, totalling 1,031 for the country as a whole. In addition there are 3,689 subsidiary branches in the West and 321 in the East. Over half of these colleges are dependent on local backing. The 25 institutions in the city-states (Berlin, Bremen, and Hamburg) have a special legal status. 220 are run by district authorities. Over two thirds of the colleges are headed by full-time specialists. In 1994 colleges of adult education had the following full-time staff: 1,019 (including 249 women) in directorial positions, 3,712 (1,957 women) in departmental managerial positions, and 3,610 (2,811 women) serving administrative functions. Some 180,000 freelance staff ran classes and courses nationwide in 1994.

The number of *Volkshochschule* courses attained a new record in that year. In the Old Laender 459,000 courses were attended by 5,967,000 participants – an average of 13 per course. In the New Laender 404,038 participated in 30,139 courses. Foreign language courses (including German as a foreign language) predominated, followed by classes in health education, arts and crafts, home economics, mathematics, natural sciences, technology, education inclusive of psychology and philosophy, administration, and business practice. Many courses also serve preparation for school qualifications.

These colleges are aimed at all sections of the population and open to diverse ideological positions. These institutions are linked at the Laender level as associations, which since 1953 have belonged to the German Adult Education Association that maintains a pedagogics centre at Frankfurt (Hansaallee 150).

Self-administering business institutions with public corporation status (chambers of industry and trade, and of skilled trades and agriculture) also provide further training with state support. Their courses are directly tailored to the needs of the economy. The trades unions, the German Trade Union Confederation, and the white-collar associations offer numerous training programmes. The political parties pursue courses in civics by way of special foundations. The SPD has the Friedrich Ebert Foundation, the CDU the Konrad Adenauer Foundation, the FDP the Friedrich Naumann Foundation, the CSU the Hanns Seidel Foundation, and the Bündnis 90 / Greens the Heinrich Böll Foundation. The adult education supported by the churches offers a wealth of courses – for mothers and parents, meetings devoted to theological or religious themes, further training, etc. The Protestant and Catholic academies developed in the post-war years play a special part as centres for discussion, reflection, and research. The courses and meetings there bring together leading figures from politics, administration, business, culture, scholarship, and the churches for consideration of contemporary issues. These academies are of great importance in terms of formation of opinion and its dissemination in many spheres of public life. They have given rise to a number of political initiatives. Discussions (generally referred to as "Loccum I-IV") between experts from the Conference of Ministers of Education on upper level reform and university entrance thus took place in recent years at the Hanover diocesan academy.

17.2 Correspondence Courses

Correspondence courses are mainly run by private firms and associations on a widely differing legal basis. Some 180 organizations offer over a thousand courses, which in 1994 were taken up by about 153,000 participants (44 % women). Of the 1,171 officially recognized courses in 1994, 121 prepare for public examinations and 88 for school qualifications (*Hauptschule*, *Realschule*, and *Abitur*).

Correspondence courses can be grouped as follows: courses in preparation for external examinations, vocational courses leading to state or other public examinations, vocational training without any recognized possibilities of assessment, and hobby courses.

In 1995 an internal study by the German Correspondence Course Association (in existence since 1969) ascertained that every second member institute works together with industrial firms. Over 2,500 companies are involved, and these have around 30,000 staff trained by way of correspondence courses. This method is thus an efficient form of advanced vocational training.

The agreement (30.10.1969) on establishment and financing of the Cologne-based State Centre for Correspondence Courses marked a first step towards introduction of supervision of such courses by the Laender. That was revised by the Laender on 20.12.1973 after the initial four-year period was over. A federal law (24.8.1976) provided protection for participants from misleading advertising, dubious representatives, and prejudicial contracts. The registration of all correspondence courses was also unified. In addition, the law opened up the possibility of involving the Berlin-based Federal Institute of Vocational Training in inspection of courses.

The 1973 law was then succeeded by another agreement (16.2.1978) to which Brandenburg, Mecklenburg-Western Pomerania, Saxony, Saxony-Anhalt, and Thuringia also became signatories on 4.12.1991. The Cologne centre's task is defined as being to observe the development of correspondence courses, to assist through recommendations and suggestions, to advise the Laender on issues within such teaching and the examination procedure for participants, to supply information about available courses and educational possibilities, and to inspect courses if so requested by the organizer. Detailed regulations cover the registration and acceptability of correspondence courses. In 1994 101 new courses were assessed and accepted – 36 business courses, 31 on mathematics and the natural sciences, and 8 new language courses. Accepted courses receive a seal of approval.

Educational programmes on radio and television (Funk- und Telekolleg), which have existed since the sixties, were used by around 20,000 people (half of them women) in 1994/95. The 29th six-month study course “Taxes – Society's Income” was launched in autumn 1995. This was transmitted on radio with accompanying study texts and sessions at colleges of adult education. Current television programmes (with accompanying direct teaching) prepare for examinations at degree-granting colleges of higher education. Six Laender are involved: Baden-Württemberg, Bavaria, Brandenburg, North Rhine-Westphalia, Rhineland-Palatinate, and Saarland.

18 Current Issues in School and University Education

In the Federal Republic of Germany educational policy is defined by a specifically federal structure, and a distinction must be made between national and regional discussions. Often regional issues are put into a national context while nationwide problems are discussed in terms of their impact on Laender policy. One example is provided by the federal constitutional court's "crucifix judgement" in autumn 1995 which led to nationwide discussion even though it only related to Bavaria. Introduction into the Brandenburg curriculum of a course on "Lifestyles – Ethics – Religious Studies" provoked headlines across the country because the status of "religious education", guaranteed in the 1949 Basic Law, was deeply affected by this new school law. Recently co-education at school, introduced in the GDR in the fifties and a decade later in the Federal Republic, has been challenged. It was initially viewed as the modern way of implementing equality of opportunity for girls and boys, but by now people recognize that this form of teaching also involves disadvantages for girls.

Only a few topics can be discussed here. In addition, such disputed issues as the status of the *Hauptschule* and never-ending discussion of the *Abitur* or university entrance examination have already been covered. On the other hand, such themes as reform of orthography (which has persisted throughout the century) or of teacher training are too complex to be sufficiently considered in this report. Discussion will thus be limited to such controversial themes as "autonomy for schools" and "long-term educational perspectives".

18.1 Autonomy for Schools

Greater autonomy for schools has been demanded for years, following the model established by universities which, although disputed, has been clarified legally in the federal university outline law and Laender university laws. Hermann Avenarius, director of the German Institute for International Educational Research, has warned against misunderstandings and illusions in the school sector: “The term ‘autonomy’ is already misleading. In legal terms it applies to the authority enjoyed by a legal entity within public law to regulate its own affairs by enacting legal norms. However, schools are not legal entities within public law; they are public institutions without legal capacity. ... One should therefore speak of schools being self-governing rather than autonomous”. Avenarius points out that the state has the task of assuring schools' religious and ideological neutrality, and asks: “Is it not strange that during the sixties the abolition of denominational schools was celebrated as great educational progress while scarcely thirty years later people promote, again under the banner of progress, the opening up of schools to new ‘declarations of faith’ by invoking supposed autonomy? ... Schools are also in danger of – and have sometimes succumbed to – becoming a battleground for conflicts between political parties and interest groups”.

The correctness of Avenarius's viewpoint becomes apparent in the light of plans under discussion in North Rhine-Westphalia. The idea of autonomy has received most comprehensive expression to date in the “Future of Education – School of the Future” memorandum (already mentioned in section 3) published in September 1995 by a commission appointed by Johannes Rau, the Land Prime Minister. This postulates a completely new kind of German school called the “House of Learning” which is conceived as being “partly autonomous” (whatever that may mean). The idea is that the traditional school administration, inspectors, and directorate with head teachers, directors of studies, and experienced civil servants should be partly replaced or augmented by such new bodies as:

1. an advisory board (for each school)
2. a community school commission
3. a regional school commission
4. an educational service which complements the individual school's constant task of “self-evaluation” by way of “external evaluation” (through Land officials).

The memorandum states:

“A fundamental re-organization of state inspection is an important component in strengthening each school's self-structuring and individual responsibility. ... One fundamental recommendation involves separation of functions involved in assessment of educational standards from legal and administrative responsibilities" (p. XXVI f.). Future teachers should no longer have civil servant status; instead their "conditions of employment and salaries" should be regulated by wage agreements. That should also apply to head teachers and members of the education service.

"Partly autonomous" schools will be obliged to devise a "school programme" following the "basic curricula" prescribed by the Land authority. They will acquire the right to "draw up an organizational statute regulating basic school issues" and "should produce projections for staffing". ... "The people running a partly-autonomous school should be in charge of personnel management and also be involved in the current responsibilities (teaching and curriculum) of the school inspectorate". ... "Partly autonomous schools have to manage their own budget and ... are entitled to seek further funding ..." (p. 162 f.). "Partly autonomous schools ... are obliged to evaluate both the processes and the results involved in their work. ... Binding regulation of the means of evaluation must be agreed with the school and then continuously developed. ... The school management's freedom of action should be extended and its position of responsibility strengthened. The school directorate should undertake its task in such a way that educational leadership becomes a shared concern for all those involved in school life" (p. 164).

Revealingly the emphasis here is on a collective "school directorate" rather than a single responsible "school director". This "partly autonomous" school directorate is answerable to the above-mentioned committees. The supposedly increased "freedom of action for the school directorate" is subject to direct intervention by new bodies, in other words restricted. The Rau commission is seeking partial "denationalization" of schools. The authors of this memorandum obviously forgot that elementary teachers waged a long struggle for "nationalization" during the 19th century. Taking schools out of control by local authorities was viewed as decisive progress. It must also be asked whether "partial autonomy" is a way of concealing a partial transfer of financial responsibility for schools from the Land to local and regional authorities. For three decades educational policy's main aim was to improve equality of educational opportunities. If in future individual schools are required to generate additional funds for themselves, there will be a greater number of "rich" and "poor" schools. The decisive factor in appointing "school directorates" will be their ability to raise funds rather than educational expertise. Disputes over trends in school policy, now being settled in Land parliaments, will be displaced onto each "House of Learning". Will teaching staff and new committees, faced with a multitude of discussions of educational policy, also be able to assure the necessary tranquillity for "school as a place of learning"? How will denationalization of schools affect standardization of qualifications? The Rau commission's proposals lack insight with regard to interventions in established structures. It is also unclear how far such changes would affect constitutional and legal regulations.

18.2 Long-Term Staffing Developments in the Old and New Laender

At present long-term staffing at schools is a cause for concern. Both the Federal-Laender Commission for Educational Planning and Advancement of Research and the Conference of Ministers of Education have devoted considerable attention to this topic in recent years. The Commission's report dated 26.9.1994 contained extensive data, which was discussed on various occasions when the Conference of Ministers of Education's departmental commission and plenum met in 1995. Particular attention was paid at the plenary meeting (28/29.9.1995) to securing schools' capacity for achievement during a phase of ongoing budgetary restraint. The Conference assumed that in the Old Laender it would be difficult to maintain pupil-teacher ratios amid budgetary restrictions and mounting numbers of pupils. If the 1992 situation is taken as a point of comparison, between 85,000 and 95,800 (or 97,640 according to the latest calculations) new teaching posts will be needed for the period from 1992 to 2005. After 2005 numbers of pupils and teachers are expected to fall again. Completely different developments are anticipated in the New Laender where the Conference forecasts a considerable drop in numbers of pupils between 1995 and 2010, leading to less demand for teachers. The Federal-Laender Commission stresses that such forecasts are based on computer models which do not permit conclusive deductions about the number of teachers actually required in specific years to cover requirements. The Commission believes that the following arguments should be taken into account when taking political decisions:

- “Social changes over the past 30 years, above all empirically demonstrated changes in family structure, have resulted in completely new demands being made on schools as places of education. Today schools have to address their pupils' general problems before they can begin to solve those related to learning. That task extends over the whole period of schooling.
- Germany needs a committed and qualified work-force if it is to remain a competitive economic power creatively oriented towards the future with economically and ecologically acceptable technologies. The education of children and young people creates the urgently necessary preconditions, to be guaranteed by appropriate educational structures.

- Those attending school today and in the immediate future will be faced with exceptionally great burdens during their later working lives. Their generational responsibility will involve providing the financial means for financing pensions for the great number of people reaching the end of their working-life. That already demands offering the younger generation suitable education and an appropriate range of training".

The Conference of Ministers of Education believes that the budgetary situation and changes in numbers of pupils necessitate decisions about how schools' future performance can be guaranteed. In addition, teachers in the Old Laender normally have the status of civil servants, which is not usually the case in the East. Legal circumstances vary considerably so decisions about modalities of employment still have to be taken.

For years the Laender have spoken about employment policy being determined by the need for savings. Job cuts in the public service may have been implemented in recent years within measures consolidating public spending (euphemistically termed "slimming"), but the number of teaching posts was largely maintained and in places even increased. However, it is true that teaching posts did not keep up with increases in pupils. That led to indirect savings measures: bigger classes and more lessons for teachers. The Conference of Ministers of Education believes that sufficient numbers of new teachers must be appointed so as to meet requirements. That is to be accompanied by reform of the law relating to teachers' duties, which basically involves changes in legislation affecting the civil service, allowing the Laender to react more flexibly to varying demands. Over the long-term efforts will be made to achieve nationwide regulation of teachers' duties so as to avoid competition between the Old and the New Laender. Experts are aware that a simple transition from civil servant status to the laws regulating white-collar employment will not solve the problems since the latter is by no means more flexible. The following issues have to be clarified:

- easing sabbaticals and part-time employment
- more flexible regulations about teachers' weekly work-load
- greater possibilities of transition between different levels of teaching
- fixed-term contracts
- reductions of work-load and early retirement.

The fundamental issue as to whether teachers should in future be taken on with public service status or as salaried employees is not at the forefront of these discussions since the Laender have differing views.

18.3 Employment Prospects for School-Leavers and Graduates

During its quarter century of existence the Federal-Laender Commission on Educational Planning and Advancement of Research has often devoted attention to this topic. On 14.3.1989 it thus approved a "Comprehensive Report on Employment Prospects after Completion of Education", looking towards the year 2000. Implementation of German unity in 1990 necessitated inclusion of the New Laender in such an overview, which was presented on 12.12.1994. Here the current situation is first outlined: general developments on the job market, qualifications possessed by employees, and unemployment. Forecasts about long-term developments in the realm of labour supply and demand at individual levels of qualification are not discussed because experience has shown that these are highly unreliable. They are replaced by computer models extending to the year 2010, which attempt to show long-term trends. Two models relating to the Old Laender are cited here:

"For youngsters completing vocational training:

- The numbers of pupils completing secondary level I and then immediately starting vocational training will increase between 1990 and 2010 from c. 41 % to around 51 %.
- Over the longer term around 25 % of the pupils qualified to enter higher education will take up vocational training under the dual system. After completing such training about half will start a university course.

For students completing higher education:

- The numbers of 18-20-year-olds qualified for higher education will increase from 32.8 % in 1990 to 42 % in the year 2000 and to 43.6 % in 2010.
- 80 % of those qualified to do so will begin higher education.
- The average time spent on studies is at present 14.6 semesters at universities and 10.2 semesters at polytechnics. That will gradually be reduced by the year 2010 to 10 (9) semesters".

Up to now all forecasts about reductions in study-times have turned out to be mistaken. The Laender heads of government took account of this report on 22.6.1995 and instructed the Federal-Laender Commission to pursue its work on correlations between education and employment. Those computer models, programmed for "growth", will probably require fundamental revision in view of the most recent developments.

19 The German Education System in the European and International Context

Wolfgang Mitter, for many years director of the Frankfurt-based German Institute for International Educational Research, has made a great contribution to international co-operation in this sphere. His views are as follows:

"For the German education system the Maastricht Treaty and the processes of transformation under way in Central and Eastern Europe signify an opening towards both 'West' and 'East'. The multidimensionality involved constitutes a radical new challenge, compelling reflection on the future of German education. ... Facing up to that challenge should be made easier for us by the fact that being embedded in European and global developments is nothing new in the history of German education. ... Reports and lectures on the German education system at present meet with great interest abroad. ... The reasons for that are complex. Germany's economic power gives rise across the world to questions about the training received by those who brought about and developed such strength. The financial strain on national and Laender budgets, which as a side-effect of the reunification process increasingly affects education, is frequently viewed by foreign observers as secondary to the great achievement of at least external adaptation of East German schools to overall developments within German education".

The following survey mainly focuses on the school system. The many links between German and foreign universities and scholarly organizations, and the contacts abroad within the sphere of adult education, are too broad a realm to be adequately covered here.

19.1 German Education in the European Context. Objectives and Significance of Foreign Language Teaching

Tables 8-10 in the appendix provide information about the development and current status of foreign language teaching. They are self-explanatory and do not require any comment (except maybe that 'Greek' refers to 'Classical Greek').

Anyone examining the role and significance of foreign language teaching in the German school system first has to put this in its historical context. European peoples have been in contact with one another for centuries, particularly such close neighbours as the French and the Germans who have influenced one another intellectually in a multitude of ways for over a thousand years. Three notable areas of influence were French Baroque culture, the large number of Huguenot refugees in Germany, and the Napoleonic era which led to complete restructuring of Germany. However, until the 20th century only a small number of German aristocrats and members of the cultivated upper middle classes (plus travelling journeymen) actually got to know other countries. A "silent revolution" has now taken place here. On the one hand, learning a foreign language became obligatory for secondary level I in all of the occupied zones in post-war Germany. On the other, during a period of economic prosperity a Europe "divided" until 1990 became accessible to Germans from East and West for the first time. Germans became Europe's "tourist nation" in an age of mass tourism.

Up to 1945 experiences of other countries were identical with war experiences for millions of Germans. Understandably, the years when German soldiers took over neighbouring states have left deep wounds – as in the Netherlands – up to the present day. For its part Germany experienced occupation by American, British, French, Soviet, and other troops after the second world war. Retrospectively, the fact that the Western allies were ready, soon after 1945 – and even as the East-West conflict developed –, to offer reconciliation to Germany still arouses astonishment. As early as the fifties such far-sighted politicians as Robert Schumann, Alcide de Gasperi, and Konrad Adenauer developed plans for economic co-operation. Jean Monnet's basic idea of establishing political security for Western Europe through economic integration initially concentrated on coal and steel, leaving aside educational policy as an integrative factor. That changed at the end of the fifties with the Rome Treaty and development of the European Economic Community, later to become the European Union. Walter Hallstein was president of the EEC Commission from 1958 to 1967 after a brilliant academic career, including an important contribution to post-war reconstruction as rector of

Frankfurt university (1946-48), followed by a time as secretary of state in the Federal Chancellor's office and then in the re-established German Foreign Office. Hallstein never lost sight of perspectives for European education. On his initiative article 9, paragraph 2, of the treaty establishing Euratom provided for the creation of an "institution with university status". The Florence-based "European University" for post-graduates was launched in 1972 and opened its doors in 1976.

From the end of the fifties, at a time when the economy was flourishing, hundreds of thousands of "guest workers" poured into the Federal Republic, and their number increased after construction of the Berlin Wall prevented East Germans from escaping or moving to the West.

As relations between states were normalized, exchanges of pupils and teachers flourished, co-ordinated by the Conference of Ministers of Education's Educational Exchange Service. The German Academic Exchange Service looked after student exchanges.

All that exerted an influence on the education system. For a modern industrial society dependent on worldwide connections knowledge of at least one foreign language became a matter of course. On 7.10.1994 the Conference of Ministers of Education approved a resolution on "A Basic Concept for Teaching Foreign Languages" and published this in conjunction with an assessment of such teaching in the Federal Republic of Germany, stating:

"European society is and will remain multilingual. Foreign language teaching in German schools is faced with the task of preparing pupils for this reality. ... Learning foreign languages at school and in vocational training has become an essential aspect of an individual's education. The future objective is thus multilingual competence. In principle as many pupils as possible should learn two foreign languages. Those aiming for higher qualifications should be encouraged and given the opportunity to learn three and possibly more foreign languages. ... Bilingual teaching, presenting some of the subject-matter in another language, is one initiative for supporting this aim".

This document of over a hundred pages offers comprehensive information about the state of foreign language teaching in Germany.

Attention must now be turned to Franco-German co-operation in schools, vocational training, and universities.

19.2 Franco-German Co-Operation in Education

Up to the first world war French predominated among modern languages in German upper schools. A 19th century bon mot – "Every civilized human being has a second homeland, and that is France" – still held good at that time. However, when English advanced to being the premier "world language", the outcome was that French increasingly slipped behind from the time of the Weimar Republic. That only affected the then limited number of pupils at upper school. Foreign language teaching for almost all children – inclusive of the upper level at elementary school (later *Hauptschule*) and even experiments at primary school – characterized post-war educational reforms. Under the influence of the occupying powers after 1945, English became the main foreign language in the British and American zones, and French and Russian in those spheres of influence. The 1955 Düsseldorf Agreement on standardization of the school system laid down that English should become the main foreign language in the Federal Republic.

The Franco-German co-operation initiated by Federal Chancellor Konrad Adenauer and General Charles de Gaulle, President of the French Republic, led to the treaty dated 22.1.1963. One of the main emphases was education and other matters affecting young people inclusive of language-teaching. Both governments agreed to strive to take "concrete steps increasing the number of German pupils learning French and of French pupils learning German". In all university language courses instruction was to alternate between the two languages. Efforts were also made towards establishing equivalence of school and university qualifications. The Franco-German Youth Office set up at that time promoted exchanges of school pupils, students, young craftsmen, and workers. It is not possible here to describe all that has been done since 1963 in implementation of the treaty, but the Franco-German Youth Office provides impressive testimony to mutual understanding.

In 1995 the Conference of Ministers of Education produced over a hundred pages of documentation of Franco-German co-operation in the sphere of education. The foreword emphasizes that this co-operation, founded on the 1963 treaty, has "proved to be extraordinarily vital and productive for over 30 years of institutional existence":

"This co-operation has resulted in schools, institutions providing vocational training, and universities in the two partner countries contributing – despite existing structural differences – to the development and further advancement of Franco-German relations. Many important initiatives have given the younger generation in both countries opportunities for learning the other language more profoundly and thus deepening mutual understanding".

This documentation refers to no fewer than 18 treaties, agreements, and joint declarations on general schooling including one on establishment of Franco-German *Gymnasia*. Other statements cover such matters as a bi-national *Abitur*, and regulation of simultaneous acquisition of the German university entrance qualification and the French Baccalauréat. An office for implementation of the bi-national *Abitur* has existed since 1988. Taking part in this experiment are *Gymnasia* at Bonn, Stuttgart, and Frankfurt/Main. The outcome is an agreement (31.5.1994) on simultaneous acquisition of the two national qualifications and integration of further schools in this programme. Eleven resolutions apply to vocational training and higher education. This documentation thus illustrates the entire spectrum of joint agreements.

19.3 Bilingual Education Courses

Bilingual education has been one of the most encouraging developments in the past two decades. The Conference of Ministers of Education has several times spoken on this issue since 1978. The objective within bilingual education is acquisition of greater knowledge of the languages of our European partners and of the countries concerned. More lessons are usually devoted to the first foreign language, which is also employed for teaching of science and arts subjects. Bilingual teaching normally begins in year 5 with more lessons in the chief foreign language. Other subjects then follow in year 7, leading to the *Abitur* at *Gymnasium*. The objective is to gain bilingual competence (apart from the mother tongue) in a foreign language, ability to communicate in both languages, and greater intercultural understanding, promoting greater choice in university courses and job mobility. 127 bilingual courses existed nationwide in 1991/92: 67 German-English, 52 German-French, 3 German-Russian, 2 German-Dutch and German-Spanish, and 1 German-Italian. In the meantime the number has further increased. Bilingual German-French courses are available in eleven Laender at: seven *Gymnasia* in Baden-Württemberg, four in Bavaria, three *Gymnasia* and two primary schools in Berlin, one *Gymnasium* in Hamburg, four *Gymnasia* and a *Realschule* in Hesse, two *Gymnasia* in Lower Saxony, eighteen *Gymnasia* in North Rhine-Westphalia, thirteen *Gymnasia* and two *Realschule* in Rhineland-Palatinate, nine *Gymnasia*, two secondary schools, and a comprehensive in Saarland, two *Gymnasia* in Saxony, and three *Gymnasia* in Thuringia. The number of schools has thus increased to 74 in just a few years.

Figures for German-English bilingual courses are only available for 1993 when 80 *Gymnasia*, 34 *Realschule*, eight comprehensives, three *Hauptschule*, and a school centre participated with a total of over 11,000 pupils. Other courses involving Polish, Portuguese, Czech, etc, are at present being developed. Advanced bilingual courses (German-English, German-French, German-Italian) are on offer at the European schools in Munich and Karlsruhe.

19.4 Education and the European Union

The Federal Republic of Germany contributes – in accordance with article 23 of the Basic Law – towards development of the European Union in order to bring about a united Europe. This contribution takes place by way of the Laender assembled in the Upper House of the German Parliament. The possibilities of exerting an impact, embodied in this article, strengthen the Laender position vis-a-vis the federal authorities with regard to European issues. Details are regulated in the law dealing with federal-Laender co-operation in this sphere (12.3.1993) and its implementation in an agreement on co-operation (29.10.1993). The Conference of Ministers of Education's European Union commission is an important means of co-ordination and responsible for all of the Conference's dealings with European questions.

This is not the place for detailed description of educational co-operation. Decisions are taken by the European Union's council of Ministers of Education which has met 29 times since 1971 – half-yearly since the mid-eighties. Preparations for these meetings are made by the education commission. The advisory committee on vocational training has played an important part since 1963. Other institutions worthy of mention are:

- the European Centre for the Promotion of Vocational Training based in Thessaloniki. Its task is to support the different levels of vocational training with information, research, and promotion of co-operation
- the Eurydice information network (by now part of the Socrates programme), based at the European Information Office in Brussels where national information services work together. This network serves to collect and distribute information about education systems, reforms, and developments – particularly for those responsible for political decisions
- ongoing co-operation between national information centres on the issues involved in equivalences in qualifications. The Laender are represented by the director of the Central Office for Education Systems Abroad, which is part of the Conference of Ministers of Education secretariat
- the European schools at Bergen, Brussels, Culham, Karlsruhe, Luxemburg, Mol, Munich, and Varese, which were set up on the basis of an agreement between member states dated 12.4.1957.

Within the European Commission executive board XXII (General and Vocational Training, Youth) is responsible for educational co-operation. The EU budget for education in 1996 was around 396 million Ecus, which is a mere 0.5 % of the total budget. 1.5 million Ecus are due to be available for educational policy by 1999.

The Maastricht Treaty, which came into force on 1.11.1993, lays down that the European Union has a limited right to take action within the sphere of education. It is limited to reaching agreement on supporting measures and making recommendations. Beyond that any attempt at harmonizing member states' legal and administrative regulations in this sphere is prohibited. The main objective is development of a European dimension within education, especially through language programmes and promotion of mobility among teachers and taught through time spent abroad.

Since 1987 the European Union has initiated exchange and mobility programmes in the spheres of vocational and university training. These include the Erasmus programme for promoting student mobility, the Lingua programme for assisting competence in foreign languages through stays abroad, and programmes for initial and further vocational training. However, these programmes are not well funded and thus limited in impact. Also worthy of mention are the joint-action Socrates programme (14.3.1995) for general education, and the Leonardo da Vinci programme (6.12.1994) for implementation of vocational training policies. All these programmes run for five years. Socrates is funded with 850 million Ecus and Leonardo with 650 million. The former continues the Erasmus education programme (for promoting student exchange) and parts of the former Lingua and Eurydice programmes.

The Frankfurt-based German Institute for International Educational Research has long been involved with the issues of "school organization, management, and administration" in member states of the European Union. Clive Hopes in particular created a network of links and analyzed systemic differences in these areas and their dynamic growth. Practitioners and researchers work together in international seminars, and their interactive analyses further the development of different levels of training for experts in school administration.

19.5 UNESCO Model Schools

100 UNESCO model schools exist in around 90 towns and cities spread throughout the Federal Republic. Across the world there are 3,000 such schools in 121 countries. The precondition for participation in this project is commitment to ongoing involvement in the UNESCO school network. These schools dedicate themselves to international understanding and intercultural learning, are open to new ideas, and participate in school twinnings, interdisciplinary teaching, and international seminars, camps, and exchange programmes. Their voluntary donations support worldwide programmes for combatting poverty and implementing human rights for

all. Protection of the environment is another central issue at UNESCO model schools. Donations from German schools support primary school children in Guatemala threatened by violence and drugs.

20 Concluding Remarks: Productive Crisis or Time for Reorientation

The Federal Republic of Germany carefully planned the reunification process and initiated reconstruction of the New Laender with financial assistance exceeding all expectations. Just a few years later it is now confronted by great economic and social challenges: four million unemployed, and mounting debts for the federal, Laender, and local authorities, compelling modifications to the welfare state and cuts in the social support-system. In a nationwide address at the end of April 1996 Chancellor Helmut Kohl emphasized: "At present we are having to make important decisions for the future of our country. ... We have had many successes, but we must nevertheless all rethink our approach in some spheres". Schools and universities are increasingly affected by lack of financial resources, particularly in Berlin with its three universities. The Laender in the West, which overnight suddenly became the "former Federal Republic", had got used to thinking that industry, welfare, and education in their state were exemplary and crisis-proof. Their progress towards an idyll of constant social progress has been brought to an abrupt halt. The structural crisis, affecting both economy and society, which has long affected such neighbouring states as France, England, and Italy, has now reached Germany too.

This crisis necessitates dedication of critical thought to recent decades in German educational policy. That may be difficult for many but the time has come for taking leave of illusions, of the utopian educational aftermath of the sixties, which determined school and university policy for many years. What are the unrealistic ideas which we must now abandon? For many the following objectives constitute unquestioned aspects of educational ideology:

- ongoing expansion of secondary schooling and the university system
- the idea that the number of youngsters with the university entrance qualification provides the classic yardstick of educational progress
- the idea that higher education automatically guarantees social advancement and crisis-proof employment
- rejection of "selection" and "achievement" at school and university.

Those issues have long been broadly discussed with crucial contributions from teachers associations, the Education and Science trade union, and the German University Association. Critical and informative articles by leading German educational journalists have exerted great influence. Kurt Reumann, Konrad Adam, and Heike Schmoll (and formerly for many years Brigitte Beer and Brigitte Mohr) of the Frankfurter Allgemeine Zeitung, Rainer Klofat and Brigitta Mogge-Stubbe of the Rheinischer Merkur, and Jutta Roitsch of the Frankfurter Rundschau can be mentioned here, standing for many committed colleagues working for newspapers and magazines, radio and television.

An attempt will made in what follows to outline aspects of new directions in educational policy.

1. University expansion in the Old Laender overturned all planning contingencies and brought about a crisis within the entire university system. What was originally conceived in 1977 as a provisional measure against overcrowding has long become a permanent fixture. For over two decades now universities have been overburdened, and the situation has clearly got worse since 1977, the year when Laender heads of government decided to "maintain access" to the system. What was the ultimate outcome of decades of discussions about university reform and all the efforts to establish a new basis for academic life by way of the university outline law? Many outstanding ministers and senators who really tried to implement careful reforms were worn out by the demands of office. In Berlin alone that happened to Peter Glotz (SPD), Wilhelm A. Kewenig (CDU), and Manfred Erhardt (CDU).

   The international reputation German universities used to enjoy was founded on extensive autonomy and the quality of the teaching. Only remnants of that autonomy remain today. Walter Rüegg, former rector of Frankfurt university and chairman for many years of the West German Rectors Conference, commented on university teachers' performance in his much acclaimed "History of the European University", written and published when he was in his eighties:

   "A university's efficiency primarily depends on the quality of its teaching staff. Good professors attract good colleagues and students, establish the importance of an area of research and teaching, open up new paths, and thereby change the structures of study programmes and research institutions. Mediocre or bad professors tend to surround themselves with others of the same character, thereby allowing their subject to atrophy in stagnation and isolation".

The efficiency of our universities is dependent on guarantees of greater autonomy (in particular financial autonomy) in future, which will allow them to compete for the best lecturers and students. Every university should be able to decide how many and which students it wishes to admit.

2. There is no lack of good suggestions for university reforms. In summer 1996 Dieter Simon, currently president of the Berlin-Brandenburg Academy of Science, used the phrase "self-inflicted blockade" to characterize the situation facing university policy, and wrote: "All possible models have been discussed at great length. What we lack is a political decision on the basic model or models of universities. ... Such a decision must be taken". It remains to be seen whether the planned revision of the university outline law will improve matters since the Laender (not the state) continue to be responsible for university policy.

   In 1991, as chairman of the Science Council, Dieter Simon had already demanded "policies that replace growth-oriented ideas, first in the universities and then in all other areas of scholarship". At that time Simon's demand was criticized in many places, but the past five years showed how justified it was. All the important planning decisions in education policy are still in thrall to belief in growth. That is shown in the previously mentioned computer models produced by the Federal-Laender Commission for Educational Planning and the Conference of Laender Ministers of Education. The University Rectors Conference also takes continuing growth in student numbers as the starting-point for its unsuperseded "Concept for the development of universities in Germany" (6.7.1992). That assumption is based on "the labour market's mounting demand for highly qualified workers". However, it must be asked whether that demand has ever been critically and comprehensively examined in recent times. There is no empirical basis for the University Rectors' assertion. Did not the Conference of Ministers of Education recently record some 14,000 unemployed young teachers in the West? That roughly accords with the number of teachers taken on by schools in 1995.

3. Quite a few people miscomprehended the "right to education" as a fundamental social right to gaining the university entrance qualification. After all, in 1965 Ralf Dahrendorf upheld the thesis that:

"With acceptance of policy directed towards implementation of the right of all citizens to participate in education, Germany is taking the path towards modernity and freedom. ... However, the most important index – and in fact the symbolic objective – of any policy of educational expansion entails increasing the number of holders of the *Abitur*". Behind Dahrendorf's proclamation of the "Right to Education" was the political conviction that looking after one's political rights and duties, and participation in public life, depended exclusively on the level of education. That momentous overestimate of the role of education got under way three decades ago. Anyone who believes that political rights and duties are only assured by education up to the *Abitur* creates a two-class society, turning an educational privilege into a political privilege. Dahrendorf saw that as a "step forward into a modern world of enlightened rationality". Those who only completed *Hauptschule*, *Realschule*, or vocational training were thus "left behind" from the very start and seen as backward social remnants of a supposedly misguided educational policy. Such an arrogant intellectual misconception must be countered.

4. The great wave of educational reforms since the sixties and broad-based strategies of educational planning and promotion were founded on the conviction that higher education guarantees social advancement and crisis-proof employment. The slogan "Advancement through Education" sounded convincing and attracted a great response among the population. Only when in the seventies Georg Picht called for the decoupling of the education system from the demands of employment did people with ears to the ground notice that a great march towards utopia was under way. Soon considerable structural problems arose, affecting the education system and employment. The current crisis intensifies all these problems. The high number of unemployed young academics (particularly teachers), and the many who are viewed as "over-qualified" and do not find a job according with their qualifications, demonstrate the questionable nature of this thesis of social advancement through education. Today qualifications no longer guarantee secure employment.

5. Disparagement of "selection" and "achievement" formed part of the discussion of comprehensive schools. The fact that a selective school system as developed in Germany since the 19th century created social problems was and remains undisputed. Such selectivity, which conflicts with our comprehension of welfare democracy, has been succeeded for decades now by a wide range of assistance for schools. However, the demand for "equality of opportunity" and "justice" leads

to a gradual levelling down of the tripartite school system in secondary level I. Anyone who calls in question or rejects the principle of selection should not be surprised if pupils' commitment and motivation dwindles, resulting in lethargy and lack of interest. A school lacking objective assessment of pupils' achievements cannot avoid a decline in quality and levelling down. Those wishing to equip our children with the knowledge and skills needed for a future Europe must also prepare them for high-level European competition. The idea of achievement underpins the tripartite school system. But have not the *Hauptschule*, the *Realschule*, the *Gymnasium*, and the comprehensive school long had reservations about "achievement"? Have not the criteria for the *Realschule* qualification and the *Abitur* constantly been reduced? Has not the time come to secure more binding unified standards for the "intermediate qualification"? Is there not otherwise a danger that the demanding *Realschule* qualification could be gained by merely "sitting out" *Hauptschule*, a comprehensive, *Gymnasium*, or a vocational school? Does not the failure of about a third of university students show that the upper level at *Gymnasium*, constantly "reformed" since 1972, obviously does not provide all holders of the *Abitur* with the basic knowledge necessary for academic studies? Is it not urgently necessary to make "capacity for studies" the main objective at upper level in *Gymnasium* as once used to be the case?

6. At the June 1995 Leipzig symposium on "University Admission in Germany", Hartmut Schiedermair, for many years president of the German University Association, spoke about the *Abitur* and university entrance examinations as follows:
   "The demands for achievement made by the *Abitur* should be raised in the great majority of Laender. In the present circumstances unified standards of achievement can only be assured through introduction of a national *Abitur* examination. Possibilities of premature selection or rejection of courses should be restricted in favour of a canon of *Abitur* subjects. The course system with its disadvantage of early specialization has not proved its worth. It should be replaced by general adherence to age-group teaching up to the *Abitur*.
   A meaningful *Abitur*, which really does mediate general capacity for studies, makes unnecessary additional admission and university entrance examinations. Conversely, entrance examinations become all the more necessary as the *Abitur* declines as demonstration of capacity for studies.
   Large-scale resort to university entrance examinations would devalue the *Abitur* once and for all, thereby destroying the *Gymnasium*. It is also not apparent how overcrowded universities would be in a

position nationwide to administer admission through entrance examinations while meeting legal requirements".

Schiedermair's concept is convincing and conclusive. Of course, courage will be required for making a break with such an educational model as the 1972 reform of upper level. However, all attempts at improving that by way of later changes of direction ultimately failed to bring results. What is basically wrong can hardly be "improved" at a later stage. Anyone who attempts to pre-empt university concepts (such as seminars) at the *Gymnasium* upper level forces the university to make initial semesters into an extension of school. That leads to loss of time and unaccustomed expenditure. On the other hand, dissolution of the course system with its high staffing levels and lack of success in ensuring "general education" and a far-reaching return to age-group classes would provide an opportunity for reducing the time spent at school from 13 to 12 years.

7. Unified criteria for the German *Abitur* presuppose co-ordinated outline curricula for the individual subjects. The historically interesting experiment of replacing the traditional canon of subjects by highly individualized education has been under way in the Federal Republic since 1972. It would be only slightly exaggerated to say that each pupil working towards the *Abitur* had his or her own course and special curriculum. That demands too much of many pupils and of the school as an institution. We should largely return – as Schiedermair suggests – to age-group teaching and a binding canon of subjects. During the 15th congress of the German Society for Educational Science, held at Halle/Saale in March 1996, Federal President Roman Herzog also spoke in favour of "the broadest possible general education as a crucial objective within education (no matter what type of school) because that is the only way to flexible thinking and responsiveness, to creative action and reaction, during times of change".

   Anyone who wants to guarantee the broadest possible general education needs co-ordinated outline curricula, which should be jointly prepared by the Conferences of Ministers of Education and University Rectors and subject-related associations. Concepts for such curricula have long existed, but mention can only be made here of Werner Heldmann's splendid (but under-appreciated) "Kultureller und gesellschaftlicher Auftrag der Schule" ("School's Cultural and Social Task"). In his study of educational theory, published in 1990, Heldmann presented a concept for schools dedicated to "social achievement" which should become the starting-point for reorientation.

8. The usual way of preparing for such reform is to appoint commissions of experts to which specialists from the former GDR should also belong. Mention should be made here of the work of Gerhart Neuner: “Allgemeinbildung. Konzeption – Inhalt – Prozeß” (“General Education. Concept – Contents – Process”, Berlin 1989). Greater use should be made of educational experiences in the GDR – but without the ideological components – than has been the case to date. What can be achieved by a modern curriculum was demonstrated in the mid-twenties by Hans Richert, a leading Prussian civil servant. Sebastian F. Müller provides an impressive account of how this last great embodiment of Prussian curricular reform was achieved through co-operation between teachers associations and the administration. Richert's curricula exerted a secret influence in the Federal Republic, through all upheavals, until the start of the sixties. As late as 1960 Eduard Spranger wrote that “this was the first reform for a hundred years to have emerged out of an educational background and can be celebrated for being founded on an idea rather than what I usually call ‘fiddling with the curriculum’”. Later people attempted to accuse Hans Richert and his curricula as being precursors of fascism. That is both unfounded and unhistorical. Would then such a committed social democrat as Adolf Grimme, the last democratic Prussian Minister of Education (and later first Lower Saxony incumbent), have devoted – in conjunction with other celebrated scholars, some of whom were forced out of office and into emigration in 1933 – a 1930 *Festschrift* to the 60-year-old Hans Richert and his predecessors, Otto Boelitz and Carl Heinrich Becker? Would a man of the stature of C.H. Becker have marked the celebration by writing: “Your work, Herr Richert, gives complete expression to the age of liberalism; it is impelled by the spirit of classical idealism”? Richert's work is only mentioned here as just one example. What is required is reappraisal of the experience of the seven decades that have passed since then.
9. If future curricula are to endure, they must be dedicated to the traditions and transformations of a European concept of education. In his great essay “The Cultural Reconstruction of Europe”, dating from 1917, Max Scheler wrote:
   “How can Europe's intellectual and ethical culture, now shaken to the foundations and fluttering in the wind like a tattered banner over fields of corpses, be reconstructed? What spirit, what convictions, must impel people to such action? What cultural shoots and educational values should be furthered ..., and what must be condemned and combatted? What kind of education, teaching, and training must a future generation receive so as to make such

reconstruction possible? ... For anyone striving to bring about a revival of European culture, there is no simpler deduction to be made from the present state of affairs than that each European nation must devote itself to upholding Classical Antiquity and Christianity as the essential and unifying foundations for all elementary and higher education and morality – more even, for endowing them with fresh life. That simple formula does not tolerate any dilution or restriction – and neither does the second which involves re-establishment of a profound awareness and feeling for the interconnections and mutual dependence of all European national cultures, furthering that everywhere through dissemination of knowledge of languages, translations, and greater cultivation of the history of culture rather than of states and their wars, and intensifying their sense of communality to the greatest possible degree".

Such Western Ministers of Education as Adolf Grimme (SPD) and Erwin Stein (CDU) were dedicated to that concept of culture after the second world war. Scheler's objective of a European dimension of general education should be adapted to our time and appropriately mediated. "European education" is non-existent without a constantly renewed "synthesis" of Classical Antiquity, Judaism, and Christianity. Creating such education out of critical sifting of German tradition and that of our neighbours is one of the central challenges confronting cultural policy today.

Federal President Roman Herzog found apposite expression for the task facing schools in his previously mentioned speech at Halle/Saale: "The second important element in schooling involves, in my opinion, learning about and experiencing community and dealings with the other: friend, fellow applicant, a person from a different ethnic background – to express myself in an old-fashioned way: education in tolerance. School offers a particular opportunity for young foreigners and young Germans to learn co-existence in a community of responsibility. ... It seems to me that over-ideologized discussion of the past is yielding to a more pragmatic attitude. One can once again call for courage in education without being accused of reactionary leanings. One can also once again remember that differentiated talents have to find appropriate forms of education. Pure equality is not an educational objective for human beings whose individuality differs. But are we drawing the right conclusions from that? Are we well advised when we eliminate entire branches of schooling and at least run the danger that some pupils come to grief with the demands of the remaining types of school and do not gain any qualifications? ... I thereby affirm my belief in the tripartite school system with co-existence of different types of school and a plurality of sources of support".

As early as 1985 Heinz-Dietrich Ortlieb, for many years director of the Hamburg-based World Economic Archive and a member of the SPD since 1931, viewed "a realistic picture of human beings" as the most important precondition for an education system doing justice to an existing situation. What is needed is an education system that "concentrates completely on untiringly facing up to reality rather than cultivating utopias. Only then can we learn to make the best of any future. That, however, entails a return to the centre which has got totally lost with the fashion for the permissiveness of anti-traditionalism, libertinism, and egalitarianism".

Unfortunately, those excellent words remained largely unheard. Do not people still prefer to cultivate utopias rather than untiringly facing up to reality? Do we not still give ourselves up to "unrealistic" ideas about education? The present crisis thus calls on us to review developments in recent decades. No kind of school, no aspect of the university system, should be excluded. Tabu zones for political parties' "favourite children" – no matter which party – should not be allowed. The more impartial and unerring this analysis is, the more likely we are to find solutions. Perhaps basic consensus, beyond all party allegiances, will even develop in education policy as happened during the post-war period. Today's crisis would then offer an opportunity for a comprehensive fresh start.

10. This stocktaking of educational policy should end with the long overdue amendment of the 1964 Hamburg Agreement on standardization of the school system. At present the situation at secondary level I (described in section 9) diverges considerably from the regulations laid down in the agreement. In recent years some Laender have introduced types of school whose designation and structure do not accord with the Hamburg provisions. The outlines of secondary level I are starting to become unclear. The Conference of Ministers of Education's spokesman on schooling, Harald Kästner, recently remarked: "The validity of the Hamburg Agreement and of associated agreements by the Conference of Ministers of Education as the joint basis for Laender schooling was expressly confirmed in the 'Treaty of Unification' dated 31.8.1990. The question now is what support does this agreement offer today for a cohesive German school system. The question now is: towards what system of joint and comparable co-ordinates are developments taking us?"

    In other words, public discussion of "chaos in the German school system" is getting under way – just like at the beginning of the fifties. The Conference of Ministers of Education's response at that time was preparation of the Düsseldorf Agreement in 1955, which preceded the Hamburg Agreement. However, very careful groundwork will be required for any amendment of the Hamburg Agreement. I speak here from experience since as schools consultant in the Conference secretariat I co-ordinated preparations for the Hamburg Agreement in 1964. Mention should be made of the fact that Hans Heckel was then very influential as a "precursor" with his "Grundordnung der deutschen Schule" ("Basics of the German School System", Stuttgart 1958). As a former leading civil servant in Hesse's Ministry of Education Heckel had years of administrative experience, and at that time he was director of the law and administration department of the former College and now German Institute of International Educational Research in Frankfurt/Main. Under the heading "Chaos or Order?" Heckel asked:

"Does the German school exist? Do we not in reality have the Bavarian school, the Berlin school, the Hesse school? Are not the *Volksschule*, *Gymnasium*, and *Berufsschule* as unfamiliar to one another as people who speak different languages? The German school does exist in the same way as there exists German history and the German language. However, since the German school is much younger than the history and language of the German people it is not yet so mature. It is still in its infancy and must first grow and become adult".

Let us leave open the question of whether during the past four decades the German school has grown up or at least become more mature. Any future "Hamburg Agreement" should not be limited to general schooling; it should also incorporate vocational schooling and teacher training. As we have seen, German teacher training will first have to be reorganized and unified as a matter of urgency. That offers an extensive sphere of operations for the Science Council.

Appendices

1. Pupils, Classes, Teachers 1995

Nationwide

a) Types of General Schools

	Type of School	Pupils	Classes	Teachers
1	**Pre-School**	40,105	2,375	2,091
1.1	Pre-classes at Special Schools	820	101	70
2	**School Kindergarten**	43,919	3,581	3,583
2.2	Special School Kindergarten	6,430	939	1,185
3	**Primary School**	3,634,340	161,708	174,010
4	**Orientation Level**	374,692	16,142	22,836
5	**Hauptschule**	1,123,634	51,016	75,880
5.1	Classes 5 and 6	381,896	16,802	23,538
5.2	Classes 7 to 9/10	741,738	34,214	52,342
6	**Integrated Classes for Hauptschule and Realschule**	368,237	16,735	24,492
6.1	Classes 5 and 6	134,353	5,744	7,653
6.2	Classes 7 to 10	233,884	10,991	16,839
7	**Realschule**	1,175,123	46,553	66,271
7.1	Classes 5 and 6	248,179	9,475	12,494
7.2	Classes 7 to 10	926,944	37,078	53,777
8	**Gymnasium**	2,164,592	–	145,895
8.1	Classes 5 to 10	1,546,117	59,980	92,274
8.1.1	Classes 5 and 6	465,814	17,250	25,037
8.1.2	Classes 7 to 10	1,080,303	42,730	67,237
8.2	Classes 11 to 12/13	618,475	–	53,621
9	**Integrated Comprehensive**	508,487	–	37,829
9.1	Classes 1 to 4	26,974	1,216	1,364
9.2	Classes 5 to 10	434,849	16,927	32,233
9.2.1	Classes 5 and 6	116,923	4,455	7,751
9.2.2	Classes 7 to 10	317,926	12,472	24,482
9.3	Classes 11 to 12/13	46,664	–	4,232

Cont.

	Type of School	Pupils	Classes	Teachers
10	**Steiner School**	63,063	–	4,463
10.1	Classes 1 to 4	22,811	783	1,205
10.2	Classes 5 to 10	30,874	1,185	2,397
10.2.1	Classes 5 and 6	11,473	430	836
10.2.2	Classes 7 to 10	19,401	755	1,561
10.3	Classes 11 to 12/13	9,378	–	861
11	**Special Schools**	390,444	38,358	58,598
11.1	For children with learning difficulties[1])	220,728	17,736	25,016
11.2	For the otherwise handicapped[1])	169,716	18,840	30,884
12	**Evening Hauptschule**	998	58	34
13	**Evening Realschule**	11,892	403	567
14	**Evening Gymnasium**	17,441	–	1,413
15	**Sixth-Form College**	14,023	–	1,424
	Total	9,930,990	–	619,386

[1]) without Thuringia

Nationwide

b) Vocational Schools

	Type of School	Pupils	Classes	Teachers
1	**Part-Time Vocational School (total)**	1,714,344	86,362	52,644
1.1	Berufsschule in the Dual System[1])	1,621,032	80,775	43,816
1.2	Preparatory Year	55,381	3,786	5,167
1.2.1	– full-time	49,985	3,365	4,978
1.2.2	– part time	5,396	421	189
1.3	Full-time Foundation Year	37,931	1,801	3,661
2	**Vocational Extension School**	3,680	185	300
2.1	– full-time	3,554	177	294
2.2	– part-time	126	8	6
3	**Full-Time Vocational School**	310,793	14,685	24,344
3.1	– full-time	298,887	14,055	23,793
3.2	– part-time	11,906	630	551
4	**Vocational/ Technical Secondary School**	3,879	189	354
5	**Technical Gymnasium**	87,622	–	7,204
6	**Technical Upper School**	78,591	3,726	5,093
6.1	– full-time	55,202	2,693	4,253
6.2	– part-time	23,389	1,033	840
7	**Technical School**	152,723	7,742	10,321
7.1	– full-time	104,241	5,239	8,616
7.2	– part-time	48,482	2,503	1,705
8	**Vocational Academy**	8,319	–	1,060
8.1	– full-time	8,168	–	1,049
8.2	– part-time	151	–	11
	Total	2,359,951	–	101,320
	Sixth-Form College	81,541	–	3,502
	– full-time	19,846	–	1,803
	– part-time	61,695	–	1,699

[1]) including co-operative Foundation Year.

Source: Kultusministerkonferenz

2. Basic structure of the Federal German Education System 1994

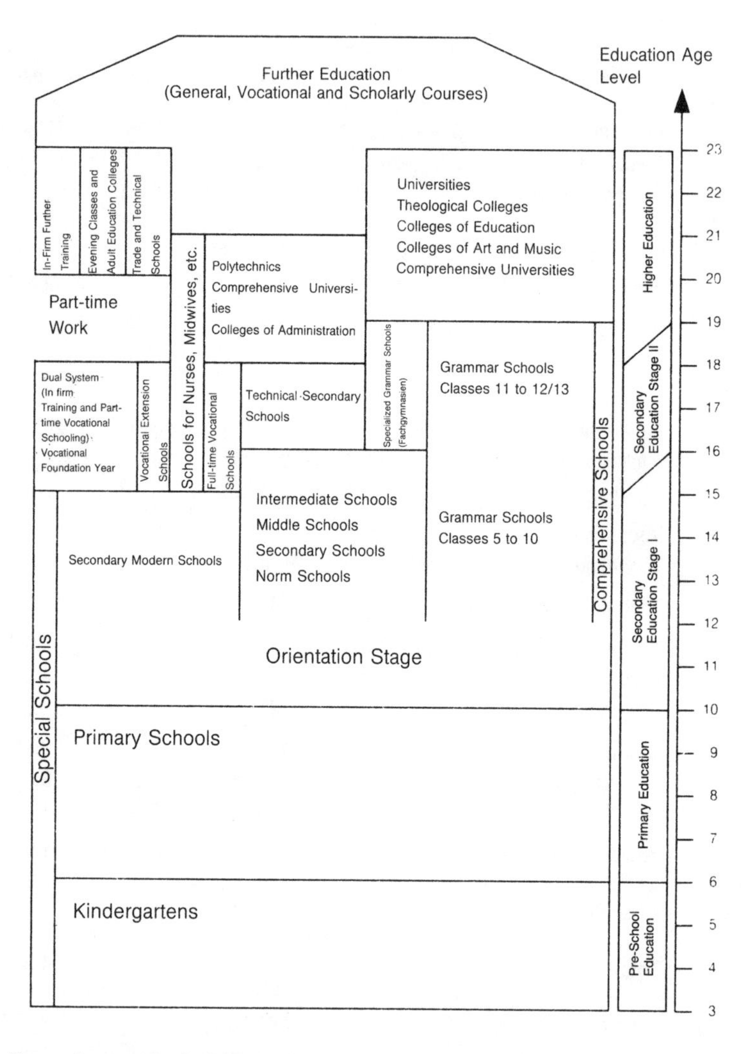

- Diagrammatic representation of typical structures in individual Laender. Variations also exist.
- The age given for attendance at the various educational institutions refers to the usual earliest possible entry.
- The size of the rectangular fields is not proportional to the number of participants.

Source: Grund- und Strukturdaten 1995/96 (BMBF)

3. Location of Universities and Art Colleges 1994

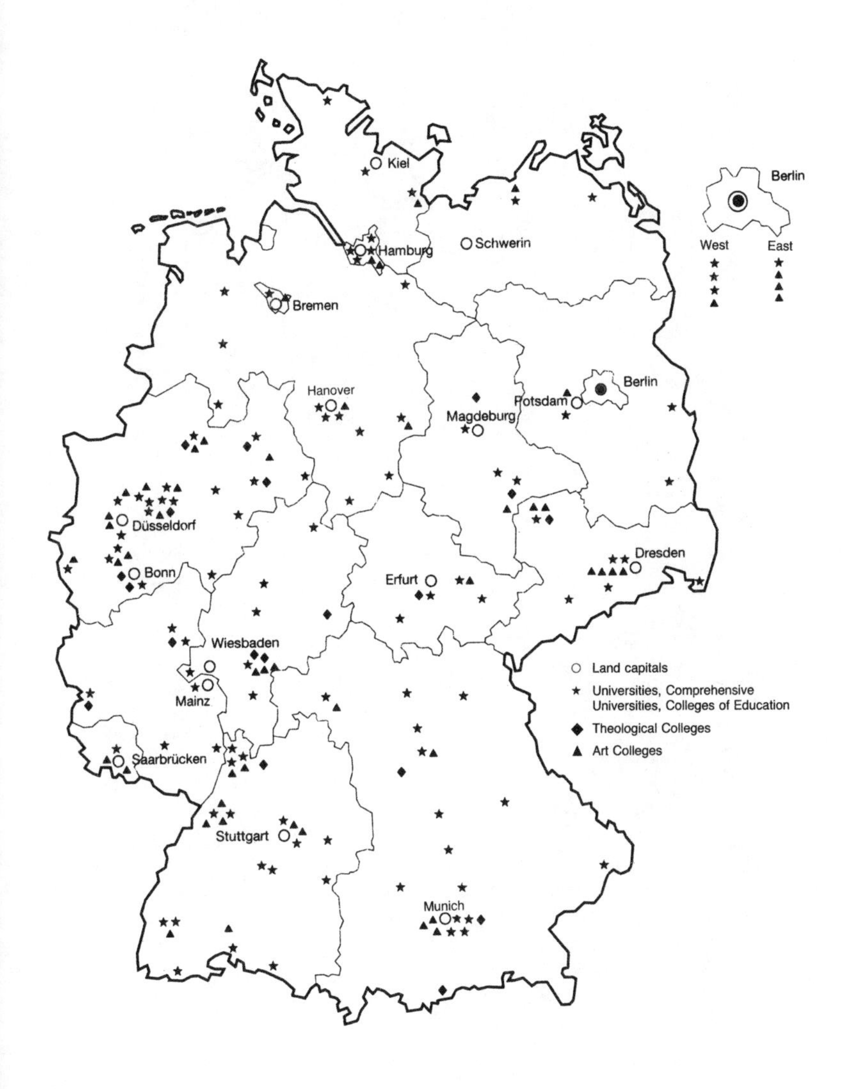

Source: Grund- und Strukturdaten 1995/96 (BMBF)

4. Location of Degree-Granting Colleges of Higher Education/ Polytechnics 1994

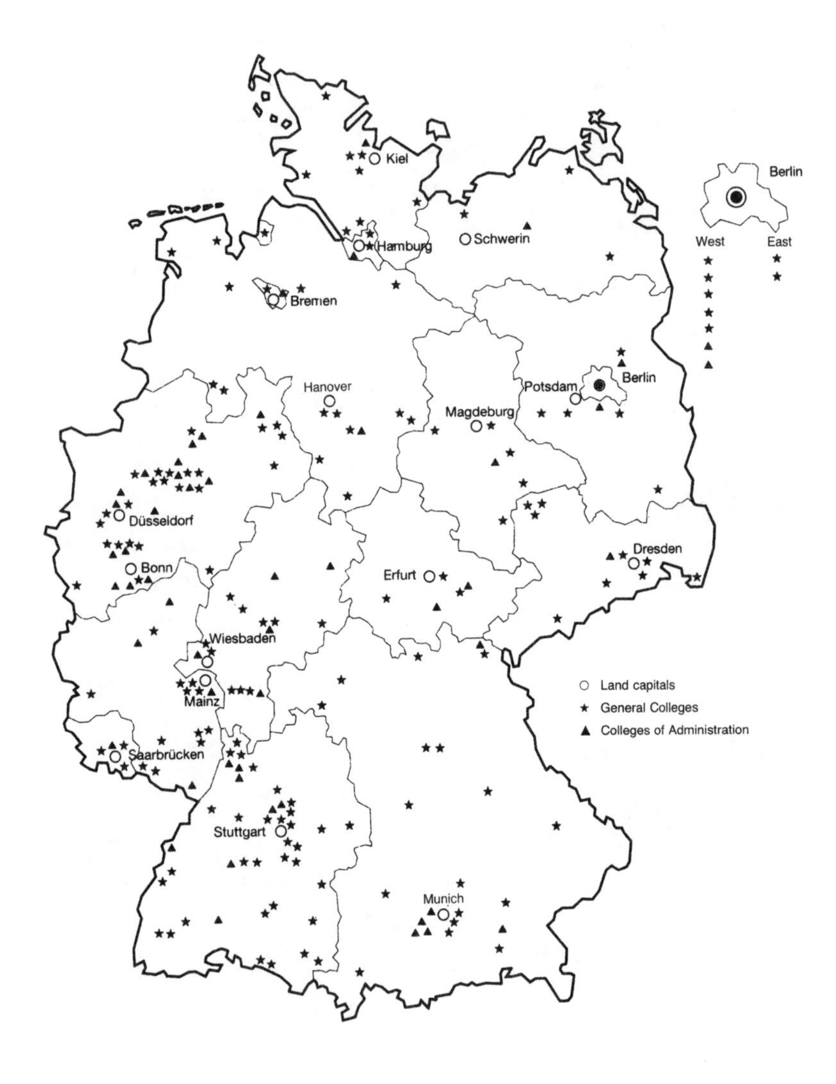

Source: Grund- und Strukturdaten 1995/96 (BMBF)

5. Pupils (in Thousands) at General Schools according to Level and Type

Year	Pupils at								
	Pre-school Level		Primary Level (Classes 1 to 4)		Secondary Level I				
	Pre-school Classes	School Kindergartens	Primary Schools	Integrated Comprehensive Schools/ Steiner Schools	Orientation Stage	Hauptschulen	Integrated Classes for pupils at Hauptschulen and Realschulen	Realschulen	Integrated Comprehensive Schools/ Steiner Schools[1])
	Old Laender								
1960	–	6.0	3096.9	3.0	–	2122.4	–	430.7	4.2
1965	–	10.9	3453.2	3.7	–	2112.5	–	570.9	4.3
1970	–	31.8	3972.5	4.7	–	2374.9	–	863.5	4.5
1975	–	84.2	3914.7	14.8	–	2510.4	–	1179.9	143.9
1980	13.0	49.2	2772.8	13.1	337.9	1933.7	–	1351.1	188.9
1981	13.8	46.9	2589.9	13.6	332.3	1853.0	–	1323.4	191.1
1982	14.4	45.4	2439.4	14.2	313.6	1748.0	–	1278.1	189.9
1983	14.6	44.1	2350.9	15.3	283.2	1611.7	–	1214.4	187.0
1984	14.5	43.7	2290.4	16.1	254.1	1460.3	–	1132.2	182.6
1985	15.3	44.8	2254.6	17.0	239.9	1332.5	–	1049.0	178.2
1986	25.5	36.8	2269.0	18.6	224.9	1227.9	–	975.5	194.5
1987	33.4	32.6	2304.0	20.0	222.9	1133.8	–	915.3	198.2
1988	32.9	33.6	2367.1	20.9	213.6	1075.8	–	875.2	207.7
1989	33.0	34.6	2448.2	25.5	210.1	1044.3	–	857.8	219.1
1990	33.7	36.3	2534.6	26.7	218.3	1054.2	–	864.6	241.1
1991	34.9	38.0	2562.7	27.4	226.8	1055.1	–	877.0	263.7
1992[3])	37.6	39.4	2669.7	28.4	264.7	1063.8	1.8	911.8	311.8
1993[3])	38.6	42.0	2731.6	29.4	267.2	1072.8	5.6	944.6	333.1
1994[3])	38.5	42.8	2816.9	29.9	266.6	1081.2	11.3	972.1	351.4
	New Laender								
1991	2.5	1.4	823.6	24.3	143.0	21.3	–	162.1	90.3
1992[4])	1.5	1.7	749.9	22.0	129.9	24.8	354.1	145.0	94.5
1993[4])	2.6	1.6	743.5	19.7	109.0	29.2	351.5	161.5	98.2
1994[4])	3.6	1.6	736.5	19.4	108.3	31.6	347.9	169.3	99.0
	Germany								
1991	37.4	39.4	3386.3	51.7	369.8	1076.4	–	1039.1	354.0
1992	39.1	41.1	3419.6	50.4	394.6	1088.6	355.9	1056.8	406.3
1993	41.1	43.6	3475.1	49.2	376.2	1102.0	357.1	1106.2	431.3
1994	42.0	44.5	3553.4	49.3	374.9	1112.8	359.2	1141.3	450.4

[1]) Classes 5 to 10. – [3]) Including East Berlin. – [4]) Not including East Berlin.

Pupils (in Thousands) at General Schools according to Level and Type (cont.)

Pupils at								Year
Secondary Level I			Secondary Level II			Special Schools		
Evening Classes at Hauptschule Level	Evening Classes at Realschule Level	Gymnasium Classes 5 to 10	Gymnasium Classes 11 to 13	Integrated Comprehensive Schools/ Steiner School[2]	Evening Gymnasium Sixth-Form Colleges	Classes for Children with Learning Difficulties	Classes for Children with Other Handicaps	
Old Laender								
–	1.9	641.7	211.7	4.2	6.9	108.5	34.4	1960
–	4.1	760.7	197.2	4.3	10.7	161.4	30.9	1965
–	8.8	1062.1	317.4	4.5	15.4	264.6	57.4	1970
–	11.5	1394.5	469.0	7.2	23.3	314.4	88.6	1975
–	8.9	1495.5	623.5	18.2	26.3	244.2	110.1	1980
–	9.4	1448.1	658.3	20.9	27.7	226.3	110.7	1981
–	9.3	1378.3	672.1	22.2	27.9	209.6	109.7	1982
–	9.2	1289.1	671.7	23.3	27.7	193.1	108.8	1983
0.7	9.1	1193.4	659.3	23.0	28.0	178.0	106.6	1984
0.7	9.1	1110.2	640.1	23.1	28.0	163.6	107.8	1985
0.6	9.8	1047.1	608.7	25.6	28.7	152.9	108.5	1986
0.7	10.9	1015.8	580.3	26.1	29.8	143.3	110.8	1987
0.7	12.8	1011.1	551.9	25.1	31.1	136.6	111.3	1988
0.7	10.7	1022.7	523.9	27.7	29.7	131.6	114.6	1989
0.8	10.8	1053.0	496.7	28.6	30.2	132.7	119.2	1990
0.8	14.9	1087.9	482.2	29.6	32.0	141.7	116.8	1991
0.9	11.3	1144.7	486.6	33.8	30.6	142.5	130.7	1992[3]
1.0	10.7	1170.6	495.9	39.0	29.0	147.0	134.2	1993[3]
1.2	11.1	1181.7	501.6	43.7	27.4	151.2	137.1	1994[3]
New Laender								
0.2	0.4	227.3	66.9	1.0	7.6	61.4	24.1	1991
0.6	0.7	340.0	75.7	2.9	4.5	62.4	24.7	1992[4]
0.0	0.7	359.9	90.0	4.4	4.2	64.2	27.0	1993[4]
0.0	0.5	356.9	108.6	6.7	4.3	66.0	28.3	1994[4]
Germany								
1.0	15.3	1315.2	549.1	30.6	39.6	203.1	140.9	1991
1.5	12.0	1484.6	562.3	36.7	35.1	204.8	155.4	1992
1.0	11.4	1530.5	586.0	43.4	33.2	211.2	161.1	1993
1.2	11.6	1538.6	610.1	50.4	31.7	217.2	165.4	1994

[1] Classes 5 to 10. – [2] Classes 11 to 13. – [3] Including East Berlin. – [4] Not including East Berlin.

Source: Grund- und Strukturdaten 1995/96 (BMBF)

6. Pupils (in Thousands) at Vocational Schools according to Level and Type

Year	Pupils at								
	Secondary Level II								
	Vocational Schools	Foundation Training Year	Basic Vocational Training Year		Vocational Extension Schools		Full-Time Vocational Schools		Berufs-, oberschulen/ Techn. Oberschulen[1])
	part-time	full-time	full-time	part-time	full-time	part-time	full-time	part-time	full-time
	Old Laender								
1960	1661.9	–	–		–	–	125.7	–	–
1965	1780.0	–	–		11.4	41.6	148.5	–	–
1970	1599.4	–	–		13.4	27.0	182.7	–	0.9
1975	1607.3	6.9	22.7		14.1	13.7	270.8	–	2.7
1980	1847.5	41.7	66.1	14.4	16.1	5.7	325.6	–	4.0
1981	1808.3	41.9	80.0	16.6	18.7	4.1	334.3	–	4.7
1982	1771.7	41.6	86.1	17.3	17.6	3.3	356.3	–	4.7
1983	1792.0	44.3	88.4	18.8	13.4	2.3	356.7	–	4.4
1984	1858.3	40.6	87.1	17.9	10.2	1.9	347.2	–	4.0
1985	1893.3	36.0	80.1	15.5	8.3	1.6	339.7	–	3.6
1986	1857.2	27.8	68.9	18.2	6.8	1.4	318.7	–	3.9
1987	1773.1	25.3	58.8	28.2	8.9	0.8	301.8	–	4.6
1988	1674.2	24.8	50.1	37.2	7.9	0.8	285.3	–	5.7
1989	1556.2	23.9	41.3	39.7	7.5	0.7	263.0	–	6.0
1990	1469.4	25.6	36.6	47.0	7.1	0.8	245.6	–	5.7
1991	1421.5	26.1	32.8	50.7	7.1	0.7	232.5	–	5.5
1992[3)]	1394.9	28.1	29.9	49.1	5.8	0.8	234.2	10.2	5.3
1993[3)]	1323.3	31.5	29.8	63.4	5.1	0.5	245.8	10.7	4.5
1994[3)]	1262.1	34.7	32.9	63.2	4.5	0.2	249.6	10.9	3.9
	New Laender								
1991	275.9	6.1	1.8	2.4	0.1	–	6.7	0.2	–
1992[4)]	283.9	9.1	1.4	0.1	–	–	19.0	0.2	–
1993[4)]	290.4	14.9	1.8	0.2	–	–	28.8	0.1	–
1994[4)]	301.7	17.0	1.9	0.1	–	–	34.5	–	–
	Germany								
1991	1697.4	32.2	34.6	53.1	7.2	0.7	239.2	0.2	5.5
1992	1678.7	37.2	31.3	49.2	5.8	0.8	253.2	10.4	5.3
1993	1613.7	46.5	31.6	63.6	5.1	0.5	274.6	10.9	4.5
1994	1563.9	51.7	34.9	63.2	4.5	0.2	284.1	10.9	3.9

[1]) Two-year full-time vocational schools awarding subject-restricted higher education entrance qualification

[3]) Including East Berlin

[4]) Not including East Berlin

Pupils (in Thousands) at Vocational Schools according to Level and Type (cont.)

Pupils at Secondary Level II: Technical Secondary Schools		Specialized Gymnasia	Trade and Technical Schools		Specialized/ Vocational Academies	Sixth-Form College[2]) (only in North-Rhine-Westphalia)		Year
full-time	part-time	full-time	full-time	part-time	full-time	full-time	part-time	
						Old Laender		
–		–	101.8		–	–	–	1960
–		–	103.9		–	–	–	1965
50.3		8.1	130.6		–	–	–	1970
90.1		28.7	100.8	6.3	9.6	–	–	1975
55.5	23.8	54.5	73.6	11.3	10.1	8.3	18.2	1980
62.9	27.0	60.7	78.7	13.4	10.5	11.2	25.2	1981
68.6	26.3	64.0	78.2	13.5	11.3	12.5	28.2	1982
63.4	23.1	63.3	73.9	14.1	11.4	13.4	34.3	1983
55.9	22.1	62.0	71.3	16.0	11.5	13.6	37.9	1984
50.5	24.2	61.1	70.5	20.2	11.5	13.1	39.3	1985
51.3	24.2	61.6	70.2	20.4	11.2	13.5	45.4	1986
54.3	24.8	62.1	74.3	23.4	10.5	13.2	44.4	1987
56.1	25.8	62.9	79.3	25.9	9.8	12.7	42.7	1988
55.5	22.2	63.0	79.7	32.2	8.1	12.9	47.6	1989
52.9	21.6	62.6	82.2	33.2	8.5	13.7	49.7	1990
54.0	21.1	63.1	84.9	35.1	8.9	14.6	52.8	1991
50.7	21.5	63.8	92.2	38.4	9.3	15.7	57.4	1992[3])
48.5	21.4	65.5	95.4	36.8	8.6	17.7	59.1	1993[3])
46.4	22.7	66.9	98.4	40.8	8.4	19.2	60.4	1994[3])
						New Laender		
1.4	0.03	7.9	20.5	5.4	–	–	–	1991
3.0	0.3	14.9	24.7	7.1	–	–	–	1992[4])
6.7	0.2	16.2	14.3	7.7	–	–	–	1993[4])
8.8	0.1	19.1	12.0	7.2	–	–	–	1994[4])
						Germany		
55.4	21.1	71.0	105.4	40.5	8.9	14.6	52.8	1991
53.7	21.8	78.7	117.0	45.4	9.3	15.7	57.4	1992
55.2	21.7	81.7	109.7	44.5	8.6	17.7	59.1	1993
55.2	22.8	85.9	110.3	48.0	8.4	19.2	60.4	1994

[2]) Schools offering general as well as vocational education.
[3]) Including East Berlin
[4]) Not including East Berlin

Source: Grund- und Strukturdaten 1995/96 (BMBF)

7. Classes and Pupil Numbers at Special Schools

Year Land	Classes and Pupils							
	Total		in classes for					
			Children with Learning Difficulties		Blind and Partially Sighted		Deaf and Hard of Hearing	
	Classes	Pupils	Classes	Pupils	Classes	Pupils	Classes	Pupils
Old Laender								
1970	19,237	322,037	14,031	264,629	254	2,544	796	7,153
1975	27,590	393,800	18,307	305,187	413	3,541	1,081	9,286
1980	29,840	354,316	17,101	244,220	494	4,026	1,378	10,858
1985	26,778	271,424	13,546	163,635	506	3,723	1,249	9,161
1990	25,624	251,897	11,455	132,668	446	3,358	1,077	7,581
1991	26,266	258,544	12,295	141,724	539	3,839	1,082	7,526
1992[1])	27,612	273,125	12,297	142,459	475	3,496	1,188	8,344
1993[1])	28,074	281,147	12,538	146,988	478	3,538	1,182	8,438
1994[1])	28,536	288,319	12,834	151,243	494	3,617	1,183	8,463
New Laender								
1990	7,329	65,488	5,579	52,416	112	854	315	2,245
1991	9,417	85,462	6,024	61,373	120	829	327	2,253
1992[2])	9,160	87,084	5,751	62,354	115	701	266	1,841
1993[2])	9,250	91,184	4,701	64,208	91	715	244	1,844
1994[2])	9,454	94,330	5,796	65,991	96	693	255	1,757
Germany								
1990	32,953	317,385	17,034	185,084	558	4,212	1,392	9,826
1991	35,683	344,006	18,319	203,097	659	4,668	1,409	9,779
1992	36,772	360,209	18,048	204,813	590	4,197	1,454	10,185
1993	37,824	372,331	17,239	211,196	569	4,253	1,426	10,282
1994	37,990	382,649	18,630	217,234	590	4,310	1,438	10,220

[1]) Including East Berlin
[2]) Not including East Berlin

Classes and Pupil Numbers at Special Schools (cont.)

Classes and Pupils in classes for: Lingustically handicapped – Classes	Lingustically handicapped – Pupils	Physically handicapped – Classes	Physically handicapped – Pupils	Mentally handicapped – Classes	Mentally handicapped – Pupils	Behaviourally disturbed – Classes	Behaviourally disturbed – Pupils	Year Land
							Old Laender	
409	5,663	515	5,499	2,060	20,455	890	12,099	1970
746	9,005	1,029	9,273	4,288	37,769	1,194	13,510	1975
1,292	14,280	1,616	13,848	5,839	47,262	1,553	14,538	1980
1,706	17,831	1,884	14,046	5,399	40,792	1,611	13,857	1985
2,047	22,168	1,967	15,144	4,922	36,988	1,838	15,692	1990
2,170	23,725	2,087	16,206	4,868	36,700	1,932	16,225	1991
2,291	24,932	2,141	16,256	4,994	37,141	2,078	17,913	1992[1])
2,335	25,550	2,164	16,654	5,159	38,843	2,094	18,013	1993[1])
2,366	26,029	2,200	16,878	5,231	39,990	2,077	17,562	1994[1])
							New Laender	
367	3,804	653	3,920	135	850	–	–	1990
430	4,698	427	2,976	1,512	9,661	217	1,644	1991
359	4,015	392	2,863	1,757	11,404	437	3,185	1992[2])
290	4,701	276	2,645	1,596	12,960	328	3,123	1993[2])
439	4,912	315	2,446	2,013	13,943	424	3,493	1994[2])
							Germany	
2,414	25,972	2,620	19,064	5,057	37,838	1,838	15,692	1990
2,600	28,423	2,514	19,182	6,380	46,361	2,149	17,869	1991
2,650	28,947	2,533	19,119	6,751	48,845	2,515	21,098	1992
2,625	30,251	2,440	19,299	6,755	51,803	2,422	21,136	1993
2,805	30,941	2,515	19,324	7,244	53,933	2,501	21,055	1994

[1]) Including East Berlin
[2]) Not including East Berlin

Source: Grund- und Strukturdaten 1995/96 (BMBF)

8. Pupils Learning Foreign Languages (Type of School and Level nationwide 1993)

Class Level		English	French	Latin	Greek	Spanish	Italian	Russian	Turkish	Other
Primary School		136,493	65,216			175	274	972		3,993
Orientation Level		371,366	3,172	1,239	30	17		227	67	138
Hauptschule		1,021,259	14,244	17	110	53	32	5,973	1,012	2,092
Integrated Classes for Haupt- and Realschulen		335,603	19,307	193		18		65,702		2,134
Realschulen		1,091,586	280,104	335	36	2,151	881	81,435	594	6,389
Gymnasium	Secondary Level I	1,481,509	662,280	439,518	6,778	14,367	5,092	157,121	726	2,376
	Secondary Level II	518,288	213,660	131,778	6,973	25,676	7,146	53,974	445	4,067
	Total	1,999,797	875,940	571,296	13,751	40,043	12,238	211,095	1,171	6,443
Integrated Comprehensives	Primary Level	1,627	66					12	129	
	Secondary Level I	394,126	80,485	16,614	103	4,508	829	43,875	5,691	632
	Secondary Level II	31,538	9,447	4,580	41	3,781	716	5,393	434	138
	Total	427,291	89,998	21,194	144	8,289	1,545	49,280	6,254	770
Steiner Schools	Primary Level	20,476	12,550			8		7,116		120
	Secondary Level I	27,936	18,832	2,522	545	5		7,336		79
	Secondary Level II	8,387	5,106	969				1,629		
	Total	56,799	36,488	3,491	545	13		16,081		199
Special Schools		31,796	757	233	15	14	1	1,584	509	105

Source: Statistisches Bundesamt 1995; W. Böttcher, K. Klemm (Ed.): Bildung in Zahlen, 1995

9. Percentages of Pupils Learning Foreign Languages at General Schools (1982 and 1993)[1]

Languages	1982 Pupils	%	1993 Pupils	%
Total Pupils	5,604,064		5,532,336	
Learning as First or Additional Language:				
English	5,241,211	93.53	5,281,598	95.47
French	1,403,013	25.04	1,306,637	23.62
Latin	805,283	14.37	597,765	10.80
Greek	27,837	0.50	14,616	0.26
Russian	23,023	0.41	422,665	7.64
Spanish	29,685	0.53	50,576	0.91
Italian	7,772	0.14	14,696	0.27
Other	21,238	0.38	27,017	0.49

1993 inclusive of the New Laender.

[1]) Without Pre-, Primary, Special, or Evening Schools.

Source: Statistisches Bundesamt, Fachserie 11, Reihe 1

10. Percentage of Pupils Learning Foreign Languages at Vocational Schools (1982 and 1993)

Languages	1982 Pupils	%	1993 Pupils	%
Total Pupils	2,596,389		2,446,961	
Learning as First or Additional Language:				
English	497,476	19.16	586,525	23.97
French	77,346	2.98	85,768	3.51
Latin	1,133	0.04	1,228	0.05
Greek	43	0.00	13	0.00
Russian	495	0.02	12,637	0.52
Spanish	27,525	1.06	35,291	1.44
Italian	310	0.01	335	0.01
Other	1,641	0.06	1,001	0.04

1993 inclusive of the New Laender.

Source: Statistisches Bundesamt, Fachserie 11, Reihe 2

11. Percentage of Girls in School-Leavers according to Type of Qualification Obtained

Year	Leavers who have completed Compulsory Full-time Schooling				Leavers with Realschule Certificate or Equivalent		
	Total	of which			Total	of which from	
		without Hauptschule Certificate		with Hauptschule Certificate		General Schools	Vocational Schools
		Total	of which from Special Schools	Total			
Old Laender							
1967	48.9	44.3	22.0	50.3	50.5	52.9	43.8
1970	47.9	44.5	22.6	49.3	51.6	52.5	49.3
1975	45.9	40.8	34.0	47.4	54.7	54.7	54.6
1976	45.6	40.5	34.5	47.3	53.7	53.4	55.1
1977	45.5	40.1	37.0	47.1	54.4	54.5	54.0
1978	45.1	39.7	38.2	46.8	55.1	55.0	55.6
1979	44.8	39.2	38.7	46.3	55.4	55.0	57.6
1980	44.1	38.1	40.0	45.8	55.4	54.7	58.8
1981	44.6	36.2	37.4	46.6	55.2	54.4	59.7
1982	43.7	38.4	39.0	45.3	55.0	53.3	60.7
1983	43.9	39.1	38.8	45.2	54.9	53.8	59.4
1984	43.5	39.2	38.1	44.5	54.7	53.7	59.5
1985	43.7	39.4	38.6	44.6	55.0	53.9	60.9
1986	43.6	39.7	38.7	44.4	53.8	52.9	58.7
1987	43.8	39.8	38.6	44.6	53.6	53.0	56.9
1988	43.3	38.9	38.9	44.3	52.3	52.7	56.4
1989	43.2	39.0	39.1	44.3	52.7	52.6	51.9
1990	43.1	38.9	39.1	44.2	52.3	52.4	52.0
1991	43.0	38.2	38.7	44.4	52.1	52.4	50.7
1992[1]	42.8	37.9	38.1	44.2	52.0	52.1	51.3
1993[1]	42.8	37.1	37.4	44.4	51.8	52.3	49.0
1994[1]	42.7	37.4	37.6	44.1	51.8	52.3	49.4
New Laender							
1992[2]	34.7	29.8	35.5	37.8	50.7	50.7	49.3
1993[2]	34.3	30.7	35.1	36.9	49.5	49.5	47.8
1994[2]	33.5	30.4	33.4	35.8	50.2	50.1	50.9
Germany							
1992	42.4	36.7	37.8	43.8	51.7	51.8	51.3
1993	41.6	35.6	36.9	43.6	51.3	51.6	48.9
1994	41.2	35.6	36.4	43.1	51.4	51.7	49.7

[1]) Including East Berlin
[2]) Not including East Berlin

Percentage of Girls in School-Leavers according to Type of Qualification Obtained (cont.)

Leavers with Entrance Qualification for Institutions of Higher Education									Year
Total			University Entrance Qualification			Polytechnic Entrance Qualification			
Total	of which from		Total	of which from		Total	of which from		
	General Schools	Vocational Schools		General Schools	Vocational Schools		General Schools	Vocational Schools	
Old Laender									
36.5	36.6	27.3	36.5	36.6	27.3	–	–	–	1967
39.4	39.6	33.8	39.4	39.6	33.8	–	–	–	1970
39.9	45.9	26.6	45.9	45.9	39.9	23.5	42.0	23.2	1975
41.7	47.2	28.2	47.2	47.2	38.7	25.7	44.4	25.3	1976
42.8	47.0	31.6	47.2	47.1	40.5	29.5	45.1	29.1	1977
44.3	47.3	36.2	47.5	47.3	40.4	37.6	43.6	35.1	1978
42.9	45.7	36.5	45.8	45.7	38.3	38.7	45.9	36.0	1979
45.4	48.3	38.1	48.5	48.3	38.5	38.5	50.3	37.9	1980
46.4	49.5	38.6	48.6	49.5	39.6	39.4	51.8	38.3	1981
46.3	49.7	37.9	48.9	49.7	40.1	38.6	52.4	37.4	1982
46.4	50.0	38.0	49.1	49.8	41.9	38.4	54.5	36.9	1983
46.9	50.6	37.8	49.6	50.5	42.2	38.4	45.5	36.7	1984
47.4	50.4	39.8	49.3	50.1	40.7	41.2	58.1	39.5	1985
47.4	50.1	40.1	49.2	50.0	40.3	41.4	55.3	40.0	1986
47.2	50.0	40.1	49.1	49.9	40.8	40.9	52.8	39.9	1987
46.4	50.0	38.0	49.1	50.0	40.1	38.3	51.5	37.4	1988
46.0	49.9	37.7	48.8	49.8	39.8	38.1	52.1	37.0	1989
46.3	50.7	37.3	49.5	50.6	39.4	37.8	50.9	36.7	1990
46.6	51.0	38.0	50.0	51.0	41.5	37.9	50.3	36.9	1991
46.7	51.4	37.8	50.4	51.5	42.0	37.4	48.5	36.4	1992[1)]
47.8	52.0	39.9	50.9	52.0	42.7	40.0	52.1	39.0	1993[1)]
48.6	52.4	41.3	51.3	52.4	43.0	41.7	51.6	40.7	1994[1)]
New Laender									
53.8	58.3	41.7	53.3	58.2	31.6	56.4	29.0	57.1	1992[2)]
56.2	59.3	43.3	57.1	59.3	37.6	51.4	60.9	50.8	1993[2)]
57.3	59.7	49.2	58.9	59.7	50.3	49.1	58.2	48.6	1994[2)]
Germany									
46.7	52.3	38.1	50.8	52.3	39.7	38.3	48.2	37.5	1992
49.1	53.4	40.2	52.1	53.4	41.8	40.7	52.5	39.7	1993
49.9	53.6	42.1	52.5	53.6	43.9	42.3	51.9	41.5	1994

1) Including East Berlin
2) Not including East Berlin

Source: Grund- und Strukturdaten 1995/96 (BMBF)

12. Teachers[1]) at General Schools according to Level and Type

Year Land	Pre-school		Primary Level (Classes 1 to 4)		Secondary Level I				
	Pre-school Classes	School Kindergartens	Primary Schools	Integrated Comprehensive Schools/ Steiner Schools	Orientation Level	Hauptschulen	Integrated Classes for Haupt- and Realschule Pupils	Realschulen	Integrated Comprehensive Schools/ Steiner Schools[4])
Old Laender									
1984	1,585	2,933	110,743	1,184	14,036	92,005	–	60,550	14,315
1985	1,579	2,968	111,538	1,227	14,101	88,885	–	59,808	14,670
1986	1,618	2,975	112,977	1,252	14,485	84,634	–	57,686	15,394
1987	1,637	3,068	115,085	1,224	15,029	80,448	–	56,052	16,152
1988	1,655	3,076	116,292	1,339	14,532	77,568	–	54,582	17,192
1989	1,728	4,252	120,786	1,352	14,368	75,224	–	53,695	18,016
1990	1,736	4,339	123,618	1,428	14,636	73,837	–	53,377	19,336
1991[2])	2,018	4,494	130,461	1,545	17,463	73,566	–	54,203	23,295
1992[2])	2,094	4,633	132,656	1,537	17,207	72,453	134	54,188	24,889
1993[2])	2,105	4,845	133,741	1,596	16,696	72,941	417	54,817	25,578
1994[2])	2,083	4,950	135,483	1,598	16,379	72,841	735	55,230	26,376
New Laender									
1992[2])	51	214	38,704	1,015	7,072	2,414	26,445	10,823	4,202
1993[2])	121	122	36,101	906	6,520	2,741	23,918	10,950	7,421
1994[2])	204	120	36,222	879	6,510	2,962	23,905	10,832	7,531
Germany									
1992	2,145	4,847	171,360	2,552	24,279	74,867	26,579	65,009	29,091
1993	2,226	4,963	169,842	2,502	23,220	75,684	24,335	65,410	33,001
1994	2,287	5,070	171,705	2,477	22,889	75,803	24,640	66,062	33,907

[1]) Full-time teachers and part-time teachers on full-time basis
[2]) Including East Berlin. – [3]) Without East Berlin
[4]) Classes 5 to 10.

Teachers[1]) at General Schools according to Level and Type (cont.)

Secondary Level I				Secondary Level II			Special Schools		Year Land
Evening Classes at Hauptschule Level	Evening Classes at Realschule Level	Gymnasium		Integrated Comprehensive Schools/ Steiner Schools[5])	Evening Gymnasium	Sixth-Form College	Classes for Children with Learning Difficulties	Classes for Children with other Handicaps	
		Classes 5 to 10	Classes 11 to 13						
								Old Laender	
26	432	67,514	55,602	2,622	1,154	1,140	19,400	20,937	1984
31	439	65,345	56,608	2,562	1,164	1,126	18,582	21,580	1985
39	427	64,547	55,712	2,659	1,200	1,168	18,022	21,763	1986
42	476	64,150	54,048	2,499	1,244	1,210	17,330	21,662	1987
50	523	64,914	51,492	2,671	1,314	1,263	16,906	21,942	1988
52	568	66,695	49,406	2,767	1,331	1,307	16,330	22,595	1989
45	613	68,970	46,981	2,843	1,380	1,349	16,505	23,204	1990
69	666	70,777	47,967	3,287	1,440	1,454	17,113	24,553	1991[2])
48	572	71,675	46,687	3,534	1,429	1,414	17,370	25,216	1992[2])
53	552	72,497	45,719	3,817	1,344	1,362	17,705	25,549	1993[2])
58	538	71,995	45,264	4,155	1,294	1,332	17,844	25,763	1994[2])
								New Laender	
–	92	20,912	6,162	264	138	74	9,094	4,579	1992[3])
–	35	20,020	7,313	367	141	147	8,100	5,074	1993[3])
–	30	19,893	8,734	581	181	136	8,162	5,335	1994[3])
								Germany	
48	664	92,587	52,813	3,798	1,567	1,488	26,464	29,795	1992
52	584	92,489	53,063	4,184	1,480	1,509	25,806	30,625	1993
58	568	91,888	53,998	4,736	1,468	1,468	26,006	31,098	1994

[1]) Full-time teachers and part-time teachers on full-time basis
[2]) Including East Berlin. – [3]) Without East Berlin
[4]) Classes 5 to 10.
[5]) Classes 11 to 13

Source: KMK; Grund- und Strukturdaten 1995/96 (BMBF)

13. Teachers[1]) at Vocational Schools according to Level and Type

Year Land	Secondary Level II							
	Voca-tional Schools	Foundation Training Year	Basic Vocational Training Year		Vocational Extension Schools		Full-Time Vocational Schools	Technical Secondary Schools
	part-time	full-time	full-time	part-time	full-time	part-time	full-time	full-time
	Old Laender							
1984	35,925	3,492	6,421	443	699	41	23,731	320
1985	37,099	3,365	6,316	435	602	39	23,608	306
1986	38,079	2,952	5,828	546	508	37	23,051	305
1987	36,849	2,954	5,756	873	673	27	23,136	381
1988	36,849	2,913	5,196	1,197	604	28	22,703	452
1989	36,716	2,971	4,791	1,322	586	27	21,583	479
1990	36,663	3,217	4,241	1,556	560	27	20,856	473
1991[2])	37,158	3,321	3,760	1,674	567	21	20,594	468
1992[2])	36,836	3,436	3,354	1,700	497	22	20,302	458
1993[2])	36,330	3,774	3,181	2,143	430	16	20,011	419
1994[2])	34,029	4,029	3,374	2,163	375	9	20,615	369
	New Laender							
1992[3])	8,856	712	110	7	–	–	1,292	–
1993[3])	8,268	874	114	7	1	–	2,134	–
1994[3])	7,816	1,118	142	2	–	–	2,601	–
	Germany							
1992	45,692	4,148	3,464	1,707	497	22	21,594	458
1993	44,598	4,648	3,295	2,150	431	16	22,145	419
1994	41,845	5,147	3,516	2,165	375	9	23,216	369

[1]) Full-time teachers and part-time teachers on full-time basis
[2]) Including East Berlin
[3]) Without East Berlin

Teachers[1]) at Vocational Schools according to Level and Type (cont.)

Secondary Level II									Year Land
Technical Upper Schools		Specialized Gymnasia	Trade and Technical Schools		Specialized/ Vocational Academies	Sixth-Form College (only in North Rhine-Westphalia)			
full-time	part-time	full-time	full-time	part-time	full-time	full-time	part-time		
							Old Laender		
3,852	691	4,655	5,115	406	872	1,035	835		1984
3,622	769	7,462	5,253	507	898	1,058	844		1985
3,730	736	4,785	5,436	573	927	1,089	1,053		1986
3,926	764	4,927	5,698	677	945	1,102	1,058		1987
4,104	792	5,081	6,133	685	939	1,107	995		1988
4,177	773	5,144	6,339	811	979	1,212	1,098		1989
4,133	758	5,230	6,442	962	999	1,307	1,231		1990
4,197	775	5,459	6,789	1,048	1,033	1,393	1,355		1991[2])
4,071	782	5,464	7,296	1,277	1,069	1,473	1,506		1992[2])
3,925	760	5,512	7,420	1,295	1,058	1,477	1,681		1993[2])
3,747	826	5,537	8,089	1,438	1,060	1,711	1,638		1994[2])
							New Laender		
223	25	1,304	1,728	123	–	–	–		1992[3])
350	30	1,223	1,071	172	–	–	–		1993[3])
523	4	1,551	932	196	–	–	–		1994[3])
							Germany		
4,294	807	6,768	9,024	1,400	1,069	1,473	1,506		1992
4,343	790	6,931	8,656	1,518	1,058	1,477	1,681		1993
4,270	830	7,088	9,021	1,634	1,060	1,711	1,638		1994

[1]) Full-time teachers and part-time teachers on full-time basis
[2]) Including East Berlin
[3]) Without East Berlin

Source: KMK; Grund- und Strukturdaten 1995/96 (BMBF)

14. Students according to Institution of Higher Education

Year[1])	Students					
	Total		of which			
			Universities	Colleges of Art and Music	Polytechnics	
					Total	of which Colleges of Public Administration
	Thousands	Per Cent[2])	Thousands	Thousands	Thousands	Thousands
	GERMAN AND FOREIGN					
	Old Laender					
1960	291.1	4.3	238.4	8.5	44.2	–
1965	384.4	6.6	299.7	8.7	76.0	–
1970	510.5	9.5	410.1	10.9	89.5	–
1975	840.8	14.1	680.2	15.4	145.2	2.9
1980	1,044.2	15.9	823.9	18.3	202.0	27.0
1985	1,338.0	18.1	1,015.1	21.7	301.3	32.4
1990	1,585.2	22.0	1,188.3	24.2	372.6	39.6
1992	1,681.1	25.2	1,259.3	24.6	397.2	44.7
1993	1,711.9	27.2	1,280.4	25.0	406.4	47.4
1994	1,676.1	28.8	1,253.4	24.5	398.2	45.3
	New Laender					
1990	132.2	8.5	126.1	6.1	–	–
1992	142.1	10.4	114.9	4.6	22.6	2.9
1993	163.3	12.5	121.9	4.8	36.6	5.4
1994	180.5	14.4	128.8	5.2	46.5	7.0
	Germany					
1990	1,717.4	19.6	1,314.5	30.4	–	–
1991	1,782.7	21.2	1,355.8	29.3	397.7	44.5
1992	1,823.1	22.6	1,374.2	29.2	419.8	47.5
1993	1,875.2	24.6	1,402.3	29.9	443.0	52.8
1994	1,856.5	26.2	1,382.2	29.7	444.7	52.3

[1]) Winter semester
[2]) As percentage of the population aged between 19 and 26

Source: Grund- und Strukturdaten 1995/96 (BMBF)

15. Number of Students (in Thousands) according to Institution of Higher Education in the Old Laender 1965–1995

Year	Universities		Colleges of Art		Fachhochschulen		Total	
	New Entrants	Total Students	New Entrants	Total Students	New Entrants	Total Students	New Entrants	Total Students
1965	61.3	299.7	2.5	8.7	21.9	76	85.7	384.4
1970	91.6	410.1	3.4	10.9	30.5	89.5	125.5	510.5
1975	119.9	680.2	2.8	15.4	42.4	142.3	165.1	837.9
1977	118.2	732.7	2.7	15.4	40.9	155.2	161.8	903.3
1980	135.6	823.9	3.1	18.3	44.8	175	183.5	1,017.2
1983	160.1	976.6	2.9	20.4	60.2	241.6	223.2	1,238.6
1985	141.3	1,015.1	3	21.7	53.5	268.9	197.8	1,305.7
1988	169.8	1,104.5	3	23.2	61.8	306.2	234.6	1,433.9
1990	194.9	1,188.3	3.1	24.2	67.5	333.6	265.5	1,546.1
1991	185.1	1,232.8	2.9	24.5	68.1	345.9	256.1	1,603.2
1992	171.7	1,263.5	3	24.6	65	352.5	239.7	1,640.6
1993	162.3	1,297.7	3	24.8	70	351.7	235.3	1,674.2
1994	150.5	1,273.5	4	27.3	64	361.7	218.5	1,662.5
1995	148.2	1,252.7	4.1	27.8	63.6	355.7	215.9	1,636.2

Source: Hochschulrektorenkonferenz

16. Staffing (in Thousands) according to Institution of Higher Education and Status (1960–1995)

Year	Staffing						
	Total	of which					
		Scholarly Staff					Non-Scholarly Staff
		Total	Students per Teacher	Professions	Other Scholarly Staff	For Special Tasks	
	Total[1]) Old Laender						
1960	62.0	19.1	15	5.5	13.7		42.9
1965	100.3	36.6	11	9.4	27.2		63.7
1970	141.9	54.5	9	14.9	39.4		87.4
1975	205.0	78.1	11	30.5	46.9		126.9
1980	214.5	79.0	13	32.9	42.6	3.6	135.8
1985	222.7	80.6	17	33.6	43.8	3.3	142.1
1986	223.7	81.0	17	33.7	44.0	3.3	142.7
1987	228.6	81.8	17	34.0	44.5	3.3	146.9
1988	232.4	82.7	18	33.4	46.0	3.2	149.8
1989	238.8	85.1	17	32.3	49.5	3.3	151.9
1990	243.3	86.5	18	33.0	50.3	3.2	156.8
1991	248.2	86.9	19	33.0	50.7	3.2	161.3
1992	254.5	89.0	18	33.8	54.3	3.0	163.0
1993	257.7	90.2	19	34.2	55.3	3.0	165.6
1994	258.8	90.3	19	34.1	55.4	2.9	166.6
1995	260.6	90.8		34.1	55.9	2.9	168.3
	New Laender						
1991	94.0	33.3	4	1.6	31.4	0.3	60.7
1992	74.8	26.7	5	7.3	19.4	0.2	47.9
1993	69.4	24.9	7	7.6	17.3	0.2	44.3
1994	65.4	23.4	8	7.6	15.6	0.5	41.7
1995	64.5	23.1		7.7	15.3	0.4	41.4
	Germany						
1991	342.2	120.2	15	34.6	82.1	3.5	222.0
1992	329.3	115.7	15	41.1	73.7	3.2	211.0
1993	327.1	115.1	16	41.7	72.6	3.3	209.9
1994	324.2	113.7	16	41.7	71.0	3.4	208.4
1995	325.2	113.9		41.8	71.2	3.3	209.7

[1]) Including staff in libraries, computer centres, administration, central facilities, etc.

Source: Wissenschaftsrat; Erhebung der Personalstellen an den in das Verzeichnis des Hochschulbauförderungsgesetzes aufgenommenen staatlichen Hochschulen; Grund- und Strukturdaten 1995/96 (BMBF)

17. University Qualifications in the Old Laender 1965–1992

Year	Diploma and equivalents	Doctorates	Teaching qualifi-cations	Diplomas at Fachhoch-schulen	Total
1965	25,500	6,971	17,100	16,200	65,771
1970	30,100	11,300	25,800	19,800	87,000
1975	33,669	11,418	40,349	31,865	117,301
1980	46,331	12,222	30,452	34,675	123,680
1983	54,766	13,637	27,368	41,893	137,664
1985	61,083	14,951	22,883	48,003	146,920
1988	74,458	17,321	13,692	53,661	159,132
1990	81,524	18,494	10,231	55,852	166,101
1991	83,007	19,022	11,057	58,855	171,941
1992	85,998	20,038	11,325	60,588	177,949

Percentages

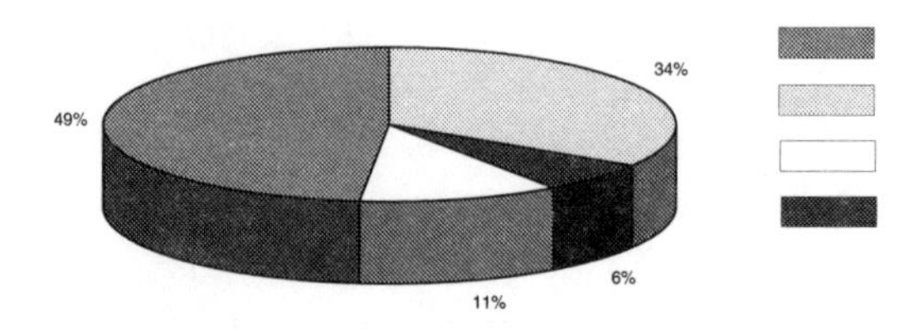

Source: Hochschulrektorenkonferenz

18. Primary School Timetable (Baden-Württemberg)

Subject[1]	Class			
	1	2	3	4
Religious Studies[2]	2	2	2	2
German	6	6	7	7
Local Studies	3	3	3	3
Mathematics	4	5	5	5
Art/Textiles and Crafts[3]	1	2	3	3
Music	1	1	1	1
Sport[4]	3	3	3	3
	20	22	24	24
Special Coaching/Remedial Teaching	2	2	3	3

[1]) Individual subjects' share in the total number of lessons can be changed for short periods in conjunction with specific projects, but balance must be maintained during the overall school year.

[2]) Weekly lessons in Religious Education accord with the church authorities without infringing religious liberties.

[3]) In classes 3 and 4 there are two lessons a week for one aspect and one for the other, alternating half-yearly.

[4]) In classes where the third sports lesson is not yet possible, this is replaced by music or art.

19. Timetable for Secondary Schools – Orientation Level (Saxony-Anhalt)

April 1993

Lessons at class level	5	6
German	5	5
1st Foreign Language	5	4
Mathematics	5	5
Biology	2	1
Physics	0	2
Geography	2	2
History	1	1
Ethics/Religion	2	2
Crafts	1	2
Sport	3	3
Music	1	2
Art	1	1
Obligatory	28	30
Remedial Teaching/Options/Study-Groups	2	2
Max. Lessons	30	32

20. Timetable for Secondary Schools – Hauptschule (Saxony-Anhalt)

April 1993

Lessons at class level	7	8	9
German	4	4	3
Foreign Language	3	4	3
Mathematics	4	4	4
Biology	1	1	2
Physics	1	1	2
Chemistry	1	1	2
Geography	1	1	1
History	2	1	1
Social Studies	0	1	1
Ethics/Religion	2	2	2
Economics/Technology	2	2	2
Domestic Science	2	2	1
Sport	2	2	2
Music	1	1	1
Art	1	1	2
Options among compulsory subjects	2	2	2
Obligatory	29	30	31
Remedial Teaching/Options/Study-Groups	2	2	2
Max. Lessons	31	32	33

21. Timetable for Secondary Schools – Realschule (Saxony-Anhalt)

April 1993

Lessons at class level	7	8	9	10
German	4	4	3	3
1st Foreign Language	3	4	3	3
Mathematics	4	4	4	3
Biology	1	2	1	2
Physics	2	1	2	2
Chemistry	1	2	2	1
Astronomy	0	0	0	1
Geography	1	1	2	1
History	2	1	2	2
Social Studies	0	1	1	2
Ethics/Religion	2	2	2	2
Economics/Technology	1	1	1	1
Domestic Science	0.5	0.5	0.5	0.5
Sport	2	2	2	2
Music	1	1	1	2
Art	2	1	2	2
Options among compulsory subjects	2	2	2	2
Obligatory	28.5	29.5	30.5	31.5
Remedial Teaching/Options/Study-Groups	2	2	2	2
Max. Lessons	30.5	31.5	32.5	33.5

22. Timetable for Classes 5–10 at General Schools (Hesse)

Weekly Schedule

	Class						
	5	6	7	8	9	10	Total
German	5	5	4	4	3	3	24
1st Foreign Language	5	5	4	3	3	3	23
Mathematics	4	4	4	4	4	3	23
Sport	3	3	3	2+2[1])	2	2	16
Religious Studies	2	2	2	2	2	2	12
Classes in the Arts							
Art	2	2	2[1])	2[1])	2[1])	2[1])	8
Music	2	2	2[1])	2[1])	2[1])	2[1])	8
Classes in the Natural Sciences							19
Biology	2	2	2[1])	2[1])	2[1])	2[1])	8
Chemistry	–	–	–	2[1])	2[1])	2	5
Physics	–	–	2	2[1])	2[1])	2	6
Classes in Social Studies							20
Geography	2[1])	2	–	2[1])	2[1])	2[1])	6
History	–	–	2	2	2[1])	2	7
Sociology	2[1])	2	2[1])	2[1])	1 } 2[2])	2[1])	7
Work Studies	–	–	2	2	1 }	2[1])	6
Options among compulsory subjects[3]) (including a 2nd and 3rd Foreign Language)	–	–	3/4	3/4	6/7	5/6	17/21
Teacher's Choice	1						
Total incl.:	28	29	30/31	30/31	30/31	30/31	177/181
Free Choice	(2)	(2)					
Lessons in the Mother Tongue	3–5	3–5	3–5	3–5	3–5	3–5	18–30

cont.

Remedial Teaching/ Options	2	2	2	2	2	2	12
Lessons obligatory and optional at full-day schools[4]) up to:	4	4	4	4	4	4	24

[1]) = half-yearly alternation

[2]) = due to be combined as a double lesson because of linked subject-matter

[3]) = with the following alternatives

either:

Class	5	6	7	8	9	10	tot.
2nd Foreign Language	–	–	4	4	4	3	15
Options	–	–	–	–	2+	2+	4

or:

Class	5	6	7	8	9	10	tot.
Options	–	–	3	3	4+2+	3+2+	17

+ = 3 lessons weekly for 3rd Language, 5 for Classical Greek.

[4]) = depending on the number of afternoons and school-concept.

23. Timetable at Hauptschule (North Rhine-Westphalia)

Class	5	6	7	8	9	10	Total no. lessons/week 180
Pupil lessons per week*)	28–30	28–30	29–31	29–31	30–32	30–32	
Subject Categories							
German	5–6	4–6	4–5	4–5	4–5	4–5	25–27
Social Studies[1][2] History, Geography, Politics	2–3	4–5	3–4	3–4	3–4	3–4	18–22
Mathematics	4–5	4–5	4–5	4–5	4–5	3–4	23–25
Natural Sciences[1][2] Biology, Physics, Chemistry	4–5	3–4	2–4	3–4	3–4	2–4	17–21
English	5–6	5–6	4–5	3–4	3–4	3–4	23–25
Work Studies[1][3] Technology, Economics, Domestic Science	–	–	2–4	2–4	3–4	3–4	11–13
Art, Music, Textile Design[1][4]	3–4	3–4	2–4	2–4	2–3	2–3	15–18
Religious Studies	2	2	2	2	2	2	12
Sport	2–4	2–4	2–4	2–4	2–4	2–4	17–19
Options among compulsory subjects[5]	–	–	2	2	2–4	2–4	8–12/5–9[6]
Extra Tuition	–	–	–	–	1–3	1–3	2–3/5–6[6]

Notes:

*) At least a combined total of 57 lessons a week is envisaged for classes 5 and 6 (KMK-Vereinbarung, 28. 2. 1974).

1) Individual subjects should be equally weighted within each category.

2) In the Social Studies (History, Geography, Politics) and Natural Sciences (Biology, Physics, Chemistry) categories, specialized courses and interdisciplinary projects alternate.

3) In classes 5 and 6 the subject-matter of the Work Studies (Technology, Economics, Domestic Science) category is included in the categories of Social Studies (economics) and Natural Sciences (technology).

4) In the category Art/Music/Textile Design at least 7 lessons weekly are envisaged for classes 5 and 6 (KMK-Vereinbarung, 28. 2. 1974). These subjects are options in classes 9 and 10.

5) All subjects can be offered in classes 7 and 8. Work Studies and Natural Sciences are available in classes 9 and 10.

6) Type A/Type B

24. Timetable at Realschule (North Rhine-Westphalia)

Class	5	6	7	8	9	10	Total no. lessons/week
Pupil lessons per week*)	28–30	28–30	29–31	29–31	30–32	30–32	180
Subject Categories							
German	4–5	4–5	4–5	4–5	4–5	3–4	23–25
Social Studies[1])[2])	3–4	4–5	4–5	4–5	3–4	3–5	21–25
History, Geography, Politics							
Mathematics	4–5	4–5	4–5	4–5	3–4	4–5	23–25
Natural Sciences[1])	3–4	3–4	3–5	3–5	3–4	3–4	21–25
Biology, Physics, Chemistry							
English	5–6	5–6	4–5	4–5	4–5	3–4	25–27
Technology, Economics, Domestic Science[2])	–	–	–	–	–	–	–
Art, Music, Textile Design[1])	4–5	3–4	2–4	2–4	2–4	2–4	16–20
Religious Studies	2	2	2	2	2	2	12
Sport	2–4	2–4	2–4	2–4	2–4	2–4	17–19
Options among compulsory subjects[3])	–	–	3–4	3–4	3–4	3–4	12–14
Options among compulsory subjects II	–	–	–	–	2–3	2–3	4–6

Notes:

*) At least a combined total of 57 lessons a week is envisaged for classes 5 and 6 (KMK-Vereinbarung, 28. 2. 1974).

[1]) Individual subjects should be equally weighted within each category. History is taught from class 6 and Chemistry from class 7.

[2]) Technology and Domestic Science are covered in options among compulsory subjects, and Economics in Social Studies and options among compulsory subjects.

[3]) French (Dutch), Social Sciences, and Technology are offered in classes 7 to 10 (options among compulsory subjects). At least 14 lessons a week are envisaged for the second foreign language. Special regulations apply to organization of options.

25. Gymnasium Timetable (Bavaria)

A. Classical/Gymnasium

Classes	5	6	7	8	9	10	11
Obligatory Subjects[1])							
Religious Studies/Ethics[2])[17])	2	2	2	2	2	2	2
German[3])	5	5	4	4	3	3	4
Latin[3])	6	6	4	4	3	3	4
English[3])	–	–	5	4	3	3	4
Greek[3])	–	–	–	–	5	5	5
Mathematics[3])	4	4	4	4	3	3	3
Physics[3])	–	–	–	2	1	2	2
Chemistry	–	–	–	–	–	–	2
Biology	2	2	2	1	2	2	–
History	–	2	2	2	2	2/1[14])	2
Geography	2	2	1	2	1	–	2
Social Studies	–	–	–	–	–	1/2[15])	–
Economics and Law	–	–	–	1	1	1	–
Art	2	3	2	1	1	1[6])	1
Music	3[5])	2	2	1	1	1[6])	1
Sport[4])[17])	2+2	2+2	2+2	2+2	2+2	2+2	2+2
	28+2	30+2	30+2	30+2	30+2	30+2	34+2

B. Modern Languages Gymnasium (Latin as 1st Foreign Language)

Classes	5	6	7	8	9	10	11
Obligatory Subjects[1]							
Religious Studies/Ethics[2][17]	2	2	2	2	2	2	2
German[3]	5	5	4	4	3	3	4
Latin[3][9]	6	6	4	4	3	3	4
English[3][9]	–	–	5	4	3	3	4
French/Italian/ Russian/Spanish[3][9][13]	–	–	–	–	5	5	5
Mathematics[3]	4	4	4	4	3	3	3
Physics[3]	–	–	–	2	1	2	2
Chemistry	–	–	–	–	–	–	2
Biology	2	2	2	1	2	2	–
History	–	2	2	2	2	2/1[14]	2
Geography	2	2	1	2	1	–	2
Social Studies	–	–	–	–	–	1/2[15]	–
Economics and Law	–	–	–	1	1	1	–
Art	2	3	2	1	1	1[6]	1
Music	3[5]	2	2	1	1	1[6]	1
Sport[4][17]	2+2	2+2	2+2	2+2	2+2	2+2	2+2
	28+2	30+2	30+2	30+2	30+2	30+2	34+2

C. Modern Languages Gymnasium (English as 1st Foreign Language)

Classes	5	6	7	8	9	10	11
Obligatory Subjects[1])							
Religious Studies/Ethics[2])[17])	2	2	2	2	2	2	2
German[3])	5	5	4	4	3	3	4
English[3])[9])	6	6	4	4	3	3	4
Latin[3])[9])	–	–	5	4	3	3	4
French/Italian/ Russian/Spanish[3])[9])[13])	–	–	–	–	5	5	5
Mathematics[3])	4	4	4	4	3	3	3
Physics[3])	–	–	–	2	1	2	2
Chemistry	–	–	–	–	–	–	2
Biology	2	2	2	1	2	2	–
History	–	2	2	2	2	2/1[14])	2
Geography	2	2	1	2	1	–	2
Social Studies	–	–	–	–	–	1/2[15])	–
Economics and Law	–	–	–	1	1	1	–
Art	2	3	2	1	1	1[6])	1
Music	3[5])	2	2	1	1	1[6])	1
Sport[4])[17])	2+2	2+2	2+2	2+2	2+2	2+2	2+2
	28+2	30+2	30+2	30+2	30+2	30+2	34+2

D. Mathematics and Natural Sciences Gymnasium

Classes	5	6	7	8	9	10	11
Obligatory Subjects[1])							
Religious Studies/Ethics[2])[17])	2	2	2	2	2	2	2
German[3])	5	5	4	4	3	3	4
English[3])[11])	6	6	4	4	3	3	4
French/Latin[3])[12])	–	–	5	4	3	3	4
Mathematics[3])	4	4	4	4	4	4	5
Physics[3])	–	–	–	2	2	3[10])	3
Chemistry[3])	–	–	–	–	3[10])	3[10])	3
Biology	2	2	2	1	2	2	–
History	–	2	2	2	2	2/1[14])	2
Geography	2	2	1	2	1	–	2
Social Studies	–	–	–	–	–	1/2[15])	–
Economics and Law	–	–	–	1	1	1	–
Art	2	3	2	1	1	1[6])	2
Music	3[5])	2	2	1	1	1[6])	1
Sport[4])[17])	2+2	2+2	2+2	2+2	2+2	2+2	2+2
	28+2	30+2	30+2	30+2	30+2	30+2	34+2

E. Arts Gymnasium (nine years)

Classes	5	6	7	8	9	10	11
Obligatory Subjects[1])							
Religious Studies/Ethics[2])[17])	2	2	2	2	2	2	2
German[3])	5	5	4	4	4	4	5
Latin[3])	6	6	4	4	3	3	4
English[3])	–	–	4	4	3	3	4
Mathematics[3])	4	4	4	4	3	3	3
Physics[3])	–	–	–	–	2	2	2
Chemistry	–	–	–	–	–	–	2
Biology	2	2	2	1	2	2	–
History	–	2	2	2	2	2/1[14])	2
Geography	2	2	1	2	1	–	2
Social Studies	–	–	–	–	–	1/2[15])	–
Economics and Law	–	–	–	–	1	1	–
Art	2	2	2	2	2	2	3
Music[3])	3	3	3	3	3	3	3
Sport[4])[17])	2+2	2+2	2+2	2+2	2+2	2+2	2+2
	28+2	30+2	30+2	30+2	30+2	30+2	34+2

F. Arts Gymnasium (seven years)

Classes	7	8	9	10	11
Obligatory Subjects[1]					
Religious Studies/Ethics[2][17]	2	2	2	2	2
German[3]	5	4	3	4	5
English[3]	5	4	3	3	4
Latin[3]	–	5	4	3	4
Mathematics[3]	4	4	3	3	3
Physics[3]	–	–	2	2	2
Chemistry	–	–	–	–	2
Biology	3	1	2	2	–
History	2	2	2	2/1[14]	2
Geography	2	1	1	–	2
Social Studies	–	–	–	1/2[15]	–
Economics and Law	–	–	1	1	–
Art	2	2	2	2	2
Music[3]	3	3	3	3	3
Sport[4][17]	2+2	2+2	2+2	2+2	2+2
	30+2	30+2	30+2	30+2	33+2

G. Economics Gymnasium (nine years)

Classes	5	6	7	8	9	10	11
Obligatory Subjects[1]							
Religious Studies/Ethics[2][17]	2	2	2	2	2	2	2
German[3]	5	5	4	4	3	3	4
English[3]	6	6	4	4	3	3	3
Latin/French[3]	–	–	5	4	3	3	4
Mathematics[3]	4	4	4	4	3	3	3
Physics[3]	–	–	–	2	1	2	2
Chemistry	–	–	–	–	–	–	2
Biology	2	2	2	1	2	2	–
History	–	2	2	2	2	2/1[14]	2
Geography	2	2	1	2	1	–	2
Social Studies	–	–	–	–	–	1/2[15]	–
Economics and Law[3a]	–	–	–	1	4	4	3
Accountancy	–	–	–	–	2	2	3
Art	2	3	2	1	1	1[6]	1
Music	3[5]	2	2	1	1	1[6]	1
Sport[4][17]	2+2	2+2	2+2	2+2	2+2	2+2	2+2
	28+2	30+2	30+2	30+2	30+2	30+2	34+2

H. Economics Gymnasium (seven years)

Classes	7	8	9	10	11
Obligatory Subjects[1]					
Religious Studies/Ethics[2][17]	2	2	2	2	2
German[3]	5	3	3	3	4
English[3]	6	4	3	3	3
French[3]	–	5	4	3	4
Mathematics[3]	5	4	3	3	3
Physics[3]	–	2	1	2	2
Chemistry	–	–	–	–	2
Biology	2	2	1	2	–
History	2	2	2	2/1[14]	2
Geography	2	1	1	–	2
Social Studies	–	–	–	1/2[15]	–
Economics and Law[3a]	–	1	4	4	3
Accountancy	–	–	2	2	2
Art	2	1	1	1[6]	2
Music	2	1	1	1[6]	1
Sport[4][17]	2+2	2+2	2+2	2+2	2+2
	30+2	30+2	30+2	30+2	33+2

I. Social Studies Gymnasium

Classes	5	6	7	8	9	10	11
Obligatory Subjects[1])							
Religious Studies/Ethics[2])[17])	2	2	2	2	2	2	2
German[1])	5	5	4	4	3	3	4
English[3])	6	6	4	4	3	3	4
French/Latin[3])	–	–	5	4	3	3	4
Mathematics[3])	4	4	4	4	3	3	3
Physics[3])	–	–	–	2	1	2	2
Chemistry	–	–	–	–	2	2	2
Biology	2	2	2	1	2	2	–
History	–	2	2	2	2	2/1[14])	2
Geography	2	2	1	2	1	–	2
Social Studies[3])	–	–	–	–	2	2/3[16])	2
Social Work	–	–	–	–	–	–	3
Economics and Law	–	–	–	1	1	1	–
Art[7])	2	3	2	1	1	1[6])	1
Music	3[5])	2	2	1	1	1[6])	1
Sport[4])[17])	2+2	2+2	2+2	2+2	2+2	2+2	2+2
Home Economics	–	–	–	–	1	2	–
	28+2	30+2	30+2	30+2	30+2	30+2	34+2

Notes

1) Priority is usually given to compulsory subjects. For exceptions see § 20 GSO.

2) See Article 26, paragraph 1 BayEUG.

3) This is a core subject.

3a) Core subject from class 9.

4) Classes 5 and 6:
Incl. 2 lessons of extended basic sport.
Classes 7 and 11:
Incl. 2 lessons for specific sports – usually in the afternoon.

5) If lack of staff prevents 3 hours of Music, there will be 2 hours of Music and 3 of Art.

6) Art or music.

7) At the Social Studies Gymnasium Art in classes 7 and 8 can be replaced by the same number of lesso
in Textiles and Crafts.

8) For practical studies (in holidays during class 11) see § 52, article 3, sentence 2 GSO.

9) The sequence in which English, French, and Latin are taken can be adapted. For bilingual French cou
ses there are different timetables which the Ministry establishes.

10) With an additional lesson.

11) Latin or French can also be accepted as first foreign language.

12) English can also be accepted as second foreign language.

13) Introduction of this third foreign language requires ministerial approval.

14) Two lessons in the first half year, 1 in the second.

15) One lesson in the first half year, 2 in the second.

16) Two lessons in the first half year, 3 in the second.

17) In special cases the Head Teacher can merge classes for lessons.

26. Gymnasium Upper Level (Sixth-Form College) – Classes 12/13 (Bavaria)

Every pupil chooses two specializations with 6 lessons weekly for each. These are accompanied by a broad range of basic courses, each with 2-4 lessons weekly. More detailed regulations provide for consolidated general education through individual balance between three main subjects. The average number of pupils per specialization was 12.8, and for basic courses (with choice among compulsory subjects) 17.3.

Most frequent combination of specializations 1990/91:

M + Ph	7.3 %
E + E/L	5.7 %
E + B	5.7 %
M + E/L	4.4 %
G + B	3.9 %
M + B	3.9 %

	Subjects	Specializations: week less.	Specializations: % of all pupils	Basic Courses: week less.	Basic Courses: % of all pupils
Language/Literature/Arts	German	6	18.4	4	81.4
	English	6	31.3	3	29.3
	French	6	15.7	3	3.7
	Greek	6	1.5	3	0.2
	Latin	6	11.1	3	2.8
	Other**	6	0.4	3	0.1
	Art	6	9.0	3	33.0
	Music	6	2.1	3	18.6
Social Sciences	Geography	6	5.0	2	42.4
	History	6	5.7	2	90.9
	Sociology	6	0.9	2	31.8
	Economics/Law*	6	19.1	2	37.5
	Sociology/ History	6	4.4	–	–
	Religious Studies	6	0,4	2	80.3
	Ethics	–	–	2	19.1
Mathematics/Natural Sciences/Techn.	Mathematics	6	29.1	3	50.1
	Biology	6	20.1	3	52.3
	Chemistry	6	8.8	3	33.0
	Physics	6	13.3	3	25.1
	Sport	6	4.8	2	93.3

* Economics and Law

** Italian, Russian, or Spanish can be taken instead of French as an advanced foreign language from year 9 at schools offering such courses.

Source: Endgültige Unterrichtsübersicht der Kollegstufe 1990/91.

27. Addresses of the Laender Ministries of Education

Baden-Württemberg

Ministerium für Wissenschaft,
Forschung und Kunst
Königstraße 46
70173 Stuttgart
Tel.: 0711/2790
Fax: 0711/279 3080

Ministerium für Kultus, Jugend und Sport
Schloßplatz 4 PF: 103442 (70029)
70173 Stuttgart
Tel.: 0711/2790
Fax: 0711/279 2810

Bavaria

Bayerisches Staatsministerium für Unterricht, Kultus, Wissenschaft und Kunst
Salvatorstraße 2
80333 München
Tel.: 089/218601
Fax: 089/2186 2800

Berlin

Senatsverwaltung für Wissenschaft, Forschung und Kultur - Bereich Wissenschaft und Forschung -
Bredtschneiderstraße 5-8
14057 Berlin
Tel.: 030/3065-3
Fax: 030/ 3065 5433

- Bereich Kultur -
Brunnenstraße 188-190
10119 Berlin
Tel.: 030/28525-0
Fax: 030/28525 450

Senatsverwaltung für Schule, Jugend und Sport
Storkower Straße 133
10407 Berlin
Tel.: 030/42140
Fax: 030/ 4214 4001

Brandenburg

Ministerium für Wissenschaft,
Forschung und Kultur
Friedrich-Ebert-Straße 4
14467 Potsdam
Tel.: 0331/8660
Fax: 0331/866-4998

Ministerium für Bildung, Jugend und Sport
Heinrich-Mann-Allee 107
14473 Potsdam
Tel.: 0331/8660
Fax: 0331/866-3595

Bremen

Der Senator für Bildung,
Wissenschaft, Kunst und Sport
Rembertiring 8-12
28195 Bremen
Tel.: 0421/361-0
Fax: 0421/361 4176

Hamburg

Freie und Hansestadt Hamburg
Behörde für Schule, Jugend und Berufsbildung
Hamburger Straße 31
22083 Hamburg
Tel.: 040/29880
Fax: 040/2988 2883

Freie und Hansestadt Hamburg
Behörde für Wissenschaft und Forschung
Hamburger Straße 37
22083 Hamburg
Tel.: 040/29880
Fax: 040/2988 2411

Freie und Hansestadt Hamburg
Kulturbehörde
Hamburger Straße 45
22083 Hamburg
Tel.:040/29880
Fax: 040/29886560

Hesse

Hessisches Kultusministerium
Luisenplatz 10
65185 Wiesbaden
Tel.: 0611/3680
Fax: 0611/368-2099

Hessisches Ministerium für
Wissenschaft und Kunst
Rheinstraße 23-25
65185 Wiesbaden
Tel.: 0611/1650
Fax: 0611/165-766

Mecklenburg-Western Pomerania

Kultusministerium des Landes
Mecklenburg-Vorpommern
Werderstraße 123
19055 Schwerin
Tel.: 0385/5880
Fax: 0385/588-7082

Lower Saxony

Niedersächsisches Kultusministerium
Schiffgraben 12
30159 Hannover
Tel.: 0511/1201
Fax: 0511/120 8436

Niedersächsisches Ministerium für
Wissenschaft und Kultur
Leibnizufer 9
30169 Hannover
Tel.: 0511/120-0
Fax: 0511/120 2801 & 120 2802

North Rhine-Westphalia

Ministerium für Schule und
Weiterbildung des Landes Nordrhein-
Westfalen
Völklinger Straße 49 a
40221 Düsseldorf
Tel.: 0211/89603
Fax: 0211/896 3220

Ministerium für Wissenschaft und
Forschung des Landes Nordrhein-
Westfalen
Völklinger Straße 49
40221 Düsseldorf
Tel.: 0211/89604
Fax: 0211/896 4555

Ministerium für Stadtentwicklung,
Kultur und Sport des Landes NRW
Breite Straße 31
40213 Düsseldorf
Tel.: 0211/8370-4
Fax: 0211/837 4444

Rhineland-Palatinate

Ministerium für Kultur, Jugend,
Familie und Frauen des Landes
Rheinland-Pfalz
Mittlere Bleiche 61
55116 Mainz
Tel.: 06131/161
Fax: 06131/16 2878

Ministerium für Bildung,
Wissenschaft und Weiterbildung des
Landes Rheinland-Pfalz
Mittlere Bleiche 61
55116 Mainz
Tel.: 06131/161
Fax: 06131/16 2997

Saarland

Ministerium für Bildung, Kultur und Wissenschaft
Hohenzollernstraße 60
66117 Saarbrücken
Tel.: 0681/5031
Fax: 0681/503 291

Saxony

Sächsisches Staatsministerium für Wissenschaft und Kunst
Wigardstraße 17
01097 Dresden
Tel.: 0351/5640
Fax: 0351/564-6040

Sächsisches Staatsministerium für Kultus
Postfach 10 09 10
01076 Dresden
Tel.: 0351/5640
Fax: 0351/564-2887

Saxony-Anhalt

Kultusministerium des Landes Sachsen-Anhalt
Breiter Weg 31
39104 Magdeburg
Tel.: 0391/567-01
Fax: 0391/567 3774

Schleswig-Holstein

Ministerium für Bildung, Wissenschaft, Forschung und Kultur
– Bereich Bildung –
Gartenstraße 6
24103 Kiel
Tel.: 0431/988-0
Fax: 0431/988-2596

– Bereich Wissenschaft, Forschung und Kultur –
Düsternbrooker Weg 64
24105 Kiel
Tel.: 0431/988-0
Fax: 0431/988 5888

Thuringia

Ministerium für Wissenschaft, Forschung und Kultur
Juri-Gagarin-Ring 158
99084 Erfurt
Tel.: 0361/5966-0
Fax: 0361/5966-320/303

Thüringer Kultusministerium
Werner-Seelenbinder-Straße 1
99096 Erfurt
Tel.: 0361/3471-0
Fax: 0361/3471-900

(Date: 18.09.1996)

28. Other National Organizations

Federal Ministry of Education, Science, Research, and Technology

Bundesministerium für Bildung,
Wissenschaft, Forschung und
Technologie
Heinemannstraße 2
53175 Bonn
Tel.: 0228/57-0
Fax: 0228/57 20 96

Conference of Ministers of Education

Ständige Konferenz der
Kultusminister der Länder
in der Bundesrepublik Deutschland
Nassestraße 8
53113 Bonn
Tel.: 0228/ 5 01-0
Fax: 0228/5 01 3 01

Federal-Laender Commission

Bund-Länder-Kommission
für Bildungsplanung und
Forschungsförderung
Friedrich-Ebert-Allee 39
53113 Bonn
Tel.: 0228/54 02-0
Fax: 0228/54 02 1 50

29. Addresses of Laender Institutes for Educational Planning, School Development, and Further Training for Teachers

Baden-Württemberg

Landesinstitut
für Erziehung und Unterricht
Rotebühlstr. 133
70197 Stuttgart
Tel.: 0711/674-1
Fax: 0711/621121

Bavaria

Staatsinstitut
für Schulpädagogik und
Bildungsforschung (ISB)
Arabellastr. 1
81925 München
Tel.: 089/9214-2359
Fax: 089/9214-3600

Berlin

Berliner Institut
für Lehrerfort- und Weiterbildung
und Schulentwicklung
Uhlandstr. 96-97
10715 Berlin
Tel.: 030/8687-1
Fax: 030/8687-266

Brandenburg

Pädagogisches Landesinstitut
Brandenburg (PLIB)
Struveshof
14971 Ludwigsfelde
Tel.: 03378/961
Fax: 03378/963

Bremen

Wissenschaftliches Institut
für Schulpraxis (WIS)
der Freien Hansestadt Bremen
Am Weidedamm 20
28215 Bremen
Tel. 0421/3506-198 (-104)

Hamburg

Freie und Hansestadt Hamburg
Institut für Lehrerfortbildung
Felix-Dahn-Str. 3
20357 Hamburg
Tel.: 040/4212-721

Hesse

Hessisches Institut für Bildungs-
planung und Schulentwicklung
(HIBS)
Bodenstedtstr. 1
65189 Wiesbaden
Tel.: 0611/342-0
Fax: 0611/342-130

Hessisches Institut
für Lehrerfortbildung (HILF)
Reinhardswaldschule
34233 Fuldatal
Tel.: 0561/8101-0
Fax: 0561/8101-100

Lower Saxony

Niedersächsisches Landesinstitut
für Lehrerbildung, Lehrerweiter-
bildung und Unterrichtsforschung
(NLI)
Keßlerstr. 52
41134 Hildesheim
Tel.: 05121/1695-0

Mecklenburg-Western Pomerania

Landesinstitut Mecklenburg-
Vorpommern für Schule und
Ausbildung (LISA)
Von-Flotow-Str. 20
19059 Schwerin
Tel.: 0385/760170

North Rhine-Westphalia

Landesinstitut für
Schule und Weiterbildung
Paradieserweg
Postfach 385
59494 Soest
Tel.: 02921/683-1
Fax: 02921/683-228

Rhineland-Palatinate

Pädagogisches Zentrum
Rheinland-Pfalz
Europaplatz 7-9
55543 Bad Kreuznach
Tel.: 0671/84088-0
Fax: 0671/84088-10

Saarland

Landesinstitut
für Pädagogik und Medien
Beethovenstr. 26
66125 Duttweiler
Tel. 06897/7908-0
Fax: 06897/7908-22

Saxony

Sächsisches Staatsinstitut für
Bildungsplanung und Schul-
entwicklung
Comenius-Institut
Dresdner Str. 78
01445 Radebeul
Tel.: 0351/832430
Fax: 0351/8324414

Saxony-Anhalt

Landesinstitut für Lehrerfort-,
Weiterbildung und Unterrichts-
forschung
Riebeckplatz 9
06110 Halle
Tel.: 0345/834-0
Fax: 0345/834-319

Schleswig-Holstein

Landesinstitut
für Praxis und Theorie der Schule
Schreberweg 5
24119 Kronshagen (Kiel)
Tel.: 0431/5403-0
Fax: 0431/5403-200

Thuringia

Thüringer Institut für Lehrerfort-
bildung, Lehrplanentwicklung und
Medienpädagogik
Hopfengrund 1
99310 Arnstadt
Tel.: 03628/7426-0
Fax: 03628/8659

30. Sources of Quotations

Sources indicated in the text are not repeated here. KMK resolutions and recommendations are contained in the ongoing and updated Beschlußsammlung. Harald Kästner's often cited "Schule in Deutschland – Bemerkungen zur aktuellen Entwicklung" (a lecture at Fulda on 21. 5. 1996) will appear in the "Zeitschrift für internationale erziehungs- und sozialwissenschaftliche Forschung" (Böhlau-Verlag, Cologne) in 1997.

P. XVIII: Theodor Haecker: Christentum und Kultur. Munich 1946, p. 15.

P. XVIII: Eduard Spranger: Verstrickung und Ausweg. Ein Wort über die Jugend. Konstanz 1947, p. 5 (Gesammelte Schriften VIII. Tübingen 1970, p. 268).

P. XVIII: Friedrich Meinecke: Politische Schriften und Reden (Werke II). Darmstadt 1966, p. 491.

P. XVIII: Ernst Jünger: Post nach Princeton. In: Merkur No. 323 (Vol. 29) March 1975, p. 226 f. (Sämtliche Werke. Stuttgart 1978. Vol. 14, p. 131 f.).

P. XVIII: Wolfgang Hildesheimer: Rede an die Jugend. Frankfurt a.M. 1991, p. 23.

P. 2: Friedrich Paulsen: Das deutsche Bildungswesen in seiner geschichtlichen Entwicklung. 3rd ed. Leipzig 1912, p. 171.

P. 3: Ernst Wiechert: Rede an die deutsche Jugend. Munich 1945, p. 1.

P. 3: Dieter Wellershoff: Deutschland – ein Schwebezustand. In: Merkur No. 372 (Vol. 33) 1979, p. 434.

P. 3: Hans Richert (Ed.): Richtlinien für die Lehrpläne der höheren Schulen Preußens, Teil 1. Berlin 1925.

P. 4: Friedrich Dickmann: Die Regierungsbildung in Thüringen als Modell der Machtergreifung. In: Vierteljahrshefte für Zeitgeschichte 1966. (Vol. 14), p. 463.

P. 4: Carlo Schmid: Europa und die Macht des Geistes. Berne, Munich 1973, p. 428.

P. 5: Karl Dietrich Bracher: Die Gleichschaltung der deutschen Universität. In: Universitätstage 1966 (Veröffentlichung der Freien Universität Berlin) 1966, p. 126 f.

P. 5f: Friedrich Heer: Warum gibt es kein Geistesleben in Deutschland? Munich 1978, p. 73 f., 68 f.

P. 6: Theodor W. Adorno: Stichworte. Kritische Modelle 2. Frankfurt 1969, p. 85.

P. 6: Gerhard Ritter: Geschichte als Bildungsmacht. Ein Beitrag zur historisch-politischen Neubesinnung. Stuttgart 1946, p. 51.

P. 7: In memoriam Peter Suhrkamp (Ed. S. Unseld). Frankfurt a.M. 1959, p. 122.

P.7: Friedrich Meinecke: Die deutsche Katastrophe. Betrachtungen und Erinnerungen. Wiesbaden 1946, p. 176 (Werke Vol. VIII. Stuttgart 1969, p. 444).

P. 7: Helmut Coing: Der Wiederaufbau und die Rolle der Wissenschaft. In: Wissenschaftsgeschichte seit 1900. 75 Jahre Universität Frankfurt. Frankfurt a.M. 1992, p. 86.

P. 7f.: Eduard Spranger: Staat, Recht und Politik. Gesammelte Schriften, Vol. VIII. Tübingen 1970, p. 342 f.

P. 8: Heinrich Deiters: Bildung und Leben. Erinnerungen eines deutschen Pädagogen. Cologne, Vienna 1989, p. 205.

P. 8: Karl Geiler: Geistige Freiheit und soziale Gerechtigkeit im neuen Deutschland. Wiesbaden 1947, p. 64.

P. 9: Theodor Heuß: Der Zeitgeist in seiner Wirkung auf die Lehrerschaft. Tübingen 1946, p. 26.

P. 9: Theodor Heuß: loc. cit.

P. 10: Walter Dirks: In: Frankfurter Hefte, Vol. 5 (1950), p. 113 f., 225 f., 942-954.

P. 10: Ludwig von Friedeburg: Bildungsreform in Deutschland. Geschichte und gesellschaftlicher Widerspruch. Frankfurt a.M. 1989, p. 282.

P. 10: Ludwig von Friedeburg: loc. cit.

P. 10: Herman Nohl: Über Leistung, Gehorsam, Pflicht (1945). Transcribed and annotated by E. Matthes. In: Neue Sammlung. Vol. 34 (1994), p. 327 f.

P. 11: Werner Conze, M. Rainer Lepsius: Sozialgeschichte der Bundesrepublik Deutschland. Stuttgart 1983, p. 12.

P. 11f.: Hans Rothfels: Zeitgeschichtliche Betrachtungen. Vorträge und Aufsätze. 2nd rev. ed. Göttingen 1959, p. 85 f.

P. 15: KMK-Dokumentation No. 2: OECD-Konferenz in Washington 1961. Wirtschaftswachstum und Ausbau des Erziehungswesens. Arbeitsunterlagen. Published by Sekretariat der KMK (Bonn) 1962, p. 27.

P. 15: Ralf Dahrendorf: Bildung ist Bürgerrecht. Hamburg 1965.

P. 16: Ludwig Erhard: Wohlstand für alle. Updated 3rd ed. Düsseldorf 1990, p. 361.

P. 16: Bedarfsfeststellung 1961-1970. Dokumentation. Publ. by Ständige Konferenz der Kultusminister der Länder in der Bundesrepublik Deutschland. Stuttgart 1963.

P. 16: Georg Picht: Die deutsche Bildungskatastrophe. Analyse und Dokumentation. Freiburg i. B. 1964.

P. 16: Beschlußsammlung der Kultusministerkonferenz No. 25.

P. 17: Heinrich Roth (Ed.): Begabung und Lernen. Stuttgart 1969.

P. 18: Theodor W. Adorno: Resignation. In: Politik, Wissenschaft, Erziehung (Festschrift für Ernst Schütte) Ed. H.W. Nicklas. Frankfurt a.M. 1969, p. 62 and 64.

P. 18: Jürgen Habermas: Protestbewegung und Hochschulreform. Frankfurt a.M. 1969, p. 147.

P. 18: Klaus R. Röhl: Der lange Marsch in die Toskana. In: Frankfurter Allgemeine Zeitung 11.12.1993.

P. 18: Gesine Schwan: Die demokratischen Impulse der 68er. Die Folgen von 1968 für die deutsche politische Kultur. In: Weltspiegel = Sonntagsbeilage des Tagesspiegels. Berlin 25.4.1993.

P. 18: Hermann Lübbe: Freiheit statt Emanzipationszwang. Zürich 1991, p. 112.

P. 19: Ludwig von Friedeburg, loc. cit., p. 412 and 454.

P. 21: Golo Mann. In: DIE ZEIT No. 51, 14.12.1973, p. 18.

P. 22f.: Georg Picht: Vom Bildungsnotstand zum Notstand der Bildungspolitik. In: Zeitschrift für Pädagogik 19 (1973), p. 677.

P. 23: Heinz-Dietrich Ortlieb: Die verantwortungslose Gesellschaft oder wie man eine Demokratie verspielt. Munich 1971, p. 118.

P. 23: Wolfgang Jäger: Die Innenpolitik der sozial-liberalen Koalition 1969-1974. In: K.D. Bracher, W. Jäger, W. Link: Republik im Wandel 1969-1974. Die Ära Brandt (Geschichte der Bundesrepublik Deutschland, Vol. 5/I). Stuttgart, Mannheim 1986, p. 133 f.

P. 23: Karl Steinbuch: Kurskorrektur. Stuttgart 1973, p. 163.

P. 24: Theses and counter-theses are printed in: Christoph Führ: Schulen und Hochschulen in der Bundesrepublik Deutschland. Cologne, Vienna 1989, p. 245 f.

P. 24: Hellmut Becker: Die Reform findet doch statt. In: Ist die Schule noch zu retten? Plädoyer für eine neue Bildungsreform. Ed.

A. Dannhäuser, H.-J. Ipfling, D. Reithmeier. Weinheim, Basel 1988, p. 91.

P. 25: Karl Czock (Ed.): Geschichte Sachsens. Weimar 1989, p. 569.

P. 34: Manfred Overesch: Die gesamtdeutsche Konferenz der Erziehungsminister in Stuttgart am 19./20. Februar 1948. In: Vierteljahrshefte für Zeitgeschichte. Vol. 28 (1980), No. 2, p. 248 f.

P. 37: Erwin Stein: 40 Jahre nach der Gründung der Ständigen Konferenz der Kultusminister. KMK jubilee lecture Bonn on 19.2.1988 (KMK press release).

P. 41: Speech by Minister Rüttgers in Hanover on 13.3.1996. In: Bulletin der Bundesregierung, 19.3.1996, p. 239.

P. 45: Bernhard Vogel: Beschränkung auf das Wesentliche. 25 Jahre BLK. In: Realschule in Deutschland. Vol. 103 (1995), No. 6, p. 3 f.

P. 46: Judgement by the Federal Constitutional Court 16.5.1995. In: Deutsches Verwaltungsblatt 1995 (Vol. 110), p. 1069-1076.

P. 52: Bildungspolitische Leitsätze der SPD von 1964, p. 7.

P. 59f: Bildungskommission NRW: Zukunft der Bildung – Schule der Zukunft. Neuwied 1995, p. 13 and XXI.

P. 66: Wissenschaftsrat: Empfehlungen und Stellungnahmen 1993. Cologne 1994, p. 7.

P. 67: Wissenschaftsrat 1957-1982. Publ. by Science Council. Cologne 1983, p. 15.

P. 68: Zukünftige Bildungspolitik – Bildung 2000. Schlußbericht der Enquete-Kommission des 11. Deutschen Bundestags. Bonn 1990, p. 13 and 765.

P. 115: R. von Carnap, F. Edding: Der relative Schulbesuch in den Ländern der Bundesrepublik 1952-1960. 4th ed. Weinheim 1966, p. 15.

P. 117: Deutscher Bildungsrat. Empfehlungen der Bildungskommission: Strukturplan für das Bildungswesen, 13 February 1970, p. 156.

P. 119: Profilierte Vielfalt: Die Realschule im bundesdeutschen Schulwesen. Bildungspolitisches Forum 30.9.1994. Verband Deutscher Realschullehrer – Bundesvereinigung der Deutschen Arbeitgeberverbände. Cologne 1994, p. 14.

P. 128f.: This brief account of the Bielefeld model school is based on its prospectus.

P. 130f.: 25 Jahre Gesamtschule – Eine Bilanz aus persönlichen Erfahrungen. Horst Wollenweber im Gespräch mit Studiendirektor a.D. Ulrich Sprenger: In: Realschule in Deutschland. Vol. 102. (1994), No. 8, p. 6 f.; Jörg-Dieter Gauger: Hat die Gesamtschule die Erwartungen erfüllt? In: Das Parlament No. 3 /4, 12./19.1.1996, p. 7.

P. 133: Hans Scheuerl: Probleme der Hochschulreife. Tutzinger Gespräche I-III (1958-1960). Heidelberg 1962.

P. 134: Ralf Dahrendorf: Bildung ist Bürgerrecht. Hamburg 1965, p. 30 f.

P. 140f.: Weiterentwicklung der Prinzipien der gymnasialen Oberstufe und des Abiturs. Abschlußbericht der von der KMK eingesetzten Expertenkommission. Publ. by Sekretariat der KMK. Bonn 1995.

P. 141f.: Positionspapier der Hochschulrektorenkonferenz zu Abitur – Allgemeine Hochschulreife – Studierfähigkeit (Presidium resolution, 16.10.1995).

P. 174: Leipziger Erklärung zum Hochschulzugang. In: Hochschulzugang in Deutschland. Ed. H.J. Meyer, D. Müller-Böling. Gütersloh 1996, p. 11 f.

P. 182: Dieter Simon's thesis is in: DER SPIEGEL. No. 50/1991, p. 52 f.

P. 182: Konzept zur Entwicklung der Hochschulen in Deutschland. Einstimmiger Beschluß des 167. Plenums der Hochschulrektorenkonferenz. Bonn, 6 July 1992 (Dokumente zur Hochschulreform 75/1992).

P. 183: Karl Jaspers: Die Idee der Universität. Berlin 1946, p. 5, 9 and 11.

P. 184: Rolf Neuhaus: Dokumente zur Hochschulreform 1945-1959. Wiesbaden 1961.

P. 184: Gutachten zur Hochschulreform. Vom Studienausschuß für Hochschulreform. Hamburg 1948, p. 3.

P. 184: Karl Jaspers: Die Idee der Universität. Berlin 1946, p. 5.

P. 184: Notker Hammerstein: Die Johann Wolfgang Goethe-Universität Frankfurt am Main. Von der Stiftungsuniversität zur staatlichen Hochschule. Vol. 1. Neuwied/Frankfurt a.M. 1989, p. 574.

P. 184f.: Loc. cit., p. 581.

P. 186f.: Helmut Thielicke: Zu Gast auf einem schönen Stern. Erinnerungen. Hamburg 1984, p. 400 f. and 418.

P. 187: Walter Rüegg (Ed.): Die Johann Wolfgang Goethe-Universität 1964. Jahrbuch 1966. Preface.

P. 189: Franz Letzelter: Die wissenschaftlichen Hochschulen und ihre Verwaltung. In: Deutsche Verwaltungsgeschichte. Ed. Kurt G. A. Jeserich, Hans Pohl, Georg Christoph von Unruh. Vol. 5: Die Bundesrepublik Deutschland. 1987, p. 661 and 666.

P. 190: Hans Dichgans: Erst mit 30 im Beruf? Stuttgart 1965, p. 9 f.

P. 192: Empfehlungen des Wissenschaftsrates zu den Perspektiven der Hochschulen in den 90er Jahren. Cologne 1988, p. 26 (here quoted from the shorter version, p. 3).

P. 192: Empfehlungen zur Entwicklung der Fachhochschulen in den neunziger Jahren. Cologne 1991.

P. 194: Konzept zur Entwicklung der Hochschulen in Deutschland. Einstimmiger Beschluß des 167. Plenums der Hochschulrektorenkonferenz. Bonn, 6 July 1992. Dokumente zur Hochschulreform 75/1992.

P. 195: Kultusministerkonferenz/Hochschulrektorenkonferenz: Umsetzung der Studienstrukturreform. 2nd ed. Bonn 1994, p. 35 f.

P. 198: Werner Thieme: Hochschule und Verwaltung. In: Wissenschaftsrecht, Wissenschaftsverwaltung, Wissenschaftsförderung. Zeitschrift für Recht und Verwaltung der wissenschaftlichen Hochschulen. Vol. 22, No. 1, March 1989, p. 9.

P. 203: Informationsbroschüre des baden-württembergischen Ministeriums für Wissenschaft und Forschung: „Berufsakademie Baden-Württemberg. Hrg. von Dr. G.G. Kinzel“. Stuttgart: March 1995.

P. 208: Rheinische Blätter für Erziehung und Unterricht. Der neuesten Folge 15. Frankfurt a.M. 1865, p. 59.

P. 219: Deutscher Bildungsrat. Empfehlungen der Bildungskommission: Strukturplan für das Bildungswesen 13.2.1970, p. 51.

P. 226: Hermann Avenarius: Rechtliche Möglichkeiten und Grenzen schulischer Selbstverwaltung. In: Schule in Verantwortung gestalten. Publ. by Senatsverwaltung für Schule, Berufsbildung und Sport. Berlin 1994, p. 11 f. and 25.

P. 228: Bund-Länder-Kommission für Bildungsplanung und Forschungsförderung: Langfristige Personalentwicklung im Schulbereich der alten und neuen Länder. Dokumentation 26.9.1994, p. I f.

P. 230f.: Bund-Länder-Kommission für Bildungsplanung und Forschungsförderung: Beschäftigungsperspektiven der Absolventen des Bildungswesens. Analysen und Projektionen bis 2010 und Folgerungen für die Bildungspolitik. 12.12.1994, p. 27.

P. 231: Wolfgang Mitter: Das deutsche Bildungswesen in internationaler Perspektive (here quoted from the manuscript in press).

P. 233: Sekretariat der Kultusministerkonferenz: Überlegungen zu einem Grundkonzept für den Fremdsprachenunterricht (mit Gutachten zum Fremdsprachenunterricht in der Bundesrepublik Deutschland). Bonn 1994, p. 3 f.

P. 234: Sekretariat der Kultusministerkonferenz: Sammlung der Beschlüsse der deutsch-französischen Zusammenarbeit in den Bereichen Schule, berufliche Bildung und Hochschule auf der Grundlage des deutsch-französischen Vertrages. Bonn 1995, p. 3.

P. 239: Helmut Kohl. In: Bild 26.4.1996; Bulletin der Bundesregierung No. 33, 29.4.1996, p. 329 f..

P. 240f.: Walter Rüegg (Ed.): Konkurrenz der Kopfarbeiter. Zürich 1985, p. 81.

P. 241: Dieter Simon: Die Stunde Null. Was eine Universität ist, muß man entscheiden. In: Frankfurter Allgemeine Zeitung 10.7.1996, p. 31.

P. 241: Dieter Simon's thesis is in: DER SPIEGEL, No. 50/1991, p. 52 f.

P. 241: Hochschulrektorenkonferenz: Konzept zur Entwicklung der Hochschulen in Deutschland 6.7.1992. Dokumente zur Hochschulreform 75/1992, p. 7 f.

P. 241f.: Ralf Dahrendorf: Bildung ist Bürgerrecht. Hamburg 1965, p. 25 and 30 f.

P. 243: Conference documentation for "Hochschulzugang in Deutschland" 22/23. June 1995. Unfortunately the organizers (the Saxony Ministry of Science and Art and the Gütersloh Centre for University Development) did not include Schiedermair's theses in the conference report, published as "Hochschulzugang in Deutschland" (Ed. H.J. Meyer and D. Müller-Böling, Verlag der Bertelsmann-Stiftung) in 1996.

P. 244: Bulletin der Bundesregierung, 26 March 1996, No. 25, p. 253 f.

P. 245: Sebastian F. Müller: Die höhere Schule Preußens in der Weimarer Republik. Zum Einfluß von Parteien, Verbänden und Verwaltung auf die Schul- und Lehrplanreform 1919-1925 (Studien und Dokumentationen zur deutschen Bildungsgeschichte, Vol. 3) 1977, 2nd rev. & expand. ed. Cologne, Vienna 1985.

P. 245: Dieter Margies: Das höhere Schulwesen zwischen Reform und Restauration. Die Biographie Hans Richerts als Beitrag zur Bildungspolitik in der Weimarer Republik. 1972, p. 138.

P. 245: Wesen und Wege der Schulreform (Ed. Adolf Grimme, with Heinrich Deiters and Lina Mayer-Kulenkampff). Berlin 1930, Preface by C.H. Becker.

P. 245f.: Max Scheler: Vom Ewigen im Menschen. Vol. 1. Leipzig 1923, p. 204 f. and 235 f.

P. 246: Bulletin der Bundesregierung No. 25, 26.3.1996, p. 253 f.

P. 247: Heinz-Dietrich Ortlieb: Reform der Bildungsreform. Anmerkungen zu ihrem Scheitern am permissiven Utopismus. Düsseldorf 1985, p. 35.

P. 248: Hans Heckel: Eine Grundordnung der deutschen Schule. Stuttgart 1958, p. 9.

31. Bibliography

The most important publications up to 1988 are included in the bibliography of my "Schools and Institutions of Higher Education in the Federal Republic of Germany" (Inter Nationes, Bonn 1989), so only titles published between 1988 and 1996 are mentioned here.

1. Educational History, Policy, and General Issues

Anweiler, Oskar et al. (Ed.): Vergleich von Bildung und Erziehung in der Bundesrepublik Deutschland und in der Deutschen Demokratischen Republik. Cologne: Wissenschaft und Politik 1990.

Anweiler, Oskar et al. (Ed.): Bildungspolitik in Deutschland 1945-1990. Ein historisch-vergleichender Quellenband. Opladen: Leske + Budrich 1992.

Avenarius, Hermann: Die Rechtsordnung der Bundesrepublik Deutschland. Eine Einführung. Neuwied: Luchterhand 1995.

Baske, Siegfried (Ed.): Pädagogische Berufe in der Bundesrepublik Deutschland und in der Deutschen Demokratischen Republik (Schriftenreihe der Gesellschaft für Deutschlandforschung Vol. XXX). Berlin 1990.

Brezinka, Wolfgang: Glaube, Moral und Erziehung. Munich–Basel: Reinhardt 1992.

Cloer, Ernst; Wernstedt, Rolf (Ed.): Pädagogik in der DDR. Eröffnung einer notwendigen Bilanzierung. Weinheim: Deutscher Studien-Verlag 1994.

Das Bildungswesen in der Bundesrepublik Deutschland. Ein Überblick für Eltern, Lehrer und Schüler. Ed.: Arbeitsgruppe Bildungsbericht am Max-Planck-Institut für Bildungsforschung. Reinbek: Rowohlt Taschenbuch 1994.

Friedeburg, Ludwig von: Bildungsreform in Deutschland. Geschichte und gesellschaftlicher Widerspruch. Frankfurt a. M. 1989 – Suhrkamp Taschenbuch Verlag 1992.

Fuchs, Hans-Werner; Reuter, Lutz R. (Ed.): Bildungspolitik seit der Wende. Dokumente zum Umbau des ostdeutschen Bildungssystems (1989-1994). Opladen: Leske + Budrich 1995.

Führ, Christoph: Zum Bildungswesen in den fünf neuen Ländern der Bundesrepublik Deutschland. Bonn: Inter Nationes 1992.

Geißler, Gert; Wiegmann, Ulrich: Pädagogik und Herrschaft in der DDR. Die parteilichen, geheimdienstlichen und vormilitärischen Erziehungsverhältnisse. Frankfurt a.M.: Peter Lang 1996.

Geißler, Gert; Wiegmann, Ulrich: Schule und Erziehung in der DDR. Studien und Dokumente. Neuwied: Luchterhand Verlag 1995.

Heldmann, Werner: Kultureller und gesellschaftlicher Auftrag von Schule. Krefeld: Pädagogik- und Hochschulverlag 1990.

Hörner, Wolfgang: Bildung und Wissenschaft in der DDR. Ausgangslage und Reform bis Mitte 1990. Bonn 1990.

Hoffmann, Dietrich; Neumann, Karl (Ed.): Erziehung und Erziehungswissenschaft in der BRD und der DDR. Vol. 1: Die Teilung der Pädagogik (1945-1965)). Vol. 2: Divergenzen und Konvergenzen (1965-1989). Vol. 3: Die Vereinigung der Pädagogiken (1989-1995). Weinheim: Deutscher Studien-Verlag 1994, 1995, 1996.

Kästner, Harald: Schule in Europa – Grundüberzeugungen und Leitlinien. In: Zeitschrift für internationale erziehungs- und sozialwissenschaftliche Forschung 1994 (Vol. 11) No. 1, p. 25-40.

Neuner, Gerhart: Allgemeinbildung. Konzeption – Inhalt – Prozeß. Berlin: Volk und Wissen 1989.

Rolff, Hans-Günther: Wandel durch Selbstorganisation: theoretische Grundlagen und praktische Hinweise für eine bessere Schule. 2nd ed. Weinheim etc.: Juventa 1995.

Schlaffke, Winfried; Weiß, Reinhold (Ed.): Private Bildung – Herausforderung für das öffentliche Bildungsmonopol. Berichte zur Bildungspolitik 1996 des Instituts der deutschen Wirtschaft, Cologne: Deutscher Instituts-Verlag 1996.

Schlaffke, Winfried; Westphalen, Klaus (Ed.): Denkschrift NRW – Hat Bildung in Schule Zukunft? Ein Symposion von Wissenschaft und Wirtschaft. Cologne: Deutscher Instituts-Verlag 1996.

Zukunft der Bildung - Schule der Zukunft: Denkschrift der Kommission "Zukunft der Bildung - Schule der Zukunft" beim Ministerpräsidenten des Landes Nordrhein-Westfalen / Bildungskommission NRW. Neuwied etc.: Luchterhand 1995.

2. Pre-Schooling

Becker-Textor, Ingeborg: Kindergarten 2010: Traum - Vision - Realität. 3rd ed. Freiburg im Breisgau et al.: Herder 1995.

Götte, Rose: Sprache und Spiel im Kindergarten: Handbuch zur Sprach- und Spielförderung mit Jahresprogramm und Anleitungen für die Praxis. 8th unrevised ed. Weinheim, Basel: Beltz 1993. (Theorie und Praxis der Schulpsychologie, Vol. 22).

Handbuch für ErzieherInnen in Krippe, Kindergarten, Vorschule und Hort. Ed. Klaus Schüttler-Janikulla. with Horst Bachmann ... Munich: mvg-Verlag, Loose leaf, updated to 1991

3. Primary School

Handbuch Grundschule. Ed. Dieter Haarmann. Weinheim, Basel: Beltz.

Vol. 1. Allgemeine Didaktik: Voraussetzungen und Formen grundlegender Bildung. - 3rd unrevised ed. 1996.

Vol. 2. Fachdidaktik: Inhalte und Bereiche grundlegender Bildung. 2nd rev. ed. 1994.

Neuhaus, Elisabeth: Reform der Grundschule. Bad Heilbrunn: Klinkhardt, 6th ed. 1994.

Rodehüser, Franz: Epochen der Grundschulgeschichte: Darstellung und Analyse der historischen Entwicklung einer Schulstufe unter Berücksichtigung ihrer Entstehungszusammenhänge und möglicher Perspektiven für die Zukunft. 2nd ed. Bochum: Winkler 1989.

4. Orientation/Mixed-Ability Level

Fördern statt aussondern: Orientierungsstufe in Niedersachsen: Dokumentation eines Kongresses der SPD-Landtagsfraktion am 1. Juni 1993 in Hannover. Hanover: SPD-Landtagsfraktion 1993.

Jürgens, Eiko: 20 Jahre Orientierungsstufe: Beiträge zu einer umstrittenen Schulform. Sankt Augustin: Academia-Verlag 1991.

5. Secondary Level: General

Arbeitsgruppe Entwicklung des Bildungswesens der Deutschen Gesellschaft für Erziehungswissenschaft: Strukturprobleme, Disparitäten, Grundbildung in der Sekundarstufe I (Ed. Peter Zedler). Weinheim: Deutscher Studienverlag 1992.

Sekundarschulbildung im Wandel: ein Vorschlag für eine zweigliedrige Schulstruktur und den Ausbau der beruflichen Bildung / Verband Bildung und Erziehung. Bonn: VBE 1992.

Sekundarschule und berufliche Bildung: Lösungswege aus der Schulstrukturkrise; Dokumentation des 4. Bildungspolitischen Kongresses, Dortmund, 19. - 20. Februar 1992 / Uwe Franke ...(Ed.). Verband Bildung und Erziehung, Landesverband Nordrhein-Westfalen. Hamm: VBE-Medien-Service 1992.

Taschenbuch Sekundarschule (Ed. Jürgen Bennack). - Baltmannsweiler: Schneider-Verlag Hohengehren 1995.

6. Hauptschule

Die Hauptschule: Materialien - Entwicklungen - Konzepte; ein Arbeits- und Studienbuch (Ed. Heinz-Jürgen Ipfling and Ulrike Lorenz). Bad Heilbrunn/Obb.: Klinkhardt 1991.

Kramer, Wolfgang: Die Hauptschule: Entwicklung, Reformbedarf, Perspektiven (Publ. by Institut der Deutschen Wirtschaft, Cologne). Cologne: Deutscher Instituts-Verlag 1993. (Beiträge zur Gesellschafts- und Bildungspolitik; 180 = 1992).

Schmoldt, Benno: Von der Volksschule zur Sekundarstufe I: ein historischer Überblick; Entwicklung und Einzelheiten einer Schulart. Baltmannsweiler: Schneider-Verlag Hohengehren 1994. (Grundlagen der Schulpädagogik; Vol. 10).

7. Realschule

Die Realschule aus bildungspolitischer, bildungstheoretischer sowie schulpädagogischer Sicht: Tagungsbericht zum 24. Mülheimer Kongress vom 11. bis 13. November 1991 / Realschullehrerverband Nordrhein-Westfalen. Paderborn: Schöningh 1992. (Schriftenreihe des Realschullehrerverbandes Nordrhein-Westfalen, RLV; No. 30) (Bildung real: Sonderdruck 1992).

Profilierte Vielfalt: Die Realschule im bundesdeutschen Schulwesen (Ed. Helmut Keim and Horst Wollenweber). Verband Deutscher Realschullehrer – Bundesvereinigung der Deutschen Arbeitgeberverbände. Cologne 1994.

Schlüsselqualifikationen in der Realschule (Ed. Horst Wollenweber; Ferdinand Bitz). Cologne: Wirtschaftsverlag Bachem 1994.

8. Gymnasium

Das Gymnasium im Aufwind: Entwicklung, Struktur, Probleme seiner Oberstufe. Arno Schmidt with Heinz Seeger. Aachen-Hahn: Hahner Verlagsgesellschaft 1991.

Heldmann, Werner: Gymnasiale Bildung und Erziehung: anthropologische und pädagogische Grundlagen. Cologne: Adamas-Verlag 1994. (Pädagogik und freie Schule; No. 46).

Max, Klemens: Das Gymnasium und seine trojanischen Pferde: eine kritische Studie zur Situation des Gymnasiums. Frankfurt a. Main: Haag and Herchen 1995.

Mitter, Wolfgang (Ed.): Wege zur Hochschulbildung in Europa. Vergleichsstudie zum Verhältnis von Sekundarabschluß und Hochschulzugang in Frankreich, England und Wales, Schweden und Deutschland (section on Germany by Ulrich Schäfer). Cologne: Böhlau Verlag 1996.

9. Comprehensive

Dörger, Ursula: Projekt Lehrerkooperation: eine pädagogische Konzeption zur Weiterentwicklung von Gesamtschulen. With Johannes Gehrmann ... Ed. & bibliography: Inge Skibba. Weinheim, München: Juventa-Verlag 1992. (Veröffentlichungen der Max-Traeger-Stiftung; Vol. 15).

Gesamtschule als Ganztagsschule: zur pädagogischen Ausgestaltung und Organisation des Ganztagsbetriebs an Gesamtschulen. Publ. by Landesinstitut für Schule und Weiterbildung. [produced by the Landesinstitut für Schule und Weiterbildung for the Ministry of Education. Ed.: Rolf Schmitz and Marga Rössler]. Soest: Soester Verlags-Kontor [1987].

10. Vocational Schooling

Berufswelt der Zukunft. Handreichungen für Lehrer. Cologne n.d..

Internationales Handbuch der Berufsbildung / Carl-Duisberg-Gesellschaft e. V. Uwe Lauterbach with Wolfgang Huck and Wolfgang Mitter. Baden-Baden: Nomos-Verlagsgesellschaft, looseleaf (Internationale Weiterbildung, Austausch, Entwicklung; 9) updated to 1995.

Raddatz, Rolf: Fünfundzwanzig Jahre Berufsbildungsforschung: Forschungsergebnisse des BBF und des BIBB im Dienst von Praxis und Politik. Bielefeld: Bertelsmann 1995.

Schreiber, Rolf: Aus- und Weiterbildungs-Handbuch: für Schule und Beruf. Ludwigshafen/Rhein: Kiehl 1992.

11. Special Schools

Das sonderpädagogische Förderzentrum: [ein Schritt auf dem Wege zu einem integrativen Schulwesen] (Ed. Dieter Gers. with Christine Pluhar ... Soltau Schulze-Soltau, 1991. (Materialien und Überlegungen zur Weiterentwicklung der Erziehung und Bildung "behinderter" Schülerinnen und Schüler; [1]).

Sonderschulen und neue Technologien Vol. 2. Bericht über die Abschlußtagung zum Modellversuch "Informations- und Kommunikationstechnologische Grundbildung in Schulen für Lernbehinderte und Schulen für Erziehungshilfe: Erfahrungen, Ergebnisse, Perspektiven"; 04. and 05.12.1989 Landesinstitut für Schule und Weiterbildung in Soest / Gerhard H. Duismann ... 1990.

Worm, Heinz-Lothar: Reparaturwerkstatt Schule: Plädoyer für einen Verbund von Kompensations- und Erlebnispädagogik; ein Konzept zur Innovation der Schule für Lernhilfe (Förderschule, Sonderschule für Lernbehinderte). Lüneburg: Ed. Erlebnispädagogik 1995. (Schriften - Studien - Dokumente zur Erlebnispädagogik; Vol. 12).

12. Free Schools (Private Schools)

Determinanten der Schulwahl: Privatschulen - öffentliche Schulen. Irmfried Speiser (Ed.). Frankfurt/Main et al: Lang 1993. (Europäische Hochschulschriften: Series 11, Pädagogik; Vol. 513).

Handbuch Freie Schulen: pädagogische Positionen, Träger, Schulformen und Schulen im Überblick (Publ. by Arbeitsgemeinschaft Freier Schulen). Rev. & expanded edition. Reinbek bei Hamburg: Rowohlt 1993 (rororo; 6323).

Kindgemäß leben und lernen: alternative Schulmodelle. Marina Kallbach, Jürgen Wichmann et al. Berlin: Altis-Verlag 1991.

13. Universities and Colleges

Aufbruch und Reform von oben: ostdeutsche Universitäten im Transformationsprozess [Max-Planck-Institut für Gesellschaftsforschung, Cologne]. Renate Mayntz (Ed.). Frankfurt/Main; New York: Campus-Verlag 1994. (Schriften des Max-Planck-Instituts für Gesellschaftsforschung, Cologne; Vol. 19).

Daxner, Michael: Ist die Uni noch zu retten? Zehn Vorschläge und eine Vision. Reinbek bei Hamburg: Rowohlt 1996.

Die deutschen Fachhochschulen. Publ. by Sekretariat der Kultusministerkonferenz. Bonn 1991.

Glotz, Peter: Im Kern verrottet? Fünf vor zwölf an Deutschlands Universitäten. Stuttgart: Deutsche Verlags-Anstalt 1996.

Hochschule im Umbruch: Zwischenbilanz Ost; Orientierungen und Expertenwissen zum Handeln. Ed. Hilde Schramm for the GEW. Berlin: Basisdruck-Verlag, 1993.

Hochschulerneuerung in den neuen Bundesländern: Bilanz nach vier Jahren [Projektgruppe Hochschulforschung, Berlin-Karlshorst]. Ed. Gertraude Buck-Bechler and Heidrun Jahn. Weinheim: Deutscher Studien-Verlag 1994.

Peisert, Hansgert; Framhein, Gerhild: Das Hochschulsystem in Deutschland. Publ. by Bundesministerium für Bildung und Wissenschaft. Bonn 1994.

Streitsache: Ost-Hochschulen im Wandel / Institut der Deutschen Wirtschaft. [Publ. by Institut der Deutschen Wirtschaft, Cologne, Hauptabteilung Bildung und Gesellschaftswissenschaften. Ed.: Winfried Schlaffke]. Cologne: Deutscher Instituts-Verlag 1992. (Streitsache; 19).

Strobel, Karl (Ed.): Die deutsche Universität im 20. Jahrhundert. Vierow bei Greifswald: SH-Verlag 1994.

Studierfähigkeit konkret. Erwartungen und Ansprüche der Universität. Ed. Thomas Finkenstaedt and Werner Heldmann for the Deutscher Hochschulverband. Bad Honnef: Bock 1989.

Wissenschaftstransfer in Deutschland: Erfahrungen und Perspektiven bei der Integration der gesamtdeutschen Hochschullandschaft. Bernhard Muszynski (Ed.). Opladen: Leske und Budrich 1993.

Wozu Universitäten – Universitäten wohin? Die Universität auf dem Weg zu einem neuen Selbstverständnis. Stifterverband für die Deutsche Wissenschaft. Villa-Hügel-Gespräch. Essen 1993.

14. Teacher Training

Ausbilden und Fortbilden: Krisen und Perspektiven der Lehrerbildung. (Ed. Hans Günther Homfeldt.) Bad Heilbrunn/OBB.: Klinkhardt 1991.

Auf dem Weg zur "Guten Schule": schulinterne Lehrerfortbildung; Bestandsaufnahme - Konzepte - Perspektiven. (Ed. Ulrich Greber ...) 2nd unrev. ed. Weinheim, Basel: Beltz 1993.

Lehrer auf die Schulbank: Vorschläge für eine zeitgemässe Lehreraus- und -fortbildung. Ed. Siegfried Bäuerle. Stuttgart: Metzler 1991.

Miller, Reinhold: Schulinterne Lehrerfortbildung: der SCHILF-Wegweiser. Revised special edition. Weinheim, Basel: Beltz 1995.

Stammberger, Jürgen: Schulleben und Lehrerbildung: Bestandsaufnahme und Perspektiven aus realistischer Sicht. Bad Heilbrunn/OBB.: Klinkhardt 1991. (Beiträge zur Fachdidaktik und Schulpädagogik; Vol. 3).

15. Adult Education

Ahlheim, Klaus: Mut zur Erkenntnis: Über das Subjekt politischer Erwachsenenbildung. 2nd ed. Bad Heilbrunn/Obb.: Klinkhardt 1992.

Arnold, Rolf: Erwachsenenbildung: eine Einführung in Grundlagen, Probleme und Pespektiven. 2nd rev. ed. Hohengehren: Schneider 1991.

Dohmen, Günther: Offenheit und Integration: Beiträge für das Zusammenwirken von Erwachsenenbildung, Wissenschaft und Medien. [Publ. by Pädagogische Arbeitsstelle des Deutschen Volkshochschul-Verbandes]. Bad Heilbrunn/Obb.: Klinkhardt 1990.

Erwachsenenbildung. Ed. Enno Schmitz; Hans Tietgens. Stuttgart. Dresden: Klett-Verlag für Wissen und Bildung 1995. (Enzyklopädie Erziehungswissenschaft; Vol. 11).

Handbuch Erwachsenenbildung, Weiterbildung. (Ed. Rudolf Tippelt). Opladen: Leske and Budrich 1994.

Oppermann, Detlef; Röhrig, Paul (Ed.): 75 Jahre Volkshochschule. Bad Heilbrunn/Obb: Klinkhardt 1995.

Thema: Weiterbildungspolitik in den Bundesländern [Publ. by: Deutsches Institut für Erwachsenenbildung (DIE), Pädagogische Arbeitsstelle des Deutschen Volkshochschulverbandes. H. Faulstich-Wieland ... (Ed.)]. Frankfurt/M.: DIE 1994. (Literatur- und Forschungsreport Weiterbildung; 33).

Weiterbildung für die 90er Jahre: Gutachten über zukunftsorientierte Angebote, Organisationsformen und Institutionen [Max-Traeger-Stiftung]. Peter Faulstich ... Weinheim, Munich: Juventa-Verlag 1992. (Veröffent lichungen der Max-Traeger-Stiftung ; Vol. 17).

16. Media-Backed Correspondence Courses

Fernunterricht, Fernstudium: Katalog der Fernlehrangebote in der Bundesrepublik Deutschland. Publ. by Bundesinstitut für Berufsbildung (BIBB); Staatliche Zentralstelle für Fernunterricht (ZFU). Bielefeld: Bertelsmann. (Informationen zum beruflichen Fernunterricht; Vol. 17). Berlin 1995.

Fernstudium - neue Initiativen in Ost und West: zeitgemässe Aufgaben und zukunftsorientierte Infrastruktur in Hochschulen und Hochschulregionen; Bericht über die Fachtagung, 27./28. November 1992, Erfurt. Herbert Asselmeyer ... (Ed.). Hildesheim: Franzbecker 1993.

Ommerborn, Rainer: Fernstudium für Behinderte: Voraussetzungen, Formen und Möglichkeiten. 2nd ed. Egelsbach et al.: Hänsel-Hohenhausen 1995. - (Deutsche Hochschulschriften; 1077).

Wissenschaftliche Weiterbildung und Selbststudium: Konzeption und Realisierung von Lehr-Lern-Modellen für das Selbststudium. Heinz Mandl; Helmut Felix Friedrich (Ed.). Weinheim, Basel: Beltz 1991. (Tübinger Beiträge zum Fernstudium; Vol. 21).